Reflections on Monetarism

To Mark Hayes
with best wishes
from Tim Congdon
2·xi·08

Reflections on Monetarism

Britain's Vain Search for a Successful Economic Strategy

Tim Congdon

Managing Director
Lombard Street Research Ltd

Edward Elgar
Institute of Economic Affairs

Published by
Edward Elgar Publishing Limited
Glensanda House
Montpellier Parade
Cheltenham
Glos GL50 1UA
UK

Edward Elgar Publishing, Inc.
William Pratt House
9 Dewey Court
Northampton
Massachusetts 01060
USA

This book has been printed on demand to keep the title in print.

A catalogue record for this book
is available from the British Library

Library of Congress Cataloguing in Publication Data
Congdon, Tim.
  Reflections on monetarism : Britain's vain search for a successful
economic strategy / Tim Congdon.
    p. cm.
  Includes index.
  1. Monetary policy—Great Britain. 2. Great Britain—Economic
policy—1945– I. Title.
HG939.5.C65 1992
338.941—dc20   92–24702
                                                                     CIP

ISBN 978 1 85278 441 6 (cased)
      978 1 85278 766 0 (paperback)

Contents

Tables and Figures

Tables

Figures

Introduction

The purpose of this collection of articles and papers is to add insights to the analysis of British economic policy in a particularly interesting period. Between the mid-1970s and the late 1980s the main theme of British macroeconomic management was the attempt to establish an efficient framework of monetary control. For much of the period this framework was provided by a target for the growth of the money supply (broadly defined, to include bank deposits). The rationale was simple: if excessive monetary growth caused inflation, targeted reductions in the rate of monetary growth would stop it.

The ideas behind the policy framework were known in public debate as 'monetarism'. The usage has become so standard that it cannot be shaken off. But there is no precise connection between policy in Britain and the theoretical proposals of the 'monetarism' associated with certain universities in the American Mid-West, particularly the University of Chicago. Academic Chicago monetarism places heavy emphasis on the advantages of monetary base control, a technique of money market management never embraced by British policy-makers, while it ignores aspects of policy formation which they saw as crucial. Two aspects of the British approach deserve special mention; first, the discouragement of bank lending as part of a larger exercise in monetary restraint and, secondly, the integration of decisions on fiscal policy with those on monetary policy. In view of the differences, it seems best to call policy developments in Britain 'British monetarism'. (The distinction is developed in some detail in the paper 'Keynes, British monetarism and American monetarism', on pp. 209–34. It was initially also broached in two articles in *The Times* in 1975, 'Price stability and the "natural" level of unemployment' and 'Making headway through the gentle therapy of British monetarism', reprinted here as 'Gradual monetary deceleration – a theme in British monetarism' on pp. 24–7 and 27–30.)

Our story falls easily into two parts – the rise of British monetarism from the mid-1970s to 1985 and its fall from 1985 onwards. My position in this story, and the background to the pieces collected here, is best explained if I give some autobiographical details. I first became interested in the relationship between monetary growth and inflation while I was working on the economics staff of *The Times* between 1973 and 1976, where I was strongly influenced by the Economics Editor, Mr Peter Jay. Mr Jay had warned in 1972 and early 1973 that the rapid monetary growth then being recorded would inevitably cause a sharp increase in inflation. He was an articulate and effective critic of the reflationary policies being pursued by the Conservative Chancellor of the Exchequer, Mr Anthony (later Lord) Barber. Having just done a degree in Modern History and Economics at Oxford University (where monetary economics was not emphasized), I was a little puzzled by his forecasts of doom and disaster. But he was right. In late 1975 inflation exceeded 25 per cent, remarkably similar to the peak rate of monetary growth three years earlier.

I became persuaded that monetary mismanagement was the root cause of the instability and high inflation from which the British economy suffered, and started to write articles urging the adoption of a more stable monetary framework. Although I moved from Fleet Street to the City in 1976, where I worked as an economist at the stockbroking firm, L. Messel & Co., I continued to write for the financial press, particularly *The Times*. (I would not want to give the impression that I learnt all my macroeconomics while I was a journalist and stockbroker. I was helped by having read, and tried to understand, such classics as Keynes's *General Theory*, Hicks's *Value and Capital* and Patinkin's *Money, Interest and Prices* both before and while I was at Oxford.)

Since exchange rates were floating in the mid-1970s, monetary policy could be sensibly quantified and formulated only in terms of domestic monetary variables, either interest rates or a money supply target. But the precise meaning of any particular nominal interest rate was difficult to interpret, mainly because of the ambiguity of inflation expectations. So the best approach seemed to me to reduce monetary growth steadily over time in order to combat inflation, while minimizing fluctuations around the monetary growth path so that the economy would avoid sharp cyclical swings in business activity. (The first two pieces, from *The Times* of 2 July 1975 and 19 January 1976, give some of the reasoning for the agenda.) These policies, which were being advocated by a number of other people, including Mr Jay and Mr Samuel Brittan of the *Financial Times*, were known in public debate as 'monetarism'. So I became a 'monetarist'. I did so without initially thinking much about what it meant, although I was well aware that I was only reflecting a general trend.

I was not alone in being uncertain about the precise meaning of 'monetarism'. Mr (later Sir) Alfred Sherman, the Director of Studies at the Centre for Policy Studies, who had liked an article I wrote about Keynes in *Encounter* (reprinted here, 'Are we really all Keynesians now?', pp. 197–209), asked me to write a pamphlet for the Centre defining the term. This appeared in

1978 as *Monetarism: an Essay in Definition*. Since the Centre was closely associated with Sir Keith (later Lord) Joseph and Mrs Margaret Thatcher, I found myself involved in the debate about economic policy in the Conservative Party. As a strong advocate of the policies described in this book as 'British monetarism', I was also inevitably described as a 'Thatcherite'. But I had no direct involvement in policy-making while Mrs Thatcher was Prime Minister.

Nevertheless, my views about monetary policy were sought by Sir Geoffrey Howe when he was Chancellor of the Exchequer between 1979 and 1983. From time to time he convened a 'brains trust' of economists outside the official machine who were sympathetic to the Government's agenda. I participated in these occasions several times and was present at the key meeting in the Treasury on 5 October 1979 when the idea of the Medium-Term Financial Strategy (MTFS) was discussed. (The material reprinted here from the June 1979 issue of L. Messel & Co.'s *Financial Analysis* (see pp. 55–65) was one of the position papers for the meeting.) Sir Geoffrey Howe proved to be a most successful Chancellor. Because he persevered with a rigorous anti-inflationary financial framework even when the overwhelming majority of press comment was hostile, he achieved the largest fall in Britain's underlying inflation rate in peacetime. In late 1975, when monetarism as an intellectual force was just emerging, Britain's inflation rate was above 25 per cent; by following a deliberate programme of monetary restraint, Sir Geoffrey Howe reduced it to under 5 per cent in 1983.

Unhappily, Sir Geoffrey Howe's successor, Mr Nigel Lawson, has a less glorious part in our story. For a variety of reasons he decided to abandon broad money targets in 1985. I was also dropped from my previous informal advisory role and was given to understand that the new Chancellor was no longer much interested in monetarism or any of its affiliated ideas. The abandonment of targets was soon followed by an acceleration in broad money growth. Because of the slack in the economy at that time and the long lag between money supply growth and rising prices, there was no immediate anxiety about inflation. But I was worried that, if broad money growth remained indefinitely above 15 per cent a year, the economy would enter an unsustainable boom and eventually inflation would take off. I expressed my concern in weekly commentaries for L. Messel & Co. and in a sequence of articles in *The Times*. This sequence of articles (of which nine are reprinted here) gave the Government ample warning, far ahead of the event, that it was heading for big trouble with inflation.

The first of these pieces ('Is Lawson heading for another Barber bubble?', 17 October 1985) tried hard to be fair to Mr Lawson, and I paid tribute to 'the seriousness of his commitment and the depth of his understanding'. I could not believe that the Conservative Party and British economists had learnt nothing from the experiences of the previous 15 years and, in particular, from the Barber boom of the early 1970s. But I was too charitable. It became clear in 1986 and 1987 that Mr Lawson was going to repeat Barber's mistakes. Of course, the Lawson boom was not identical to the Barber boom, but there were several remarkable (and depressing) similarities. Rapid growth in credit and the money supply stimulated a sharp upturn in private expenditure, particularly on housing, consumer durables and office construction. Whereas in the early 1980s I had been one of the few loyal supporters of the Thatcher Government's economic policies, I became in 1986 and 1987 a lonely critic. With hardly any exceptions, the policy-making establishment in the Treasury and the Bank of England, British academic economists and City editors in the newspapers approved of Mr Lawson's expansionist policies.

I was described as 'the City's last monetarist'. This was an exaggeration, because it overlooked a small band of other City economists with similar views. But it served as a pointer to where I stood. In 1987 my research team at L. Messel & Co. forecast that inflation would move up to the 8 to 10 per cent level and stay there for some time. It also said that, if the credit boom was to be broken, base rates (9 per cent at the time) would have to increase to 12 per cent and remain there for at least six months. Both these forecasts were dismissed by mainstream British economists as pessimistic to the point of eccentricity, even laughable. (What about the 'small band of other City economists with similar views'? Mr David Smith of the brokers, Williams de Broe, and Mr Paul Turnbull and Mr Roger Nightingale, both of Smith New Court, were certainly worried about excessive monetary growth. Professor Gordon Pepper, then of Midland Montagu, gave warnings from mid-1987 onwards. I should also mention my close colleague at L. Messel & Co. and Shearson Lehman, Dr Peter Warburton, who shared my views and helped me to develop them. L. Messel & Co. was taken over by Shearson Lehman in 1987 and I was Shearson's chief London economist for a short period. Finally, I must make an obvious tribute. The articles I wrote in *The Times* between 1985 and 1988 about the Lawson boom echoed, very self-consciously, the articles Mr Jay wrote in *The Times* between 1972 and 1974 about the Barber boom. There was nothing particularly original in giving warnings about 'booms that must go bust'.)

Everyone involved in the debates of the 1980s will agree that they were difficult. Many observers may want to shrug their shoulders and say that the differences will never be resolved. They will argue that no completely objective appraisal of economic policy is possible, certainly not so soon after the event. I find this agnosticism strange and unacceptable. In my view there is little doubt that monetarism was responsible for Britain's financial rehabilitation in the ten years from 1976, when money supply targets were first introduced, to 1985, when they were abandoned. (Three articles reprinted here – 'Winning the economic war' from *The Spectator* of 29 May 1982, 'Following Friedman' from *The Spectator* of 28 May 1983 and 'Alternatives galore, but none of them better' from *The Times* of 28 September 1985 – were written when monetarism appeared to have won the argument.) There is also little doubt, I believe, that the abandonment of money supply targets in 1985 was responsible for the change from the relative macroeconomic stability and falling inflation of the 1981–86 period to the macroeconomic upheavals and rising inflation of the 1986–91 period. For that reason the abandonment of money supply targets was a dreadful mistake. This may be the most controversial message of the book.

The articles and papers collected here were written at different times, for different audiences and at different levels of technical difficulty. I hope that the story running through them is nevertheless consecutive and easy to follow. An attempt has been made to ease the exposition by prefacing all the pieces with a short comment. Many of them were written at great speed, often to a newspaper deadline in only two or three hours, and this shows in some cases. I have therefore felt free to carry out extensive editorial changes, although without altering the original sense. There is in fact only one piece ('Monetarism and the budget deficit', on pp. 38–49) where I would now want to change the substance of the argument radically. But I have left it much as it was, partly because of its role in the development of the MTFS and partly because it could be seen as a rough draft for the more satisfactory paper on 'The analytical foundations of the Medium-Term Financial Strategy', published in *Fiscal Studies* in 1984, which is reprinted on pp. 65–77.

I hope that the collection will be read by academic economists and policymakers. None of the pieces are technically complicated and the whole book should be easy for any interested layman to follow. Indeed, I expect that many non-economists will be puzzled and dismayed by the story that the book tells.

The last 20 years have seen three boom–bust cycles – the Barber boom of 1972 and 1973, followed by the recession of 1974 and 1975; a period of above-trend growth in 1978 and 1979 (which might be called 'the Healey boomlet', after Mr Denis Healey, the Chancellor of the Exchequer at the time), followed by the manufacturing slump of 1980 and 1981; and the Lawson boom of mid-1986 to mid-1988, followed by the recession of 1990 and 1991. Each of these cycles has been accompanied by great disturbance to business and industry. The false optimism of the boom has given way to the disappointment of expectations in the recession. Speculative fortunes have been made and lost, people have been recruited unwisely and then sacked for no good reason, bad businesses have been established on invalid assumptions about continuing boom, and good businesses have been closed down on equally invalid assumptions about never-ending recession. In short, there has been immense and unnecessary waste. Indeed, it is not going too far to say that the lives of many decent, hard-working people have been ruined by Britain's macroeconomic volatility.

All of the cycles were associated with – and, in my view, mainly caused by – large swings in monetary growth. If policy-makers had over the whole 20-year period concentrated on stabilizing monetary growth at a low rate, the cycles would have been smaller and less harmful, and inflation would have been lower. Of course, this claim cannot be proved beyond contradiction. Perhaps fortunately, laboratory experiments are not possible in economics. But an unfavourable comparison with Germany, also a middle-ranking European industrial nation, is easy to draw. There the Bundesbank has concentrated since the early 1970s on stabilizing monetary growth at a low rate, and business cycles have certainly been smaller and less harmful, and inflation consistently lower, than in Britain.

The questions arise, 'why were so many blunders made?' and 'how could successive governments have been so foolish?'. One answer is to pin the blame on politicians, particularly on three Chancellors of the Exchequer: Barber, Healey and Lawson. But I believe that is a mistake. Politicians are far less important than they like to think. Their decisions rarely come from their own intuitions or judgement, but are taken on the basis of advice from a wide range of sources. This pattern of advice depends, in turn, on a climate of informed opinion which is strongly influenced by the consensus of academic views, particularly (in Britain) by academic views from Oxford and Cambridge. If we want to understand why Britain has had three destructive boom–bust cycles in a 20-year period, it is to this climate of informed opinion and this consensus of academic views that we must look.

The root of the problem is that the majority of British academic economists do not believe that the behaviour of the money supply is relevant to macroeconomic outcomes. They also pay little attention to other monetary variables, such as bank credit to the private sector, and sometimes argue that interest rates are of only marginal importance for decisions to save and invest. How – the puzzled layman might ask – can they hold these views, which have been so thoroughly refuted by the events of the last 20 years? The standard answer of the British academic economist is 'I am a Keynesian', as if – by invoking the name of the greatest economist of the 20th century – he exonerates himself from having to think about such painful topics as credit, the money supply and interest rates.

The third part of the book therefore considers the relationship between Keynes and monetarism. The subject turns out to be complicated and controversial, but one point is clear. This is that Keynes was fascinated, throughout his career, by the interrelationships between monetary and real variables, and saw the behaviour of credit and money as fundamental to macroeconomic outcomes. The attitude of most British economists towards credit and money then becomes even more of an enigma. I used the opportunity of an inaugural lecture at Cardiff Business School (where I became an honorary professor in 1990) to explore this enigma. (The lecture is reprinted on pp. 234–55).

The argument of the lecture is that for most of the 19th and early 20th centuries leaders of informed opinion thought that the ideal monetary policy for Britain should be specified in terms of the sterling price of gold or, in other words, the exchange rate; not in terms of quantities of credit or money. Although the emphasis moved away from gold after the Second World War, Britain participated in the Bretton Woods system of fixed exchange rates and monetary policy remained focused on the exchange rate. Hence, there was no compelling need for British economists to consider the domestic aspects of monetary policy. Ironically, Keynes himself had always favoured a 'managed currency' in which these domestic aspects would have been paramount. (That was the key point of his early essay *A Tract on Monetary Reform* and explains his lifelong antagonism towards gold.)

The neglect of monetary economics can also be blamed on the long period – from 1939 to the mid-1950s – when much of the British economy was subject to direct controls of one sort or another. Extensive controls originated in the War, but they were retained far longer than strictly necessary for military purposes. In fact, a large number of influential intellectuals on the left of British politics wanted them to be retained indefinitely after the War, as a way of building socialism. In a planned economy of the type they favoured, monetary policy would have been of little importance in macroeconomic management and interest rates would have been otiose in the allocation of resources.

The denigration of monetary economics can therefore be attributed, at least in part, to the impact of such socialist thinkers as G. D. H. Cole, R. H. Tawney and the Webbs on a generation of British economists. Roughly, this was the generation educated between 1940 and 1965, who were most active in teaching and policy advice in the 1970s and 1980s. If the conjecture seems far-fetched, I would direct the reader to p. 245, which mentions an important book on *The Labour Government's Economic Record: 1964–70*. This book, published in 1972 with contributions predominantly from Oxbridge economists, had only one index reference to 'the money supply', but no less than 41 to the National Plan and 'planning'. Is it an accident, in view of the declared interests and attitudes of these influential British economists at the start of the Barber boom, that the 20 years after 1972 were to see gross monetary mismanagement?

There is no point being mealy-mouthed about this subject. The great majority of British academic economists have no time for either monetarism narrowly understood, or for monetary economics as a whole. They sometimes deny the relevance or meaningfulness of monetary policy in any shape or form whatsoever. It is hardly surprising, therefore, that the academic economics profession should have been appalled by the Thatcher Government's commitment to monetary control in its early years. In 1981 two Cambridge economists were able to assemble 364 signatures from academic economists to protest, in a letter to *The Times*, against the allegedly 'monetarist' Budget of that year. The letter claimed that the Government's policies would 'deepen the depression...and threaten' Britain's 'social and political stability'.

The 364 economists were wrong, but that does not mean their letter was unimportant. As I said in the Cardiff lecture, the letter 'accurately reflected the overwhelming consensus of British academic opinion. Whenever officials from the Treasury or the Bank of England took part in academic conferences, both in these years [i.e., the early 1980s] and later, they were subjected to a barrage of scorn for obeying their political masters and implementing money supply targets'. As money supply targets encountered various technical and measurement difficulties, these officials became thoroughly weary of the whole subject. They were delighted that Mr Lawson agreed to scrap them in 1985. When the monetary excesses of 1986, 1987 and 1988 followed, neither the academic economics profession nor the official advisers close to the Government were prepared to ring the alarm bells about future inflation. Moreover, most of them were not at all sorry about the increase in inflation which occurred in 1989 and 1990. On the contrary, it is a fair guess that a good 90 per cent of the 364 were jubilant that rising inflation ruined the reputation of Mrs Thatcher and her Government for basic managerial competence in economic policy. In this sense the Lawson boom was the revenge of the 364.

The larger message of my lecture was therefore that the macroeconomic volatility of the 1970s and 1980s was due to 'British economists' lack of recognition of how credit and money affect demand, output, employment and inflation' or, in a phrase, to 'a great vacuum in intellectual understanding'. The consequent indictment of 'an entire profession, the profession of academic economists in this country' was not meant in fun, but as a serious comment on a tragic national failure.

The non-academic reader may wonder precisely what has happened to British macroeconomics over the last 50 years. After all, Keynes's *General Theory*, published in 1936, is undoubtedly one of the greatest contributions to macroeconomic understanding this century. How could its endowment to British economics have been so thoroughly squandered? It seems to me that the *General Theory* should be seen, as the inaugural lecture says, as 'both the climax and the terminus of the 19th-century tradition of trade cycle theorizing, in which credit and money had been so important'. Such great economists as Henry Thornton, John Stuart Mill, Bagehot and Alfred Marshall, and Keynes's contemporaries, Dennis Robertson and Ralph Hawtrey, belonged to the tradition, and it was surely the dominant strand of British monetary thought until (say) 1950. May I suggest that the pieces brought together here are a small attempt to rescue some of its key ideas? If so, they are not really monetarist at all. Perhaps it is a pity that they will, inevitably, receive the 'monetarist' label.

Two period pieces complete this collection. They do not fit neatly into the chronology of the story, but are included because they introduced themes which were important at various times in the public debate about economic policy.

Because this collection brings together work over a period of more than 15 years, I will not be able to acknowledge everyone who has helped or influenced me. My first debt of gratitude (as will be clear from this Introduction) is to Mr Peter Jay, who offered me a position on the economics staff of *The Times* in 1973. I also owe a great deal to Lord Rees-Mogg, who, as Editor of *The Times* in the mid-1970s, took a close interest in my work and has subsequently helped me in several ways. Important influences have been Professor Charles Goodhart and Professor David Laidler, who (I feel) are two lonely representatives of the great tradition of British monetary economics; Sir Alan Walters and Professor Patrick Minford, but (as we shall see) my disagreements with them are profound; Sir Terence Burns and Sir Peter Middleton, with whom I had such fruitful discussions in the late 1970s, although I have not spoken to them so much recently; and Dr Walter Eltis, Mr David Gowland and Professor Douglas McWilliams, who have been an intellectual stimulus for over 20 years.

I have benefited from the friendship (and occasional rivalry) of many City economists and financial journalists. I would particularly like to mention two former colleagues, Mr Paul Turnbull and Dr Peter Warburton, and two former competitors, Mr Richard Coghlan and Professor Gordon Pepper. Lord Joseph has taken a close interest in my work since the mid-1970s and I much value his continuing support. It is not an accident that most of my pamphlets have been published by the Centre for Policy Studies. I am deeply grateful to Professor Christopher Green and Dr Kent Matthews, whom I met through the Money Study Group, for recommending that I be appointed to an honorary professorship at the Cardiff Business School.

I have a number of other thanks in connection with my work in the City, first to the other partners of L. Messel & Co., for (more or less) allowing me to proceed unhindered with my analysis and propaganda for such a long time, and to the directors of Gerrard & National, for providing me with a new City home in the last three years. Mr Brian Williamson, the Chairman of Gerrard & National, has been particularly helpful. My colleagues at Lombard Street Research Ltd, Mr Jonathan Morris and Mr Simon Ward, have also been more easy-going than I deserve. I owe a special debt of thanks to my secretary, Miss Grace Graham, who has worked with me now for almost ten years. She has helped in the preparation of this book with her usual diligence and cheerfulness. Mr Gabriel Stein also gave invaluable help in the delicate task of transferring files between disks

I should emphasize that none of the above is responsible for any factual errors remaining in the book or necessarily agrees with the views expressed.

I am grateful to the various editors for permission to reprint these pieces again.

Last, but certainly not least, I must thank my wife, Dorianne, for her loyal support, tolerance and affection. The preparation of this book coincided with the arrival of our first child, Venetia, and – like my pamphlet, *For a Stable Pound*, last year – it is dedicated to Dorianne and Venetia.

PART ONE

The Rise of British Monetarism

1. Setting the agenda

Two events in 1971 and 1972 radically changed the context of British macroeconomic policy-making. First, in September 1971 the Bank of England implemented a set of reforms known as Competition and Credit Control (CCC), which ended quantitative restrictions on bank lending. These quantitative restrictions had been in force for most of the period since 1945, with the purpose of keeping the growth of credit consistent with Britain's exchange rate commitment (i.e., the fixed exchange rate between the dollar and the pound at $2.80 from 1949 to 1967, and at $2.40 from 1967 to 1971). But they had been crude and inefficient, and were widely believed to have distorted the financial system. They required the banks to limit their lending to a particular figure at a particular date, regardless of customers' demands for finance or the banks' own preparedness to supply credit. The second was Britain's departure in June 1972 from the European 'snake', which had fixed the exchange rates between a number of currencies (notably the Deutschmark and French franc) in a narrow, snake-like band. The snake had been designed to maintain currency stability in Europe despite the breakdown of the previous Bretton Woods system, in which exchange rates had been pegged to the dollar.

By abandoning the use of administrative controls in monetary policy, the CCC reforms raised new questions about how monetary policy should be conducted. Most observers agreed that the level of interest rates, which was set by the Bank of England, would become a more important instrument, perhaps the most important instrument of all. But was it sufficient to relate interest rates to ultimate target variables such as inflation? Or could a case be made for an intermediate target specified in terms of the money supply?

The decision to leave the snake inaugurated almost 20 years of floating exchange rates. This also raised new questions about the conduct of monetary policy. Traditionally, the Bank of England had varied interest rates mostly in order to keep the pound stable on the foreign exchanges, with only a side-glance at the effects of interest rate variations on domestic economic activity. But in an era of floating exchange rates the exchange rate no longer provided a reliable guide to interest rate decisions. What should guide interest rates instead? Was the quantity of money (the sum of notes, coin and bank deposits in the economy) appropriate as a target? Or should the exchange rate still have a role, even if secondary to the money supply?

These were some of the questions I tried to answer in two articles in *The Times* on 2 July 1975 and 19 January 1976. It needs to be emphasized that they were written when the annual inflation rate was well over 20 per cent and when memories of the collapse in share prices in 1974 were still vivid. In this environment a fixed exchange rate (against the currencies of countries with inflation under 10 per cent) would have been folly, while nominal interest rates had lost much of their signalling function for policy-makers. Money supply targets seemed to me to be the right policy response.

Money Supply Targeting vs Interest Rate Targeting

From an article 'The money supply – more meaningful than interest rates as a policy goal' in The Times, *2 July 1975.*

The argument of the article was that interest rate targeting – in the sense of holding interest rates steady in order to give stability to asset prices and the financial system – is inappropriate in an inflationary economy. Entrenched and volatile inflationary expectations make it difficult to know what level of interest rates is most appropriate to achieve desired macroeconomic objectives. In such circumstances money supply targeting is 'plainly much more sensible', since a target set slightly 'beneath the going rate of inflation' should in due course 'bring inflation down without disturbing financial markets more than necessary'.

The article said that 'a new style of monetary policy [i.e., British monetarism, with money supply targets] has gradually developed which...may result in big improvements in stabilization policy in future'. In view of the adoption of money supply targets in the following year and the progress in inflation over the next ten years, this was a good surmise. (See 'A perspective on a decade of progress' on pp. 111–14.)

Cynics might claim that the sole objective of central banks is to minimize criticism. If so, the Bank of England has failed lamentably in recent years. Few institutions have been attacked so frequently or so strongly. The official memoirs industry will no doubt thrive on future disclosures about the conduct of monetary policy during the 'Barber boom' of 1972 and 1973 when the money supply exploded upwards by 25 per cent a year. The question 'how could it have happened?' has become almost an opening gambit of conversation between economists. It is a way of recognizing like-minded people.

There may now be unanimity that the rates of monetary expansion found in 1972 and 1973 must never be repeated. But has the Bank of England mended its ways? Has it learnt lessons of permanent value from recent unhappy experiences? It will be argued here that the Bank has been forced by the pressure of events to modify its approach to monetary control. As long as there is no back-sliding for reasons of political expediency, the traumas of the Barber boom have had a beneficial effect by exposing the errors contained in some ancient and highly durable banking prejudices. A new and better style of monetary policy has gradually developed. It may result in big improvements in stabilization policy in future.

But, before presenting this argument, two basic truths have to be noted. They are not controversial, but tend to be forgotten in the heat of debate. The first is that one of the Bank of England's main functions is to oversee and manage the Government's finances. It has to ensure that, if the Government is spending more than it is receiving in taxation, the deficit is covered by borrowing from other agents in the economy.

Secondly, money supply targets and interest rate policy have to be consistent. A particular money supply target requires that interest rates be set at a certain level, and a particular interest rate policy involves certain money supply behaviour. One entails the other and vice versa. For example, the Bank of England cannot clamp down on money supply growth and hope that interest rates will not rise. The financial system will find that because of official policy it does not have enough liquidity to meet the demands placed on it by trade and industry. It must therefore raise interest rates to hold back that demand. If the Bank of England tries to stop this normal commercial response by artificial restrictions on lending, it is liable to distort financial markets and discourage competition.

The interaction between interest rates and money supply policy suggests alternative styles of monetary control. One approach, which might be called the 'new style', is to emphasize the money supply as the vital target variable. This approach is found in the United States and West Germany, where the central banks announce in advance a target for money supply growth. Although mindful of interest rate movements, they do not allow immense government borrowing needs to frighten them from large bond sales if necessary. This policy can be partly justified on the grounds that, if interest rates go up, the industrial demand for loans will be choked off. Because of the extra room created in the economy, a large budget deficit may not cause excess demand.

The alternative 'old style' of monetary management accords primacy, instead, to interest rate targets and treats money supply behaviour as incidental. The emphasis on interest rates is a by-product of beliefs about the functions of a central bank which have been held by Bank of England officials for generations. Maintaining interest rate stability lends support to the market value of gilt-edged securities, which should also be reasonably steady over time. Gilts are the key to asset values generally. If they are steady, equities and property should be steady, too. This steadiness of asset values is important for the soundness of the financial system. As long as asset values are not rushing wildly upwards or downwards, banks can be confident that their loans have adequate collateral and there is little danger that several of them will become over-extended simultaneously. In this way interest rate stability is a means of ensuring the coherence and integrity of the entire financial system.

'Old style' central bankers did nevertheless, on occasion, contemplate large changes in interest rates. A run on the pound might force an increase in Bank rate to check speculation on the foreign exchanges and to sustain the exchange rate. In extreme emergencies the stability of the exchange rate had higher priority than the steadiness of asset values. A rational justification for this worship of the exchange rate might lie in the role of a fixed exchange rate in forcing a country to adopt and persevere with responsible anti-inflationary monetary policies. However, the external value of sterling was typically seen as the ultimate arbiter of foreign 'confidence' in Britain and an essential component of national prestige, and it still holds this status in market gossip.

The sanctification of sterling by the 'old style' is regarded by 'new style' central bankers as little better than superstition. To them interest rates are principally devices for guiding the demand for and supply of credit in domestic financial markets. They concede that interest rates may have a subsidiary function in influencing international capital flows, but they believe that the exchange rate should be governed, first and foremost, by demand and supply in the foreign exchange markets. If hostile pressure builds up against the sterling exchange rate, the right response is to drop the exchange rate until it is realistic.

Has the 'old style' fallen out of favour? And, if so, why? The crucial flaw in the 'old style' was exposed in 1972 and 1973. The floating of sterling in June 1972 weakened the external constraint on monetary policy and enabled the Bank of England to pursue its traditional policy of interest rate stability more or less without regard to the state of the pound. At the same time the Government began to run a huge budget deficit on a scale quite unprecedented in peacetime.

The coincidence of a large public sector borrowing requirement (PSBR) and a new interest rate permissiveness set the scene for an explosive growth in the money supply. The Bank of England seemed bewildered by the rapid increase and attributed it to an institutional adjustment in the wake of Competition and Credit Control. Its arguments, which had always seemed a little contrived, became totally implausible in late 1973. Lax monetary and fiscal policies led to a colossal balance-of-payments deficit. After a particularly bad set of trade figures in December 1973 a 2 per cent jump in Minimum Lending Rate (a neologism for Bank rate) became necessary. High interest rates ruled for another year. As 'old style' central bankers would have expected, the result was a collapse in asset values and serious worries about the solvency of many City of London institutions.

But, once the genie of financial irresponsibility had been let out of the bottle in 1971 and 1972, the troubles were inevitable. The scale of monetary disequilibrium in late 1973 was such that a crisis of financial solvency could have been avoided only by allowing a take-off into hyper-inflation. Interest rate stability may be a sensible policy if the price level also is fairly stable and if governments balance their budgets. But it is altogether misguided once the inflationary process is under way and gathering momentum. Interest rate stability is then not even a recipe for keeping asset values steady, because inflation causes a re-assessment of the attractiveness of different assets. If gilt prices are artificially supported by official purchases, the Bank of England may find itself financing a runaway speculative boom in reputedly inflation-proofed assets such as property.

In the present condition of the economy, with high and volatile inflation which is forecast to last indefinitely into the future, a money supply target is much more sensible than a dogged commitment to interest rate stability. The target should be related to prevailing inflation expectations, being set a few percentage points beneath the going rate of inflation. In due course this should bring inflation down without disturbing financial markets more than necessary. Equally, the use of interest rates to buttress a particular exchange rate is folly, when inflation rates in Britain are out of line with those abroad. The adjustment should instead take place through a downward float of the exchange rate. A rigid adherence to a particular exchange rate, whatever its symbolic appeal, might destroy several soundly-based financial institutions, and have subsequent needlessly severe effects on output and employment.

To conclude, the pressure of events over the last four years has prompted a re-appraisal of methods of monetary management by the Bank of England. A 'new style' has emerged, not so much because intellectual arguments convinced policy-makers of its virtues as because the disarray created by the alternative 'old style' obliged the authorities to adopt new approaches. However, the conversion will be complete only when the Bank of England acknowledges money supply targets in the same way as the West German Bundesbank and the American Federal Reserve. The readiness of Bank economists to quibble with 'monetarism' should also give way to a more open recognition of the inadequacy of interest rates as target variables in present conditions.

Money Supply Targets vs Fixed Exchange Rates

From an article 'A conflict of objectives in the Government's monetary policy' in The Times, *19 January 1976.*

This article foreshadowed many of the controversies of the next 15 years. Taking its cue from Keynes's Tract on Monetary Reform *(published in 1923), it argued that a money supply target (i.e., a monetary policy focused on the internal price level) might sometimes be inconsistent with a fixed exchange rate. The point was to criticize a statement in Mr Healey's letter of application to the International Monetary Fund (IMF) for a stand-by facility. This statement had been that interest rates were set in relation to 'external as well as domestic objectives', which seemed to me 'useless' and muddled. The themes of the article recur in other papers here, notably in the inaugural lecture to Cardiff Business School in 1990. The comment that a fixed exchange rate leaves 'internal inflation and employment objectives at the mercy of foreign central banks' would, of course, have been equally relevant ten or 15 years later in the the debate about Britain's attitude towards the European Monetary System (EMS).*

A money supply target and a fixed exchange rate are incompatible. Indeed, the point is more general than that. Any monetary policy geared to the requirements of the domestic economy is inconsistent with a concern for 'external factors', whether these be the rates of inflation or the levels of interest rates abroad. It would encourage confidence in the British Government's monetary policy if it would recognize these tensions in official policy statements. Because it is not clear at present what objective the Government is pursuing, financial markets have difficulty interpreting policy moves and unnecessary instability is engendered.

The argument is readily developed by looking at the influences on monetary growth. Nowadays cheque payments are many times larger than payments in notes and coin, and the money supply consists predominantly of bank deposits. Deposits are, of course, sums of money owed by the banks to their customers. Deposits on the liabilities side of the balance sheet increase whenever banks are able to expand their assets by lending more. Three main influences on monetary growth can therefore be identified – more lending to the private sector, more lending to the Government (or other public sector agencies) and more lending overseas.

The role of overseas lending, and other external contributors to monetary growth, can be extremely complicated. But some definitional ideas are easy enough to explain. When a country runs a balance-of-payments surplus, it increases its claims on the rest of the world. If some of these claims are registered in the banking system, the money supply rises. In particular, when the exchange rate is fixed, the central bank is almost continually active in the foreign exchanges, buying or selling the currencies of other nations. Consequent changes in its foreign exchange holdings can have a significant effect on the money supply. It is only in a system of purely floating exchange rates that no such official operations are conducted and no such impacts on the money supply are possible.

This analysis is the essence of the claim that a fixed exchange rate conflicts, inevitably and necessarily, with a money supply target. It demonstrates that floating exchange rates are required if countries are to have fully autonomous monetary policies. However, external considerations can intrude on domestic policy-making even if the exchange rate is floating. The possibility arises because the central bank may alter interest rates in response to events abroad. These changes in interest rates may repercuss on the avowedly domestic influences on monetary growth, namely bank lending to the private and public sectors.

In the British context the Bank of England may change Minimum Lending Rate (the old 'Bank rate') because of 'the state of the pound'. Through familiar mechanisms, monetary growth is then affected. Consider, first and most simply, bank lending to the private sector. In their borrowing behaviour companies and individuals are plainly concerned about the costs involved. If interest costs are excessive they are deterred from incurring new debt. Secondly, interest rates have a powerful, if more indirect, effect on bank lending to the public sector. Sales of new government debt (or 'gilt-edged securities') to the non-bank public are undoubtedly related to the level of interest rates. The higher are interest rates, the lower is the price of gilt-edged securities and the more gilts the Bank of England can sell. As a result, the Government's deficit (also known as the 'public sector borrowing requirement') can be financed to a smaller extent from the banking system and money supply growth is contained.

Some dealers in the gilt-edged market argue that the Bank of England can sell gilts only 'on a rising market', that is, when interest rates are falling. They go on to assert that increases in interest rates do not boost official gilt sales. Taken to extremes, this piece of market lore becomes absurd, as it would imply that the Bank could attract buyers now if it reduced interest rates to 5 per cent or even 2 per cent. Given present inflation rates, that is clearly not correct. There is a grain of truth in the 'rising market' argument – namely, that gilt sales are easier to make if interest rates are expected to decline. But expectations of a decline in rates should be stronger the higher their current level.

There is no real doubt about the link between interest rates and money supply growth. High interest rates dampen monetary expansion and low interest rates stimulate it. Clear confirmation of the link, and an emphatic refutation of the 'rising market' argument, has been provided in recent months. The jump in Minium Lending Rate in the autumn enabled the Government to conduct a massive gilts selling campaign in November and December, which has now been fully reflected in the money supply figures.

The undeniable connection between interest rates and monetary growth has a vital implication. If interest rates are used for purposes other than the attainment of money supply targets, those targets may be missed. In particular, if interest rates are raised whenever the pound comes under pressure in the foreign exchange market, the rise in rates interferes with domestic monetary policy.

Suppose, for example, that the money supply is growing at 3 per cent a year while the target is 7 per cent, but that the pound at a $2 exchange rate is being sold heavily on the foreign exchanges, even though the Bank of England is committed to a $2 exchange rate. Since the pound is being pushed down, external factors indicate the need for higher interest rates. But, obviously, an increase in interest rates would reduce money supply growth further and make it depart even more from the 7 per cent target. Domestic and external objectives are on a collision course.

Although the defence of sterling may cause slow output growth (or falling output) and more unemployment, supporters of a fixed exchange rate sometimes claim that it is needed as 'a discipline'. Because a particular numerical ratio, $2.80 to the pound, $2.40 to the pound, $2.00 to the pound, or whatever, acquires an aura of inviolability if it lasts for several years, it is said to act as an effective obstacle to a spendthrift and inflationary government. In the circumstances of post-war Britain this may be a valid point. But it is a comment on politicians, not a technical proposition in international monetary economics. Quite apart from its disciplinarian hairshirt connotations, the statement that a $2 parity would act as an obstacle to inflation is equivalent to the statement that the British Government has to be as financially responsible as the American Federal Reserve decides. More succinctly, to adopt a fixed exchange rate is to abandon the independence of monetary policy. It leaves internal inflation and employment objectives at the mercy of foreign central banks.

The consistent approach to monetary policy is to combine a money supply rule with floating exchange rates. The purer the float, the more consistent the policy. Mr Healey's recent letter of application to the International Monetary Fund contained the statement that interest rates policies 'are formulated with regard to external as well as domestic objectives'. This is useless. It leaves financial markets completely in the dark as to which objective is uppermost in the authorities' minds at any particular moment.

It will no doubt be said, as if it were a smear, that the combination of a money supply rule and a floating exchange rate is 'monetarist'. That label may be justified, but, if so, Keynes was a monetarist before it became fashionable. Indeed, the classic statement of the potential incompatibility between foreign and domestic monetary objectives is given in Keynes's *Tract on Monetary Reform*, published in 1923. In its words, the exchange rate 'cannot be stable unless both internal and external price levels remain stable. If, therefore, the external price level lies outside our control, we must submit either to our own internal price level or to our exchange being pulled about by external influences. If the external price level is unstable we cannot keep both our own price level and our exchanges stable. We are compelled to choose.'

It is a pity that, after 50 years of muddle and confusion, the British Government still has not chosen.

2.   Some key themes

The adoption of money supply targets was announced publicly on 22 July 1976, although the Bank of England has claimed that it had in fact been privately following the money supply for two or three years before this. Money supply targets had repercussions on all areas of macroeconomic policy. Most obviously, as we saw in the previous section on 'Setting the agenda', there were implications for interest rates and exchange rates. Monetary targets required both that interest rates be readily adjusted to changing trends in money supply growth and that the exchange rate be allowed to float, in order to avoid possible inconsistencies between external and domestic objectives. But there were other problems. The various themes come back, at various points and in a number of guises, later in our story.

First, if monetary growth was fixed by a pre-ordained target, how could the Government alter demand in the economy and ensure full employment? The stock monetarist answer was that attempts to reduce unemployment beneath the so-called 'natural rate of unemployment', determined by structural characteristics of the labour market, would lead not to a stable high inflation rate, but to an ever-accelerating inflation rate and ultimately to hyper-inflation. I set out this view, which originated in Professor Milton Friedman's presidential address to the American Economic Association in 1967, in an article in *The Times* on 22 January 1975. In practice, the British Government effectively abandoned the objective of full employment in the mid-1970s, and employment considerations were not a major influence on macroeconomic policy at any point in the late 1970s or 1980s. (Of course, I am not denying that they were very important in the public debate on economic policy.)

An important corollary of the concept of a natural rate of unemployment needs to be spelt out. If a rate of unemployment maintained continuously beneath the natural rate leads to hyper-inflation, a rate of unemployment continuously above the natural rate leads to ever-falling inflation and eventually to price declines. (Technically, when unemployment is above the natural rate, the short-run inflation–unemployment trade-off improves indefinitely into the future, i.e. the short-run Phillips curve keeps on moving to the left. If unemployment is constant over a sequence of such short-runs, inflation must keep on falling.) I picked up this point in an article in *The*

Spectator, entitled 'Following Friedman', on 28 May 1983, arguing that it pointed to extremely favourable prospects for growth and inflation in the mid-1980s.

The natural rate argument does not mean that the supporters of monetarism in the 1970s were indifferent to the suffering caused by large swings in economic activity. A central element in British monetarism was that large fluctuations in monetary growth should be avoided, since they were liable to cause extreme fluctuations in output and employment. In the mid-1970s the Manchester Inflation Workshop, led by Professors David Laidler and Michael Parkin, urged the case for 'gradualism', partly because they were worried that drastic monetary deceleration would cause an unnecessarily steep rise in unemployment. In fact, Professor Laidler was highly critical of the abruptness of the monetary slowdown between 1973 and 1974, and argued that it was the main cause of the intensity of the recession in early 1975. I reported on 'gradualism' and the work of the Manchester Inflation Workshop in an article in *The Times* on 29 April 1975. (Note that the theme of gradualism had also been present in Friedman's own advocacy of stable monetary growth, although it had been not articulated in quite these terms. Friedman had grown up in the Great Depression of the 1930s.)

Finally, money supply targets altered the role of fiscal policy and questioned the validity of the Treasury's approach to economic management in the late 1960s and early 1970s. In this approach, the level of demand in the economy was adjusted by short-run changes in the fiscal position, usually at Budget time but sometimes at other points in the financial year. The direction and scale of such fiscal fine-tuning were determined by forecasts of future economic activity. These forecasts were derived from an elaborate econometric model containing many hundreds of equations. The practice of macroeconometric forecasting was relatively new in the mid-1970s, with the full-scale, computer-based Treasury model dating only from 1968.

Advocates of monetary targets regarded the Treasury's macroeconomic forecasts as of little help in taking the right decisions. This stemmed partly from a deep-seated scepticism that enough was known about the economy for the sort of enterprise on which the Treasury had embarked. But it also reflected the apparent inability of the Treasury model (and other macroeconometric models) to incorporate monetary influences successfully. In fact, the Treasury failed abjectly to foresee either the harshness of the 1975 recession or the increase in inflation to over 25 per cent. By contrast, the Manchester monetarists were roughly right in predicting both. My article in *The Times* of 28 August 1975, 'A lesson from the Treasury on how to be precisely wrong', concluded that, 'Unless and until conventional models incorporate monetary variables they will fail to capture some of the most important influences on the economy'. This theme re-surfaced in the late

1980s, when, once again, Treasury forecasts became hopelessly wrong following a marked change in monetary growth. (See, in particular, 'The importance of money in macroeconomic forecasting – part 2', based on an article in *The Spectator* of 11 March 1989, on pp. 191–4.)

Price Stability and the 'Natural' Level of Unemployment

Reprinted from an article of the same name in The Times *of 22 January 1975.*

The article sets out Friedman's argument about the natural rate, with little additional comment. But it is worth mentioning that the then Economics Editor of The Times, *Mr Peter Jay, had observed over a sequence of business cycles from the late 1950s, a continual deterioration in the unemployment–inflation trade-off. Friedman's analysis seemed to provide an explanation for this deterioration, as the gradual embedding of adverse inflation expectations would increase the unemployment cost required to achieve any given reduction in the inflation rate. (The original version of this article, which suffered badly from sub-editing, has been revised substantially.)*

One sentence towards the end of the article is worth highlighting. This is the observation that, assuming no regime change which would banish inflationary expectations 'quickly and decisively', inflation could be cured only after 'four or five years' hard slog', with unemployment held above the natural rate for that length of time. This already hints at the time-scale of the Medium-Term Financial Strategy.

It is a commonplace that the Government faces a choice between inflation and employment objectives. Less unemployment, associated with policies which keep up demand in the economy, is also associated with rising wages and prices. It is perhaps less widely recognized that if the Government is too ambitious – if, for example, it aims to keep unemployment at extremely low levels – its options can deteriorate progressively. The price to be paid for driving unemployment down to unsustainable levels is not a once-for-all rise to a higher rate of inflation, but an ever-accelerating rate of inflation.

The dynamics of inflation may be unstable. Thus, it may be that if, in the first year, 3 per cent unemployment is accompanied by 5 per cent inflation, it will in the second year be accompanied by 5 per cent plus a little extra to make, say, 8 per cent, and in the third year, by 8 per cent plus a little extra to make 12 per cent, and so on. The process of degeneration is cumulative. 'Creeping inflation' (of 5 per cent a year or less) slides into 'strato-inflation' (20 per cent a year plus) and 'strato-inflation' culminates in 'hyper-inflation' (50 per cent a month or more). The theory that this is how the economy behaves, while a profoundly depressing one, is also rather suggestive. There is at least a case for saying that a move from creeping inflation to strato-inflation is precisely what has happened in Britain since the late 1960s. Serious commentators have even started to warn that, if nothing is done, Britain may end up with hyper-inflation.

The argument hinges on the idea of a 'natural level of unemployment'. This is the level which keeps supply and demand in the labour market balanced and at which unions, management and other labour market participants reach pay bargains similar to those prevailing in the past. If the level of unemployment drops beneath this rate, pay bargains tend to rise. The essence of the problem is that, once a particular rate of inflation has occurred and is expected to continue, the groups involved in collective bargaining make an allowance for it in their negotiations. This expectation of inflation is added to next year's pay settlements, pushing up the inflation rate; the higher inflation rate is then again embedded in pay bargainers' expectations and added to the following year's settlements, which pushes up the inflation rate further; and the yet higher inflation is again embedded in expectations and added to another year's settlements; and so on, until the economy suffers from hyper-inflation.

Economists used to call the old relationship between unemployment and wage increases the Phillips curve, after an economist at the London School of Economics who reported some of the historical statistics on the subject in a famous academic article. But, by recognizing the role of expectations, they now talk about a new relationship, 'the expectations-augmented Phillips curve'. It is explicitly understood that any unemployment rate less than the natural rate leads to ever-rising wage awards and ever-deteriorating inflation.

There are two sources of instability in this story. The first is the Government's commitment to a level of 'full employment' which is unsustainable because it forces unemployment beneath the natural rate. The second is the generation of inflationary expectations. Of course, if everyone were to believe that 5 per cent inflation this year will be succeeded by no inflation next, the progressive escalation to higher inflation rates could be avoided.

The Government can try to escape from this dilemma by restricting demand and permitting unemployment to increase. But here is the rub. Once inflationary expectations have contaminated the system, it is not sufficient to raise unemployment to the natural rate. To repeat, the natural rate is accompanied not by stable prices, but by stable pay increases and stable inflation. To reduce inflation, unemployment has to rise above the natural rate. Once an economy has experienced an inflation rate above 20 per cent, it probably has to undergo several years of deflationary agony, with very high unemployment, to restore inflation of 5 per cent or less. The effect of a few years of constantly rising inflation is to worsen the inflation–unemployment trade-off confronting the Government. A government which accords an excessive priority to high employment may, finally and ironically, have to 'trade' far more unemployment to keep inflation down than a government which is openly indifferent to the plight of the unemployed.

The theories of the natural rate of unemployment and the expectations-augmented Phillips curve, which were put forward in American academic journals in 1967 and 1968, have some rather striking and obvious parallels with the real world of the early and mid-1970s. They were also at the centre of the discussions at an Institute of Economic Affairs (IEA) seminar last September, which have now been brought together in a new pamphlet. (*Inflation: Causes, Consequences, Cures*, published by the IEA in 1974.) The occasion was a field-day for Professor Milton Friedman, the most vigorous and well-known protagonist of these ideas.

Sceptics might reasonably ask: what is this 'natural rate of unemployment?'. It has a faintly mystical ring. What determines it? How is it to be measured? The discussion at the IEA seminar was largely concerned with these questions. It was argued that trade unions mattered because they distorted the working of the labour market and raised the natural rate. The potential relevance of the trade unions is easy enough to explain, at least in principle. Trade unions ask for higher wages than an unorganized labour force. In those parts of the economy where unionism is prevalent, the effect is artificially to raise the wage level. The inevitable by-product is higher unemployment. When governments try to counter the unemployment by stimulatory policy, it could be argued that the trade unions are the true source of the trouble and the real culprits for rising inflation.

Another possible determinant of the natural rate is a prices and incomes policy. Defenders of such a policy would argue that, both through its favourable effects on expectations and through direct compliance with the rules it lays down, it improves the inflation–unemployment trade-off. In the IEA discussion Professor Friedman showed himself extremely reluctant to acknowledge any importance in these qualifications. In his view, they were merely the institutional forms which the inflationary problem assumed. As Professor Friedman remarked, anything might be the first symptom of instability. In his words, 'It might on one occasion be the creation of a few trade unions. It might be a change in the terms of trade. It might be the loss of an export industry. There is a sense in which you can say in each of these cases that "the cause" of the inflation was a strong trade union or a trade deficit. But surely it is analytically cleaner to say that the fundamental cause of the inflation in all these cases is the adoption of a destabilizing monetary policy, namely, of an attempt to use a monetary weapon to fix something which it cannot fix.'

After years of counter-inflation programmes, industrial relations Acts, special cases, 'norms' and 'ceilings', it is hard not to feel that Professor Friedman is right. If he is right, there are only two ways to cure the problem of inflation. The first is not 'two years' hard slog', but 'four or five years' hard slog', as unemployment held above the natural rate, combined with the cost-reducing effect of productivity increases, brings inflation down to more reasonable levels. The second is for the Government to make some gesture which would banish inflationary expectations quickly and decisively. This is the way hyper-inflations are eventually resolved, with the Government introducing a new currency and announcing draconian budgetary measures to make it credible. No such outcome is necessary or inevitable in this country, but it may help to maintain a sense of perspective to remember that reforms like these have taken place in both France and West Germany since the Second World War, and they don't seem to be doing so badly now.

Gradual Monetary Deceleration – A Theme in British Monetarism

From an article 'Making headway through the gentle therapy of British monetarism' in The Times, *29 April 1975.*

This article is largely self-explanatory, but there are two points of particular interest. First, contrary to the reputation in public debate of monetarists as people who 'grow horns and breathe fire', the Manchester monetarists were acutely concerned in early 1974 that the slowdown in monetary growth was too sharp and too deflationary. Secondly, the article begins my practice of differentiating between British and American monetarism. The distinction is developed most fully in 'British and American monetarism compared', given at the annual Keynes seminar at the University of Kent in 1987 and reprinted here on pp. 209–34.

'Monetarism' has become a vogue word. It is frequently used in political debate, sometimes almost as a term of abuse. Indeed, it would seem not only to have lost the precise technical meaning it once possessed, but to have become a term without any exact meaning whatsoever.

In popular use the word normally has two connotations. According to the first, a monetarist believes that higher unemployment reduces wage demands and inflation; the second connotation is that savage cuts in public spending are required to help the Government balance its books and prevent excessive 'printing of money' if there is a deficit. There is a grain of truth in describing these attitudes as 'monetarist', but to think this is all that monetarism involves is grossly unfair. Perhaps the ease with which monetarism has been distorted reflects the American origins of the school of thought.

The home of modern monetarism is Chicago and its most well-known advocate is Professor Milton Friedman. There has been no strong British tradition to defend the purity of the term. However, monetarist economists are to be found in England and, contrary to a common misconception, they do not grow horns and breathe fire. The centre of monetarist studies is the University of Manchester, where a research project known as the Inflation Workshop has been under way for more than five years. It is under the direction of Professors David Laidler and Michael Parkin, and there are about 20 university lecturers and research assistants associated with it. They have built up a long and impressive list of publications.

At the outset it was not clear what tendency the Workshop's studies would take. The team's members were of all political persuasions, and of all the economic creeds and theologies which have been fashionable in recent years none was particularly dominant. Professor Parkin himself was a self-confessed Keynesian; he believed that changes in taxation and government spending were more effective ways of controlling the economy than changes in interest rates and the money supply. However, five years later all this has changed. The team's members are still of all political persuasions, but on economics they are united – or, at least, as united as economists are ever likely to be in their areas of professional competence. Money, they agree, matters; and if the outbreak of double-digit inflation is to be explained, the explanation is to be sought in governments' neglect of traditional canons of monetary and financial responsibility.

Because the root cause of inflation is regarded as lax monetary and fiscal policy, members of the Workshop favour, in present circumstances, the application of the brimstone and treacle of fiscal and monetary restraint. But this emphatically does not mean that they favour strict control of the money supply regardless of the consequences for demand and employment. Indeed, in early 1974, as the Healey money supply squeeze began, Professor Laidler was one of its most outspoken critics. The expansion of the money supply at rates of more than 25 per cent a year in 1972 and 1973 may have been responsible for the outbreak of excess demand pressures. But it would be folly, he argued, for the authorities to reduce the money supply growth rate to 10 per cent a year.

This rate of money supply deceleration would be too sharp. It would conflict with the system's inflationary expectations, cause a severe liquidity squeeze and result in a larger and more abrupt increase in unemployment than was necessary. In other words, Professor Laidler specifically rejected the idea that unemployment for its own sake was an objective of policy. Unemployment might be an unavoidable cost of overcoming inflation, but policy should be careful and considerate. As far as possible, it should minimize disruptive effects in the labour market.

One of the key words in the monetarist vocabulary at Manchester, as at Chicago, is 'gradualism'. The rise in the money supply should neutrally and steadily reflect the growth of the productive capacity of the economy, and should never alter abruptly. The justification for gradualism is that businesses and individuals form expectations about the economic outlook which depend crucially on current conditions. If government acts in such a way that current conditions are violently transformed within the space of a few months, the expectations created earlier will be inappropriate. Mistakes will tend to become more common and conflicts will arise from the mismatch between what people think they should have and what they can be allowed to have.

The most vivid and most discussed illustration of this general problem is in collective bargaining and in the process of wage formation as a whole. The starting-point of the Manchester economists is that inflation encourages people to expect continuing inflation. Pay settlements today will, therefore, tend to reflect yesterday's price increase. If price increases have been at an annual rate of 25 per cent and the government sits on the money supply so that it rises at only 10 per cent, trade unions will ask for 20 or 25 per cent pay rises while companies' bank deposits are rising much less. The two possible consequences are strikes and labour militancy if companies refuse to match the pay demands, or unemployment if wages are allowed to move out of line with companies' ability to pay. Neither of these consequences is desirable. It would be better to slow down the money supply slowly – reducing growth to 15 or 20 per cent a year – so that expectations can be brought into a closer relation with the behaviour of demand.

The Manchester Workshop's analysis of expectations formation is probably its most distinctive contribution to economic debate. Some Chicago economists think of people forming expectations in a rational way, which implies a quick adjustment of attitudes to every twist and turn of policy-making. If inflation last year stood at 10 per cent, and the government continues to conduct macroeconomic policy in much the same way, people will assume – according to the rational expectation theorists – that inflation this year will also be 10 per cent. The Manchester economists regard the formation of expectations as more complicated. When inflation is running at 10 per cent they believe that people adjust to the existence of this inflation rate, but not completely. In their view, the typical reaction is to assume (from memories of previous non-inflationary years) that inflation will run at a particular fraction of 10 per cent – say 6 or 8 per cent. The analysis of the economy's behaviour and the development of theoretical models is made much more difficult by this pragmatic approach to the importance of expectations. Arguably, it is also made more realistic.

Although expectations are emphasized as part of the inflationary process, other factors, particularly excess demand, are also regarded as vital. A belief in the effectiveness of market forces and a conviction that policies to restrain demand will eventually curb price and wage increases are two of the most typical attitudes of the Manchester economists. Monetarism as a political fashion may or may not be here to stay, but henceforward it need not be regarded as exclusively an American import.

The Importance of Money in Macroeconomic Forecasting – Part 1

From an article 'A lesson from the Treasury on how to be precisely wrong' in The Times, *28 August 1975.*

The indictment of Treasury forecasting in this article is harsh. In effect, the article said that the resources and effort devoted to macroeconomic forecasting by the Treasury were a waste of public funds, essentially because its model failed to take proper account of the role of the money supply. A contrast is drawn between the Treasury's 'precisely wrong' forecasts and the Manchester monetarists' 'roughly right' forecasts. The Manchester monetarists reached their conclusions without the need for a large and expensive computer-based forecasting model. Like Mr Jay with his prediction of a 'boom that must go bust' in 1972, they were successful because they had a good basic understanding of the importance of money to macroeconomic outcomes.

Macroeconometric forecasting was given a subordinate position in Treasury policy-making when money supply targets were being followed in the early 1980s, but it became important again in the mid and late 1980s after the targets had been abandoned. Serious forecasting mistakes, similar to those in 1974 and 1975, were made in 1987 and 1988. As I argue in 'The importance of money in macroeconomic forecasting – part 2' (see below pp. 191–4) the forecasting errors in the Lawson boom had the same origin as the forecasting errors in the Barber boom, namely the failure of the Treasury model to attach sufficient importance to monetary variables.

One fortunate result of writing this article was that, as part of my research for it, I talked about the problems of economic model-building to several leading forecasters. These included Mr Terence (later Sir Terence) Burns, who prepared the London Business School's macroeconomic forecast jointly with Professor James (later Sir James) Ball. We met quite frequently for lunch in the next two or three years, as the London Business School's forecasting approach became, according to the media, steadily more monetarist. One of the topics we discussed most actively was how to specify fiscal policy when monetary targets were the centrepiece of macroeconomic management.

Economic forecasting has been one of the rare growth industries of these troubled times. Not only have companies and financial institutions become increasingly interested in its output, but government departments have also felt obliged to set up distinct forecasting functions. The Treasury, the power-house of British economic policy, has had a 'model' since the early 1960s. It has had a computer, capable of solving large simultaneous equation systems, since 1968. Assisted by this electronic gadgetry, the model has expanded at a far more spectacular rate than the economy it pretends to describe, and now consists of about 700 equations and identities.

But all is not well with the Treasury model. In the last five years the Government's handling of the economy has not been very happy and its public pronouncements on the future behaviour of major economic variables have usually been wrong. The latest example has been politically sensitive and, for that reason, more than usually newsworthy. To quote Mr Denis Healey, the Chancellor of the Exchequer, in his April Budget speech, 'The pressure of demand in the United Kingdom will continue easing and unem-ployment will continue to rise for the remainder of the year. I must warn the House that it could be touching a million by the end of the year.' But unemployment has misbehaved. It amounts to one-and-a-quarter million on some definitions and, on the central definition mentioned by Mr Healey, seasonally adjusted for the United Kingdom, it reached 1,008,800 on 11 August, several months before schedule.

The abrupt and frightening change in labour market conditions has taken the Government by surprise, embarrassed ministers and caused some red faces among Treasury officials. The Government was nevertheless given advance warning by some independent forecasters. In early 1974 Professor David Laidler, then of the University of Manchester Inflation Project, fore-told a sharp rise in unemployment in 18 months' time. His colleague, Professor Michael Parkin, was more definite. Unemployment, he said, would reach one million by July 1975.

The Treasury's estimates – or, rather, 'guesstimates' – of future inflation rates have been even more lamentable, and the consequences have in some ways been just as disturbing. It has clearly been bewildered by the speed of pay and price increases since early 1974. This has been the basic reason for runaway public spending and the present disarray in public sector finances. But the Manchester economists had said that 20 per cent inflation was inevitable some time before it happened. Professor Laidler's evidence to the House of Commons Expenditure Committee on 26 June 1974, was quite firm on this point. 'I would be surprised', he said, 'if the inflation rate stopped accelerating before mid-1975 on the basis of past form. This means the rate of inflation will be over 20 per cent as things are going now. I wrote an article in March in which I said that we would be lucky to keep the rate below 20 per cent.'

The contrast between the Treasury and these independent outside observers should not be pressed to caricature. It is not a quarrel between devils and archangels. The Treasury is a large organization and it must be a struggle to reach a compromise between all the doctrinal positions represented. Some officials may well have agreed with the Manchester economists' warnings when they were given. But the fact remains that most officials did not, and that the Treasury as a whole was badly wrong. What is the matter with its forecasting procedures? Is there some fundamental weakness in its approach or is the work on the right lines but incompetently performed?

The Manchester economists have one great advantage over the official model. They believe that 'money matters', whereas most of the economists who developed the model regard money as an incidental extra to be ignored or remembered according to personal taste. It is possible to find forecasters in the Treasury who deny any connection between the 25 per cent rates of money supply growth in 1972 and 1973 and the 25 per cent rates of inflation found in 1974 and 1975. If one looked hard enough, it might even be possible to find forecasters who deny any connection between the Barber money supply explosion and the property boom or the growth of secondary banks.

It may be that such events are too close to the 'real world' to be of much interest to the Treasury. But official forecasters – and, indeed, private forecasters who also exclude monetary variables from their models – do have some good reasons for adopting their position. Their distrust of 'monetarism' arises from a belief that it has only one equation, that which links the money supply and the money national income. For Treasury purposes such a narrow approach is not much help. The Government needs to know what the prospects are for the major demand categories of consumption, investment and exports and for scores of minor sub-categories.

When monetary variables are incorporated in a detailed model they tend not to be as efficient for forecasting as traditional variables of the so-called 'Keynesian' kind. The relationships between interest rates, for example, and housebuilding or investment tend to be volatile and unreliable. They are not sufficiently stable for inclusion in a model which aims at exactitude and precision. The 'monetarists' do not dispute the variability of particular monetary relationships, although it does not worry them particularly. Whatever the difficulties of detail, they insist on the central connection between the money supply and money national income.

Most 'monetarists' reject the practice of 'fine-tuning' the economy – that is, of trying to keep demand close to a hypothetical full employment level by marginal adjustments of government spending and taxation – as over-ambitious and basically misconceived. They are, on the whole, equally unenthusiastic about particular micro-interventions of the kind facilitated by detailed forecasting. These are some of the ways 'monetarism' coincides with a liberal approach to politics and economics generally.

It should also be said, at a more technical level, that a volatile relationship may still be a powerful one. No one in the Treasury believes – or at least, one hopes that no one in the Treasury believes – that interest rates and other financial factors do not affect housebuilding and investment. The fact that relationships jump up and down does not mean that the relationships are not there or that the money supply can be pumped up at unprecedented rates without influencing economic behaviour.

Moreover, there are plausible explanations for difficulty in accommodating monetary variables into forecasts. Equations are stable if the behaviour they describe is stable and if the institutional framework in which they operate varies little over time. But British monetary policy since the early 1960s has not created a continuous institutional framework. On the contrary, policy has been implemented by a succession of 'ceilings' on lending and directives on credit priorities. These adornments would inevitably have upset the data from which the equations were estimated, even if the underlying behaviour had been stable. If monetary institutions had been left alone, the responses of firms and individuals to financial signals might well have been regular and predictable.

In any case, to recall an old dictum, it is better to be roughly right than precisely wrong. Precise models without money seem to have been badly wrong in the last two or three years, while rough models with money seem to have been more or less right. The growing discontent with the full-blown several-hundred-equation system type of forecasting has encouraged interest in a less formal, but much more pragmatic and simple, approach. This relies on the use of certain statistical series as advance indicators of future economic developments.

The Central Statistical Office (CSO) has developed the technique and begun to publish the results in its monthly *Economic Trends*. These consist of four composite indices of indicators (two indices of leading indicators, one of coincident and one of lagging). If the index of leading indicators goes up it suggests that the economy is likely to revive in several months' time; if the index of lagging indicators increases it suggests that the economy was approaching a peak several months ago. If full-blown computer forecasting has pretensions to being a science, leading indicator forecasting is very definitely an art, above all, an art of selection and emphasis. It is essential to select those indicators which give a good guide to the way the economy is moving and to accord them the appropriate relative emphasis. Both selection and emphasis are improved if they spring from an integrated and complete theory of 'how the economy works'.

This is where 'monetarism' or, at any rate, a belief that monetary and financial variables are crucial to economic behaviour, scores well. The four components of the first CSO leading indicator index are the number of housing starts, the rate of interest on three-month bank bills, the corporate sector's acquisition of financial assets and the *Financial Times* ordinary share index. It is striking that all four are 'monetary', in the sense that they are profoundly influenced by monetary variables. The significance of monetary policy could hardly be more spectacularly confirmed. The same is true, though to a slightly lesser extent, of the second leading indicator index. This is influenced by four variables – the total increase in hire purchase debt, the number of insolvencies, wages per unit of output and new car registrations. Of these, only one (wages per unit of output) is not directly affected by credit and monetary conditions.

A 'Keynesian' forecaster would have great trouble fitting the success of these monetary variables into his world-view. To him the ups and downs in economic activity depend on a highly restricted range of 'exogenous variables', primarily world trade, public expenditure, tax rates and incomes policies. But the success of monetary variables in the leading indicator approach surely casts doubt on the validity of a several-hundred-equation computer approach which excludes them or refers to them only peripherally.

Interest in the leading indicator approach is likely to be furthered by a book, *Cyclical Indicators for the Postwar British Economy*, by Desmond O'Dea, published last month by the Cambridge University Press as an occasional paper for the National Institute of Economic and Social Research. It is particularly notable because it has come out under the aegis of the National Institute, a bastion of Keynesianism and the home of one of the biggest computer models in the United Kingdom. One finding of the study is that the level of share prices is one of the best signals of future economic development. A number of other indicators are awarded points according to their frequency and consistency in preceding changes in output and employment. The *Financial Times* dividend yields and ordinary share indices achieve some of the highest points totals. Other high scorers are the balance of payments, the price of raw materials purchased by industry and the Confederation of British Industry survey of business opinion.

It should surely be uncontroversial that the level of share prices depends very much on the conduct of monetary policy. The automatic reaction of any stock exchange in the world is to lower prices after an officially induced increase in interest rates. It is very difficult indeed to see how a conventional forecaster can both agree with the conclusions of leading indicator studies and believe that monetary policy is of little relevance to economic performance. However, the National Institute and the Treasury may not be especially concerned about the efficiency of monetary variables as predictive tools. The National Institute, which is considering the preparation of its own leading indicator index, seems untroubled by the inconsistency of publishing data on leading indicators and preparing standard forecasts in which these indicators play no role. Civil servants in the Treasury are most unlikely to start looking at the level of share prices to help them in the formulation of policy.

Unless and until conventional models incorporate monetary variables they will fail to capture some of the most important influences on the economy. Instead, the models will have to rely, as they do now, on assumptions, many of them highly political in nature, plucked out of thin air. The people who construct them will continue to see inflation as determined by erratic changes in the community's level of greed and envy (or 'union militancy') and output by violent and inexplicable swings in business optimism. In short, while Treasury forecasters deny that 'money matters', their forecasts will continue to have much in common with astrology. As laymen may have realized, both economic forecasting and astrology are based on a great deal of hunch, speculation and amateur psychology.

3. The rationale of the Medium-Term Financial Strategy

The recession of late 1974 and early 1975, which followed the Barber boom, was the deepest in the post-war period until then. Like most recessions, it had a highly adverse effect on public sector finances, reducing tax revenues and increasing such items of expenditure as unemployment benefits and subsidies to nationalized industries. Partly as a result of these influences and partly because of an underlying increase in public expenditure as the new Labour Government honoured its election pledges, the budget deficit soared in 1974 and 1975. In the first quarter of 1975 the public sector's borrowing requirement reached 12 per cent of gross domestic product, the highest-ever level in peacetime. (It may give a sense of perspective to note that a PSBR/ GDP ratio as high as this today would imply a PSBR of approaching £75 billion.)

The surge in public borrowing created a danger of long-run fiscal unsustainability. Concern about potentially explosive increases in debt interest was expressed in a number of reports from the House of Commons Expenditure Committee in 1974 and 1975. The large budget deficit in 1974/75 added to existing public debt and therefore increased debt interest costs in 1975/76. It was obvious that, unless there were economies in non-interest expenditure or higher taxes, these higher debt interest costs would raise the budget deficit in 1975/76, which would again increase debt interest costs and the budget deficit in 1976/77, and so on.

I reported on the Committee's activities for *The Times* and, as a result, became aware of the long-run debt interest problem. I had already learnt from attending the Committee that the practical operation of fiscal policy was very different from that described in the textbooks. In particular, the Committee had criticized the Treasury in 1974 because it had heavily under-spent on certain capital programmes in 1973. This under-spending, motivated by a wish to avoid paying too much on land and construction costs (which were at ludicrous levels because of the Barber boom), had been similar in size to the 'Budget judgement' in the 1973 Budget. (The Budget judgement is the amount that the Chancellor of the Exchequer injects into or withdraws demand from the economy by changing taxes.) I realized from this episode that very large expenditure slippage and/or revenue miscalculation were common, and that in the hurly-burly of the real world the idea of precise fiscal fine-tuning was an illusion. My criticisms of Keynesian demand management, and my preference for monetary rules, were strongly influenced by these visits to the Expenditure Committee.

It seemed to me that a minimum requirement for a sustainable fiscal policy in the long run was that interest on public sector debt should not grow at a faster rate than national income. The idea is far from startling and can hardly be controversial. However, a tight constraint on fiscal policy is implied. With the ratio of debt to national income given at a moderate level (say, 50 per cent), and an official commitment to price stability (i.e., that the rise in nominal national income should be equal to the long-run real growth rate), it is easy to work out that the maximum sustainable ratio of the budget deficit (i.e., the PSBR) to national income is very low in a slow-growing economy like Britain's. (Formally, the maxium ratio of the budget deficit to national income is equal to the ratio of debt to national income multiplied by the growth rate in long-run steady state. If the debt/income ratio is 50 per cent and the growth rate is 2 per cent a year, the maximum deficit/income ratio compatible with price stability is a mere 1 per cent.)

I was also interested in the relationship between fiscal and monetary policy. In the mid-1970s the large PSBR was a threat to monetary restraint. When the Government was unable to finance the PSBR by sales of gilt-edged securities to non-banks, it had to borrow from the banks, which increased the money supply. Reductions in the PSBR seemed essential if monetary growth were to be reduced over the medium term. Of course, a large PSBR could be reconciled with low monetary growth if the private sector were discouraged from borrowing from the banks, either by quantitative credit restrictions or by high interest rates. But in that event anti-inflationary monetary policy would work only by 'crowding-out' private borrowers from the banking system and perhaps reducing private investment. I wrote a number of articles for *The Times* on 'crowding-out' in 1974 and 1975. (None of these articles is reprinted here.)

These two problems – the problem of potentially explosive growth in debt interest and the problem of crowding-out – argued that large reductions in the PSBR would be vital if inflation were ever to be brought under control. A PSBR/GDP ratio of 12 per cent was certainly not sustainable in an economy with a low inflation rate. The disaster of the Barber boom also emphasized that short-run discretionary adjustments of the fiscal position were inappropriate as a means of managing the economy. It would surely be better to lower the PSBR (or the PSBR/GDP ratio) gradually, so that financial policy as a whole (i.e., both the money supply target and the PSBR/GDP ratio) could be consistent with falling inflation over the medium term. Ideally, the Government should commit itself in advance to a declining path for both monetary growth and the PSBR/GDP ratio, so that irresponsible reflationary episodes such as the Barber boom would never be repeated. At least, if politicians were to repeat them, the breach of the Government's own anti-inflationary guidelines would be clear and public, and would happen some quarters ahead of any resurgence in inflation.

These were some of the key ideas behind the Medium-Term Financial Strategy, which became the centrepiece of the Thatcher Government's anti-inflation programme in the early 1980s. The evolution of the ideas can be seen in my writings of the late 1970s. I benefited from my discussions with Mr Burns at the London Business School, who supported the principle of medium-term financial planning. I was delighted when he was appointed Chief Economic Adviser to the new Thatcher Government in 1979. The first MTFS was announced in the 1980 Budget. It was then regularly up-dated, with some revisions to the forward targets in the light of circumstances, throughout the 1980s. The 1981 Budget, which raised taxes in the middle of a recession and gave new credibility to the Government's anti-inflation programme, would have been inconceivable without the MTFS. Sadly, the revisions of the mid-1980s heavily diluted the financial restraint implicit in the original version. By the late 1980s it had become virtually meaningless as a constraint on politically-motivated monetary adventurism. The story of the breakdown of the MTFS is taken up later in the book.

Monetarism and the Budget Deficit

Paper given to the Money Study Group conference at Brasenose College, Oxford, on 14 September 1976. Not previously published.

This paper, which was written in a great hurry so as to be available in time for the 1976 Money Study Group conference, was very unsatisfactory in several respects and has not previously been published. It is perhaps best seen as a working paper for the final version of the paper 'The analytical foundations of the Medium-Term Financial Strategy', which was published nearly eight years later and is reprinted here on pp. 65–77.

However, the paper was important in two ways. First, it asked a newly pertinent question, 'if it is accepted that money supply targets should be central to macroeconomic policy, what is to be done about fiscal policy?'. Chicago-style monetarism had become rather vague about this issue by the 1970s. Secondly, it answered the question in terms of a long-run steady state, borrowing a technique commonly found in growth theory. (I had been interested in growth theory when I was at Oxford, where I had been fortunate to have some tutorials from Dr Walter Eltis.) The trick here was to take the ratios of certain stocks to income (in this context, the ratios of public debt and money to income) as constant, so as to work out the implications for a flow variable (of the PSBR) to income. One consequence was to think about fiscal policy not as an aspect of a short-run stabilization problem, but as constrained by long-run stability considerations. In particular, it had to be consistent with anti-inflationary monetary policy. The shift of focus was vital in establishing a rationale for medium-term financial planning. (Incredibly, in the mid-1970s there were still some British economists who thought fiscal policy should be addressed to short-run demand management while the PSBR was over 10 per cent of GDP!).

The paper has had to be tidied up in various ways. First, the algebra behind the numerical answer (that, to defeat inflation, 'the maximum permissible ratio between the budget deficit and national income is between 2 and 2¹/₂ per cent') was a mess and has not been reprinted. (The reasoning, roughly, was that − with a debt/income ratio of 0.6 and a long-run real growth rate assumed optimistically at 3¹/₂ per cent − a budget deficit of 2.1 per cent of GDP would be sustainable. In addition, the paper conjectured − I now think wrongly − that the banking system needed some public sector assets for its reserve asset position, which justified a little extra deficit financing.) Secondly, I argued that budget deficits were required to support monetary growth, because banks had to have a proportion of safe, liquid assets (i.e., public sector obligations free from default risk) in their balance sheets for prudential reasons. These could increase, in line with economic growth, only if the Government ran a budget deficit. I now believe that this argument is incorrect. A portfolio of commercial bills 'accepted' by two good banking names should be quite sufficient, in normal circumstances, to provide the banking system with prudentially appropriate assets. But I have left the passage in, as the discussion is interesting.

The last few paragraphs, on 'the re-entry problem', are not a model of literary clarity. But there is no simple rule to fix the 'best' public debt/ income ratio. To that extent, this approach to determining the right level of the budget deficit is arbitrary, as the paper concedes.

One of the most important changes in thinking about British economic policy in recent years has been a reaction against discretionary adjustment of the Government's financial position to control fluctuations in activity. Scepticism about 'fiscal fine-tuning' has developed partly because of its conspicuous inadequacy to meet the cyclical problems of the 1970s and partly because the current large public sector borrowing requirement is seen as a threat to financial stability. A preference for automatic rules, to be obeyed by the Government irrespective of the cyclical conjuncture, has been expressed in some quarters.

Public debate has concentrated on two main rule prescriptions. These are the monetarist recommendation that the money supply be regulated in order to keep its rate of growth in line with that of productive capacity, and the 'new Cambridge school' doctrine that the budget deficit be geared to medium-term balance-of-payments targets, being set equal to the private sector's equilibrium net acquisition of financial assets, which is said to exhibit considerable stability through time.[1] These two rules are concerned with different policy variables and they focus on different objectives. One consequence is that monetarism appears to give no guidance on the desirable size of the budget deficit. This impression is confirmed by the haphazard reference to the budget position from its supporters. Some monetarists seem to believe that fiscal rectitude consists of the restoration of balanced budgets; others profess an almost total indifference to the scale of the Government's borrowing needs.[2]

The purpose of this paper is to show that monetarism, loosely understood, can generate a framework for determining the permissible size of the budget deficit in relation to national income. The framework is theoretical, but it has direct policy applications. It accords high priority to the attainment of price stability. By contrast, other policy goals, such as full employment and balance-of-payments equilibrium, are not recognized in the analysis. Their exclusion could be justified on the assumptions that labour markets are self-equilibrating and that floating exchange rates are a sufficient answer to external imbalance. Some economists might disagree with these assumptions. However, they would probably accept that, if the budget deficit indicated by the present discussion is inconsistent with full employment or payments equilibrium, serious problems would arise for the conduct of economic policy. The viability of pursuing simultaneously the three objectives would be challenged.

The notion of 'monetarist equilibrium' is central to the analysis and must be defined at the outset. It is not to be understood as equilibrium in a behavioural sense; although it may be compatible with stable asset acquisition patterns, it is not intended as a partial specification of portfolio balance. Instead, it should be considered as equilibrium in a policy sense; it pertains to a state of affairs in which the Government is achieving price stability and can expect to continue doing so indefinitely into the future.

In the next two sections the conditions for monetarist equilibrium are discussed. They are that money supply growth should be related to the growth of productivity capacity and that the rate of increase of interest on the national debt should be equal to the rate of increase in national income. Given the institutional context in Britain and most other industrial countries, these conditions can only be satisfied if the budget deficit is of a particular size. Monetarist equilibrium may obtain in a stationary or growing economy, but it is most interesting when set against the background of economic growth. The analysis is close, therefore, to the models of 'steady-state' expansion which play such a major role in the theoretical interpretation of growth. In the fourth section the problem of moving from the current disequilibrium towards equilibrium is considered.

In Britain the money supply is tied to a number of government liabilities and its growth is largely determined by the public sector borrowing requirement. Although the linkages may be familiar, they are important to the present argument and it may be helpful to recall them in more detail.

The money supply has two components, notes and coin in circulation with the public, and bank deposits. The first component is a liability of the Bank of England and, indirectly, of the Government. Since the public cannot ask for redemption except in the form of other notes and coin, this characterization may seem artificial. But it is at least true that a gap between the Government's expenditure and revenue is necessary for an increase in the issue of notes and coin; and, apart from Friedman's helicopter, no other route whereby they may enter the economy has been suggested.

Bank deposits are a liability of the banking system. However, the propensity of the banks to extend credit and add to both sides of their balance sheets is constrained by the quality of their assets. In particular, the structure of the financial system is such that deposit creation depends on the quantity of reserve assets in their portfolios, and reserve assets are preponderantly liabilities of the public sector. Consequently, deposit creation is related to the public sector's financial position.

It is instructive – and essential to the argument – to note that the private sector is unable to conceive on a sufficient scale either notes and coin or reserve assets. The objection to the private issue of notes and coin is that, when enforced by law, the seigniorage accrues to a company or institution; and it is not clear that any private body merits such an advantage. On the other hand, if private issue is not enforced by law it is not credible and cannot perform the function of a medium of exchange. The possibility of reserve assets being provided by the private sector is more substantial. Indeed, commercial bills, as high-quality private sector paper, do rank as reserve assets in Britain. But it is unlikely that the banks would feel safe if their operations were ultimately founded on the reputations of a small number of leading industrial companies. They must have government paper on their books. Only central government liabilities are altogether free from default risk.[3]

It follows, therefore, that a budget deficit is required to achieve money supply growth and that a deficit of a particular size is necessary for growth at a particular rate. It follows also that the monetarist recommendation of stable monetary expansion has definite implications for fiscal policy.

Some remarks on the monetarist rule may be relevant here. The rule is normally proposed in the form 'the money supply should grow at a steady 3 to 5 per cent a year in line with the underlying rate of growth of national output'. This formulation is based on the observation that the money supply and money national income tend to move together over time. But to state the problem in this way has a drawback: the demand for money arises for private expenditures, not for money national income as a whole. Because the Government can 'print' money, the transactions under its control are not covered by running down holdings of bank deposits and it has no need to keep liquid assets of any type. Hence, if the share of national income accounted for by public expenditure increases, the demand for money declines. There are some difficulties with this assertion. For example, the private sector does build up balances in advance of tax payments and the status of public corporations and local authorities, which are not altogether protected from risk and therefore have some demand for liquidity, is uncertain. But these difficulties are incidental to the main argument and may be avoided by making the assumption that the ratio between public and private expenditure is constant. Until the last three years the assumption would have been realistic in the British case.

Although the demand for money may bear a stable relationship to private expenditures, it does not, of course, necessarily grow at the same rate. The income elasticity of demand for money may differ for one; and technical progress in the financial system may enable companies and individuals to economize on their liquid balances. These points are not incorporated in the relationships in the appendix [not published here], but the qualification is not important. If equilibrium obtains only when the money supply is increasing at a steady rate different from productive capacity the budget deficit necessary for monetary reasons may be adjusted accordingly.

One interesting, if obvious, outcome of the discussion so far is that balanced budgets and a monetary rule are not consistent, apart from the special case of a static economy. In general unbalanced budgets are appropriate and the degree of imbalance is a positive function of the growth rate. An exception would be feasible when illiquid liabilities of the Government, incurred in previous deficit phases, are coming due for redemption as the option to redeem in notes and coin, or reserve assets, would then be available. However, such a policy would have effects on the burden of debt interest, and it is to this topic that attention must now be directed.

The results of large national debts have been controversial for centuries and the subject remains among the most unsettled in economics. The purpose of this section is not to revive the disputes, but to outline the reasoning behind the rather unsurprising principle that interest on the national debt must never, for any prolonged period of time, be allowed to grow at a faster rate than national income.

One of the more ancient perceptions of economic science is that a nation cannot be in debt to itself. In this trivial sense the national debt can never, no matter how large, impose a burden on society. But this does not mean that the size of the debt and its rate of growth can be ignored. The simplest and most entertaining demonstration of the dangers of a burgeoning national debt is to attempt the description of an economy where interest on the debt is equal to national income. The tale is an improbable one and perhaps it does not need to be said that the economy would break down long before debt interest had become so large. We may distinguish two cases – one where the debt interest is met from direct taxation; and one where it is met from indirect.

If debt interest is financed only from direct taxation, the rate of tax has to average at least 50 per cent on both earned and unearned income. With a 50 per cent rate the national income accounting identities are satisfied, as long as there is no Government expenditure apart from debt interest. Further expenditure would necessitate an even higher tax rate. It is doubtful that an efficient pattern of incentives would survive with these tax rates in force, but a decline in national income would exaggerate the problem. The piquancy of the Government's dilemma is heightened by distinguishing between the working taxpayer and the rentier. (The rentier is also a taxpayer, but he does not have to do anything to receive his income.) The working taxpayer obtains no return from half his output and probably has no compunction about evading tax. But, if the Government does not raise the revenue required, the rentier feels cheated, particularly as he has saved and made sacrifices to acquire his bonds.

If debt interest is paid for by indirect taxation the situation is a little easier. A 100 per cent rate of value added tax would again satisfy the national income accounting identities. The working taxpayer would still be doing half his day for no reward, but he might be under the optical illusion that he was being paid in full because there would be no deductions from his payslip. The snag here is less one of work incentives than of the attractiveness of carrying out transactions by barter or cash to avoid identification by the tax authorities. Successful evasion would, as in the direct tax case, magnify the Government's difficulties. The situation is untenable.

Clearly, there are upper bounds to the ratio between interest payments on the national debt and the national income. The binding constraint on deficit financing is that, when taken to extremes, it sows the seeds of social conflict beween the taxpayer and the rentier.

These conclusions are not new. Indeed, they were a commonplace in the 1920s and 1930s and constituted the most persuasive justification for sound finance and balanced budgets. The effectiveness of sound finance principles in public debate at that time was largely attributable to the force of 'the limits of taxable capacity' argument. The financial traumas of several European governments after the First World War, which had left a legacy of enormous national debts, remained vivid in the minds of most contemporary economists. In France in the mid-1920s, for example, the greater part of government revenue was levied on behalf of the rentier, and the resulting social stresses became intolerable. Keynes wrote an article in *The Nation and Athenaeum* of 9 January 1926, with the rather impudent title 'An Open Letter to the French Minister of Finance (whoever he is or may be)', suggesting that a deliberate inflation of between 60 and 80 per cent be engineered to diminish the real value of the debt-servicing burden.[4] The memory of this phase of its financial history may be responsible for France's high ratio of indirect to direct taxation and for its failure [until the 1980s] to establish an effective market in long-term government bonds.

If, therefore, debt interest threatens to rise indefinitely as a proportion of national income, corrective measures have to be taken and policy is not in equilibrium. There would, however, be no objection to keeping debt interest and national income growing at the same rate. This condition is chosen here as a characteristic of monetarist equilibrium.

It is important to note that the condition is not necessarily optimal; it may be that a large national debt occupies too prominent a position in the private sector's portfolio and 'crowds out' other asset holdings, such as equities and debentures, which would otherwise match a greater accumulation of real capital goods. But a situation in which debt interest and national income are growing at the same rate is sustainable and, for the purposes of this paper, that is what matters. The analysis is intended to find out the maximum size of the budget deficit compatible with zero inflation and political stability, not to indicate the economic results of having a smaller deficit.

The rule that debt interest should grow no more quickly than national income was mentioned in most manuals of public finance before the onset of Keynesian macroeconomics. It has tended to be disregarded since *The General Theory* because the popular assessment of Keynes's work is that uninhibited deficit financing is warranted by a deficiency of aggregate demand. In fact, no leading economist of Keynes's generation – and certainly not Keynes himself – thought that the size of the budget deficit could be divorced entirely from considerations of financial prudence. Indeed, the 1944 White Paper on *Employment Policy*, often described as the charter of discretionary demand management, contains an excellent paragraph on the approach towards controlling the national debt in the long run. It deserves to be quoted in full:

> Not only the national dead-weight debt in the narrow sense, but other public indebtedness which involves directly or indirectly a charge on the Exchequer or on the rates, reacts on the financial system. Interest and other charges thus falling on the Exchequer are often regarded as in the nature of a transfer income in the hands of the recipients and as imposing no real burden on the community on the whole. But the matter does not present itself in that light to the taxpayer, on whose individual effort and enterprise high taxation acts as a drag. At the same time, proper limits on public borrowing also depend on the magnitude of the debt charge in relation to the rate of growth of national income. In a country in which money income is increasing, the total debt can be allowed to increase by quite appreciable amounts without increasing the proportionate burden of the debt Owing to the prolonged decline in the birth rate and the present age distribution of the population we can no longer rely, as in the past, on an increase in national income resulting solely from an increase in the number of income-earning persons. On the other hand, these difficulties would be more than offset by continued progress in technical efficiency, which is the dominating factor in the growth of real national income.

More remarkably still, the previous paragraph closed with the words: 'To the extent that the policies proposed in this Paper affect the balancing of the Budget in a particular year, they certainly do not contemplate any departure from the principle that the Budget must be balanced over a longer period'; and the following paragraph, almost anticipating what has been termed the 'fiscal frenzy' of 1974 and 1975, opened with the warning that, 'Both at home and abroad the handling of our monetary problems is regarded as a test of the general firmness of the policy of the Government. An undue growth in national indebtedness will have a quick result on confidence. But no less serious would be a budgetary deficit arising from a fall of revenues due to depressed industrial and commercial conditions.'[5]

The two conditions for monetarist equilibrium are combined in an appendix [not published here] and a simple algebraic solution for the maximum permissible ratio between the budget deficit and money national income is reached. The ratio depends on the growth rate and the income elasticity of demand for money, which cannot be manipulated by the authorities; and on the reserve asset ratio, and the ratios of private expenditure and the national debt to national income, which can be partly influenced by government action.

The role of the ratio of national debt to national income – or debt/income ratio, for short – is awkward, because it and the budget deficit interact. An argument could be made, that, since the ratio is an inheritance of history it could reasonably be regarded as a datum, for present purposes. But this is unsatisfactory because, when the economy is out of monetarist equilibrium, the budget deficit causes variations in the ratio. Only in equilibrium is the ratio constant.

The interpretation of the debt/income ratio is critical for selecting the correct budget deficit figure. It obstructs the immediate application of the analysis to policy formation because the formula is not valid outside an ideal equilibrium context. The current state of affairs diverges rather conspicuously from such an ideal. More specifically, it would make little sense to favour stability of the ratio of debt interest to national income (debt interest/income ratio) in the present circumstances. Were inflation to be overcome, interest rates would fall sharply, perhaps to 3 or $3\frac{1}{2}$ per cent on the type of assets which constitute the bulk of the national debt. Since the average rate of interest on the nominal value of the debt is at present about $7\frac{1}{4}$ per cent, a constant debt interest/income ratio would imply a doubling of the debt/income ratio. But this, in turn, would imply several years of deficit financing.

Two approaches to the 're-entry problem', of moving from disequilibrium towards equilibrium, might be suggested. The first is to take the debt/income ratio as a desideratum in its own right. It is most likely that the policy-maker would choose one close to the current ratio between the nominal value of the national debt and the national income (or nominal debt/income ratio). This course is recommended here because it minimizes disturbance to public sector finances and has the merit of simplicity. But there is a second approach which highlights the economic significance of policy options and might lead to a more reasoned discussion of alternatives. It is to note the essential respects in which equilibrium and disequilibrium differ.

There are two such respects. First, in equilibrium the nominal and market values of the national debt are identical, because interest rates are constant; in disequilibrium they may not be equal. Secondly, in the comparison of equilibria it is of no importance whether the debt interest/income ratio or debt/income ratio is chosen because they differ by equal proportionate amounts, but in the comparison of disequilibrium and equilibrium the choice of ratio affects the issue because changes in the ratios may not be proportional. This contrast hints at three possible objectives for a policy-maker faced by the re-entry problem:

1. Stability of the debt interest/income ratio. On the path to equilibrium the nominal debt/income and market debt/income ratios adjust.
2. Stability of the market debt/income ratio. The debt interest/income and nominal debt/income ratios adjust.
3. Stability of the nominal debt/income ratio. The debt interest/income and market debt/income ratios adjust.

In discriminating between these three objectives the policy-maker may have several considerations in mind. He may have political preferences for a low debt interest/income ratio from sheer dislike of the rentier class. Alternatively, he may feel that a high market debt/income ratio 'crowds out' the accumulation of capital goods by the private sector and discourages investment by satisfying savers' asset demands too completely. Another option is to decide that an abundance of public debt instruments adds flexibility to the financial system and, because of their suitability as collateral, encourages the taking of risks in industry and commerce. It is impossible to resolve these issues in the space available here. A much fuller and rather different discussion would be required before they could be adjudicated.

It is surely natural, nevertheless, for the Government in Britain today to pay most attention to the nominal debt/income ratio and to insert its present value – about 0.6 – into the formula. Stability of the debt interest/income and market debt/income ratios do not bear examination as objectives, unless wild upheavals in the Government's financial position on the path to equilibrium can be contemplated with equanimity.

If, therefore, the Government wants to pursue a permanent and sustainable anti-inflationary policy, the maximum permissible ratio between the budget deficit and national income is between 2 and 2^1/2 per cent. This fiscal recommendation is designed as an accompaniment to the monetary rule. It may be regarded as a step towards the more complete specification of monetarist stabilization policy.

The argument that the Government should rigidly adhere to a budget deficit of at most between 2 and 2^1/2 per cent year after year has not been made in this paper, but the reader may guess (rightly) that the author is in favour of this course. It would be strange, but not necessarily inconsistent to support an automatic monetary rule and discretionary fiscal policy. But even to a defender of fiscal 'fine-tuning' the paper's results may be valuable. In particular, an indication has been given of the average level around which the budget deficit may be allowed to fluctuate through each cycle if monetarist equilibrium – or, less tendentiously, price stability – is to be preserved from one cycle to the next.

It could be objected that the conclusion depends on an arbitrary value of the debt/income ratio. The objection is valid. But the argument could be hardened by appealing more definitely to the 'crowding-out' hypothesis that an increase in public debt substitutes for private debt issues that would otherwise have occurred, and thereby reduces investment. If this hypothesis is accepted the paper has effectively reinstated the pre-Keynesian 'Treasury view' that the inevitable results of increases in government expenditure, when unmatched by taxation, are higher inflation, less private expenditure or some combination of the two.[6]

Notes

1. See 'Public expenditure and the management of the economy' by F. Cripps, W.A.H. Godley and M. Fetherston in 9th Report from the Expenditure Committee *Public Expenditure, Inflation and the Balance of Payments* (London: H.M.S.O., 1974, particularly p. 4). No behavioural explanation for the stability of the private sector's acquisition of financial assets has been provided by the new Cambridge economists, an omission unsurprising in view of their neglect of monetary economics. Perhaps because of this weakness the new Cambridge school was unable to provide an explanation of the improvement in the balance of payments in 1975, concurrently with a marked widening of the public sector financial deficit. In any case the theory does not stand up as an insight into payments imbalance because it takes no account of the fiscal position in trade partners. Would Britain have a current account deficit equal to 3 per cent of national income if its public sector financial deficit were 4 or 5 per cent and that in other countries were 10 per cent?

    The new Cambridge economists have performed a service, however, by pointing out the need for a theory of private sector asset acquisition. I would suggest that it can be divided into two parts – the acquisition of liquid assets; and the acquisition of illiquid assets. The acquisition of liquid assets in equilibrium is stable through time. This, after all, is the kernal of monetarism. The behaviour of illiquid asset acquisition is more uncertain. It clearly is influenced by both interest rates and changes in the value of private sector wealth. In 1974 and 1975 interest rates rose to unprecedented levels and the market value of most asset holdings collapsed. Perhaps it is not surprising that private sector acquisition of financial assets was very different from that in the 1960s and early 1970s.

    A much fuller macroeconomic picture – incorporating the effects of monetary policy on economic activity and, hence, on the public sector's financial position – would be needed to assess the new Cambridge arguments properly.

2. Calls for balanced budgets are legion. For an example of indifference to the budget position see S. Brittan's comment in the *Financial Times* of 5 February 1976. 'Events in the last few months have shown that monetary control is the important element of "sound finance" and that the balanced budget doctrine is, for a thousand and one different reasons, as absurd as Keynes once thought it to be.'

3. The argument in this paragraph has an obvious relevance to Professor Hayek's advocacy of 'laissez-faire' in money in *Choice in Currency* (London: Institute of Economic Affairs: 1976). In fact, the historical evidence is that, by a process of natural selection, the financial system chooses one money, the liabilities of 'the lender of last resort'. The lender of last resort is always banker to the Government because it is the strongest and most reliable financial institution.

4. Reprinted in *The Collected Writings of John Maynard Keynes* vol. IX *Essays in Persuasion* (London: Macmillan, 1972), pp. 76–82.

5. White Paper on *Employment Policy* (London: H.M.S.O., 1944) pp. 25–26, paragraphs 77–79. The phrase 'fiscal frenzy' is used by David Rowan in a recent *Banca Nazionale del Lavoro Review*. I also recommend that the reader have a look at Sir Herbert Brittain's *The British Budgetary System* (London: Allen & Unwin, 1959), where the purpose of the above-the-line and below-the-line distinction is outlined by a traditional 'Treasury knight'. On p. 53 there is a pellucid explanation of the need to keep borrowing above-the-line under control. 'Over a period of years the Budget should certainly be balanced above-the-line; otherwise that part of the debt not covered by new assets will increase indefinitely.' The exceptional economic stability of the 1950s – the heyday of the so-called 'Keynesian Revolution' – may well have been the product of sound finance of a rather orthodox variety.

6. Three further sets of observations may be relegated to a final note.

    First, there is the important practical question of the appropriate budget deficit concept. The vital distinction here is between public sector expenditures which are expected to be covered by taxation, and public sector expenditures which are expected to be covered by ongoing commercial operations and the associated receipts. Borrowing incurred by nationalized industries should not be included in the budget deficit if it will be repaid by a subsequent financial surplus arising from such receipts.

Secondly, it has been pointed out to me that there is already a large literature on fiscal and monetary policy in long-run equilibrium, based on Tobin's model of portfolio balance. I can only say that such examples of this literature as I have read pay scant attention to institutional realities. Money drops like manna from heaven, bonds are issued to buy machines which are rented back to the private sector, and so on. That would not matter if more realistic assumptions were difficult to model – but, as I hope this paper shows, they can be analysed quite simply.

Thirdly, some interesting questions would arise for international finance theory if the budget deficits indicated by the present analysis differed from country to country. I suspect it could be shown that the conditions for monetarist equilibrium could not be satisfied in a fixed exchange rate world where different countries had different growth rates. See Robert A. Mundell *International Economics* (London: Macmillan, 1968), pp. 126–129, for a tentative account of the implications of growth rates for budget policy and the balance of payments. Mundell's analysis – in these pages, at least – is confined to the budget deficit necessary for monetary reasons, and does not take account of more long-term debt issues and the wider portfolio balance problems they would raise.

A Proposal for a Medium-Term Financial Plan

From a memorandum on the Expenditure White Paper, Cmnd 7049, submitted to the General Sub-Committee of the Expenditure Committee of the House of Commons in 1978.

After I left The Times *in 1976 and stopped reporting on its proceedings, the Expenditure Committee of the House of Commons invited me to submit evidence on various aspects of the economic situation. The next paper is taken from a memorandum I wrote on the 1978 Expenditure White Paper. It set out more explicitly than the 1976 paper on 'Monetarism and the budget deficit' a proposal for a medium-term financial plan. But the sentence, 'If non-inflationary money supply growth and propitious conditions for business investment are to be achieved by the early 1980s, the PSBR must be reduced to about $2^1/2$ per cent of national income', clearly recalled one conclusion of the 1976 paper. The frequent references to the 'new industrial strategy', one of the then Labour Government's hobbyhorses, played to the political gallery. But the basic point – about the inconsistency between a large budget deficit and ample private sector finance for industry – was right.*

The latest Public Expenditure White Paper gives much useful information on certain recent developments of great importance to the British economy, notably the size of the fall in expenditure in the 1976/77 and 1977/78 financial years. The fall has been much greater than envisaged in previous

White Papers, and is likely to attract considerable comment. However, in this note the emphasis will be placed rather on a new departure in the presentation of the White Papers – the attempt to place expenditure projections within the broader fiscal context and, more particularly, to provide estimates of the Government's borrowing needs in future financial years. Later in the memorandum a proposal is advanced for medium-term financial planning, in which borrowing requirement forecasts play a central role. The proposal is designed to achieve a better co-ordination of fiscal and monetary policy. It is particularly pertinent now that the Bank of England has committed itself to money supply targets and described them, in its July 1977 *Quarterly Bulletin*, as possibly marking 'a major step in the evolution of monetary policy'.

The main purpose of the concept of the public sector borrowing requirement is financial: it indicates the size of the gap between the public sector's incomings and outgoings which has to be covered by borrowings from other agents in the economy. Its significance for monetary policy has always been well understood. However, it has perhaps not been sufficiently noticed that the new practice of announced money supply targetry may be co-ordinated with budget deficit projections to form a medium-term financial plan, with many wide implications for macroeconomic policy.

It is generally agreed that if inflation is to be overcome, money supply growth will have to be brought down to that of productive potential, currently believed to be about $3^{1}/_{2}$ per cent a year. But there is a common view that too abrupt a deceleration from current rates will cause unnecessary reductions in output and employment, because of the shock to expectations. In the 1974/75 financial year, sterling M3 rose by 7.7 per cent; in 1975/76, by 7.1 per cent; and in 1976/77, by 7.8 per cent. In the present financial year an acceleration to about 10 or 11 per cent looks probable. It seems reasonable to propose as targets 8 per cent growth in 1978/79, 6 per cent in 1979/80 and 4 per cent in 1980/81. There would then be a real chance of achieving price stability in the early 1980s.

Money supply growth may be regarded as the sum of three credit counterparts – the PSBR minus sales of public sector debt to the non-bank public (the public sector contribution); bank lending to the private sector minus the increase in banks' non-deposit liabilities (the private sector contribution); and the increase in bank deposits arising from a variety of external transactions, of which the most important is usually intervention by the Exchange Equalization Account in the foreign exchange markets (the external contribution). In the next few years, the external contribution is likely to be small and positive, because of the need to acquire foreign currency to repay Britain's international debts. The key to medium-term financial planning is therefore to obtain the right balance between the public and private sector contributions.

In paragraph 55 of volume I, the White Paper observes that, 'Along with a satisfactory balance of payments, the first claim on higher output must be investment. A rise in the proportion of national income devoted to industrial investment is essential both for underpinning a faster growth rate and more generally for increasing industrial efficiency and providing more employment.' The connection between this observation and the Government's financial intentions is not made evident. But, in fact, the connection is direct. An increase in investment can be financed either from companies' internal sources, principally retained profits, or external sources. With current low levels of industrial profitability, reliance has to be placed to a great extent on external sources, such as bank borrowing and sales of equity and fixed interest debt.

Here is the crux of the problem. For any given money supply target, the higher is the public sector contribution to monetary growth the lower must be the private sector contribution; and a lower private sector contribution entails less bank borrowing by industry, checking the recovery in investment. It might be argued that this does not require that the PSBR be reduced to make room for industry's financial needs because the public sector contribution as a whole can be reduced by sufficiently large sales of public sector debt to the non-bank public, for example, by skilful and adroit management of the gilt-edged market.

However, there are three objections to this argument. The first is that large sales of public sector debt constitute a major drain on the financial resources of the leading savings institutions, the pension funds and life assurance offices. These institutions therefore have less money available for buying debt issued by the corporate sector. It may be difficult for companies to raise capital by rights issues or offers of debentures and loan stock. The resulting inability to maintain a satisfactory ratio between long-term and short-term debt, and between equity and fixed interest liabilities may also inhibit companies' willingness to borrow from the banks.

Secondly, the rate of interest needed to promote the quantity of gilt-edged sales compatible with a money supply target may prohibit a significant revival in lending to industry. For example, in the December 1976 Letter of Intent to the International Monetary Fund, lip-service was paid to 'the essential needs of industry' as one of the desiderata of monetary policy. But the interest rates prevailing at that time – with Minimum Lending Rate at $14^3/_4$ per cent – were, although necessary to stimulate buying of gilts, certain to prevent any significant increase in bank loan demand.

Thirdly, a situation in which both the budget deficit and industrial demand for loans are high is liable to generate considerable financial instability. If, because of a disappointing set of economic news, the gilt-edged market is reluctant to buy 'tap' stocks (i.e., new issues of government debt), the strength of the expansionary monetary forces is likely to cause bad money supply figures very quickly. The market's trepidation about the authorities' response exaggerates the difficulties in selling stock as pessimism becomes self-reinforcing. A sharp rise in interest rates is needed to restore confidence. The abrupt interest rate movements which have occurred on a number of occasions in the mid-1970s exemplify the problem. Interest rate volatility is in itself an evil, both because of the uncertainty engendered in business planning and because of the administrative inconvenience to financial institutions and their customers.

It follows, then, that large budget deficits, monetary restraint and the revival in lending to the private sector which is a precondition for industrial recovery cannot be reconciled. There should be progressive reductions in the PSBR in the next three years in order both to ensure monetary deceleration and to leave scope for increased availability of investment finance. The point can perhaps be given a more pungent and polemical tone by saying that 'expansionary' Keynesian fiscal policy and the 'new industrial strategy' are incompatible – unless the money supply is again to be allowed to grow at over 25 per cent a year as in 1972 and 1973.

In Table 3.1 an example of a medium-term financial plan is given. It respects both the aim of slowing monetary growth and allowing scope for a big rise in lending to the private sector.

No sophisticated justification for the figures suggested in Table 3.1 can be provided, and its primary function is illustrative. Nevertheless, a number of comments seem in order.

Priority is given in Table 3.1 to the private sector's borrowing needs. The greater part of bank advances are to productive concerns – roughly 30 per cent of the total is to industry, 25 per cent to services and 13 per cent to 'other production' – and, if they are to expand, the finance must be available. It is worth pointing out that the £3 billion totals for bank lending to the private sector which have been typical in recent years do not, in fact, necessarily represent finance for new projects. The reason is that interest charges – which will amount to about £3 billion to £3½ billion this year on a sterling bank advances total for the UK banking system of £30,013 million (16 November 1977) – increase banks' assets and liabilities even if there has been no genuine loan demand for investment or stockbuilding purposes.

One salient message from Table 3.1 is that, if non-inflationary money supply growth and propitious conditions for business investment are to be established by the early 1980s, the PSBR must be reduced to about 2½ per cent of national income. This conclusion may be contentious, but it follows from logic and arithmetic, not dogma and theory. The projections made in a

Table 3.1 A medium-term financial plan

	1967–77 outturn [(£m)]	1977–78 estimate [(£bn)]	1978–79 estimate [£bn]	1979–80 projections [(£bn)]	1980–81 projections [(£bn)]
			All figures in current price terms		
1976–77 figures from *Financial Statistics*					
Sterling M3 (unadjusted) – end of financial year	40,439	44.7	48.3	51.2	53.2
Increase in year	7.6%	10.5%	8%	6%	4%
Amount of increase	2,828	4.2	3.6	2.9	2.0
Causes of increase					
1. Public sector contribution					
–PSBR	8,770	6.7	5.4	4.8	3.8
–Debt sales to non-banks	–7,450	–8.0	–6.0	–5.9	–5.5
2. Private sector contribution					
–Lending to private sector	3,414	3.3	3.6	3.9	3.9
–Lending to overseas	218	0.6	0.6	0.7	0.7
–Non-deposit liabilities	–776	–1.0	–1.0	–1.1	–1.1
3. External contribution	–1,348	2.6	1.0	0.5	0.2
Total	2,828	4.2	3.6	2.9	2.0

medium-term financial plan highlight the nature of the options facing the Government – and perhaps most important of all, they emphasize that fiscal, monetary and industrial policy should be viewed as an integrated whole.

There is an urgent need for the closer harmonization of monetary and fiscal policy. For much of the mid-1970s the two branches of macroeconomic policy have been in conflict. In 1974 and 1975, for example, Government expenditure rose dramatically, the budget deficit widened and fiscal policy was extremely lax. Monetary policy, on the other hand, was tightened with almost unparalleled severity. The British economy was being driven like a car with one foot on the accelerator and the other on the brake – and it is not surprising that the engine, the private industrial sector, responded badly.

The proposal for a medium-term financial plan accords with the spirit of the comment in the December 1977 Bank of England *Quarterly Bulletin* that, 'Both fiscal and monetary policy affect demand; there are thus important inter-connections between the two branches of policy. A more expansionary fiscal policy would increase the Government's borrowing requirement. One consideration is that beyond a point this would be difficult to finance without either leading to an expansion of the money stock that would seem excessive, or alternatively raising interest rates. The latter would in turn have negative effects on the private sector, partially offsetting those of the Budget itself. For these reasons fiscal and monetary policy need to be decided as part of a single policy.'

The approach being suggested here cannot be regarded as radical, 'extreme' or 'monetarist'; it would not represent a great departure from existing practice; it is simply a common-sense attempt to ensure that expenditure policy decisions, tax decisions and monetary decisions are not taken independently. Future annual expenditure White Papers could serve as a focus for public discussion of the interdependence of these decisions.

The latest Expenditure White Paper should be commended for its joint publication of figures for both revenue and expenditure. This may eventually prove to have been rather more than a minor presentational reform. Indeed, it may foreshadow a great improvement in the co-ordination of fiscal and monetary decisions in this country. After the inconsistencies and conflicts which have marred economic policy in recent years, this would be a very encouraging development.

Our recommendation of a medium-term financial plan designed to restore price stability and industrial prosperity by the early 1980s has implications which many economists would not like. For example, it would abolish discretionary fiscal policy as the prime instrument for regulating aggregate demand. Moreover, the pursuit of price stability by one country in an inflationary international environment might, according to some observers, create structural adjustment difficulties for industry. At any rate, it is heartening that the annual Expenditure White Papers may now become the forum for a more well-informed debate on these and other issues.

The Medium-Term Financial Implications of North Sea Oil

From the June 1979 issue of L. Messel & Co.'s quarterly forecast of financial flows, Financial Analysis.

The economic prospect was changed radically in 1979 by two developments; the election of a radical right-wing Conservative Government under Mrs Thatcher, and a sharp rise in the price of oil following the Iranian Revolution. The new Government was more receptive to monetarist ideas than its predecessor. Meanwhile, the higher level of oil prices had made it easier to implement the fiscal element in the monetarist package, because it increased the value of tax revenues on North Sea oil profits. The ambitious fiscal agenda set by my 1976 Money Study Group paper and the 1978 proposal to the Expenditure Committee, which had seemed 'politically impossible', now became viable.

The following paper was published in the June 1979 issue of the L. Messel & Co. publication, Financial Analysis. *It took the proposal for a medium-term financial plan quite a bit further, including more detail than the 1978 version submitted to the Expenditure Committee of the House of Commons. It was used as briefing material for a meeting of outside economists at the Treasury on 5 October 1979, where the idea of a Medium-Term Financial Strategy was discussed.*

The paper provides a forward projection of a number of key financial variables, particularly the credit counterparts (the PSBR, gilt-edged sales, bank lending to the private sector) to broad money growth. In retrospect, the comments on the public sector contribution to monetary growth and external influences on the monetary situation were remarkably prescient. The section on the public sector's contribution clearly anticipated the later so-called problem of 'overfunding', with sales of public sector debt to non-banks ahead of the PSBR. The surmise that excess institutional liquidity might have to find its way into overseas assets, after the abolition of exchange controls, was also correct.

However, two parts of the projection were very wrong. First, bank lending to the private sector was much higher than I had foreseen, which made it virtually impossible to bring broad money growth into single digits in the early 1980s in the way that I had hoped. Secondly, instead of the ratio of broad money to national income falling in the early 1980s (as it had done in the late 1970s), it rose substantially. Both these errors – which were also made by the Government and other analysts – damaged the image of the MTFS. The consequences of the presentational embarrassments are discussed in more detail later on pp. 83–104.

The Conservative Government is committed to sound finance. Although, in his first Budget, Sir Geoffrey Howe placed more emphasis on restoring incentives than on setting the right financial climate, there has undoubtedly been a shift from the reluctant, 'pragmatic' monetarism of Mr Healey to a more full-blooded version. The effective £9$^{1}/_{4}$ billion PSBR in 1979/80 (i.e. after including £1 billion public sector asset sales) is disappointingly high and, in the next two years, the Government will face the same kind of difficulties as its Labour predecessor in reducing the budget deficit and money supply growth. However, its task thereafter will be considerably eased by tax revenues related to North Sea oil.

According to the Treasury, these revenues are expected to be about £4$^{1}/_{2}$ billion (at 1977 prices) by the mid-1980s. In current price terms, and given that the recent rise in oil prices sticks, the amount involved could be much larger. Unless the money is squandered on tax reductions or increases in public expenditure, Britain's financial position could be revolutionized. The public sector borrowing requirement might fall sharply, particularly as a proportion of national income, and the implications for financial markets would be exciting. The present paper concentrates on these possible medium-term developments.

The exercise could be criticized as an imaginative extravagance, since it depends on political decisions over the next few years. Some investors seem to prefer hearing gloomy prophecies about a 'confrontation' between union leaders and the Government, leading to an election within two years and another Labour Government which will spend the oil revenues on miscellaneous welfare hand-outs and wholesale nationalization. It could happen. But the balance of probabilities is against it and, extrapolating from Mr Healey's policies in 1976 and 1977, even a Labour Government would be likely to use the oil money in part to cut the PSBR. The consequences of a big reduction in the budget deficit over the next few years must be discussed. They are particularly important for long-term savings institutions whose strategy must look beyond the next 12 or 18 months.

Confidence in medium-term financial trends would be improved if the Government were to announce PSBR and money supply targets for several years ahead. These targets could serve as a barrier against ambitious spending ministers and opportunistic tax cuts in the later years of the present administration; they would strengthen the Chancellor's hand in the Cabinet. However, even if the Government's economic strategy is not to be determined by quantified targets, we have decided to present a central case with specific numbers as a 'par for the course'. It helps as a benchmark for discussion and enables the analysis to be focused effectively. The numbers are in no sense precise forecasts, but they give some notion of the orders of magnitude involved.

The major unresolved issue can be stated straight away. In the 1978 calendar year, inflows into life offices and pension funds were £8,353 million. In the 1983/84 financial year, on plausible assumptions about inflation, they will approach £14 billion. Purchases of public sector debt by the institutions amounted to £3,988 million in the 1978 calendar year and, given the burst of gilt-edged buying in February and March, to perhaps £4,500 million in the 1978/79 financial year. With the PSBR declining to probably under £5 billion by 1983/84, compared to £9.2 billion in 1978/79, where will institutional cash be allocated? At first sight, there appears to be an impossible problem of reconciliation here. However, we will argue that developments such as a revival of debenture issues and outward portfolio investment after the abolition of exchange controls could make the numbers add up.

The analysis is important not only as a signpost to future changes in financial markets, but also to explain how the economy would respond if the PSBR were cut sharply. It is sometimes argued – notably by the more stalwart Keynesian economists at the National Institute of Economic and Social Research – that a reduction in the PSBR would be deflationary because private sector demand would not compensate for lower public expenditure. But our analysis shows there are several ways in which the financial markets will promote spending by companies and individuals. Indeed, the long-run effect of cutting the PSBR would be to transfer the task of allocating resources from the public sector, through industrial subsidies, employment grants and so on, to private financial institutions. The eventual benefits to productivity growth could be substantial.

Reductions in the PSBR form only one part of a sound financial policy. They are important not merely in their own right, but because they enable money supply growth to be lowered. In this section the implications for monetary growth over the medium term of lower budget deficits and control over other contributors to monetary expansion are analysed. The paper includes some specific numbers in a medium-term financial projection. The projection is given in Table 3.2. These numbers are generated by an analysis based on the money supply equation:

Increase in sterling M3 = PSBR – sales of public sector debt to the non-bank private sector + bank lending to the private sector and overseas – external and foreign currency finance – increase in non-deposit liabilities

Table 3.2 A medium-term financial projection

All figures in £bn	1979/80	1980/81	1981/82	1982/83	1983/84
Public sector borrowing requirement	+8.3	+6.1	+5.5	+4.3	+3.1
Public sector debt sales to non-banks	−8.2	−5.8	−5.3	−4.1	−2.9
Bank lending to private sector and overseas	+5.6	+5.3	+5.0	+4.6	+4.3
External and foreign currency finance	nil	nil	nil	nil	nil
Increase in non-deposit liabilities	−1.0	−1.0	−1.0	−1.0	−1.0
Increase in sterling M3	+4.7	+4.6	+4.2	+3.8	+3.5
Outstanding sterling M3 at beginning of year	51.3	56.0	60.6	64.8	68.6
Percentage rise in sterling M3	9.2	8.2	6.9	5.9	5.1

Notes
(1) The PSBR figures are illustrative, but are much influenced by the prospective rise in North Sea tax revenues.
(2) The outstanding total of bank lending to the private sector and overseas was about £45 billion at the beginning of the 1979/80 financial year. It is assumed to rise in line with the money national income figures given in Table 3.3.

The projection identifies the constraints on the authorities and explains the interaction between them. Clearly, the higher is the public sector contribution to monetary expansion, the less room there is for bank lending to the private sector within a given monetary target. The prospects for each of the components of the money supply equation are discussed in the following subsections.

The public sector contribution to monetary growth (PSBR – sales of public sector debt to the non-bank private sector)

The link between the budget deficit and monetary growth is familiar. It has become part of monetarist folklore in recent years and, as such, has quite rightly received much publicity. However, the public sector contribution to money supply growth need not be worrying if the authorities are able to sell substantial quantities of public sector debt outside the banking system. In these circumstances, an excess of government expenditure over revenue does not raise bank deposits or necessarily cause problems of monetary control. Indeed, such has been the success of the funding programme in Britain in the last three financial years that it has tended to offset the PSBR almost entirely. It follows that the main advantage of reducing the budget deficit would not be that money supply growth could be cut directly. The real benefit would instead be that the headaches created by the need to sell substantial quantities of public sector debt would be eased. Consequently, the interest rate levels required to control private sector credit could be lower and more stable.

The PSBR forecasts in Table 3.2 are to be regarded as a reasonable central case. A discussion of their political plausibility would be dominated by projections of North Sea oil revenues and here we will concentrate only on their economic implications. It will be seen from Table 3.2 that the PSBR declines from just over 5 per cent of gross domestic product in 1979/80 to about $1^{1}/_{2}$ per cent in 1983/84. In the 11 years from 1955 to 1966 the ratio averaged just over 3 per cent and was comparatively stable; in the subsequent 11 years, to 1977, it averaged about $4^{3}/_{4}$ per cent and was highly volatile from year to year. In other words, there is a distinct possibility that the PSBR/GDP ratio will be lower by the mid-1980s than has historically been normal. Indeed, a determined effort might succeed in eliminating the PSBR completely.

It could be argued, however, that a zero PSBR is an inappropriate objective because the public sector includes the nationalized industries. These are commercially run enterprises and, if they were in the private sector, it would be expected that over a period of years they would on balance incur financial liabilities to match their investment in fixed assets. The solution to this problem is to derive a separate budget deficit measure which is more specifically related to the central government and local authorities. It would be more sensible to aim for a balanced budget on this measure, while investment by the nationalized industries was financed by long-term borrowing in the market. However, this point is perhaps a detail in comparison to the distinct possibility that the PSBR/GDP ratio will be much lower in future than it has been for most of the 1970s.

But what about sales of public sector debt outside the banking system? The simplest approach in estimating their future level would be to assume that the same proportion of institutions' cash flow is allocated to gilt-edged securities as in the recent past, that personal sector investment in national savings grows roughly in line with inflation, and that sales of the miscellaneous forms of public sector debt (certificates of tax deposits, local authority bonds, Treasury bills, etc.) rise steadily. The difficulty is that, on any plausible projections of savings inflows into the institutions, this would soon lead to an impossible result.

The only way in which sales of public sector debt to the non-bank private sector can exceed the PSBR is by the Government reducing its indebtedness to either the banks or the overseas sector. This is the obvious result of accounting identities; it is just another way of saying that to every creditor there must be a debtor and that 2 plus 3 cannot make 4. Institutional cash flow in the early 1980s will exceed £10 billion. In recent years nearly 50 per cent has gone into public sector debt, principally gilts. If the same proportion were to continue, the acquisition of public sector debt by the institutions would be about £6 billion to £8 billion, compared with a PSBR declining to £4 billion in 1982/83 and £3 billion in 1983/84. Obviously, the two cannot be reconciled. In our estimates we have assumed, therefore, that public sector debt sales will be just less than the PSBR. The implication, even in this case, is an almost continuous reserve asset squeeze on the banks, since the Treasury bill issue should not rise much if the PSBR is more or less fully matched by gilt sales. An easy solution would be to increase the number of eligible commercial bills or banks' money-at-call with the discount houses.

The result is that the public sector contribution to monetary growth is tiny throughout the period. The explanation is that the private sector's appetite for government debt is so strong relative to the available supply. This may sound an extreme suggestion, but it is by no means unrealistic in view of recent experience. In the six banking months ending on 18 April this year, the non-bank private sector purchased about £5 billion of central government debt, a massive figure which exceeded the Central Government borrowing rate over the same period by a wide margin. The institutions and general public have become so habituated to investing in public sector debt in the 1970s that it will take some time before they switch to alternative savings outlets.

Bank lending to the private sector
In the 1970s bank lending to the private sector has been one of the most volatile components of monetary growth. A phase of very rapid expansion in the early 1970s was followed by contraction in the mid-1970s and more steady growth in 1977 and 1978. The fluctuations reflected both the swings in economic activity and the somewhat erratic conduct of interest rate policy by the Bank of England. We have assumed that in the early 1980s the outstanding total of bank advances rises in line with money national income and that it does so without deviations from its trend year by year. This seems the most neutral approach and is, to that extent, the most easy to defend. However, it has a significant and perhaps disappointing consequence. As the decline in inflation can be expected to follow the deceleration in monetary growth only with a lag, and as bank lending reflects inflation by assumption, it remains relatively high and is by far the biggest contributor to monetary growth throughout the early 1980s. It would be feasible to restrain bank lending more aggressively, and therefore bring money supply growth down to the 3 or 4 per cent level compatible with price stability more quickly, but only by obliging companies to reduce the real value of their bank borrowings. That would be more positively deflationary than the central case we have assumed.

There are grounds, nevertheless, for thinking that bank lending might show a weaker trend in the early 1980s than in the 1970s. Rapid inflation encourages borrowers because, of course, the real value of their liabilities is being continuously eroded. Were inflation to slow down markedly, as seems quite possible, there might be a change in corporate debt patterns with less reliance on bank debt and more on shareholders' funds or fixed interest bond debt. As we have seen, there would be a real problem in finding a destination for institutional funds if the PSBR were to decline drastically. An escape valve would be provided if some of that money went into the corporate sector via new equity, loan stock or debentures. Insofar as companies meet their external financing requirements in these ways, they have less need to resort to the banks, bank lending to the private sector can be lower and so, too, can money supply growth. Indeed there is a sort of virtuous circle at work here. Lower inflationary expectations discourage the incurral of bank debt which helps monetary trends. This contributes to, and therefore reinforces, the deceleration of inflation. The process becomes self-validating.

External and foreign currency finance
The external contribution to monetary growth is the most difficult to predict, partly because it is contingent on exchange rate policy and partly because it is susceptible to monetary developments in other countries. There is also a major imponderable about official economic policy in this area as Britain

has a large volume of foreign debt coming due for payment in the early 1980s. It has not yet been decided whether the amounts involved will be paid back or 'rolled over'. In a speech in 1977, Mr Gordon (later Lord) Richardson, the Governor of the Bank of England, pointed out that the debts total about $20 billion and they are heavily concentrated in the three years from 1982 to 1984. To eliminate them without dipping into the reserves, the Bank of England would have to be a persistent seller of sterling and buyer of other currencies in foreign exchange markets over the next few years. If this did happen, it would raise the money supply; and the more complete the attempted repayment of debt, the greater the problems of monetary control. In practice, it seems unlikely that the Government will make a determined effort to pay back the debt, partly for these monetary reasons and partly because of the rather persuasive welfare argument that the real value of the debt is falling every year because of inflation.

It follows that the assumption of a modest external impact on monetary growth is the most convincing. This would be consistent with the authorities allowing the exchange rate to float, with only slight intervention on occasions to smooth out what are deemed to be erratic fluctuations in the exchange rate.

External and foreign currency finance has three components – external financing of the public sector (mostly official intervention in the foreign exchange markets), the change in overseas sterling deposits, and the change in banks' net foreign currency deposits. There is a long-term tendency for foreign holding of sterling deposits to rise because they are mainly intended to meet the trading needs of multi-national companies, and these needs rise steadily with inflation. Thus, between 21 March 1973 and 21 March 1979, overseas sterling deposits rose from £2,457 million to £5,567 million, roughly matching the growth in money national income over that period. As a rise in overseas sterling deposits enables banks to increase their sterling assets without affecting the money supply, such increases are a negative influence on monetary growth. With inflation they can be expected to amount to about £500 million a year.

If so, the other two elements of external and foreign currency finance could be slightly positive. There is no systematic tendency in either direction in the banks' net foreign currency position, so it would be possible for external financing of the public sector to be slightly positive over this period without external factors having any overall effect on the money supply. Any resulting accruals of foreign currency could go some way towards repaying official debt.

Perhaps it does not need to be said that all this is rather academic given the turbulence of foreign exchange markets. It has frequently happened in recent years that official intervention on one either to support or to depress the exchange rate has exceeded £200 million in one day. The difficulty is that it is impossible, from the standpoint of June 1979, to foresee what the scale, timing and direction of sterling crises (if any) will be in 1982 and 1983. So we just have to assume that they won't happen.

The projection in Table 3.2 is an indication of economic possibilities: what will actually happen depends on politics. However, a strong argument for formalizing such a projection into an official medium-term financial plan can be made. The argument has two aspects. First, it would act as a political constraint on spending ministers in future years. The present enthusiasm for cost-cutting exercises in the departments will almost certainly wane and, if spending growth is resumed, it will be difficult to hold down the PSBR. The other danger is that the revenue from North Sea oil will be used to cut income tax rather than reduce the PSBR. Sir Geoffrey Howe's statement in the Budget that the standard rate should be cut to 25p in the pound, presumably over a period of years, was ominous. A medium-term financial plan would, if publicly announced, serve as a check on political opportunism of this sort.

Secondly, a medium-term plan would indicate to industry that the Government is committed to sound financial policies. Of course, government ministers have often pledged that monetary restraint is here to stay, but fine words are not a substitute for quantified targets. A medium-term plan would help businesses to plan ahead and would give them reassurance about the continuity and rigour of financial policy over the next few years. It might also have a benign effect on inflation expectations and, in the battle to overcome inflation, the moulding of expectations is almost as important as the adoption of the appropriate underlying policies. If inflation expectations were lowered, the deflationary impact of monetary deceleration would be moderated.

Nevertheless, to plan the Government's finances several years ahead would involve several difficulties of both estimation and implementation. Not the least of these is that the PSBR varies with the level of economic activity. It follows that to forecast the PSBR several years ahead it is also necessary to forecast economic activity. In the past, such forecasts have not proved very successful. This problem could be evaded by estimating the PSBR on a constant employment-basis and stating the targets in those terms. They might then become politically sensitive if the degree of unemployment assumed was higher than 'socially acceptable'. However, this raises wider issues and it should be pointed out that our projections already incorporate a highly pessimistic view about unemployment.

In implementing PSBR targets, there have always been serious problems because the PSBR is the difference between two very large flows – the Government's expenditure and revenue. It may be asked what value a PSBR target two or three years ahead would have if the Government has enough trouble in meeting a target only 12 months away. But the imprecision of a target variable does not mean that it is either unimportant or uncontrollable. Indeed, if PSBR targets cannot be attained, it would be difficult to see what value any quantified policy objectives would have. The argument degenerates into economic nihilism. In particular, Keynesianism, which relies on the 'fine-tuning' of fiscal policy and is usually advanced as the main alternative to focusing on monetary targets, would be invalidated.

The Government should consider publishing a medium-term financial plan because of the political and psychological benefits that would ensue. The estimation and technical problems in preparing it are not particularly serious and can be overcome.

In conclusion, a few words are needed on the economic consequences of the numbers given in the medium-term financial projection. Over the whole period the money supply grows more slowly than money national income, implying a persistent squeeze on real money balances (see Table 3.3). This might be thought to point to a continuous recession. However, the velocity of circulation has been rising steadily over recent years, perhaps because of technical progress in the financial system. If velocity is on a rising trend, the slight fall in real money balances should not prove difficult to accommodate. Indeed, the path portrayed in Table 3.3 is very stable in comparison to the violent swings in monetary conditions in recent years. It would produce a much more settled economic environment.

Table 3.3   Implications for velocity of circulation

	Percentage rise		
	Sterling M3	Money national income	Velocity of circulation
1979/80	9.2	13.1	+3.6
1980/81	8.2	11.0	+2.6
1981/82	6.9	9.3	+2.3
1982/83	5.9	8.0	+2.0
1983/84	5.1	7.0	+1.8

The main proviso relates to the next 18 months, when the pressures on the economy's liquidity are most severe. In 1979/80 we have assumed a 13.1 per cent rise in money national income, which may be thought on the low side, but is realistic. However, the demand for money may rise more than this because of the rise in VAT to 15 per cent, announced in the 1979 Budget. (Higher indirect taxes increase the money value of transactions and so also the amount of liquidity needed to finance them.) In other words, a recession will occur in late 1979 and early 1980, as forecast by the Treasury in the *Financial Statement and Budget Report 1979/80*, and by most private forecasting bodies.

The Analytical Foundations of the Medium-Term Financial Strategy

From an article of the same name in the May 1984 issue of the Institute for Fiscal Studies' journal, Fiscal Studies.

This paper developed in an analytically acceptable way the ideas which had begun in the 1976 paper for the Money Study Group conference. Ironically, by 1984 they were of interest for their retrospective insight into past government decisions, not because they provided background reasoning for current policy. I did not know this when I was writing the paper and was only to recognize the early signs of the disintegration of the MTFS in early 1985. In the 1985 Budget speech Mr Lawson, the Chancellor of the Exchequer, said that: 'There is nothing sacrosanct about the precise mix of monetary and fiscal policies required to meet the objectives of the MTFS'. But the whole point of the MTFS had been to restrict the Government's scope to vary the budget deficit. Mr Lawson had therefore challenged the basic rationale of the centrepiece of the Government's economic strategy. More fundamental changes, particularly to targets for monetary growth, were to follow.

In truth, Mr Lawson saw no virtue in price stability as an objective of official policy and never had done. Deep down, he had always been a 'growth-man' of 1960s vintage, someone who wanted the Government to push Britain higher up the international league tables of economic growth. I realized this gradually in late 1984 and 1985, as a sequence of curious announcements came out. By mid-1986 I was extremely worried that he might throw away the Thatcher Government's two great economic achievements – the sharp drop in inflation and the restoration of a degree of stability to Britain's much-troubled economy.

Strangely, the one area where Mr Lawson did make a positive contribution was fiscal policy. The boom he presided over in 1987 and 1988 resulted in large budget surpluses and enabled the Government to repay debt for the first time in 20 years. Mr Lawson finally announced in the 1988 Budget that the Government would follow a rule of balancing the budget over the economic cycle. Perhaps the MTFS did some good after all.

Since the mid-1970s macroeconomic policy in Britain has changed in two main ways. First, the Government's overriding aim has become the reduction of inflation by financial control, in contrast to the previous emphasis on full employment. Secondly, both ultimate objectives (the inflation rate) and intermediate target variables (money supply growth and the budgetary position) have been specified over a medium-term time-horizon, usually three to five years. This represents a clear break from the practice of annual adjustments to the budget deficit associated with Keynesian fine-tuning in the 1960s and early 1970s.

The two changes are related. The rationale for a medium-term policy specification is to be sought in scepticism that any worthwhile impact on the inflation rate can be achieved by monetary restraint lasting only one year. The length and unreliability of lags in monetary policy suggest that the Government should instead adhere to a programme of money supply control lasting several years. It has also been argued that, although there is no mechanical link between the PSBR and money supply growth from year to year, the two variables are related over the medium term.[1] A logical accompaniment to setting monetary targets for some years ahead is therefore to state PSBR guidelines over a similar extended period.

These ideas were implicit in the Medium-Term Financial Strategy announced by Sir Geoffrey Howe in the March 1980 Budget. They remain highly relevant to the appraisal of Mr Lawson's 1984 Budget. In the *Financial Statement and Budget Report* (FSBR) published with the Budget, the Government mentions a 3 per cent figure for the GDP deflator in 1988/89. This is not exactly a target, but it is probably intended as rather more than a working assumption. The Government's eventual goal is purportedly to establish price stability. In evidence to the Treasury and Civil Service Committee on 28 March, Mr Lawson indicated that it was a ten-year aim.

In this paper we shall consider, in loosely theoretical terms, the relationship between fiscal policy and inflation. The purpose of the exercise is to provide analytical foundations for the Medium-Term Financial Strategy and a means for assessing the consistency of the Government's macroeconomic programme with its inflation objectives. The latest version of the MTFS, contained in the 1984/85 FSBR, is clearly central to this assessment, but a few passages in the Green Paper on *Public Expenditure in the 1990s* are perhaps of even greater interest. In conclusion, some remarks are ventured on where fiscal policy might go in the future.

Two possible channels of linkage between fiscal policy and inflation will be examined here. The first relates to the interaction between budget deficits and the debt interest burden. It was recognized many years ago and remains logically compelling. The second, which relies on the credit counterparts arithmetic so basic to the conduct of monetary policy in Britain, may be more controversial.

One of the most ancient perceptions of economic science is that a nation cannot be in debt to itself. In this sense, the notion of a debt burden is a misunderstanding. However, interest has to be paid on government debt and taxation collected to meet the interest payments. Such taxation has the usual disincentive and allocation-distorting effects. If the national debt is 'too large' these effects become serious and people may be reluctant to pay their tax bills. Since difficulties in raising revenue discourage investment in government bonds, a higher real interest rate must be paid. The resulting increase in debt-servicing costs further aggravates taxpayer discontent. Sooner or later the situation deteriorates into ungovernability, with open political tension between the taxpayer and rentier classes. There is no absolute criterion for deciding when the debt interest/income ratio is excessive, as much depends on the structure of taxation and taxpayer ethics. France between the two World Wars illustrated the problem of unacceptable rentier claims with particular clarity.

The difficulties which arise from an increasing debt interest/income ratio have been discussed in a recent paper by Sargent and Wallace.[2] In their work an upper bound on the public's demand for government bonds is derived from an overlapping generations model of savings behaviour. The constraint on the debt interest/income ratio therefore stems from assumptions about the savings function rather than taxpayer resistance to rentier claims. The conclusion that there is a limit to the debt interest/income ratio – and so to the debt/income ratio – is reinforced by their alternative approach.

It is important to notice that both the constraints on the debt interest/income ratio identified here are 'real'. They would apply whatever the rate of money supply growth. However, the result of excessive budget deficits must still be inflation. If a government's budget deficit is so large that debt interest is increasing faster than money national income, the maximum debt interest/income ratio will eventually be reached. At that stage if the debt interest/income ratio is to remain constant, and the trend growth of productive capacity is unchanged, the rate of inflation must rise.

This argument suggests the principle that the maximum budget deficit/income ratio for a stable inflation rate (or stable prices) is one compatible with a constant debt interest/income ratio in the long run. The point was recognized in the 1944 White Paper on *Employment Policy*, but in the 1950s and 1960s it was more or less forgotten because the budget deficit was quite low and inflation eroded the real value of the national debt.[3] But more recently they have become important. Table A.7 in the Green Paper shows that the ratio of net debt interest to gross domestic produce rose from 2.2 per cent in 1975 to 3.7 per cent in 1981 and 3.4 per cent in 1982.

A simple algebraic argument can be outlined to determine the budget deficit/income ratio consistent with a constant debt interest/income ratio. If we assume that the interest rate is fixed, a constant debt interest/income ratio implies a constant debt/income ratio. Let 'a' denote the constant ratio of the national debt to income. Then:

$$D = aY$$

and

$$\Delta D = a\Delta Y$$

where D is the national debt and Y is national income and signifies changes in the variables. But the change in the debt is the same as the budget deficit (denoted by B), and so:

$$B/Y = a.\Delta Y/Y$$

Here $\Delta Y/Y$ is, of course, the rate of increase of money national income and is equal to the increase in prices plus the increase in real output, which may be denoted by i (inflation) and g (growth), respectively. We therefore have:

$$B/Y = a.(i + g)$$

As long as the budget deficit/income ratio is kept equal to the right-hand side of this equation year after year, the debt interest/income ratio will be constant.[4]

This is a useful result. Clearly, if the government wants to have stable prices (i.e, i = 0), it must keep:

$$B/Y = a.g$$

In an economy with a low underlying rate of economic growth, the message is that the government's scope for running budget deficits is very limited. The ratio of the national debt to income has never exceeded 2 for long periods in Britain. If we regard the economy's growth rate in the very long run as 2 per cent, the maximum budget deficit/income ratio consistent with stable prices and a constant debt interest burden at any state in our history emerges as 4 per cent. At present, the national debt/income ratio is about $1/2$. If we follow the Treasury's suggestion in the Green Paper of $2^1/4$ per cent a year growth until 1988/89, and $1^1/_2$ to 2 per cent a year between 1988/89 and 1993/94, the implied maximum budget deficit/income ratio would seem to be about 1 per cent. In fact, the mechanical application of the formula is not legitimate because the average rate of interest on the national debt will undoubtedly change in coming years. However, the exercise does identify variables relevant to the specification of a medium-term fiscal strategy for inflation control.

Before moving on to the relationship between the fiscal stance and monetary growth, we should note the concept of the budget deficit relevant to the debt interest problem. Government debts matched by interest-paying financial assets (e.g. claims on the private sector) or which lead to investment in profitable or self-financing enterprises (e.g. public corporations' capital spending) should be deducted from the budget deficit since they have no net effect on the interest burden. In Britain the general government financial deficit is the closest approximation to this underlying idea.

The general government financial deficit is not, however, the appropriate concept for tracing the link between fiscal policy and money supply growth. Here the right measure is the potential addition to the money supply attributable to the budgetary position. This measure is the public sector borrowing requirement, since it is one item in the well-known credit counterparts identity for sterling M3:

Change in sterling M3 = PSBR + bank lending to private sector − sales of public debt to non-bank public − external items − increase in non-deposit liabilities

This identity can be expressed more concisely as:

$$\Delta M = B - \Delta S + \Delta L \tag{1}$$

where S is the stock of government debt held by the non-bank public and L is the outstanding total of bank advances to the private sector. This formulation excludes the external items, the analysis of which would introduce unnecessary complications. In developing another brief algebraic argument we shall make use of the monetarist assumption that the rates of growth of money national income and of the money supply are equal in the long run:

$$\Delta Y/Y = \Delta M/M \tag{2}$$

Now let us consider a steady-state situation in which the ratios of government debt and of the outstanding bank advances total to money national income have constant values denoted by α and β, respectively.[5] Then:

$$S = \alpha Y \tag{3}$$

$$L = \beta Y \tag{4}$$

Taking differences in (3) and (4), and substituting into (1) gives, after division by Y:

$$\frac{\Delta M}{M} \frac{M}{Y} = -\frac{B}{Y} - \alpha \frac{\Delta Y}{Y} + \beta \frac{\Delta Y}{Y}$$

From (2), $\Delta M/M$ equals $\Delta Y/Y$ in long-run equilibrium, and hence:

$$\frac{\Delta M}{M} = \left\{\frac{1}{(M/Y) + \alpha - \beta}\right\} \frac{B}{Y} \tag{5}$$

Equation (5) shows that the rate of money supply growth is a positive function of the PSBR/GDP ratio if:

$$\frac{M}{Y} + \alpha > \beta$$

This will always be true since the money stock is higher than the outstanding bank advances total. The equation also says that an increase in the PSBR/GDP ratio can – in a long-run steady state – be accompanied by no increase in the money supply growth rate only if one or other of the following three conditions is satisfied:

1. There is an increase in the ratio of the money supply to national income.
2. There is an increase in the ratio of public sector debt holdings to national income.
3. There is a reduction in the ratio of bank advances to national income.

As with the previous exercise, it is important to realize that the current values of the variables mentioned cannot be inserted mechanically in the equation to obtain the PSBR/GDP ratio consistent over the next few years with a particular growth rate of the money supply and money national income. The equation applies in a long-run steady state, a condition which does not prevail in the British economy today. The advantage of the exercise is again that it identifies influences on the relationship between the budget deficit and money supply growth, and so gives analytical leverage on the theoretical issue. Real-world application is more problematic.

There are two particular hindrances to estimating the PSBR/GDP ratio consistent with a given inflation rate or price stability over the long run. First, considerable uncertainty exists about the determinants of the demand for public sector debt. It is not clear whether wealth-holders are more concerned about the market value or the nominal value of the debt. The natural assumption would seem to be that they focus on the market value of debt issued in the past, but the budget deficit represents new additions to the nominal value of the debt. The successful passage of the economy from high to low inflation would reduce interest rates, increasing the market value of the national debt but having no effect on the increase in the nominal debt associated with a particular budget deficit. More fundamentally, the national debt/income ratio has varied substantially in the post-1945 period. The London Business School has shown that the nominal value of public sector debt fell from 73 per cent of GDP in 1963 to 41 per cent in 1979.[6] The decline would have been even greater if market value had been used instead.

Secondly, the ratios of both the money supply and bank lending to national income are not immutable for all time. The ratio of broad money to money national income has varied within a relatively narrow band (from 0.35 to 0.45) over the last 20 years, but the ratio of bank advances to national income has risen steadily. The rise in the bank advances/national income ratio reflects the attractiveness of bank finance for companies relative to capital market finance throughout the 1970s. The 1984 Budget has altered the balance again, since the scope for leasing business will decline after 1986 and the need to pay deferred tax will, by eroding banks' capital adequacy, tend to restrict lending growth. At present the bank advance/national income ratio is about 0.35, a figure unlikely to be exceeded for the foreseeable future.

The provisos about the real-world application of the equation must be recognized and understood. Nevertheless, some indication of the order of magnitude of the PSBR/GDP ratio consistent with different money supply growth rates can be given. The matrix in Table 3.4 relies on realistic assumptions about the money supply/money national income and bank advances/national income ratios to derive possible outcomes.

Is the 1984 version of the Medium-Term Financial Strategy consistent with the Government's inflation objectives until 1988/89?

In the 1984 Budget Mr Lawson decided that most of the Thatcher Government's hard work on reducing the budget deficit had been completed. Para-

*Table 3.4   The relationship between the PSBR/GDP ratio and the growth
rate of broad money: possible outcomes*

Debt/income ratio (%) \ PSBR/GDP ratio (%)	1	2	3	4	5
0	20.0	40.0	60.0	80.0	100.0
25	3.3	6.7	10.0	13.3	16.7
50	1.8	3.6	5.5	7.3	9.1
75	1.3	2.5	3.8	5.0	6.3
100	1.0	1.9	2.9	3.8	4.8

Note
The figures in the matrix show the percentage growth of broad money associated with
particular PSBR/GDP and debt/income ratios. For example, with a PSBR/GDP ratio of 2%
and a debt/income ratio of 50%, broad money should grow by 3.6% a year. These calculations
use equation (5) of the text.

Assumptions
(1)   Ratio of broad money to money national income: 0.40.
(2)   Ratio of bank advances to money national income: 0.35.

graph 56 of the Green Paper on Public Expenditure states that, disregarding
net debt interest, 'the tax burden for the non-North Sea sector can be reduced
to the extent that public expenditure falls more than North Sea tax revenues
as a share of GDP'. In other words, success in controlling public spending
other than debt interest will lead to tax cuts, not a lower PSBR/GDP ratio.
This is a major change of direction from the unswerving commitment to
PSBR reduction when Sir Geoffrey Howe was Chancellor of the Exchequer.

According to the Medium-Term Financial Strategy set out in the 1984/85
Financial Statement and Budget Report, the PSBR/GDP ratio is intended to
decline from $3^1/4$ per cent in 1983/84 to $2^1/4$ per cent in 1984/85 and 2 per
cent in 1985/86. Although figures of $1^3/4$ per cent are given for 1987/88 and
1988/89, the difference between $2^1/4$ and $1^3/4$ per cent is less than the margin
of error, and for all practical purposes can be ignored. Mr Lawson is, in
effect, planning to stabilize the PSBR/GDP ratio at about 2 per cent for the
rest of the Thatcher Government's second term.

The stabilization of the PSBR/GDP ratio contrasts with the aims to lower
both the growth rate of broad money and inflation. The target range for
sterling M3 growth is 6 to 10 per cent in 1984/85, falling by 1 per cent a year
to 2 to 6 per cent in 1988/89. This is a significant deceleration. More modest
are the inflation goals. The GDP deflator is put at $4^3/4$ per cent in 1984/85,
$4^1/4$ per cent in 1985/86 and 4 per cent in 1986/87, and finally at 3 per cent in

1988/89. Curiously, these figures are assembled at no one point in the PSBR, almost as if the Government wanted to hide something, or at least confuse the outsider about its intentions. The GDP deflators in the years up to 1986/87 are presented in Table 5.5, while the 3 per cent number for 1988/89 appears in paragraph 2.19. Our own Table 3.5 brings together the various items in the 'programme', if such it may be called.

Table 3.5   *The Government's Medium-Term Financial Strategy and inflation programme 1984/85 to 1988/89*

	1984/85 (%)	1985/86 (%)	1986/87 (%)	1987/88 (%)	1988/89 (%)
PSBR/GDP ratio	$2^{1}/_{4}$	2	2	$1^{3}/_{4}$	$1^{3}/_{4}$
Growth of broad money as measured by sterling M3	6–10	5–9	4–8	3–7	2–6
Inflation rate as measured by GDP deflator	$4^{3}/_{4}$	$4^{1}/_{4}$	4	$3^{1}/_{2}$	3

Source: *1984/85 Financial Statement and Budget Report*

Whatever the reservations about applying the theoretical steady-state result to an actual situation, it is striking that the Government's fiscal plans and inflation objectives are very much in accordance with the 'ballpark' numbers given in Table 3.4. The national debt/income ratio is currently about $^{1}/_{2}$. Moreover, the market and nominal values of the debt are not at present very different, which simplifies analysis. Table 3.4 shows that, with a debt/income ratio of $^{1}/_{2}$, a PSBR/GDP ratio of 2 per cent would be accompanied – if realistic assumptions are made about the ratios of money and bank advances to GDP – by a rather low growth rate of broad money, about $3^{1}/_{2}$ per cent a year, in long-run steady state. This is beneath the target bands for 1985/86 and 1986/87 and within them for 1987/88 and 1988/89.

An alternative approach, which is a standard technique of financial analysis in Whitehall, the Bank of England and the City, is to consider the credit counterparts arithmetic in any particular year, making 'guesstimates' about the main components. The purpose is to find out how large official gilt sales must be if the money supply target is to be achieved. If required official gilt sales are excessive in relation to institutional cash flow, fiscal policy is deemed inconsistent with the money supply target and so with the Government's inflation objectives. There appears to be no major problem of reconciliation in 1984/85. Table 3.6 demonstrates that, with plausible assumptions about items

Table 3.6 *The credit counterpart arithmetic in 1984/85: the consistency between the PSBR and money supply targets*

£M3 growth	PSBR	£5.2bn	£7.2bn	£9.1bn
6%		6.1	8.1	10.1
8%		4.0	6.0	8.0
10%		2.0	4.0	6.0

Note
The above matrix shows the level of official gilt-edged sales required in 1984/85, for varying PSBR totals, to achieve the sterling M3 growth stated in the left-hand margin. The figures are required official gilt sales in £billion. They relate to annual periods and not the 14 months in which the target is stated. The estimates rely on the assumptions given below.

Assumptions
(1) Bank lending to UK private sector: £13.5bn
(2) Sales of other public sector debt: £3.0bn
(3) External and foreign currency finance: –£1.5bn
(4) Increase in banks' non-deposit liabilities: £2.5bn
(5) Sterling M3 at mid-February 1984: £102 bn

in the credit counterparts identity, required official gilt sales are unlikely to have to exceed the total of £8.8 billion actually sold in the year to January 1984. Two qualifications to this sanguine conclusion should be mentioned. The first is that money needed for privatization issues will represent a bigger drain on institutional cash flow in 1984/85 than in any previous year; the second is that bank lending may be significantly above the £13.5 billion figure assumed if the economic recovery gathers more momentum than expected.

The path for the PSBR to 1988/89 set out in Mr Lawson's first Budget is, then, fully consistent with the Government's stated inflation goals. What about the general government financial deficit which, we argued earlier, is the appropriate budget concept for the debt interest problem? Is there any danger that the debt interest/national income ratio will rise even though money growth and inflation are under control? In fact, not much trouble is likely in this area. The national debt is dominated by gilt-edged securities, with the total amount in issue about £108 billion. Of this total, £66 billion was issued with coupons of $10\frac{1}{2}$ per cent or more. It seems unlikely that debt with a coupon much above $10\frac{1}{2}$ per cent will be needed over the next four years, as long as the Government's inflation projections are met. It follows that the debt interest/national income ratio should be declining as a result of lower coupons on stock issued to match redemptions. The size of this effect is such that the increase in the debt interest burden due to persisting deficit financing should be manageable.

A PSBR/GDP ratio of about 2 per cent is consistent with stable inflation of 5 per cent or a little less in the period up to 1988/89. But what fiscal policy is needed for price stability? And would the long-run fiscal policy described in the Green Paper be compatible, eventually, with price stability?

Perhaps the first point to emphasize is that these questions have clearly exercised the authors of the Green Paper. Paragraphs 53 to 56 are a brief statement of principles on 'Debt interest and public sector borrowing'. But the brevity of the remarks should not be taken as indicating that policy-makers attach little importance to them. Paragraph 56 makes the key statement about the intention to translate successful public expenditure restraint into tax cuts. Some very interesting sentences also appear in paragraph 55. 'There is inevitably some uncertainty about the precise PSBR path which would be consistent with the government's aims on inflation. But given the aim of stable prices, the scope for varying the PSBR as a share of GDP is relatively limited. If a higher path were followed a good deal of the apparent scope for increased spending or lower taxes would be pre-empted in the event by higher debt interest payments.' The Treasury is evidently well aware of the medium-term constraint on budget deficits imposed by the debt interest problem. Detailed work on the probable development of the debt interest/national income ratio is presented in Annex 4. Although this is the final section of the Green Paper, it takes up five pages and must have been the product of considerable thought.

Paragraph 8 of Annex 4 is optimistic about the debt interest burden over the next decade. The PSBR/GDP ratio 'is assumed to be low compared with the assumed growth of money GDP. Together with an assumed decline in both nominal and real interest rates as inflation is brought down further and pressure in financial markets eases, this implies a reduction in net debt interest payments'. Table A.8 quantifies the reduction as being from $3^1/2$ per cent of GDP in 1983/84 to $1^3/4$ per cent in 1993/94. It is this improvement which allows the Treasury to envisage a PSBR/GDP ratio of only 1 per cent in 1993/94, despite the official intention to use any decline in the ratio of public expenditure, apart from debt interest, to national income for tax cuts. To put the point more simply, the Government has in mind a clear dichotomy between genuine public expenditure programmes and debt interest. Success in controlling programmes will lead to tax cuts; success in reducing debt interest will lower the budget deficit.

A PSBR/GDP ratio of 1 per cent would be consistent with price stability. About that there can be no doubt. Table 3.4 shows that a budget deficit as small as that would, with a debt/income ratio of $1/2$ be accompanied by broad money growth at an annual rate of only 1.8 per cent. That is clearly no higher than the trend growth of productive capacity. Changes in assumptions about the debt/income and money supply/income ratios could alter the numbers, but the overall conclusion about the compatibility of such a low budget deficit with stable prices is surely robust. The general government financial deficit is usually less than the PSBR. If it were nil or a mere $1/2$ per cent of national income there would be no worries about an increasing debt interest burden. In this respect too, the Government's fiscal plans for the 1990s are consistent with price stability.[7]

The Government's medium-term fiscal strategy and its long-range expenditure plans for the 1990s can be reconciled with its inflation objectives. The Treasury has clearly recognized the debt interest constraint and thought about the need to make its fiscal programme consistent with declining money supply growth.

But Mr Lawson could have done more. PSBR/GDP ratios of 1 to 2 per cent are low not only in relation to the post-1945 average; they are also very small in relation to the margin of error in PSBR estimates. The announcement of a balanced budget rule, on either the PSBR or general government financial deficit definitions, would therefore have meant little difference in practical terms. But it would have had a far more worthwhile impact on expectations than the indefinite extension of the Medium-Term Financial Strategy. Mr Lawson apparently wants to give himself as much room as possible, within financial constraints, for tax cuts. As a journalist twenty years ago his enthusiasms were tax cuts, tax reform and economic growth. He had no time for sound money nostrums. In a *Sunday Telegraph* article on 11 March 1962 he wrote against 'the Eisenhower school of economic commentators, who see mystical significance in an overall budget balance, since this is a muddled amalgam of Gladstone and Keynes without the logical consistency of either'; on 28 April 1963 he judged that 'The great social justification, to my mind, for a mildly inflationary economy is that a society in which borrowers do better than lenders of money is fundamentally more attractive than one in which the reverse is true.'[8] The quotations might be dismissed as those of a young man trying to cut a dash. But there are two reasons for taking them more seriously. First, in evidence to the House of Commons Treasury and Civil Service Committee on 28 March 1984, the same Mr Lawson said: 'There is no particular magic about a balanced budget'. Secondly, in the first Budget he presented as Chancellor of the Exchequer he sanctioned the continuation of mild inflation for the next five years.

But tax cuts do not change the burden of public expenditure. The increase in the budget deficit they must involve means merely that the burden damages the private sector in different ways (higher interest rates, higher inflation, debt debasement) from the disincentive effects associated with overt taxes raised by the Inland Revenue or the Customs and Excise.[9] And, more fundamentally, what is the point of perpetuating the national debt? In a long-run steady state the only beneficiaries of deficit financing are tax inspectors (who have to collect taxes to pay the interest), gilt-edged stockbrokers (who receive commission on transactions in the debt instruments) and macroeconomists (who pontificate on the pros and cons of particular fiscal policies). There is more useful work for these worthy members of society to do. A really radical Chancellor would think about extinguishing the national debt by a policy of deliberate budget surpluses. Financial markets could then concentrate on the important task of channelling the nation's savings into profitable and efficient private sector investments.

Notes

1. A. Budd and T. Burns, 'The role of the PSBR in controlling the money supply' *Economic Outlook* (Gower Publishing for the London Business School), November 1979, pp. 26–30. The subject was also considered in T. G. Congdon, 'Monetarism and the budget deficit', paper given to the fifth Money Study Group conference at Brasenose College, Oxford, in September 1976, and reprinted in this volume on pp. 38–49.
2. T. J. Sargent and N. Wallace, 'Some unpleasant monetarist arithmetic' *Federal Reserve Bank of Minneapolis Quarterly Review*, Fall 1981, pp. 1–17.
3. See above, p. 45.
4. The result is far from new. See p. 64 of M. Feldstein, *Inflation, Tax Rules and Capital Formation* (Chicago and London: University of Chicago Press, 1983) for an alternative derivation. The similarity with the Domar model of public debt, which says that in the limit the ratio D/Y tends towards B/Y divided by $\Delta Y/Y$, is also apparent.
5. The algebraic argument is also given at the end of the third chapter of T. G. Congdon, *Monetary Control in Britain* (London: Macmillan, 1982).
6. A. Budd and T. Burns, 'The role of the PSBR', pp. 26–27.
7. A PSBR/GDP ratio of 1 per cent was given as a prescription for long-run price stability in A. Budd and G. Dicks, 'A strategy for stable prices' *Economic Outlook* (Gower Publishing for the London Business School), July 1983, pp. 18–23.
8. R. Shepherd, 'Lawson's words for eating' *Investors Chronicle* 9 March 1984.
9. The argument was developed in T. G. Congdon's 'What's wrong with supply-side economics?' *Policy Review* (Washington: Heritage Foundation), Summer 1982.

4. Britain's monetarist experiment – initial setbacks followed by triumph

Although money supply targets were introduced in 1976, the Labour Government led by Mr James Callaghan honoured them as much in the breach as in the observance. The key policy problem in 1977 – as on so many occasions before and since – was how to reconcile domestic monetary priorities (as expressed in the targets) with exchange rate stability. Strong upward pressure on the pound emerged at various times in the year, obliging policy-makers to choose between exchange rate appreciation and above-target monetary growth. Until late in the year the Government tried to hold the pound down, both by heavy foreign exchange intervention and by cutting interest rates. As a result, the money supply target (which had been for growth in sterling M3 of between 9 and 13 per cent) was exceeded by a significant margin. Moreover, the very low interest rates reached in late 1977 gave a strong boost to credit demand, notably to the demand for mortgages. House prices rose sharply in 1978.

Because of these monetary developments, the economy grew quite strongly in 1978 and early 1979, and inflationary pressures gathered momentum. The Conservative Government elected in June 1979 was very articulate about the need to reduce monetary growth and pledged itself to stick to its broad money target. By late 1979 it was clear that the only way this could be done was by a large rise in interest rates. Minimum Lending Rate (i.e., the old Bank rate) was raised to 17 per cent on 15 November. Because interest rates in other industrial countries were much lower, sterling became an attractive currency to hold and it appreciated strongly during 1980. By undermining industry's international competitiveness, the substantial currency appreciation was the immediate cause of a slump in the foreign demand for British products and a sharp fall in industrial output. Meanwhile the money supply target was again exceeded in the 1980/81 financial year, largely because of the abolition of an artificial scheme (the so-called 'corset' on bank liabilities) for limiting the size of banks' balance sheets.

By early 1981 the British economy appeared to be in a shambles. The slide in output and employment was the worst in the post-war period, while the new monetarist policy framework seemed far from working according to plan. Deep pessimism about Britain's economic prospects coincided with ritual media abuse of 'monetarism' as the 'ideology' which was to blame. The first piece in this section, 'When Balogh was wrong', reprinted from *The Spectator* of 14 March 1981, was intended as a corrective to the prevailing mood.

It pointed out that the German currency reform of July 1948 had also received a hostile reaction, particularly from the Oxford economics don, Mr (later Lord) Thomas Balogh, in a pamphlet published in April 1950. Five years later, in the midst of the German *Wirtschaftswunder*, Balogh's remarks seemed ludicrous. My point was that the critics of the 'Thatcherite monetarist experiment', such as commentators in *The Observer* and *The Sunday Times*, might look equally silly by 1985. No one in Britain should have been surprised that a determined anti-inflation programme would have bad effects on output and employment in the short run. But the programme was medium term in nature and explicitly described as such (the 'Medium-Term Financial Strategy'). The commitment to responsible financial policies had to be for an extended period of time if it were to be convincing enough to change inflationary expectations.

Nevertheless, there was a need for a more considered discussion of the problems of 1980 and 1981, and I wrote two articles for *The Banker* on 'Why has monetarism failed so far?'. The first of these articles discussed the missed monetary targets and identified the buoyancy of bank lending to the private sector as the main culprit. As is obvious from my proposals for a medium-term financial plan (see pp. 55–65, especially p. 61), the strength of private sector credit in the early 1980s surprised me.

The second article was concerned with the persistence of inflation despite severe monetary restraint. Part of the explanation was the long lag between monetary action and inflation response, but I highlighted another aspect of the problem. This was that monetary conditions had only indirect relevance for public sector inflation. Excessive pay awards in the public sector had therefore, in the article's words, been partly 'responsible for the poor unemployment–inflation trade-off' of the early 1980s.

At no point in the early 1980s did I have any serious doubts about the validity of the Government's economic policies. Having been much influenced by Laidler and Friedman in the mid-1970s, I had always expected the pay-off to be over a long period, such as five or ten years. I did not realize how much damage the embarrassments and setbacks of 1980 and 1981 caused to the monetarist approach. Many of the politicians and officials who had supported monetary targets in the late 1970s decided that the events of the early 1980s demanded a radical policy re-assessment. In the 1982 Budget Sir Geoffrey Howe indicated that the Government would pay more attention to the exchange rate and 'narrow money' in future. The retreat from monetarism had begun. I did not initially appreciate the full significance of these changes. ('Narrow money' consists of a limited range of monetary assets, either notes and coin alone (M0) or notes and coin plus bank deposits which can be used without giving notice (M1). It contrasts with 'broad money', which includes all bank deposits, including deposits with quite long periods of notice. Broad money had been the understood meaning of the phrase, 'the money supply', in the late 1970s.)

At any rate, broad money targets were retained in 1982, 1983, 1984 and early 1985. Inflation fell to an annual trend rate of 5 per cent and the path of output growth became more stable. As these years were quiet ones for the economy, the controversy about economic policy-making died down. Monetarism seemed to have triumphed. A crucial turning-point had been the re-election of Mrs Thatcher's Government in 1983, which appeared to make possible the continuity that the monetarist programme had always needed. There is no point denying that the 'Falklands factor' had been vital to the Conservatives' success in the 1983 election, and so to the durability of the monetarist approach. I noted the point in an article in *The Spectator* on 29 May 1982, 'Winning the economic war'. The two articles, 'Following Friedman' from *The Spectator* of 28 May 1983 and 'Alternatives galore, but none of them better' from *The Times* of 28 September 1985, celebrate the apparent achievements of monetarism in this relatively peaceful period.

The Need for a Medium-Term Perspective

From an article 'When Balogh was wrong' in The Spectator, *14 March 1981.*

This article was a journalistic polemic, but it made the important point that ultimately successful programmes of financial control and market liberalization often appear to be failures in the short run.

The last two years of British economic policy have purportedly been an experiment in free markets and sound money. If the newspaper editorials are to be believed, the experiment is in a mess. Indeed, many leader-writers are saying that it should be abandoned as soon as possible and something more 'moderate' (usually left unspecified) put in its place. There is also a tendency to regard the British trial-by-monetarism as special and unique. This is wrong. Several countries have in the past followed economic programmes with similar intentions and methods. Some have lasted much longer than two years. What kind of mid-term reports did they receive?

Perhaps the most celebrated example of economic liberalization was the West German in 1948. Like its British counterpart today, it soon attracted comment and criticism. At almost exactly the same two-year stage now being reached here, an assessment of its progress was made by Thomas Balogh in a pamphlet entitled *Germany: an Experiment in 'Planning' by the 'Free' Price Mechanism*. The pamphlet, based on a talk given to a German trade union conference in April 1950, was published in Oxford in September of that year.

Before quoting from Balogh's little work, we should briefly describe the events it attempted to analyse. In July 1948, after a period in which some basic necessities could be obtained only by barter, the German Central Economic Administration introduced the Deutschmark in a comprehensive currency reform and abolished nearly all price controls. A consumer spending-spree developed which had a highly favourable effect in encouraging production, but also threatened rapid inflation. In November 1948 the central bank, then known as the Bank Deutscher Lander (later the Bundesbank), took conventional restrictive measures and adhered to them, with little inter-mission, for the next three years. Although production and exports continued to grow quickly, unemployment quadrupled between June 1948 and January 1950. In early 1950 unemployment averaged over 10 per cent of the labour force in West Germany as a whole, while in some regions it exceeded 20 per cent.

Balogh was scornful of the central bank responsible for this deflation. In his view, 'its leaders were hagridden by obsolete monetary theories'. Even worse, he thought, was the institutional framework created to stop politicians from meddling with monetary policy. The thinking behind the constitutional checks on political interference was 'a mixture of quaint opinions, those of the 19th century on budget management and of the late Mr Montagu Norman on the proper role of a central bank'. Balogh admitted that production was increasing, but he doubted that the liberalization policy deserved any credit. On the contrary, 'the market mechanism is an exceedingly tardy and imperfect means of readjustment'. The policy would require continued deflation, even though this would be 'insufficient' to restore balance on trade with other countries. It was 'evident' that unemployment would 'not be permitted to decline much from the 1.25 to 1.5 million level'.

The pamphlet was not confined to purely economic issues, for Balogh was also despondent about Germany's political viability. The central weakness of the 'iniquitous new German economic and social system' was that the currency reform had favoured the rich at the expense of the poor. There was a resultant lack of the mass-consumption demand appropriate to the country's industrial structure. It followed that 'when the attempt is made to recreate mass demand and to wrench the productive system into another shape, a serious crisis and terrible social costs will be inevitable'. For this reason, the consequences of the currency reform were 'immense and immensely lamentable'. In Balogh's opinion, 'the reform had put money into the hands of hoarders and speculators, while the middle classes and workers had lost cash, confidence and respect for their conquerors'. He concluded that 'German society is less stable than ever'.

If Balogh was long on foreboding, he was not short of advice. 'Nothing but fast reform by free men can prevent the Western Germans from deserting political moderation for the militant extremes of right and left.' The first priority, according to him, was therefore an immediate co-ordinated reversal of economic policy. The choice was between further deflation and controls. As controls could be framed with the assistance of the trade unions and directed towards a more equal income distribution, they were clearly preferable. As for the autonomous central bank, that also should be brought under government supervision. Its independence would, according to Balogh, 'generate intolerable delays and frictions' in economic policy-making, 'the consequences of which menace political stability'. In short, Balogh wanted the German Government to desert the supporters of sound money and collaborate with the trade unions.

This may sound familiar to students of the British political scene in the last 20 years. It may, therefore, come as no surprise to the reader to learn that the Balogh who wrote such a fierce indictment of the German free market system in 1950 was the same Balogh who acted as personal adviser to Harold Wilson in the 1964–70 Labour Government, starred as an economic wizard in the Crossman diaries and was later given a life peerage for his services.

As it happens, the question of how Germany would have responded if its Government has taken his advice is not one of the might-have-beens of recent economic history. The assumedly crass, myopic and incompetent free market did rather well. Industrial production rose five times in the ten years after the currency reform, while the unemployment total dropped to 350,000 and the unemployment rate to 2 per cent. The allegedly archaic monetary ideas of the Bank Deutscher Lander were quite good at achieving financial stability. In the five years to 1955 the German price level went up by about 1 per cent a year, and trade surpluses were recorded continuously from 1952 onwards. On the whole, the Germans are probably glad that their rulers ignored Balogh's denunciation of their experiment in '"planning" by the "free" price mechanism'.

If anyone became unemployed as a result of German economic liberalization, it was the architect of the policy, Dr Ludwig Erhard. He was made redundant by its success. Throughout the 1950s he was in the rare and happy position, for an economics minister, of having almost nothing to do. Perhaps, he reflected, like Mae West, that too much of a good thing can be wonderful.

But there was one point he had in common with Lord Balogh. He also wrote a book about German economic policy. Entitled *Prosperity Through Competition*, it was published in English in 1958 and contained several passages on the early years of the experiment. Criticism, even within Germany, had been heavy and sustained. The trade unions tried to organize a general strike on 12 November 1948. Fortunately, they obtained little public support. But Erhard acknowledged that the trade unions were not the only critics,

> as a glance at the newspapers of those days proves. 'Pessimism reigns everywhere', 'Erhard at the end of his tether', 'Chaotic picture of prices', 'Economists in favour of a return to planning', were some of the headlines. Even worse, perhaps, was that within the economy one side began to insult the other. Everyone was ready to ascribe the fault to someone else –industry to trade, trade to industry, the urban dweller to the peasants and vice versa.'

This also sounds familiar. It is the sort of stuff which one now finds every week in *The Observer* and *The Sunday Times*, the two newspapers which have most noisily and repetitively opposed the Government's economic policies.

It seems that contemporary comment on the West German free market experiment was, at the two-year stage, very similar to that on Britain's today. The contexts are, of course, quite different. It would be silly to claim that, because liberalization in West Germany was initially unpopular and eventually successful, it will also work here. The sad truth is that monetarism, like taking exercise, is only good for you if it hurts. At the moment it is hurting. Naturally enough, people are complaining and saying it must stop.

The one lesson we can draw from Balogh's 1950 pamphlet is that they are not necessarily right.

Why did Monetarism have so much Trouble in the Early 1980s?: 1. The Missed Targets

From an article 'Why has monetarism failed so far?: 1. The missed targets' in The Banker, *March 1982.*

The rapid growth of bank lending to the private sector in the recession of 1979–82 was unexpected. It was the principal reason that monetary growth exceeded target. The article blamed the vigour of the private sector's demand for credit on the interaction of financial deregulation with a tax system which was too friendly to borrowers. It therefore pointed an accusatory finger at such features of the tax system as full deductibility of business interest as an expense and of mortgage interest from personal incomes. Some of these aspects of the British tax system have subsequently been changed, with, for example, the 1984 Budget lowering the standard rate of corporation tax, and so making borrowing and leasing less attractive to companies.

Monetarism has received a great deal of criticism and even a certain amount of mockery over the last two years. A few months ago many journalists were deriding it as intellectual junk which, because of its association with the deepest recession since the 1930s and the resulting unemployment, could never be salvaged. Although signs of a more cautious and ambiguous assessment are now emerging because of the tentative recovery in the economy, something has clearly gone wrong. There is no doubt that British economic policy has been broadly monetarist in character in recent years and that it has not matched its supporters' original expectations. Economists need to ask in what respects and for what reasons monetarism has failed so far.

Most indictments of monetarist policies have been marked by great vigour, but also a curious inconsistency. On the one hand, they have emphasized the Government's inability to meet its own targets. As heavy political capital was invested in sterling M3 and the public sector borrowing requirement as symbols of successful financial policy, the charge seems to be that the Government has been incompetent according to criteria it recognizes. On the other hand, the losses of output and employment in 1980 and 1981 have been condemned as too high a price to pay for too small a reduction of inflation. As the Government's main aim was to lower inflation and it never denied that higher unemployment might occur, this second charge focuses on a policy objective to which the Government did not – at least initially – pay all that much attention. The critics' inconsistency arises because, if the financial targets had been met, their first point would not apply, but the jobless total would have been far worse and their second point even more emphatic. A logical anti-monetarist cannot simultaneously level both charges against official policy.

However, a monetarist sympathizer should consider each of the two problems. The missed targets and the mass unemployment have been equally embarrassing, if in different ways. Although the two disappointments are related, we shall examine only the failure to achieve monetary targets in the present article. This failure has been essentially in the operation of monetary policy. In a subsequent article [reprinted here on pp. 95–104] we shall consider the question of why the consequences of the particular monetary stance chosen by the Government have been so damaging for the 'real' economy.

There has been a persistent tendency to exceed official money supply targets in the last two years. Previously they were met, if not very convincingly. In 1978/79 sterling M3 went up by 10.9 per cent against a target band of 8 per cent to 12 per cent, and in 1979/80 by 11 per cent against 7 per cent to 11 per cent. Only in 1980/81, when sterling M3 surged by 20.9 per cent compared with another 7 per cent to 11 per cent target, did control disintegrate. Another large overshoot seems likely in 1981/82. The main headache for the money supply managers in 1980/81 and 1981/82 was the obstinate refusal of private sector demand for bank credit to decline despite a very depressed economic background. Every new loan creates a new deposit and every new deposit counts in sterling M3.[1] With bank lending to the private sector at record high levels, the sterling M3 targets were wrecked. This much is well known and familiar. What is far less certain is why loan demand remained – and indeed remains – so buoyant.

There is a temptation to suggest an explanation merely by providing a narrative of events. The first sign of serious trouble came in August 1980 when, following the abolition of the 'corset' in June, the full scale of credit growth over the previous two years was revealed. This credit growth had been channelled into some very obscure interstices of the financial system and no one appreciated how large it had been. Most of it had gone to the corporate sector. Despite the ruinous impact on the money supply targets, the furore caused by the abolition of the corset had died down by early 1981. With many observers confident that loan demand had begun to subside, Minimum Lending Rate was cut to 12 per cent in the March Budget. By September and October it was clear that, once again, the problem had been underestimated. Bank lending was surging forward at an underlying rate of over £1 billion a month, with personal sector borrowing for house purchase this time being the most dynamic element.

But to focus on the sequence of specific episodes which together constituted the Government's policy failure evades the serious issues. It implies that bank lending could have been curbed if the Bank of England had changed its tactics a little on one or two critical occasions. This is almost certainly an illusion. A persuasive explanation for the strength of loan demand should instead relate it to deep-seated structural characteristics of the economic system. As it happens, a good argument can be made that the credit boom of 1979 to 1982 was the culmination of powerful trends which had been working, although often artificially suppressed, for over 30 years. To understand these trends it is necessary to recall Britain's economic situation in the 1950s and 1960s.

In those years the Government's priority was to raise economic growth by encouraging investment. A succession of legislative changes gradually improved the tax advantages of owning capital assets. Capital allowances of 100 per cent on plant and machinery became accepted by the early 1970s and, in the November 1974 mini-Budget, the principle was extended to stocks as well. These changes were designed to stimulate the acquisition of real assets, if necessary by the incurral of paper liabilities. Other characteristics of the fiscal system, notably the tax deductibility of interest payments, were of long standing, but strengthened this effect. With inflation rates creeping upwards, the attractions of holding real assets increased further. Interest payments became equivalent to early repayments of capital, but they had the merit that a proportion of the cost was effectively borne by the Exchequer. There was a gradual spread of understanding about the most efficient methods of minimizing tax bills and maximizing protection against inflation. The answer, as more and more people realized, was to borrow money and invest in goods or property.

The combination of more worthwhile government investment incentives and rising inflation expectations generated a growing demand for credit. The problem had already surfaced by the mid-1950s. At that time, with economic policy subordinated to the need to maintain a fixed exchange rate, an early consequence of excessive credit expansion was to cause a run on sterling. A characteristic 'stop–go' pattern developed. Rapid credit growth would lead to a sterling crisis, forcing the introduction of direct restrictions on bank credit. As the balance of payments convalesced, these restrictions would be withdrawn and another burst of credit would be unleashed, only to end in another sterling crisis.

There was a definite incoherence in official policy. Repeated statements were made by politicians, businessmen and financiers on the need to increase investment and raise Britain's position in the league table of economic growth. Tax legislation was progressively altered in response to this clamour. By the mid-1970s Britain's investment incentives were the most generous of any advanced industrial nation. But the Government did not allow companies or individuals to take full advantage. Whenever the private sector began to invest heavily, imports of capital goods jumped and the balance of payments went into deficit. Quantitative restrictions on bank credit would then be imposed, neutralizing the effect of the investment incentives. There was a continuous unsatisfied demand for credit which would have passed through the banking system if it had been free to do so. The favourable tax treatment of investment collided head on with the monetary authorities' desire to restrain bank credit.

Quantitative limits on bank lending in the 1950s and 1960s had several harmful consequences. They handicapped banks subject to them, particularly the clearing banks, in their rivalry with other banks; they penalized the banking system as a whole in its competition with non-bank financial intermediaries; and they obstructed the efficient distribution of credit to profitable borrowers prepared to pay high interest rates. The concept of 'financial repression' has been proposed by Professor McKinnon, an American economist who specializes in developing countries' monetary systems, to describe how government interference with interest rates and credit allocation can hamper economic growth by reducing total investment and directing the investment which does occur to the wrong places. Britain is not a developing country, but an argument could be made that its economy suffered from several features of financial repression throughout the stop–go era.

Because of the restrictions on the banks, the demand for credit was met by other institutions. Medium-term finance was available from the capital markets, with new debenture issues being particularly active in the late 1960s. Mortgages for house purchase were provided by building societies, while hire purchase companies and finance houses answered the personal sector's need for consumer credit. The banks continually lost ground to these other intermediaries.

In 1971 the Bank of England, with the full approval of the Government and most academic economists, decided that the process had gone too far. The Competition and Credit Control reforms were intended to put banks and non-banks on a more equal footing in their struggle to capture an increased share of financial intermediation. All restrictions on bank credit were abolished. Over the two years from September 1971, bank lending to the private sector doubled and was largely responsible for two consecutive years of 25 per cent money supply growth. The rapid monetary growth lay behind a powerful boom in economic activity, which by late 1973 was causing sharp deterioration in Britain's overseas payments position. The authorities reverted to direct quantitative restrictions on banks' balance sheets by introducing the 'corset'. Although specified in terms of deposit liabilities, the corset's aim – and, to some extent, its effect – was to check the expansion of bank lending.

But the Competition and Credit Control reforms had not been entirely pointless. Although lending to the personal sector, a boom area in 1972 and 1973, showed little growth in the mid-1970s, the banks' entry into the market for medium-term finance was a permanent change. Whereas in the 1960s a company requiring medium-term finance would try to raise money through a debenture issue, in the 1970s its first step was to apply to a bank. The character of banks' liabilities adjusted to this innovation in their lending. An increasing proportion of their deposits was 'wholesale' money, typically with a one-month or three-month term, in contrast to the traditional current accounts and seven-day deposits. The banks were so successful in satisfying the need for medium-term credit facilities that the debenture market was snuffed out. Partly as a result of the Competition and Credit Control reforms, the banks had taken opportunities for financial intermediation away from the capital markets.

Between 1973 and 1980 the banks continued to be subject to a range of official interferences which hampered their expansion. The most obtrusive was the corset, which was in force, if over three separate phases, for more than half the period from December 1973 to June 1980. But also important were qualitative guidelines discouraging credit to the personal sector, including loans for house purchase. As a result, the building societies' expansion was – almost without interruption in the 1970s – at a faster rate than the banks'. Apart from these direct constraints on banks' balance sheets, they also suffered from the costs of the reserve asset ratio and, like other businesses, from the exchange control regime. The reserve asset ratio obliged them to keep part of their assets in relatively unprofitable investments, while exchange controls prevented them from lending in sterling overseas. In addition, the clearing banks suffered from the minor irritation of having to maintain $1^1/_2$ per cent of their eligible liabilities in non-interest-bearing balances at the Bank of England.

Since 1979 all these regulations have been scrapped. The third instalment of the corset was withdrawn in June 1980. The circumstances in which this occurred were very humiliating for both the Bank of England and the Government when it became known that sterling M3 had risen by 5 per cent in July. The 1980/81 money supply target was ruined by just one month's figures. The banks concluded that the corset would never be imposed again. In consequence, they felt free to market their corporate lending facilities even more aggressively than they had done in the 1970s, with leasing being one new area of business which showed particular promise. The ending of all restrictions on lending to companies in 1980 was followed by the ending of nearly all restrictions on lending to persons in 1982. No formal announcement was made, but the banks were given to understand that they would be allowed to give mortgage finance to house-buyers, while more conventional personal sector borrowing would no longer be hindered. The distinction implicit in many earlier Bank of England announcements, between wicked lending to persons for consumption and benign lending to companies for investment, seemed to have been forgotten. Other reforms also expanded the banks' opportunities for business. The abolition of exchange controls in October 1979 gave them the chance to lend sterling to foreign borrowers. Initially most loans were directed to foreign banks in the Eurosterling market, but there has been an increasing tendency to direct funds to ultimate borrowers through syndicated credits. This development was certainly unexpected when the Conservatives came to power in May 1979, but even more so was the outcome of the debate on monetary control. Although its theoretical focus was supposed to be the merits of monetary base control, its practical effect was to remove regulations on bank balance sheets. The reserve asset ratio and the $1^1/_2$ per cent cash requirement on the clearing banks lapsed in August 1981.

Although informal understandings about banks' appropriate liquidity norms remain, these changes have left the British banking system relatively little burdened by central bank superintendence of its assets. In most countries the central bank enforces direct restrictions on the amount and the allocation of new lending business; in the United States and West Germany, two countries where such restrictions are absent, banks are required to maintain central bank reserves much above their true business needs. The contrast between either arrangement and the existing very liberal regulatory framework in Britain is sharp. It is not hyperbole to say that banks in Britain now operate in a freer and more relaxed environment than anywhere else in the world.

The sequence of liberalization moves between 1979 and 1981 may be interpreted as the second stage of a process begun by the Competition and Credit Control reforms in September 1971. Their motivation was to establish equality of competition between different kinds of financial intermediary, as it was felt – notably by senior Bank of England officials – that the quantitative bank lending limits of the 1950s and 1960s had unfairly penalized the banks and benefited their rivals. The great freedom currently enjoyed by the British banking system has arisen as a reaction to the excessive, if rather spasmodic and diffident, interventionism which characterized the 40 years until 1979.

Before 1971 the gradual increase in investment incentives provided by the tax system was not fully translated into credit growth because of crude quantitative controls on bank lending. Between 1971 and 1973 the banks were free from restraint – and the result was monetary bedlam when the Heath Government botched 'the dash for growth'. Interventionism, although in a milder form than before 1971, was renewed between 1973 and 1979. Since 1979 all restraints have been taken away. The precise date at which the new freedom began is open to question. Arguably, the ending of exchange controls in October 1979 was the turning-point because it rendered the corset ineffective as a device for controlling bank credit. (Banks merely lent to British companies from an offshore branch, bypassing the controls on their domestic activities.) But in some ways the August 1981 changes, in conjunction with the virtual demise of official guidelines against personal sector credit, were more important.

In the 1950s and 1960s there was persistent – and indeed growing – incompatibility between the ever more helpful tax treatment accorded to purchases of plant, equipment, houses and other capital assets, and the authorities' anxiety about the damage to the balance of payments from excessive credit growth. Over the last two years this incompatibility has been progressively reduced. It is now non-existent. Here, in a nutshell, is the explanation for the bank credit boom of 1979 to 1982. Whereas the credit demands fomented by the tax system were for long either frustrated or

Table 4.1 The growth of sterling advances in 1981

	Total			Increase	
	At 19 Nov 1980 (£ million)	At 19 Aug 1981 (£ million)	At 18 Nov 1981 (£ million)	Year to 18 Nov 1981 (%)	Quarter to 18 Nov 1981 (%)
Total advances to UK residents	48 483	55 329	58 298	20.2	5.4
of which:					
Manufacturing	13 004	13 052	12 909	−0.7	−1.1
Other production	6 041	6 883	6 856	13.5	0.3
Financial services	5 979	6 752	6 899	15.4	2.2
Professional, scientific and miscellaneous	14 420	17 149	18 817	30.5	9.7
	5 947	7 555	8 439	41.9	11.7
Persons	9 040	11 543	12 816	41.8	11.0
House purchase	2 755	3 809	4 714	71.1	23.8

Note
The 'advances' figure does not cover all lending, which also includes acceptances. Acceptance lending over the year to November 1981 was largely to manufacturing, which helps to rectify the sharp divergences between sectors shown by the 'advances' totals.

Source: Financial Statistics

90

channelled through non-bank intermediaries, over the last two years they have passed through the banks. There is no sign that these credit demands are fading away. On the contrary, they seem to be accelerating. In the three months to January, sterling bank lending to the private sector and overseas was increasing at about £2 billion a month. This may somewhat overstate the underlying position, but a trend figure of £20 billion a year is not a wild exaggeration. The outstanding total of sterling bank lending at the end of the third quarter of 1981 was about £72 billion. It follows that, if the £20 billion a year figure is right, banks' loan books are currently growing by nearly 30 per cent a year.

Heavy emphasis has been placed in this article on the tax system as a prime culprit for the lending boom of 1979 to 1982. Can this be substantiated by the evidence? Have tax-sensitive types of credit seen the most rapid expansion in the last two years? Some relevant statistics are given in Table 4.1. It shows how different sectors' bank advances increased over both the year and the quarter to the mid-November 1981 make-up day. This quarter is particularly interesting as it was the first after the final liberalizing changes last August.

The salient feature is the wide variation between the borrowing behaviour of different sectors. Advances to manufacturing industry barely changed in the two periods under consideration. Manufacturing has always been deemed a virtuous activity, high on the list of government priorities. As a result, loans to it have not been thwarted by official restrictions, and there was no major backlog of suppressed credit demand at the end of 1980. The 'other production' and 'financial' categories also registered quite moderate growth rates in 1981, with a tendency towards deceleration.

There were only two conspicuous growth areas – 'services' and 'persons'. But the expansion of loans to the service sector was driven by one particular sub-category, 'professional, scientific and miscellaneous'. Over the year to mid-November this sub-category went up by 41.9 per cent and in the final quarter by 11.7 per cent, equivalent to an annual rate of 55.7 per cent. 'Professional, scientific and miscellaneous' sounds like a rag-bag and so appears to say nothing about the business motivation behind the loans. But the explosive growth of this type of lending is almost entirely attributable to one constituent – leasing.

The detailed logic behind leasing is quite complicated, but its essence is simple. An industrial company which is investing as much as its taxable profit cannot reduce its tax bill further by increasing capital expenditure. It has fully exploited the fiscal incentives for investment. But a financial institution, such as a clearing bank, benefiting from high interest rates, may have a taxable profit much above the sums needed for its own investment programme. Of course, if the financial institution could buy capital goods, it could cut its tax bill as effectively as the industrial company. The solution is for the financial institution to buy capital goods and to lease them to the industrial company which needs them.

The rental charged in the lease has two elements, one amount to recover the capital outlay and another which represents the rate of interest due on the investment. Because the financial institution receives a 100 per cent capital allowance, its tax bill (at a 52 per cent corporation tax rate) is halved and this interest rate may be 8 per cent rather than the 16 per cent implied by 14 per cent base rate plus a margin. Leasing has created, in effect, a market in tax allowances. It is clear that all bank loans which result from it are a by-product of the tax system and, in particular, of the exceptionally favourable treatment of investment.

The amount of new lending for leasing purposes is difficult to estimate precisely, but it is a plausible surmise that it accounted for £500 million to £600 million of the additional advances to the 'professional, scientific and miscellaneous' sub-category in the quarter to mid-November. At that stage it was growing at an annual rate of about 60 per cent. In 1982/83 new lending for leasing may approach £3 billion, which by itself would cause a $3\frac{1}{2}$ per cent increase in sterling M3. Against tax-subsidized opponents like these, money supply targets of 5 per cent to 9 per cent, or even 7 per cent to 11 per cent, are hopelessly outnumbered. There is also no chance of a revival of the debenture market. From the leasing subsidiary of a clearing bank, a company can obtain medium-term finance at 8 per cent or 9 per cent (sometimes fixed rate); from the capital markets similar money would cost 16 per cent.

Although leasing is growing quickly, far more public comment has so far been directed at the banks' entry into housing finance. The figures in Table 4.1 indicate why. In the three months to mid-November bank advances for house purchase rose by almost a quarter. At present they are running at about £300 million a month or $£3\frac{1}{2}$ billion a year, again very large in relation to official money supply targets. Part of the reason for such heavy borrowing by individuals is the tax benefit of having a mortgage. As is familiar, all interest on a mortgage up to £25,000 can be deducted from taxable income. However, this is not altogether persuasive as an explanation because many bank loans for house purchase are bigger than £25,000. Continuing expectations of house price appreciation above the rate of interest, combined with the amenity value of living in a larger home, seem to have been the main influences on the heavy demand for mortgage finance. As building society lending has not fallen much, the big increase in funds channelled to the housing market appears to be attributable to the removal of official restrictions on the banks.

The buoyancy of lending for leasing and house purchase, both responding to tax advantages, confirms our thesis. The credit boom of 1979 to 1982 was caused by the liberalization of the financial system interacting with a fiscal regime designed to promote investment. Its origins are to be sought in two characteristics of the British economic debate in the 1960s – widespread dissatisfaction with the repercussions of quantitative bank lending restrictions on the efficiency of financial intermediation; and a very general anxiety about the presumed link between low investment and low economic growth.

The Government's failure to meet its money supply targets has almost nothing to do with its refusal to introduce monetary base control, as many academic monetarists, particularly from the American Mid-West, believe. These academics often seem to regard monetary base control as a universal panacea, regardless of the local context. As we have seen, the causes of the missed targets are instead parochial and specific; they can be understood most easily by an economist who has followed British governments' persistent tendency, over many years, to pursue irreconcilable economic objectives with a great deal of noise, enthusiasm and naivety. (Ironically, the Conservatives' record in controlling the monetary base is immaculate. In the period from June 1980 to November 1981 it increased by 3.1 per cent, compared with 29.6 per cent for sterling M3. It is since June 1980 that academic monetarists have complained most loudly about the Bank of England's supposed incompetence and blamed it on the absence of monetary base control machinery.)

The question arises of what the Government should have done at the beginning of the whole process. Surely, critics might claim, the Treasury and the Bank of England are full of clever people who should have realized that financial liberalization would cause the release of pent-up credit demands and a switch of business towards the banks, which together would lead to rapid growth in bank deposits and the destruction of official sterling M3 targets. Perhaps these clever people should have realized, but no one outside these institutions foresaw what was coming.

In fact, the authorities were in an impossible dilemma. The sequence of reforms introduced from October 1979 (the abolition of exchange controls) to August 1981 (the ending of balance sheet requirements for the banks) were all desirable. Whereas the financial system was subject to quite severe restriction for most of the 40 years to 1979, it is now exceptionally free from government regulation. There is much evidence from developing countries that liberalizing the money side of the economy has favourable effects later on the 'real' side.[2]

But suppose that in mid-1979 Sir Geoffrey Howe, aware that liberalization would cause a credit boom, had said: 'Our sterling M3 targets in 1980/81 and 1981/82 will be 13 to 17 per cent and 12 to 16 per cent. These are much higher than recent rates of increase, but reflect the distortions arising from a number of forthcoming measures intended to strengthen competition in the financial system, and should not jeopardize the Government's objective to achieve a lasting reduction in the rate of inflation. We cannot measure the distortions exactly, but believe they will be large'. Who would have taken the statement seriously? How could a government, publicly branded as monetarist, have announced that it would allow an acceleration of money supply growth?

Of course, neither Sir Geoffrey Howe nor his cohorts of advisers inside and outside the government machine appreciated in advance the potential scale of the 1979 to 1982 bank lending explosion. As a result, the presentation of policy has suffered a heavy blow. One objective of the Medium-Term Financial Strategy, declared in the 1980 Budget, was to mould inflation expectations favourably by projecting a gradual deceleration in target money supply growth in future years. That objective has not been fulfilled. But there have been pluses as well as minuses. It was because of the Medium-Term Financial Strategy that the Government raised taxes so vigorously in the 1981 Budget, a very courageous move which has had the effect of making Britain's public sector finances stronger than most other industrial countries'; and it was because money supply targets were in being that the authorities kept interest rates so high for so long. Without these interest rates, credit and money growth would have been even faster – and inflation would not now be heading for single figures. The decision to keep interest rates at such levels was broadly correct.

If the argument of this article is right, there will continue to be severe difficulties in reconciling money supply restraint with a free financial system, a tax system promoting investment and high inflation expectations. Because of the benefits a free financial system gives to the real economy, it would be a mistake to return to the interventionism of the 1950s and 1960s. Arguably, the tax system is too friendly to investment and is the main culprit for the recent credit boom. Its reform might make some contribution to solving the problem of monetary control.

Notes

1. The implied approach to monetary control is to regulate the credit counterparts to bank deposits. This approach, which is broadly that adopted by the Bank of England, is very different from the banking multiplier theory found in the textbooks and academic monetarist writings. An account of how the credit counterparts approach works (if not very well) is given in T. G. Congdon, *Monetary Control in Britain* (London: Macmillan), 1982.

2. There may be a connection between the 1979–82 credit boom, relatively high capital investment and the recent rapid growth of productivity. The possibility was analysed in 'The boom in bank lending: is it related to the surge in productivity growth?', accompanying the 22 January 1981 issue of *Messel's Weekly Economic Monitor.*

Why did Monetarism have so much Trouble in the Early 1980s?: 2. The Public Sector Problem

From an article 'Why has monetarism failed so far?: 2. The public sector problem' in The Banker, *April 1982.*

The article had a straightforward argument. One weakness of monetary control as an antidote for inflation is that it has little effect on the public sector. Since the Government can extract resources from the rest of the economy at will (by taxation or printing money), it has no need to hold money balances. There is no particular connection between monetary growth and public sector inflation. The large size of Britain's public sector (relative to, say, the USA) was therefore one reason for both the obstinacy of the British inflation problem in the 1970s and for the severity of the 1980/81 recession.

The Conservative Government may have failed to control the money supply, but it has succeeded in curbing inflation. The 1981/82 pay round seems likely to finish up in the 6 per cent to 8 per cent area. It will be the lowest since the 1977/78 round, which was artificially and unsustainably depressed at the tail-end of an incomes policy. There can be little doubt that underlying inflationary pressures are weaker now than at any time since the late 1960s.

But has this achievement been bought too dearly? Over the last three years the unemployment total has climbed to three million, while hundreds of thousands more have at some stage or other been worried that they also might find themselves without a job. Too small a reduction in inflation seems to have been gained at too great a cost in terms of lost employment. More-over, this failure does not matter only to the competing monetarist theologians who have bickered incessantly about the rival merits of different money supply definitions and agonized over the vagaries of sterling M3. It has directly affected many ordinary people. Most of them have no interest in the technical mechanics of monetary control and can be plausibly represented as the innocent victims of a government policy they do not understand. Surely, the critics argue, if monetarism works so badly there must be a better alternative.

There are two ways a monetarist might attempt to answer this charge. The first is to say that no one knows what determines the unemployment–inflation trade-off. But, whereas the Government cannot in the long run control the level of unemployment (which depends on labour market institutions), it is responsible – again in the long run – for the level of inflation (which depends on the central bank's regulation of the money supply). This cogent, but highly pessimistic, interpretation of the economic system was implicit in

Friedman's 1967 exposition of the 'natural rate of unemployment', given as a presidential address to the American Economic Association. The natural rate is that at which there is no tendency for wage increases either to accelerate or to decelerate. It is consistent with stable inflation. 'Unfortunately,' Friedman warned, 'we have as yet devised no method to estimate accurately and readily the natural rate of unemployment.'[1] The corollary was that active attempts to manipulate unemployment beneath the natural rate would lead to ever higher inflation. The right approach was therefore to confine monetary policy to its proper role of achieving price stability. The unemployment repercussions, however dire, would have to be ignored.

The second response is more equivocal. It recognizes that the unemployment–inflation trade-off can be affected by government policy. According to this line of monetarist thinking, the key variable to operate on is inflation expectations. The reasoning is straightforward. If people expect low inflation, the adjustment of behaviour to a fall in inflation from a high level is easy and painless. On the other hand, if they expect rapid inflation, the same adjustment not only takes time, but also tends to be accompanied by setting the 'wrong' prices in product and labour prices. These 'wrong' prices include excessive wages, which then lead to unemployment.

Monetarism was never intended as a form of corporal punishment on the British economy. No one wanted unemployment to reach three million and, as is clear from forecasts made in 1979 and 1980, no one expected it to do so. Whatever some Sunday papers may say to the contrary, all monetarists would have preferred the unemployment–inflation trade-off to be more favourable. The question arises of what went wrong and whether anything could have been done to improve the situation. The argument of this article is that a very important cause of the adverse unemployment–inflation relationship was the movement of public sector wages and prices in the first two years of the present Government's period in office. This suggestion may not by itself be new or controversial. But I want in this article to propose a perhaps more provocative extension: it is that monetary policy has almost no relevance (except at several removes) to the containment of public sector inflation. Original monetarist hopes that the inflation problem could be solved solely by reducing the rate of money supply growth were naive. Because the money supply prescription neglected the public sector, it was incomplete. This is the sense in which monetarism was not – and is not – enough. (Sir Keith Joseph wrote an influential pamphlet *Monetarism is not Enough* for the Centre for Policy Studies in 1978, which argued that control over government spending had to accompany monetary restraint, if inflation were to be brought down. But it did not highlight the problem of public sector wages.)

If the moderation of inflation expectations is necessary to mitigate the unemployment arising from restrictive financial policies, the Government made its first mistake in the June 1979 budget. The increase in value added tax from 8 per cent to 15 per cent had an immediate effect on the retail price index and wage-bargainers regrettably decided to incorporate it in the 1979/ 80 pay round. This was despite the large accompanying cut in income tax. It should perhaps be said, in the Government's defence, that at the time there was a strong body of informed opinion behind a shift from direct to indirect taxation. For example, the Meade Committee Report for the Institute for Fiscal Studies recommended a big rise in VAT as one part of its proposal to introduce an expenditure tax.

But more serious than the VAT increase was the surge of public sector inflation from mid-1979 until early 1981. It had two aspects. The first was the deliberate raising of public sector prices above the general rate of inflation. In the year to August 1980 the increase of the prices of goods and services produced mainly by the public sector was 26 per cent, while the retail price index as a whole went up by just over 16 per cent. The second was the tendency to grant public sector wage increases much higher than those in the private sector. The evidence on this point is abundant and persuasive. According to official figures published in the Treasury's December 1981 *Economic Progress Report*, the ratio of public to private sector earnings rose from 101.5 (1970 = 100) in 1979 to 108.4 in 1981. An independent assessment in the August 1981 *National Institute Economic Review* had earlier reached similar conclusions.

Retrospective moralizing always sounds smug and patronizing. In this case, it is particularly unhelpful. To say that the Government should have controlled public sector pay and prices better in 1979 and 1980 is all very well, but it shows little appreciation of the local and specific justifications for excessive public sector inflation in those two years. The justifications were usually sound and sometimes compelling. It would have been difficult for any government, even one commanding widespread public support, to resist them. As it happened, the Conservative Government did not command such support and had to acquiesce in numerous pay and price changes it disliked.

The objections to holding down nationalized industry prices were both microeconomic and macroeconomic. In the last two years of the Callaghan administration there had been a politically- motivated failure to raise these prices. A consequent danger was gross resource misallocation with demand being inappropriately encouraged in areas where goods were supplied at beneath cost. The size of the required price adjustment was further aggravated by the second oil shock which pushed up energy bills. Nearly all the nationalized industries in Britain are either energy suppliers or highly sensitive to the price of energy. In addition to the need to prevent microeconomic distortion, the Government was worried that, if nationalized industries kept prices too low, their deficits would rise and jeopardize its goal of reducing public sector borrowing. Whatever the short-run once-for-all impact on the retail price index from higher nationalized industry charges, a macroeconomic priority was to cut the PSBR as part of the long-run strategy to contain money supply growth and inflation.

If the economic logic behind big increases in public sector prices was convincing, the political expediency of large public sector pay rises was undeniable. The most awkward of these rises stemmed from the Clegg Commission's activities and affected the earnings of groups, such as the teachers, the civil servants and the local authority manual workers, who account for a high proportion of total public sector employment. As the Conservatives had agreed to honour the Commission's awards before the 1979 election, not much could have been done – without patent breaking of pledges – to avoid paying up. In the context of 1979 to 1981, which saw several major public sector strikes anyway, refusal to match the increases recommended by Clegg would have invited at best widespread disruption and at worst open confrontation between the Government and trade unions.

But, however good the reasons for particular public sector wage and price increases, the effect on inflation expectations was very unfortunate. Many nationalized industry price rises were intended to change relative prices, correctly reflecting a sharper increase in the cost of their inputs, like energy, than in other industries. But there is a tendency, particularly in a country as easily swayed by newspaper headlines as Britain, to interpret price movements in certain major industries as symptomatic of a general trend. When 25 per cent or 30 per cent rises in the price of electricity, gas, coal and so on were announced in late 1979 and the early part of 1980, businessmen thought these were indicative of prospective changes in the absolute price level.

They therefore decided that there would not be much of a penalty, in terms of lost sales, if their own prices were hoisted by similar percentages. They soon discovered that they had made a miscalculation. In the second quarter of 1980 demand for nearly all kinds of industrial product collapsed. It was a classic example of government policy causing private sector decision-takers to set the 'wrong' prices. Similar forces were at work in the labour market. Employment in the public and private sectors can be readily differentiated as a matter of definition, but comparisons between the two are frequent and inevitable. Moreover, the functional dividing-line is rather blurred. Many unions are strongly represented in both and expect them to have similar wage levels, while job interchanges are quite common. When large public sector increases took place in 1979 and 1980, private sector employers felt obliged to give similar rises, irrespective of their own ability to pay. Once again the Government's approach to controlling public sector inflation was responsible for employers and employees deciding 'wrong' prices which, in this case, meant wage levels inconsistent with the preservation of jobs.

The term 'administered prices' has been suggested for those prices set less by market forces than by bureaucratic decision. Although it may be a misunderstanding to think that the prices of any product can be analysed without reference to supply and demand, there is little doubt that many public sector prices and charges are administered, at least in the sense that the people responsible are not much bothered by the subsequent effect on the quantity sold. The Government's programme to raise administered prices in 1979 and 1980 worsened inflation expectations. At the same time, monetary policy was being tightened to slow down the rise in market prices. The conflict between policy towards public sector administered prices and private sector market prices was total. There was a head-on collision between price-making behaviour in the two different parts of the economy. The smash contributed to the biggest increase in unemployment since the early 1930s.

At this stage of the argument an academic monetarist might start to complain. Surely, he would say, the remedy for excessive public sector inflation is the same as for excessive private sector inflation. It is to reduce the rate of money supply growth. There is nothing special or unusual in the problem.

Here is the mistake. What the academic monetarist fails to understand is that much of the public sector is completely immune to tight monetary policy – or to lax monetary policy, for that matter. It is quite easy to identify mechanisms whereby a reduction in money supply growth checks inflation in the private sector. Slower money growth means that companies' bank deposits are not increasing as much as before; they may perhaps be rising at less than the going rate of inflation. If companies continue to raise wages and carry out investment plans on the same scale as previously their balance sheets come under strain. Their most liquid asset – their balance at the bank – may fail to grow in line with their liabilities, notably bank borrowings and trade creditors.

If this mismatch intensifies, they may be bankrupted. Measures to improve the bank balance are therefore necessary. Such measures may include cutbacks in stocks, lay-offs of workers and deferment of investment, all of which are likely to restrain price and wage increases. The nature of the link between a deceleration in money supply growth and slower inflation is fairly obvious in the private sector, whatever the controversy about its strength and timing. But compare this with the public sector. The civil servants in government departments who manage expenditure do not have to worry about a bank balance. They receive their money from the Treasury and the Treasury can borrow at will from the Bank of England. This power to borrow is, of course, equivalent to a licence to print Bank of England notes. The notes are legal tender and must be accepted as payment for goods.

It follows that most of the government sector does not have to keep bank deposits as a liquidity reserve to meet unexpected bills. It also follows that slower growth of the total amount of bank deposits has no effect whatever on those individuals whose daily task is to control government expenditure. Although monetary policy acts as a powerful constraint on (or stimulant to) businessmen in the private sector, it is useless and irrelevant as an instrument for influencing civil servants in the public sector. A reduction in the rate of money supply growth cannot solve the problem of public sector inflation.[2] Indeed, the situation is rather worse than that. Suppose that the overall inflation rate is 16 per cent – with public sector inflation at 26 per cent and private sector inflation at 10 per cent. (This broadly describes Britain's position in mid-1980.) Unsympathetic journalists and Opposition politicians are bound to deride 'the failure of monetarism', the apparent inadequacy of monetary restraint as a method of lowering inflation; 16 per cent is, after all, a rather disappointing performance.

The only answer an academic monetarist could propose would be to reduce the money supply growth even more. But it is clear from the numbers what would happen. The private sector, already burdened by its inability to offer wages competitive with government employment and by higher electricity, gas, water, transport and other nationalized industry bills, would have to reduce its inflation rate to 8 per cent or 6 per cent. The imbalance between it and the public sector would be exaggerated. More companies would go into liquidation, more workers would join dole queues and, as long as the public sector pressed on with big wage and price increases, more gloomy inflation news would be announced. (This broadly describes Britain's position in early 1981.)

The academic monetarist might protest that money supply control does eventually feed through to the public sector. Government employees will, in their expectations about what constitutes a reasonable wage award, take note of settlements in the private sector, while the sales revenue of nationalized industries is determined largely by business conditions in the economy as a whole. These are fair observations. But there is an implied recognition that monetary policy has its direct and immediate effect on the private sector alone; it is afterwards that the public sector has to adjust. Even when the adjustment comes, it is not because of anxiety about balance sheets, liquidity, interest rates and so on; it is because of earlier anxiety about these variables by private sector decision-takers.

Indeed, a case can be presented that to control inflation in a mixed economy by monetary means is almost certainly unfair to the private sector. The inequity can be mitigated by such devices as 'cash limits' on public expenditure, set in accordance with money supply targets or expected private sector inflation. Another possibility is that a formal incomes policy may be more effective in the public sector than the private, helping to redress the discriminatory impact of monetary policy.[3] Both cash limits and incomes policies can be regarded as virtuous confidence tricks, which would mould expectations favourably and help to stop the private sector setting the 'wrong' prices. Whatever the merits of these particular arguments, there is no doubt that textbook versions of monetarism – both as they were available in May 1979 and as they are available today – are silent about the problem of public sector inflation. This silence is symptomatic of a larger weakness in the monetarist position, a haziness about the precise transmission mechanisms by which changes in the money supply influence changes in the price level. Earlier in the article a brief account was given of how companies might be forced to take inflation-reducing action in response to balance sheet difficulties caused by slow money growth. But this was merely a sketch. In the real world there is a rich diversity of other mechanisms at work.

If the monetarist story is to be persuasive, it should explain how these interact with each other, which is the quickest to take effect, which is the most powerful and so on. Instead, monetarists seem to be preoccupied with what are termed 'reduced form' econometric exercises, which try to discover the relationship between one big number (money national expenditure) and another big number (the money supply), ignoring the thousands of little numbers in between. This habit is partly responsible for the tendency to look at the money national expenditure as a whole and to overlook the contrasting behaviour of its two constituents, public expenditure and private expenditure.[4]

A further dimension of the topic needs to be emphasized. Some influential monetarist research was carried out by the Manchester Inflation Workshop, under Professors Parkin and Laidler, in the mid-1970s. Two of its most insistent themes were that inflation was a monetary phenomenon and that what it termed the sociological school, which analysed wage increases in terms of relative bargaining power, was mistaken.[5] The main drawback to the Manchester view is that it regards all wage increases as taking place in the same institutional environment, which is clearly incorrect. In the private sector, market forces are at work and monetary policy is the main determinant of inflation. But in the public sector, market forces are remote from the bargaining process. The money supply does not matter in settling the pay of civil servants, health workers, teachers and so on, but relative bargaining power does. There are economic techniques for analysing bargaining situations, but no definitive theory has been derived. So it is necessary, unfortunately, to pay attention to sociological variables like the political attitudes of trade union leaders. This is messy, untidy and not to the taste of rigorous monetary economists, but it is also the real world.

The waywardness of public sector inflation is a nuisance not merely for analytical reasons. It also gives rise to the serious practical question of how it should be controlled. If money supply restraint is not the solution, what is?

The major nationalizations and the establishment of a large permanent public sector were completed during the Attlee administration of 1945 – 51. At that time Labour Party intellectuals had few doubts about the problem of public sector pay. Their judgement was that, with so much of the economy in state hands, it would be possible to replace arbitrary market forces by the sweetness and light of responsible centralized wage bargaining. They hoped that at long last incomes could be determined by the ideal of social justice. Ever since governments and trade unions have squabbled about what 'social justice' involves. For the particular producer group affected it normally means 'more for us' and 'less for them'. The determinant of public sector pay is not sweetness and light, but who is the bigger and better bully.

The downfall of the Heath Government in 1974, after a disastrous contest with the coalminers and narrow defeat in a general election, encouraged the belief that public sector unions are very good at bullying. The memory of this experience was largely responsible for the sharp improvement in the public sector's relative pay, both in 1974 and 1975, and in the period from 1979 to 1981. It is no surprise that the present Government should have been worsted so badly. The advice it received from its friends was 'control of the money supply is sufficient for control of inflation'. They did not warn that control of the money supply is insufficient for the control of inflation arising in the public sector.

The solution, as more people have come to realize, is for the Government to strengthen its bullying position. There are, of course, many illustrations of the likely success of this course of action. In Communist countries, as there is only a tiny private sector, the problem of inflation reduces to the problem of public sector inflation. Governments maintain tight restrictions over the trade unions, which are merely accomplices of political repression, so that the risk of excessive wage demands is eliminated without further ado. In several Latin American countries, again with large public sectors, the power of independent trade unions has been smothered by military dictatorships.

If these examples are reliable, there is no difficulty about curbing inflation even given the dominance of public sector employment. The Government has only to make itself nasty enough. According to opinion polls, trade union leaders are very unpopular in Britain today. Any government, facing insubordination by a powerful public sector group, would probably command extensive support from the general public if it showed itself prepared to take the necessary counter-measures.

What are these counter-measures? So far British governments have displayed a certain lack of imagination about the methods available. Recently, however, Professor Meade has outlined some possibilities in his book on *Wage-Fixing*. A union which failed to accept the arbitration of an independent pay tribunal and went on strike should, Meade suggests, be subject to certain sanctions. These might include the withdrawal of the right to redundancy money, the impounding of union funds and the payment of supplementary benefits only in the form of loans. Once a government began to go down this path, it is difficult to see where it might stop. In the last resort, it could evict recalcitrant strikers from council houses or end their right to state pensions. If any union thinks that it is necessarily a bigger and better bully than the government, it is making a serious mistake. The record of many autocratic regimes in the Communist world and elsewhere is testimony to this melancholy but inescapable truth.

There is no easy solution to the problem of public sector inflation. A reduction in the size of the public sector would obviously make the area of potential dispute smaller. The implied recommendations are further denationalization and subjecting public sector employees to market disciplines similar to those already operating in the private sector. There might be disagreement about how these disciplines are to be specified, interpreted and applied, but the objective of parity of treatment in the public and private sectors seems reasonable. This approach might be criticized as too 'ideological'. But, if it is ideological to want to remove an active source of social tension which in many countries has contributed to the establishment of political tyranny, then 'ideological' is surely a term of approval.

Public sector inflation is a political issue and it can be tackled only by political means. The failure of monetarism in the last three years owes much to misunderstanding on this point. Monetary policy did curb private sector inflation. But, because public sector wages and prices rose quickly as a result of Government decisions, inflation expectations were stimulated and 'wrong' prices were set in many parts of the economy. This was responsible for the poor unemployment–inflation trade-off – and so for the increase in the jobless total to three million. The hope must be that in the next few years the trade-off becomes more benign. There are cases, such as West Germany in the early 1950s, where unemployment and inflation declined together. The exercise of restraint by public sector unions may be a precondition for a similar outcome in Britain in the mid-1980s. Much depends on the political situation, particularly the result of the next general election.

Notes

1.   The concept of the natural rate of unemployment was advanced in Friedman's 1967
     presidential address to the American Economic Association. The paper, 'On the role of
     monetary policy', was reprinted in M. Friedman, *The Optimum Quantity of Money* (Lon-
     don: Macmillan), 1969.
2.   The point was strongly emphasized on p. 58 of T. G. Congdon, *Monetarism: an Essay in
     Definition* (London: Centre for Policy Studies), 1978.
3.   The sequence of 'on–off' periods of incomes policy can be interpreted in terms of the
     differential impact of monetary policy on the public and private sectors. See T. G.
     Congdon, 'The incomes policy cycle in Britain: an attempt at explanation', *The Banker*,
     December 1980.
4.   The link between money and private expenditure is, however, noted on p. 30 of D. Smith,
     'The counter-inflation strategy in historical perspective' in the London Business School's
     February 1981 *Economic Outlook*.
5.   See, particularly, D. Laidler and D. L. Purdy (eds), *Inflation and Labour Markets* (Man-
     chester: Manchester University Press), 1974.

The Value of a Long-Term Anti-Inflation Programme

From an article 'Winning the economic war' in The Spectator, *29 May 1982.*

*Because of the 'long and variable lags' between monetary restraint and
lower inflation, about which Friedman warned so clearly, any successful
anti-inflation programme had to last for several years. A crucial problem for
the Thatcher Government in its first term was that it would run out of time,
with not enough benefits emerging from its policies after five years to make
its re-election possible. In this context the Falklands War of 1982 was a
godsend. Some extraordinary and totally unexpected events in Argentina
and the Falklands led to Mrs Thatcher's re-election, giving the monetarist
programme the time it needed to work.*

While the fighting has intensified in the South Atlantic, there has been a
curious lull in hostilities on the home front. Critics of the Government's
economic policies have gone rather quiet. It is not hard to explain why. The
main weakness of the Thatcher experiment has been its time-scale. Sound
money and free market policies have worked in many countries and on many
occasions, but they have always taken a long time. In their early years
programmes of economic liberalization can be very painful. Perhaps the
most celebrated example, the Erhard currency reform of 1948, was considered as late as 1951 to have been a serious mistake for the West German
economy. It was only in the mid-1950s that people began to talk about the
Wirtschaftswunder.

The Thatcher Government's opponents have assumed that the British
electoral term is too short. Many of them secretly admit that the policies

would succeed if pursued with enough determination for a sufficiently long period, but they doubt the political staying-power of such an abrasive approach. Until two months ago they took it for granted that the Conservatives would lose their parliamentary majority in the next general election. The Thatcher experiment would therefore be scuttled before any of its benefits might emerge.

Now the position has changed. The probable outcome of the Falklands crisis would have been to strengthen the Government's popularity even if the Opposition had handled the affair with some degree of political competence. In the event the Labour Party has bungled terribly. As a result there is a distinct possibility that Mrs Thatcher will win the next general election and that the policies with which she is so closely identified will have the time they need to reach a favourable conclusion. There has also been helpful economic news. By chance the timing of the landing in San Carlos Bay coincided almost exactly with that of the announcement of the April retail price index. It showed a 9.4 per cent rise in the previous 12 months. The Government has achieved one of its symbolically most important objectives – single-figure inflation. Over the period to the general election the rate of price increases is likely to decelerate further.

Viewed from an historical perspective the cost of controlling inflation has been appalling. If an economist had been told in 1967 that there would simultaneously be three million' unemployed and 9.4 per cent inflation 15 years later, he would have regarded the forecast as a macabre joke. But attitudes have shifted. From an electoral standpoint the crucial issue may prove to be not the level of unemployment, but the direction of change at the time voting takes place. Here, too, the trends are reassuring. The rate of increase in the jobless total has slowed down sharply in recent months. There is a good prospect that the numbers out of work will stabilize or start falling by early 1983. With skilful editing of history and suitable phrasemaking about leanness and fitness, it may even be feasible to present 1980 and 1981 as a period of great advance by British industry. That would be a caricature, but a few marginal voters may be persuaded.

And what would happen if the Conservatives were re-elected in 1983 or 1984? It is an unattractive and perhaps a callous thought, but the three million unemployed would be a potential economic asset instead of a persistent electoral liability. The reason is that at some stage they will seek new jobs and so provide the manpower for a sustained period of rapid economic growth. In the 1950s and 1960s the binding constraint during the expansion phase of the stop–go cycle was invariably a shortage of labour, expressed in excessive wage increases. Because of the resulting lack of competitiveness there were frequent balance-of-payments difficulties. In the late 1980s there should be no labour shortages and no balance-of-payments difficulties.

All this is a horrifying prospect for the tribe of leftish leader-writers, SDP activists, morally indignant trade union leaders and Sir Ian Gilmour, who have warned us so often that the Government's policies would end disastrously. Their favourite target has been 'monetarism', about the meaning of which they have, however, been a little vague. With the aid of certain Sunday newspapers they have led us to believe that the vagaries of sterling M3 have no effect on inflation, but are responsible for misfortunes as diverse as race riots in Brixton, inner-city problems in Toxteth and the threatened closure of aluminium smelters in Invergordon.

What proposals will the reflationists start peddling now? Will the realization that they are no longer on the offensive, force them to strengthen their analysis and add fresh bite to their polemic? The impression given by their most recent statements is that it will not. Take, for example, a column by Mr Peter Shore in *The Observer* of 23 May. He summarizes his recommendation as the replacement of 'passive government' by 'active government'. 'We shall,' so he says, 'have to plan for economic growth and industrial change, and intervene in the economy to achieve them...Human intelligence, with all its imperfections, must once more be brought to bear on the forces of the market.' He fills out his allotted eight hundred words with a few remarks about 'a range of measures' to rig interest rates, the exchange rate and the international flow of capital, but otherwise does not introduce any ideas of substance to his readers. Of course, no one would question the prerogative of politicians to write empty bluster like this. But there is at least an expectation that the bluster will be entertaining. The objection to Mr Peter Shore, Sir Ian Gilmour and their associates is not so much that they are wrong, but that they have ceased to be interesting. There is something risible about pontificating on the need 'to plan for economic growth and industrial change' nearly 20 years after George Brown set up the ill-fated Department of Economic Affairs.

Keynesianism became boring about 15 years ago, monetarism became boring about three years ago, and today the critics of monetarism have become boring too. In consequence, the economic debate is shifting from labels and terminology to weighing the advantages and disadvantages of particular institutional arrangements and policy approaches. Wreckage from earlier theoretical battles is still littered over the newspapers, but there is a developing consensus that the size of the budget deficit and the rate of money supply growth are important economic variables. Monetarism, if in a diluted and flexible form, is securely entrenched. Because of this, and signs that the economy is recovering without deliberate reflation, the Government will adhere to the broad outlines of its original strategy. There may be minor tactical adjustments here and there, but they will not amount to much. As the critics' arguments become more hackneyed and their language more dreary, the intellectual opposition will seem increasingly unconvincing.

It may seem ugly and even a little ghoulish to suggest that the Government's domestic policies will receive another chance as a side-effect of a military dictatorship's delinquent behaviour which has led to a silly war and unnecessary loss of life. When considered with detachment, the whole business is miserable and ludicrous. It should certainly not be a pretext for national self-congratulation, let alone rejoicing. But as the cogency of the case for what Sir Ian Gilmour calls 'the good old expansionary measures' is waning, it would not be too unjust if the Government's economic policies were allowed to continue and Mrs Thatcher was re-elected thanks to General Galtieri.

A Confident Forecast of Prosperity in the Mid-1980s

From an article 'Following Friedman' in The Spectator, *28 May 1983.*

This article emphasized the obverse of the monetarist gloom about ever-rising inflation while unemployment was held beneath its natural rate. (See pp. 24–7, the article 'Price stability and the "natural" level of unemployment', reprinted from The Times *of 22 January, 1975.) As long as unemployment remained above the natural rate, inflation would keep on falling. Indeed, it ought to be possible, in principle, to combine falling unemployment and lower inflation for a period. The argument was the basis for an optimistic forecast of the medium-term economic prospects. This forecast was, in fact, fully justified by the rapid output and employment growth, and moderate inflation, of the next five years.*

Sadly, the remark in the penultimate paragraph (that 'We can rely on economic commentators to invent more adventurous programmes and so create a climate of opinion in which governments will tend to stray...from the narrow path of financial prudence') was also fully justified by events.

Until 1979 all post-war governments failed to achieve their economic objectives. The problem of how to reconcile financial stability, as indicated by the inflation rate and the balance of payments, with a strong 'real' economy, measured by output growth and the level of employment, proved too difficult.

The Thatcher administration, unlike its predecessors, has achieved its objectives. But this success has been made possible not by particular cleverness, skill or luck, but because it has redefined the economic problem. It has concentrated on the financial side and abandoned targets for the real economy. This approach, implicit from the start, was made explicit with the announcement of the Medium-Term Financial Strategy in March 1980. The strategy proposed gradual declines in the ratio of the budget deficit to national income and in the rate of money supply growth, with the eventual aim of a substantial reduction in inflation. Broadly speaking, that is what has happened. The budget deficit and money supply growth have been cut, and inflation is lower now than for 15 years.

The focus on financial targets had its intellectual origins in a theory advanced by Milton Friedman in his 1967 presidential address to the American Economic Association. He said that there was one rate of unemployment, the 'natural rate', towards which the labour market would settle in the absence of outside intervention. This was the only rate compatible with stable inflation. If any government misguidedly tried to drive unemployment beneath the natural rate, inflation would not be constant at a high level, but would accelerate explosively, culminating in hyper-inflation and the collapse of political life.

It followed that monetary policy should be confined solely to the task of maintaining price stability and should not be used to pursue an arbitrarily-defined full employment target. Friedman's argument was a radical challenge to the orthodoxy, dating from the 1944 *Employment Policy* White Paper, that governments had an overriding commitment to full employment. It was pessimistic, and widely understood to be pessimistic, in its denial that politicians could do much good by manipulating macroeconomic levers. But it was also optimistic in its underlying premise that, if unemployment rose above the natural rate, the economy contained innate mechanisms that would bring actual unemployment back into line with the natural rate. This optimistic strand has been almost unnoticed in public debate.

Mrs Thatcher herself has repudiated the notion of a natural rate of unemployment. In a House of Commons exchange on 26 March 1981, Mr Foot asked her, 'Will she explain what is meant by the "natural rate of unemployment" that Treasury spokesmen mentioned to a Select Committee? Is it not wrong to introduce the idea that there is a natural rate of unemployment of about 5 per cent?' She answered that, 'It is not a Treasury concept. It is an academic concept invented some time ago. I have never agreed with it or thought it sound.' The reply may not have been altogether frank. The concept with which she is supposed to have 'never agreed' is the only analytically rigorous and intellectually convincing justification for the single-minded concentration on financial variables which has been the hallmark of her administration's economic policy.

Mrs Thatcher's refusal to endorse the natural rate idea should be blamed not on ingratitude to her intellectual mentors, but on political circumspection. The phrase 'natural rate of unemployment' is objectionable because of its connotation that there is something pre-ordained and unavoidable about

people being without jobs. No politician could ever admit this. Her preference has been to dress up technical economics with homespun morality.
Instead of referring to the need for money supply restraint and a low public
sector borrowing requirement, she talks about sound money and good house-
keeping. For public relations purposes this is almost certainly right.

The Government has also benefited from a widespread recognition that
unemployment stems from the elimination of industrial inefficiency. There is
a great deal of common sense in this. Monetarism can be castigated for
many things, but not for over-manning at Port Talbot, unofficial strikes at
Halewood and bloody-mindedness at Liverpool Docks. People voted for the
present Government because they wanted to stop the more eccentric tribal
customs of the British trade union movement. It would have been naive to
imagine that this process would not involve heavy unemployment, at least
for a time.

The Government's record can be summed up briefly: in its first term it has
done the dirty work either for its second term or for its successor. Rightly or
wrongly, perseverance with sound finance and the closure of unproductive
factories have created a pool of three million jobless workers. It is here,
paradoxically, that we come to the optimistic side of the natural rate theory.
The point is that the brute fact of mass unemployment has created labour
market pressures – in the form of long job queues and passive union leaders
– for a decline in inflation. While unemployment is above the natural rate,
these pressures will persist. Indeed, unless unemployment falls to the natural
rate, inflation will decelerate year after year until actual declines in the price
level are recorded. This is the counterpart to the proposition that inflation
will accelerate explosively if unemployment is beneath the natural rate.

There can be little doubt that in Britain today unemployment is above,
possibly very much above, the natural rate. Wage settlements and inflation
have been declining since late 1980 when the jobless total was one-and-a-
half million. So the natural rate of unemployment must be below two million. It follows, by the logic of Friedman's theory, that unemployment could
go down by a million and there would still be a tendency for inflation to fall.
The economy can look forward to the happy combination of lower unemployment and lower inflation.

A suggestion of this kind is regarded as fantasy by middle-of-the-road
forecasters at organizations like the National Institute and the London Business School, which both establish and reflect the economic consensus. As far
as they are concerned, the future is mostly an extrapolation of the past. Any
suggestion that it might be much different is considered an imaginative
indulgence. So their typical procedure when making a medium-term forecast
is to examine the economic data for the last ten years, add them up, divide

by ten and then assume that the resulting numbers will be average performance in the next few years.

Not much insight is required to see that, although this may be economic
forecasting, it is not serious thinking. If the method were legitimate, any
decade of economic history would closely resemble the decades before and
after it. But economic history is not like that. The more optimistic assessment
of current prospects generated by the natural rate theory is, unlike the standard forecasts, based on the idea that individuals' response to economic
conditions varies as those conditions vary. For example, it appeals to the
simple hypothesis that someone out of work will look for a job. Whatever
the econometrics of the matter may be, this seems plausible as an observation
on human nature.

The conventional economic forecast also suffers from an obsession with
aggregates, big numbers like 'consumption', 'investment' and 'public expenditure'. It cannot easily handle the shift of manpower and investment
from smokestack to sunrise industries which has been a feature of Mrs
Thatcher's first period in office. Between June 1978 and September 1981,
the numbers employed in metal manufacture fell by 31 per cent from 459,000
to 314,000, while the numbers employed making computers rose by 42 per
cent from 43,000 to 61,000. In 1982 and 1983 the change in the relative
importance of the two industries has continued and will improve Britain's
long-term economic prospects. An econometric model which assumes that
future output growth will be the same as the average of the last ten years, a
period characterized by mindless subsidization of metal manufacture and the
rest of Britain's supposedly 'essential industrial base', is very likely to be
wrong.

The Conservatives have in fact been successful in strengthening the supply
side of the economy. The rate of productivity increase has clearly improved
relative to previous trends, particularly in manufacturing. There is an apparent irony here because the Government has, of course, placed most emphasis
on sound finance and the fight against inflation. But there is no inconsistency. Evidence of the better productivity performance helps to legitimize a
policy approach in which the Government takes responsibility for financial
variables and abdicates from the management of the 'real' economy. It
should be said, in partial qualification, that neither Sir Keith Joseph nor Mr
Patrick Jenkin has ended the philanthropic activities of the Department of
Industry, although these are possibly less misdirected today than they were
four years ago.

If a commitment to sound finance has dominated the Conservatives' economic policy in their first term, and served them reasonably well, how
should this commitment be maintained if they are elected for a second, third
and fourth term? The logical completion of the Medium-Term Financial

Strategy would be a balanced budget, a rate of monetary expansion always equal to the underlying growth rate of productive capacity and price stability. The Conservative manifesto does, indeed, refer – if rather sheepishly – to price stability as an ultimate objective. There is, however, a fatal weakness in this set of policies: they are so simple, straightforward and obvious that they would leave economic commentators with nothing to say. We can therefore rely on economic commentators to invent more adventurous programmes and so create a climate of opinion in which governments will tend to stray – every now and again – from the narrow path of financial prudence.

But, if occasional wobbles from sound money are an inevitable part of our economic future, that is still much better than our position in the past. In the 1960s and 1970s Britain was the chronic invalid of the industrialized West. The Thatcher administration's most salient economic achievement is to have restored a measure of financial self-respect. Sterling crises, like country lanes and historic inns, used once to be part of the British way of life. They will not be in the next five years if the Conservatives are re-elected on 9 June.

A Perspective on a Decade of Progress

From an article 'Alternatives galore, but none of them better' in The Times, *28 September 1985.*

This was the last article I wrote which was strongly supportive of the Thatcher Government's economic policies. I still thought – wrongly in late 1985 – that the Government was committed to monetary control. My argument was that, despite many problems, the framework of financial control introduced by Healey in 1976 and consolidated under Mrs Thatcher had led to a significant improvement in Britain's economic circumstances. Over most of the period sterling M3 had been the focus of monetary targeting. I urged that it be retained in future.

A craving for intellectual novelty does not improve economic policy. If people are to understand what the Government is doing, the framework of policy should be simple and stable. Frequent shifts from one framework to another weaken confidence that the Government believes in its own rules, undermine official targets and reduce the effectiveness of policy.

So much is obvious. But that has not stopped much hostile comment on the present approach to economic policy, with its emphasis on joint control of the budget deficit and money supply. The critics' most familiar refrain at the moment is that monetarism, sterling M3 and the public sector borrowing requirement have all, in their different ways, become 'meaningless'. Sometimes they claim that full British membership of the European Monetary System (EMS) would be superior to monetary targets; sometimes they say that fiscal policy should stabilize 'public sector net worth' (the difference between the public sector's assets and liabilities); sometimes they have no alternative to suggest. But they are agreed on the desirability of replacing current arrangements with something new. There is a danger that this sort of comment will be accepted uncritically merely because it has captured so many column inches and been repeated so often. It is important to check whether the existing system has performed well or badly.

Contrary to folklore, the system began in late 1976, not May 1979. In July 1976 Denis Healey, then Chancellor of the Exchequer, said that a money supply 'guideline' was to be followed. This was soon firmed up into a target. In December 1976 the Government announced a Letter of Intent to the International Monetary Fund (IMF) which contained conditions for domestic credit expansion and public sector borrowing. There have been targets for the PSBR and money supply growth ever since. A reasonable way of assessing the system is to compare the major economic indicators at about the time it was introduced with the same indicators today. The facts are summarized in Table 4.2. For every variable under consideration the situation is better now than it was a decade ago.

Table 4.2   *Britain's economic performance: a comparison of the mid-1970s and the mid-1980s*

	1975	1976	1984	1985
Inflation – (% increase in prices)	25.3	15.0	4.9	$5^3/_4$
Balance of payments –				
(current account as % of GDP)	−1.6	−0.7	+0.3	$+^3/_4$
Output – (% change in GDP)	−1.2	+2.7	+2.4	$+3^1/_2$
Employment – (change in labour				
force, in '000s)	−90	−212	+380	+250

Note
Inflation is increase in retail price index in year to fourth quarter; balance of payments is current account deficit/surplus as % of GDP at factor cost, current prices; output is change in GDP as factor cost, average estimate, year over year; employment is change in employed labour force (inc. self-employed) from mid-year to mid-year.

Figures for 1975, 1976 and 1984 are actual; figures for 1985 are estimates based on recent experience and consensus forecasts.

Source: Economic Trends

The improvement is clearest on the financial side. Inflation is down to about 5 per cent, only a quarter of the 20 per cent it averaged in 1975 and 1976. The balance-of-payments current account, at present in modest and satisfactory surplus, was then in significant deficit. Indeed, if we extend the period of comparison back to 1974, the current account deficit amounted to almost 5 per cent of gross domestic product, the worst figure in our peacetime history.

Output and employment, the so-called real variables, have also behaved more favourably in the two years, 1984 and 1985 than in the two years, 1975 and 1976. Inflation and external payments figures in the mid-1970s were not the unhappy financial counterpart to a cheerful record of growth and employment. The employment total was falling steadily and at the end of 1976 the unemployment rate was at its highest since the 1930s. Although unemployment today is even worse, the numbers in work are rising. The increasing demand for labour reflects a well-defined and quite strong upturn in economic activity which should cause growth in 1984 and 1985 to be the highest in any two-year period since the Barber boom of 1972 and 1973.

Given the dreadful starting-point in the mid-1970s and the need to tame inflation expectations, the unemployment cost may have been inevitable. If any government had tried to cut unemployment by deliberate demand stimulus in the early 1980s, inflation and the balance of payments today would be worse. Unemployment might nevertheless be just the same because the government would be forced to halt and then undo the stimulus to prevent the financial variables running hopelessly out of control. This may sound like bold and untestable conjecture. It is certainly conjecture, but the experience of several European countries suggests that it is far from bold or untested. France, Italy, Spain and Ireland have all at various times in the last decade indulged in supposedly unemployment-reducing demand reflation. Today their average unemployment rate is above Britain's.

Their reflation had to be reversed for the sake of monetary rectitude, but inflation and the balance of payments remain poor. The evidence seems to be that financial policy is powerless to affect real variables in the long run, but that it can be effective in controlling financial variables. That is the precise thinking, the exact rationale, behind the original shift towards the new set of policy rules in 1976. Since the present system has a satisfactory track record, strong arguments have to be adduced if the Government is to abandon it. The benefits of joining the EMS, targeting public sector net worth or adopting seat-of-the-pants pragmatism are hypothetical and impossible to quantify. The benefits of the existing arrangements are known and substantial.

It would be particularly foolish to reject the PSBR and sterling M3 because the figures have generated problems of interpretation. Sterling M3 cannot be 'meaningless'. It consists of bank deposits, notes and coin, and no one in his right mind can believe that their holdings of these assets do not affect the behaviour of individuals, companies and financial institutions. The relationship between sterling M3 and national income wobbles from year to year and forces policy-makers to exercise discretion in monetary management. But it is about as wrong-headed for economists to claim that bank deposits are meaningless as it is for a meteorologist to dismiss the sun and moon as empty baubles.

The current approach to financial control has not been an unqualified triumph: it has not (yet) created a new Jerusalem of price stability and full employment. But neither has it been an absolute failure. The Government can fairly answer the critics by highlighting the advantages of PSBR and money supply targets. In particular, it can point to the facts and emphasize that the last decade has seen considerable improvement in Britain's economic circumstances.

PART TWO

The Fall of British Monetarism

5. Early warnings

In the middle of 1985 British monetary policy changed radically. The Government stopped its previous practice of adjusting the quantity of official gilt-edged sales to meet its broad money target. Without active use of this policy instrument (known as 'funding'), broad money growth accelerated sharply. In the Mansion House speech of 17 October 1985 Mr. Lawson announced the 'suspension' of the broad money target. In fact, the speech signalled the end of broad money targeting. Although a broad money target was included in the 1986 Budget, it was not taken seriously and was also 'suspended' when it became inconvenient.

I was dismayed by this turn of events. Even worse was to follow. In all official statements over the next few years the Government insisted that it still paid attention to the behaviour of credit and broad money in its assessment of monetary conditions. In fact, it neglected credit and broad money totally. The growth rate of sterling M3 increased from about 10 per cent in late 1984 and early 1985 to the high teens in late 1985 and 1986, and then on to over 20 per cent in 1987 and early 1988. Predictably, the economy started to grow quickly in late 1986. By mid-1987 it was booming. Mr. Lawson, commonly described as 'the architect of monetarism', seemed intent on repeating in the mid- and late 1980s the same mistakes made by Barber in the early 1970s. The Lawson boom continued unchecked until mid-1988. In its sheer bravado and dash, Mr. Lawson's performance was remarkable. In effect, he defied everything that the Thatcher Government had represented in economic policy when it had been elected in 1979.

All through these years I expected an announcement that the Government was re-considering its approach and would restore broad money targets. But nothing of the sort happened. I wrote a sequence of articles in *The Times*, roughly from October 1985 to October 1988, urging a return to the original principles on which the Thatcher Government's anti-inflation successes had been based. As remarked in the Introduction, these articles in *The Times* echoed, very self-consciously, the articles Peter Jay had written between 1972 and 1974 about the Barber boom.

The warnings contained in the first three articles republished here were carefully measured. The economy in late 1985 and early 1986 still had high unemployment and a substantial margin of slack. As a result, rapid monetary growth would impact on output and employment first, and might have little effect on inflation. My worry was what would happen if rapid monetary growth persisted 'for a year or more' (see the article of 17 October 1985). It also seemed to me that 'a mini-boom based on fast credit and money growth' (see the article of 9 January 1986) was a betrayal of the Thatcher Government's commitment to price stability and a sound currency.

It is quite untrue that, in the early stage of the game, I gave an unequivocal forecast of an imminent return to inflation over 10 per cent. I want to emphasize this. In 1987, and even in 1988, some mainstream economists decried my warnings on the grounds that I had been too alarmist about inflation in 1985. It is very clear from the articles that my warnings were long term in nature. To repeat the lessons of Friedman's classic empirical work, the first effects of an acceleration in monetary growth are on output. The damage to inflation comes through after 'long and variable lags' which, in the British case, can be as much as three or four years.

The decision to abandon broad money targets was defended by most leading economists, including Professor Sir James Ball, who had made the London Business School so well known for macroeconomic forecasting in the 1970s and encouraged such important figures as Sir Terence Burns and Professor Alan Budd. (Burns was the Government's Chief Economic Adviser from 1979 to 1990; Budd is currently Chief Economic Adviser.) In the 1988 Deloitte Haskins and Sells lecture at the Cardiff Business School, Ball said that the instability of the relationship between broad money and nominal national product in the early 1980s had made broad money targets 'look pretty silly'. Seven years after the abandonment of those targets one has to wonder whether the severe macroeconomic instability of the late 1980s, with the wild boom of 1987 and 1988 followed by a rise in inflation to over 10 per cent and the most severe recession since the 1930s, has not made a number of British economists also 'look pretty silly'.

Is Lawson Heading for Another Barber Bubble?

From an article of the same name in The Times *of 17 October 1985.*

The article is self-explanatory. I believe that it was the first time the phrase 'the Lawson boom' was used.

Memories of the Barber boom haunt the Conservative Party. It began merrily enough, with rapid growth in bank credit and the money supply encouraging a speculative surge in property values, a vigorous boom in output and much superficial prosperity. It ended in misery, with inflation reaching the highest levels in our peacetime history and the Heath Government suffering a humiliating electoral defeat.

When the Chancellor of the Exchequer, Mr Nigel Lawson forecast 4 per cent inflation by mid-1986 in his speech to the Conservative Party conference last week, he and his audience took it for granted that the Barber boom could never happen again. If the Thatcher Government stands for anything, it stands for the prevention of the follies of the early 1970s. The conference delegates had no doubts that Lawson believes in monetary control and that he will act on his beliefs. Tonight Lawson faces a more sceptical audience at the Mansion House dinner. The assembled bankers and financial experts will know that in the last six months the rate of money supply growth has been similar to that in the first six months of the Barber boom. They will also expect the Chancellor to indicate, at least in general terms, what he is going to do about it.

The offending aggregate is the broad measure of money known as sterling M3. Since the Budget in March it has been advancing at an annual rate of 18¹/₂ per cent, far ahead of the official target range of 5 to 9 per cent (see Table 5.1). There has been only one other six-month period since the Barber boom that has seen a faster increase; the Healey boomlet in late 1977 and early 1978. As with Barber the early stages were enjoyable, with output moving ahead nicely, unemployment falling and inflation not reacting too badly. But the later stages were again very unhappy. A 20 per cent annualized rate of increase in sterling M3 in the six months to April 1978 was followed by a 20 per cent inflation rate in early 1980. There were other influences at work – such as the increase in value added tax in the 1979 Budget – to

Table 5.1   The acceleration in money supply growth in 1985

	Increase in sterling M3 in month (%)	Annualized increase in previous six months (%)
February	0.3	11.6
March	0.9	10.8
April	2.9	16.4
May	0.5	12.4
June	2.3	16.9
July	–0.8	12.8
August	2.0	16.6
September	1.75	18.5

Source: Bank of England

explain the jump in inflation, but the coincidence still needs to be mentioned.

Given the record and the facts, the 18$\frac{1}{2}$ per cent annualized growth rate in sterling M3 in recent months is certain to arouse critical comment. In one respect, moreover, the figures are slightly worse today than under Healey. Over the last few years inflation has been lower than in the late 1970s. In consequence, a high rate of increase in sterling M3 generates a faster rate of increase in the real money supply – the actual money supply adjusted for inflation. At the peak of the 1977/78 monetary acceleration the real money supply was about 7$\frac{1}{2}$ per cent up on a year earlier; today the figure is 8 per cent.

Despite all the unfavourable arithmetic, it would be unfair and wrong to start talking about the 'Lawson boom'. The Chancellor is genuinely concerned about money supply numbers. He also has a far stronger grasp than his predecessors of the theoretical justification for monetary control and the institutional technicalities involved. It is precisely because of the seriousness of his commitment and the depth of his understanding that the City regards tonight's speech as one of the most important he has had to make since becoming Chancellor. He has to reassure financial markets that the recent overshoot on money supply targets of the recent past will not have the same dire effects as earlier misdemeanours. He also has to outline the Government's attitude towards sterling M3 and the future mechanics of monetary management.

There is a chance that the latest burst of high money growth will not be damaging in the long run. The economy has a reasonable margin of spare machine capacity and, with unemployment so high, there are no shortages of labour. If all goes well the latest phase of above-target money growth may lead solely to more output and not at all to higher prices. Further, it can be argued that the relationship between sterling M3 and the economy is changing. (Lawson will probably endorse this argument tonight.) Because of the competitive and deregulated financial system Britain is now fortunate to possess, the banking system may be expanding faster than the economy as a whole. Its deposit liabilities may increase permanently as a proportion of national income. If so, there need be no inflationary risk if these liabilities, which account for most of sterling M3, grow quickly for a short period.

However, they cannot be allowed to grow at the recent very rapid rates for a year or more. Despite the many difficulties in interpretation, sterling M3 must not be cast aside because its monetary message has become inconvenient. Lawson's task tonight is the old, familiar and necessary one of maintaining financial confidence. He knows very well that the City will be more difficult to convince than the Conservative Party conference.

Why the European Monetary System is no Easy Option

From an article of the same name in The Times *of 22 November 1985.*

In late 1985, at a session of the Cabinet's economic committee, Lawson and Sir Geoffrey Howe pressed Mrs Thatcher to agree to an important change in economic policy. They wanted the pound to join the exchange rate mechanism (ERM) of the European Monetary System. Mrs Thatcher said no. Although the proceedings of the Cabinet committee did not become known until some years later, there was a widespread understanding at the time that the EMS option was under careful consideration. The trouble was that a fixed exchange rate (of the kind implied by EMS membership) might at times conflict with the requirements of domestic monetary policy, as expressed in money supply targets. (See the article 'Money supply targets vs fixed exchange rates', on pp. 18–21, from The Times *of 19 January 1976, for a simple statement of the point.) It seemed to me that the debate about the EMS symptomized 'an apparently predestined cycle of economic management and mismanagement'.*

A few weeks ago there was a chance that Britain would become a full member of the European Monetary System in the same manner as it had acquired an empire, out of sheer absent-mindedness. Full membership would have involved sterling's participation in the semi-fixed exchange rate system known as the 'exchange rate mechanism'. A powerful and vocal lobby in favour was forming. The Government could easily have agreed that the EMS was a 'good idea' and that 'something should be done'.

The process was obstructed by a sceptical verdict on the EMS in the Treasury and Civil Service Committee's latest report. But the debate is not over yet. The Confederation of British Industry and influential groups of economists, notably the London Business School, have recently declared their support for membership. Their enthusiasm can be seen as a response to disillusionment with the Medium-Term Financial Strategy. The MTFS has, in fact, been gradually de-emphasized for some time. It is far from clear that this was intended or desired by Nigel Lawson and the Treasury. Nevertheless, the result of a sequence of policy announcements, each quite minor, is that no one takes the MTFS at face value any longer.

The first stage in the process was the proposal of a target for M0, a narrow money measure, in the 1983 Mansion House speech. The City regarded the new aggregate as an upstart and maintained its allegiance to sterling M3. In the 1985 Mansion House speech Lawson completed the usurpation, saying the sterling M3 target would be suspended until the next Budget. While monetary targets have been side-stepped, the fiscal arithmetic has been conducted more casually. The 1985 Budget speech suggested that the precise mix of monetary and fiscal targets should no longer be regarded as 'sacrosanct'. This was directly contrary to the analytical basis of the MTFS, in which gradual reductions in the public sector borrowing requirement were seen as an essential support to the targeted deceleration in money supply growth.

The most recent blow to the MTFS was the admission in the Autumn Statement last week that the Government's targets for spending, taxation and borrowing in both 1985/86 and 1986/87 would not be achieved. If a medium-term financial strategy is not to impose some sort of discipline on finances in the medium term, it is difficult to see what purpose it serves.

It is against this background of doubt about the MTFS that the case for joining the EMS has become persuasive. Two years ago the Government's sound-money supporters were, almost to a man, absolutely loyal to money supply and PSBR targets, and regarded EMS membership as a third or fourth-best option. Today many of them think that the MTFS has been so thoroughly compromised that an exchange rate target would be preferable. Their change of attitude should not be interpreted as a softening on inflation control. It cannot be emphasized too strongly that, by establishing a tie between the pound and the Deutschmark, Britain would be obliged to bring its inflation rate into line with West Germany's.

That would prove hard work after the slippage on financial control of recent years. It is ironic that 'wet' critics of the Government should advocate EMS entry as an alternative to the rigours of the MTFS. They do not seem to understand that a Deutschmark-dominated exchange rate system could prove much more financially rigorous than a Treasury-determined monetary strategy. In any British Cabinet, spending ministers heavily outnumber Treasury ministers. The consequence is that spending and borrowing have a persistent tendency to run ahead of target. The corrective is a financial crisis which for a period (not usually very long and never before a general election) forces the Prime Minister to give the Chancellor of the Exchequer wholehearted support. The Chancellor is then all-powerful. He can cut spending, reduce borrowing and restore the nation's finances to order.

For a generation and more Britain had an exchange rate target. The benign and necessary financial crisis took the form of a run on sterling which threatened the rate against the dollar ($2.80 until 1967; $2.40 afterwards). This check was removed by the decision to float the pound in 1972. Four years of economic anarchy followed, including the highest inflation rate and balance-of-payments deficit in our peacetime history. A new system of control, organized around money supply and PSBR targets, began in 1976 under IMF guidance. It reached its apogee in the early years of the MTFS in 1982 and 1983, when it succeeded in curbing inflation to 5 per cent. But Lawson, perhaps unintentionally, has let it fall into disrepair. Britain looks as if it might once again adopt an exchange rate target, now focused on Europe rather than the US.

None of this is to be understood as a recommendation for EMS membership. It is only a description of an apparently predestined cycle of economic management and mismanagement. If Britain were governed by logic rather than by whim, there could hardly be a sillier time to join the EMS than now, when oil prices are liable to fall sharply any day and hit sterling hard on the foreign exchanges.

A Forecast of a Lawson 'Mini-Boom'

From an article 'Why Lawson must repent' in The Times *of 9 January 1986.*

Like its predecessor, 'Is Lawson heading for another Barber bubble?' of 17 October 1985, this article is self-explanatory.

As Treasury ministers and officials meet at Chevening this weekend to discuss Budget strategy, their main problem is less economic than moral. They must decide whether, having sinned, they should enjoy it or repent.

There can be no doubt that, according to the strict canon of the monetarist creed to which they were once so committed, they have sinned. In the year to December sterling M3 rose by 15 per cent, far ahead of the top end of the Government's original target of 5 to 9 per cent growth. In his Mansion House speech last October Nigel Lawson reacted to the overshoot by suspending the sterling M3 target band, claiming that this measure of the money stock gave a misleading guide to monetary conditions.

Every day more evidence becomes available that the rapid growth of sterling M3 is not misleading, but is having standard and predictable effects on economic behaviour. Most obviously, cash-rich companies are using their spare bank deposits, which are included in and bloat sterling M3, to expand by acquisition rather than organically. If sterling M3 were under proper control, they would not have such a high level of bank deposits and could not so easily embark on expensive takeover struggles. Meanwhile, if surplus cash in the corporate sector is financing takeovers and so driving up share prices, surplus cash in the personal sector is starting to affect house prices. When people have more money in the bank than they need, they transfer it to building societies, which lend it out for mortgages. A substantial increase in mortgage lending tends to raise property prices. In 1985 house prices went up by about 10 per cent, much above the general inflation rate. Most of the increase was in the second half of the year as a strong upturn in the volume of mortgage lending gathered pace. The process has further to go: at the end of November the building societies' outstanding commitments to lend stood at £6.2 billion, an all-time record and 30 per cent higher than a year earlier.

As with so many government misdemeanours, the initial results of excess monetary growth are pleasurable. High takeover activity and buoyant house prices are classic symptoms of an economy in the early stages of a cyclical upswing and contradict the large number of forecasts that the economy will expand more slowly in 1986 than in 1985. Already the employment situation is improving in sympathy with a better outlook for demand and output. Unemployment fell in each of the three months to November, despite continuing growth in the number of people of working age, while the latest survey by the Institute of Directors indicates that more companies are considering new recruitment in the first half of 1986 than for many years. Lawson and his colleagues must welcome the short-term employment gains from their monetary trespasses more than they fear the long-term inflation dangers. After all, if higher inflation comes after the next general election, it is politically harmless.

The remoteness of the inflation risk is perhaps the major argument for enjoying the monetary overshoot fully and shamelessly. Indeed, a case could be made that these inflation risks – even after the usual 18-month to three-year lag – should not be all that great. At present the economy can plausibly be said to have 'too much money chasing too few assets'. But it is nonsense, while unemployment remains above three million, industry has abundant spare capacity and there is scope to increase output, to say that 'too much money is chasing too few goods'.

There is a chance that the monetary excesses of 1985 and early 1986 will, in the end, impact only on output and employment, and not at all on price levels. If that turns out to be right, they could be regarded as wholly benign, giving a phase of unsustainable demand stimulus similar to that urged on the Chancellor by his Keynesian critics years ago. Ironically, the stimulus would have been in the monetary form he once deplored instead of the fiscal variety they advocated.

But is a mini-boom based on fast credit and money growth what Lawson said he would achieve? Was not his principal policy objective in his first Mansion House speech in 1983 the attainment of price stability? Have not both he and Mrs Thatcher subsequently and frequently said that further reductions in inflation remain their foremost economic goal? If Lawson wants to restore credibility to his old statements, he must not boast about the mini-boom, but apologize and repent. He has to bring back the Medium-Term Financial Strategy in all its former glory. In policy terms, that would have two main implications.

First, he has to reintroduce a target for broad money. Sterling M3 has several drawbacks, but so do the alternatives, and it has the important virtue that the financial markets are familiar with it. In fact, in the Mansion House speech Lawson did say that a target for broad money would be announced in the Budget. It is realistic to expect some sign of penitence in this area. Yesterday's 1 per cent increase in base rates could be regarded as an earnest of good intent. Secondly, he has to re-emphasize that fiscal policy will support monetary restraint. In the 1985 Budget he flirted with the idea of changing the mix between fiscal and monetary policies. Some observers have interpreted this, understandably enough, as a shift towards 'Reaganomics', with an increased budget deficit supposed to be boosting demand and high interest rates protecting the exchange rate.

It is far from clear that any such shift was either intended or achieved. But the ambiguity of Lawson's statements has led to much confusion in market thinking, with no one really sure whether he is more concerned about the exchange rate or domestic monetary trends in interest rate decisions. Even worse, there has been an erosion of confidence as the apparently more pragmatic view on public sector borrowing has been accompanied by asset sales and falling oil prices. Critics have remarked that, without the receipts from asset sales, the public sector borrowing requirement in 1986/87 would be £4³/₄ billion higher than the £7 billion envisaged in the Government's economic forecast. Some asset sales were always part of official plans, but not on the present scale, and to return to the spirit of the original medium-term strategy it would be necessary to reduce the PSBR to about £5 billion.

No one outside the Whitehall machine expects that, as it would limit the scope for tax cuts too severely. But some brave soul at Chevening – perhaps John MacGregor, the new Chief Secretary – might suggest that a gesture towards fiscal probity would be appropriate, with the PSBR down to, say, £6 billion. The viability of the lower figure in practice would depend as much on the Organization of Petroleum Exporting Countries' (OPEC) ability to hold the current level of oil prices as on anything the British Government can do.

But at present the Treasury's worst impieties are monetary, not fiscal. A firm, clear-cut decision to reinstate a broad money target and to stick to it would be more fundamental than the most inspired guess about how much room a fall in oil prices will leave for tax cuts.

Broad Money vs Narrow Money

From an article 'Time to take a broader view of money' in The Financial Times
of 16 April 1986.

*An important influence on economic policy-making during the Lawson boom
was the Group of Outside Economic Advisers (GOEA). It met over dinner at
No. 11 Downing Street every few months, with the Chancellor of the Exchequer in attendance. The central debate within the GOEA was between advocates
of British membership of the ERM (led by Mr Samuel Brittan) and supporters of narrow money targets (led by Professor Patrick Minford). No one in
the GOEA favoured broad money targets or regarded the rapid growth of
broad money as likely to cause rising inflation. The meetings of the GOEA
were confidential, but it has become known who was saying what and why.
(In view of its inglorious record and despite its considerable contemporary
influence, the GOEA may not be mentioned in the history books. It should
be. It demonstrates only too clearly that important policy debates should be
conducted by means of written statements open to public scrutiny, preferably
under parliamentary auspices. No wonder policy blunders were made during
the Lawson boom if the Chancellor formed his views on the basis of casual,
off-the-record remarks delivered over port and brandy.)*

*In early 1986 I had no idea that the GOEA was in existence, but I was
well aware that the Government was listening to Minford and paying attention to his views on narrow money. I therefore wrote an article on the
relative virtues of broad and narrow money ahead of a speech by Lawson to
the Lombard Association in the City of London.*

The Battle of the Aggregates has been one of the most hard-fought intellectual
struggles in the Government's long anti-inflationary campaign. Its objective
has been to determine which measure of money is most suitable as a target
for monetary policy. In his speech to the Lombard Association tonight Mr
Nigel Lawson, the Chancellor, will give an official verdict on the latest
tussles between the two sides.

The supporters of broad aggregates have normally favoured sterling M3,
which includes all bank deposits as well as notes and coin. For much of the
period since 1976 (when monetary targets were first introduced) sterling M3
was in virtually total command of the battlefield. However, its hegemony
was undermined in 1981 and 1982 when several commentators urged that
narrow money, as measured by either M1 or M0, had a more reliable relationship with national income. (M1 includes sight deposits and notes and
coin; M0 only notes and coin.)

Their views were reflected in official statements, particularly after Mr Lawson became Chancellor, and the Government began to stress that M0 and sterling M3 played an equal role in determining interest rates. It appeared that sterling M3 was in headlong retreat and would soon be judged unfit for combat. However, the M0 camp has also recently suffered an embarrassing reverse. At the end of last year some of its adherents tried to use M0 for forecasting purposes. Most notably, Professor Patrick Minford of Liverpool University claimed in a Centre for Policy Studies publication in December that, as M0 had grown at a 'miserable' $1\frac{1}{2}$ per cent over the previous six months, 'we now have the tightest monetary policy we have ever had'. He warned that 'a stalling in the growth rate' was 'increasingly likely' unless immediate action was taken to reduce interest rates.

In fact, interest rates were raised slightly in the first quarter of 1986, but there is almost no sign of the slowdown Professor Minford predicted. The most telling counter-evidence is the buoyancy of the housing market and the resilience, at high levels, of retail sales and car registrations. Indeed, in January new orders for private residential construction – widely recognized to be a good lead indicator for the economy as a whole – were stronger than for three years.

But it would be unfair, in a criticism of M0, to concentrate on one particular forecasting error. The failure of prognosis here is the result of a more general drawback of all narrow money aggregates. Narrow money – in either its M0 or M1 versions – does not determine important economic variables, such as prices and output, but is determined by them; it follows rather than leads the economy. The reason for this subordinate role is easy to explain. Consider the behaviour of an average individual with a bank or building society deposit. Every week or fortnight he draws some cash from his deposit to suit the flow of his minor transactions. The amount of cash he has adjusts to the value of his transactions, not the other way around.

More generally, M0 – which, to repeat, consists only of cash – is determined by what is happening in the economy now; it does not determine what will happen to the economy in future. To use M0 as a predictive tool indicates a rather serious misunderstanding of how money interacts with the economy. For this to be valid, ICI would have to base its investment plans on fluctuations in its petty cash tills and Prudential Assurance would have to alter asset allocations in accordance with the value of the notes held by its staff canteen and sports club.

The recent behaviour of sterling M3, unlike that of M0, has given many useful clues to the economy. When the Government abandoned overfunding last summer, the growth rate of broad money accelerated. As is usually the case in the early stages of any monetary upswing, most of the extra bank deposits were held by companies and financial institutions, not by the personal sector. In fact, companies and financial institutions had more bank deposits than they needed and have been trying hard to get rid of their excess liquidity. In particular, they have been buying financial assets with great enthusiasm. The takeover boom, and the 20 per cent surge in share prices in the first quarter, can be interpreted as the direct consequence of the recent misbehaviour of sterling M3.

In the Budget speech Mr Lawson sanctioned a target range for sterling M3 of 11 to 15 per cent in the 1986/87 financial year, after a 12-month period in which it had increased by $16^1/_2$ per cent. It may take another year to 18 months before such fast monetary growth is reflected in higher inflation in terms of goods and services, but it has already been reflected in higher inflation in terms of asset prices. If he is to show himself a prudent monetary general, Mr Lawson should concede some ground to sterling M3 in his speech tonight. If he instead tries to end the Battle of the Aggregates once and for all by relegating sterling M3 from target status, he will find that its supporters in the City can put up a staunch defence.

6. A typical Tory boom

The Lawson boom was very similar to previous Tory booms in the post-war period. For adventitious reasons, notably the weakness of the dollar, there was no perceived external constraint on monetary policy in 1986 and 1987. With the external constraint in abeyance, the leaders of the Conservative Party did not want to be reminded that expansionary domestic monetary policy would inevitably lead to inflation. As on numerous other occasions since 1951, they were hallucinated by the many signs of prosperity into thinking that they had accomplished an 'economic miracle'. These signs, which were very familiar to anyone who could remember the Barber boom, included get-rich-quick property speculators and young men driving expensive cars on the profits from rising house prices. As in the Barber episode, the Government ignored the domestic symptoms of monetary excess. It changed policy far too late, in mid-1988, and then only because the external constraint had returned. An abrupt and unforecast deterioration in the balance of payments aroused fears that the pound would soon weaken sharply on the foreign exchanges. As in other stop–go cycles in the post-war period, the Lawson boom was brought to an end because of foreign disapproval of the conduct of British macroeconomic policy.

The performance was made all the more pathetic by the contrast with the stated intentions of the Thatcher Government in 1979, when the emphasis had been very much on defeating inflation and preventing stop–go cycles. Although Lawson prided himself on his early advocacy of the Medium-Term Financial Strategy, he had evidently not understood its most essential characteristic – that financial targets were to be stated in terms of domestic variables, not the exchange rate, so that the Conservative Party could never again indulge in silly booms like 'Butler's in 1956, Heathcoat-Amory's in 1960, Maudling's in 1964 and Barber's in 1974'. (The key 'domestic variable' was, of course, the money supply on the broad definition.) As my article 'The return of stop–go?' in *The Times* of 20 October 1987 said, it was not going too far to describe the Thatcher Government's record in the central area of economic policy as 'bewildering to the point of perversity'.

In the late 1970s I had proposed a medium-term financial plan, in the hope that financial targets laid down several years in advance would constrain electoral opportunism and prevent a recurrence of the stop–go cycle. By mid-1987 it was evident that the Medium-Term Financial Strategy was not working in this way. In an article in *The Spectator* of 27 June 1987 I noted that: 'The main message of the latest phase of financial excess, so depressingly similar to many other episodes in the post-war period, is simple: monetary policy is too serious to be left to politicians'. I therefore concluded that monetary policy should be entrusted to an independent Bank of England.

Macroeconomic policy in the late 1980s was full of rich and wonderful ironies. But perhaps the most opulent and fantastic came in a House of Commons speech by Mr Lawson in late 1989, the first after his resignation from the Cabinet. For over six years he had been an opinionated and domineering Chancellor of the Exchequer, consistently disdaining the views of the Bank of England. But from the backbenches he declared himself to be strongly in favour of granting the Bank of England greater independence from government!

Will the House-Buying Boom Save Thatcher?

Reprinted from an article of the same name in The Times *of 17 June 1986.*

As is well known, the mortgage boom of 1986 and 1987 helped Mrs Thatcher's Conservative Party to its third successive general election victory. But it was also inconsistent with the Thatcher Government's commitment to gradual reductions in monetary growth to restore a sound currency. This piece should be read in conjunction with the paper on equity withdrawal on pp. 274–87 and the more alarmist article, 'Even the housing boom can turn to bust', in The Spectator *of 14 May 1988.*

The Conservatives are asking themselves how they can secure re-election. Unless the economy recovers more vigorously, unemployment will remain at over three million and the Government will appear to have failed on the most important social issue of the day. But its self-imposed rules of financial management, with limits on public sector borrowing and money supply growth, prevent an active programme of economic stimulus.

How does it escape? Is there any mechanism still available for strengthening demand and improving business conditions in time to swing enough votes in its direction? For an answer we should look at certain financial antecedents to the last general election. Between 1980 and 1983 lending for house purchase virtually doubled from £7.3 billion to £14.4 billion. The pace of the housing finance boom was fastest in late 1982, as banks joined in on a large scale.

As always, an upturn in housing activity was followed by more spending on consumer durables and then by a general revival in retail demand. In 1983 consumer expenditure rose by 3.9 per cent, sufficient to generate a satisfactory growth rate for the economy as a whole and to check the increase in unemployment. It was not an exciting economic background, but it was enough for the Conservatives to win.

Almost unnoticed in most political commentary, a similar process is at work today. In the first quarter of 1986 net mortgage advances by the building societies, at £3,814 million, were up 26.8 per cent on the same period of 1985. Figures published on Friday show that in April and May combined they were £3,157 million, an increase of 28.9 per cent on the same period of 1985. The surge will undoubtedly gather momentum in the rest of 1986 and in 1987. In April the building societies committed themselves to lend £3,664 million – 64.3 per cent more than in April 1985 – and in May £3,761 million (up 57.1 per cent). This big injection of credit will enliven the housing market in the summer and autumn.

Moreover, the building societies are not the only organizations enjoying the mortgage party. They have been joined not only by the clearing banks and insurance companies, but also by a number of foreign-owned institutions who have no previous experience of lending to the British personal sector. Together they could lend £24 billion for house purchase in 1986, £6 billion more than in 1985. The immediate effect will be a faster increase in house prices (now about 11 per cent). Home-owners will feel better off and, as in 1983, improved consumer confidence will boost spending in the shops, initially on carpets, furniture and other items connected with moving to a new house, but eventually on all consumer goods.

Overall this should result in an appreciably higher growth rate in 1987 than in 1986. If, and at present it seems quite a big if, the world economy moves forward more briskly as well, 1987 could see the fastest rate of economic expansion since the early 1970s. In these circumstances unemployment could well fall by anything up to 300,000. In relation to a total of over three million out of work, that would not represent great progress. But in relation to the media stereotype of where Conservative economic policies are leading, it would seem little short of miraculous. The change in perceptions and expectations would significantly strengthen the Tories' election chances.

It may seem exaggerated to place so much emphasis on housing finance as the key area determining Britain's economic prospects and its political future. But today 63 per cent of adults are owner-occupiers. Not only are they the highest paid 63 per cent of the population (accounting for possibly 85 per cent of all income received), but also their house is for the majority of them the most valuable single asset they own. Indeed, Britain has almost passed the stage of property-owning democracy to become a property-trading democracy. As Mark Boleat noted in his *National Housing Finance Systems: A Comparative Study* in 1980, 'over 50 per cent of households with a head of household aged between 25 and 29 were owner-occupiers, double the proportion of other developed countries.' In consequence, most people buy and sell houses several times during their lives.

Left-wing parties will find it increasingly difficult to sustain the political appeal of rhetoric about wealth redistribution in a society where most people already have some wealth. Denis Healey has quipped that the Conservative Party has been hijacked from the landowners and given to the estate agents. Possibly, but does this not reveal Labour's secret anxiety?

Economists could protest that the housing credit boom is irresponsible. It is an associate – perhaps, one should say, an accomplice – of the excessive growth of sterling M3 in the past year. Nigel Lawson has played down the significance of the above-target money supply expansion by muttering about distortions, institutional changes and the like, but there can be no doubt that the recent behaviour of mortgage credit is contrary to both the spirit of the Government's Medium-Term Financial Strategy and to the letter of its original monetary targets. What now do we hear about price stability as even an 'ultimate' objective? How could the Chancellor plausibly commit himself to that while living in a city where residential property values have soared by 60 per cent in the last two years, and in a country where credit to stoke up similar house price increases has never been more readily available?

The excesses will be forgiven – at least within the Conservative Party – if the mortgage boom proves a successful ingredient in the election campaign. Moreover, it could be argued that the Government is merely responding to those ancient and familiar demands for reflation. But, instead of the reflation being achieved by extra public sector borrowing to finance improvements to the infrastructure, it is being conducted through extra private sector borrowing to finance additions and improvements to the housing stock. Indeed, it may not be too facetious to invent a new concept called the private mortgage borrowing requirement (or PMBR) as a complement to the PSBR. The £6 billion increase in the PMBR in 1986 must have official blessing and could, without caricature, be regarded as old-fashioned pump-priming. Is the British economy entering a new era of Thatcherite Keynesianism?

Why Lawson should have Re-Introduced a Broad Money Target in Late 1986

From an article 'Why Lawson must stick to his target' in The Times *of 31 October 1986.*

A year after the 'suspension' and effective abandonment of broad money targets in the 1985 Mansion House speech, I wrote another article in The Times *about the need to curb monetary growth. It was important to comment on a speech from Mr Leigh-Pemberton, the Governor of the Bank of England, which had argued that financial liberalization had invalidated broad money targeting. In this article I suggested, on the basis of 'a very modest grasp of elementary arithmetic', that 'the message must be that inflation will accelerate in the next few years, perhaps to as much as 10 per cent'. This was right in the end, as inflation went above 10 per cent in 1990. But see the article below, on pp. 143–50, 'The Lawson boom in the light of the Crash', for more discussion of the inflation rate.*

Monetary statistics were first prepared in their present form in 1963. Since then broad money, on the familiar sterling M3 definition (which includes notes and coin, and all sterling bank deposits), has risen by about 12 times, and money national income by about $12^1/_2$ times.

Targets for the growth of broad money were introduced in July 1976 to restrain inflation. The inflation rate then, as measured by the annual increase in the retail price index, was 13.3 per cent, and rising. Today it is 3 per cent. In more general terms, monetary targets have been instrumental in reducing the trend inflation rate from 15 per cent in the mid-1970s to 5 per cent at present.

The crude facts of the link between broad money and national income, and the apparent success of the system of monetary control established a decade ago, suggest that official targets for broad money should be retained. As the Americans say: 'If it ain't broke, don't fix it'. But the Government has a different view. Broad money targets are now practically defunct and will soon, perhaps in the Chancellor's Autumn Statement, be formally abandoned. The thinking behind this change was explained in a speech by Robin Leigh-Pemberton, Governor of the Bank of England, at Loughborough University last week. His central argument was that technical change in the financial system has disturbed the relationship between broad money and national income so radically in the 1980s that it is 'fair to ask whether a broad money target continues to serve a useful purpose'. Perhaps, to quote his words, 'we would do better to dispense with monetary targetry altogether'.

This argument has considerable force. There is no doubt, for example, that the more attractive interest rates now available on bank deposits should encourage people to hold a higher share of their wealth in this form. But there are at least two reasons for scepticism, perhaps even cynicism, about the Government's decision.

The first is that technological advance in banking and other financial services has been continuous since the early 1960s. Some of the innovations have reduced the amount of money people need to keep (as a proportion of income) in their banks, while others have increased it. But over the whole period their effects have broadly cancelled out. Although the rate of change may have accelerated in recent years, and there does appear to have been some rise in the desired ratio of money to national income, the 1980s are not obviously special or unusual. An unhappy memory is that the Bank of England made excuses for very high growth rates of broad money in the early 1970s by attributing them to technical and institutional developments it could not easily interpret. But confusion about the meaning of the statistics should not have been a pretext for nihilism about the right way to conduct policy. In 1975 the inflation rate exceeded 25 per cent, the highest in Britain's peacetime history. Technical and institutional developments today should not be used to justify any rate, no matter how rapid, of broad money growth. It is one thing to say that the liberalization of mortgage finance, the internationalization of company finance, the Big Bang and various other upheavals have altered the relationship between money, income and expenditure. It is something quite different to claim that, in the new circumstances, there is no such thing as an excessive rate of broad money growth which will cause inflation.

The second worry is related to the first. If broad money was being demoted at a time when the Bank of England was meeting its targets with reasonable precision, there would not be much suspicion in the City about the Government's motives. But, in fact, broad money growth is not only far ahead of the official target range, but also – at almost 20 per cent in the last year – higher than at any time since the Barber boom. There may be grounds for expecting broad money to increase by 3 or 4 per cent a year more than national income for quite a long period. That would, indeed, explain why the 11 or 12 per cent increases in broad money recorded between 1981 and 1985 were typically accompanied by real growth of 3 per cent and inflation of 5 per cent. But how can 20 per cent rises in sterling M3 be reconciled with the Government's objectives?

A very modest grasp of elementary arithmetic is sufficient to suggest that, if the pattern of the early 1980s persists, 20 per cent increases in broad money imply that money gross national product will eventually rise by about 15 per cent. Since it is fantasy to imagine that real growth can be much above 5 per cent, the message must be that inflation will accelerate in the next few years, perhaps to as much as 10 per cent.

In short, the fact of financial change does not in itself rule out the possibility of excessive monetary growth, while the latest numbers suggest disturbingly that monetary growth has indeed become excessive. It may be convenient for Nigel Lawson that he can discard a major barrier to stimulatory policies so close to a general election. But, after the experience of the Barber boom and its sequel, no one should be surprised if seemingly good political tactics in the short run prove to be electorally unrewarding and bad economic strategy in the medium term.

The Credit Boom and the Case for a More Independent Bank of England

From an article 'Mr Lawson's secret inflation' in The Spectator *of 27 June 1987.*

Credit growth, by both banks and building societies, was higher in real terms in 1986 and 1987 than in the notorious Barber boom years of 1972 and 1973. The argument of this article was therefore that politicians could not be trusted to control inflation. The job had to be given to an independent Bank of England.

Much has gone wrong with the management of the British economy in the last two years. The growth of credit amd money is too high, the economy is expanding too quickly and interest rates are too low to prevent the return of inflationary pressures. Indeed, the scale of the present credit boom is without precedent. In terms of the amount of money being lent by both banks and building societies, it is larger than the notorious Heath/Barber boom of the early 1970s. The main message of the latest phase of financial excess, so depressingly similar to many other episodes in the post-war period, is simple: monetary policy is too serious to be left to politicians. Britain should follow West Germany's example by giving the Bank of England as much independence from government as is currently enjoyed by the Bundesbank.

That, in brief, is the argument of this article. It is an expression of deep scepticism about the ability and willingness of British governments to conduct financial policy in a consistent, stable and non-inflationary way. Their monetary performance over the last 40 years has been too unreliable for them to be trusted in future. Alternative arrangements, which as far as possible take macroeconomic policy outside the political domain, are needed.

True enough, three or four years ago such scepticism seemed unjustified. Mrs Thatcher's first term had succeeded in bringing inflation down from over 20 per cent in early 1980 to under 5 per cent by mid-1983, while confidence in the permanence of responsible financial policies was buttressed by targets for monetary growth and public sector borrowing in the Medium-Term Financial Strategy. There appeared to be a consensus that monetary policy had been anti-inflationary and would remain so, at least as long as the Conservatives stayed in power. The breakdown of that consensus has a complicated story, in which many of the details are technical. But the main points are not particularly abstruse. They should not be allowed to frighten away readers who have a hunch that the subject is important and deserves to be understood, but are sometimes deterred by commentators who make it seem more confusing than it actually is.

One of the most important debates in British monetary policy in recent years has related to the significance of narrow money as compared to broad money. Narrow money consists of notes and coin held by people and companies, plus (on some definitions) bank deposits which can be drawn on without notice; broad money consists of notes and coin, and all bank deposits. Holdings of bank deposits are many times larger than holdings of notes and coin. When the first monetary targets were announced by Mr Healey in 1976 and again after 1980 in the early versions of the Medium-Term Financial Strategy, monetary policy was stated in terms of broad money. Indeed, for a few years the phrase, 'the money supply', was virtually synonymous with broad money. The reliance on broad money could be explained partly by the reasonably close connection it had had with total spending in the economy in the 1960s and 1970s.

This approach had a very important practical result. Bank deposits make up 90 per cent of the broad money total, but banks can expand their deposits on one side of the balance sheet only if they can expand their loans on the other. A target for broad money therefore contains, at least by implication, a limit on the growth of bank credit. In consequence, the period of broad money targets involved careful monitoring of credit to both the public and private sectors. Credit to the public sector was curbed by reducing the Government's budget deficit and credit to the private sector by maintaining an appropriately high level of interest rates. This system of monetary control was a success. Contrary to all the sneers in the media, and despite many awkward teething troubles in its implementation, it worked on the only test that really mattered: it brought a sharp fall in inflation to a country which had seen rising inflation, comparing one cyclical peak with another, for over 20 years. In 1984 and 1985 there was no need to change it. It could – and should – have been left alone.

However, officials at the Treasury and, to a lesser degree, at the Bank of England, were concerned about certain changes in the relationship between broad money and money national income. Control over broad money may have achieved lower inflation, but they were mystified that a particular growth rate of broad money seemed to be associated with less inflation in the 1980s than it would have been in the 1970s. There was enough of a puzzle for them to recommend to Mr Lawson that the Government shift its attention towards narrow money. Mr Lawson accepted their view and abandoned broad money at some stage in the middle of 1985.

This may have seemed, to those uninitiated in the subtleties of monetary management, a petty detail in the political life of the nation, a point of some interest to the financial artisans who work the parish pumps of Lombard Street and Threadneedle Street, but of none to the more dignified citizens of Westminster and Whitehall. In fact, the move away from broad money is fundamental to explaining both subsequent developments in the economy and the Conservatives' success in the general election. With broad money targets no longer the focus of policy, the Government was excused from the need to limit the growth of bank credit. Whether by accident or by design, Mr Lawson had set the scene for the largest boom in private credit this country has ever seen. It is this boom which, more than anything else, has been responsible for the recent upturn in the economy, for the sense of well-being undoubtedly felt by the majority of voters (particularly those owning homes) and for the Government's re-election.

The Government may not have realized, as preparations were made for the credit boom, just how spectacular it would prove to be. The growth of private credit had been high throughout the early 1980s, largely because of the removal of a variety of restrictions on the banks and other financial institutions, but it was not out of control. Sterling bank lending to the private sector was steady at about £13 billion in 1982, 1983 and 1984, with the growth rate under 20 per cent a year and falling. After adjustment for inflation, the amount of bank lending was appreciably less than in the Heath/ Barber boom of 1972 and 1973. But in 1985 and 1986 the position changed radically. Bank lending doubled in just two years to reach £30 billion, a level far higher than ever before in nominal terms and about 25 per cent more in real terms than at the previous peak in 1972.

The extra credit was not sprinkled evenly over all parts of the economy, but channelled particularly into the housing market. A substantial portion of the record bank lending total was accounted for by mortgage credit, as the banks tried to gain market share from the building societies. Nevertheless, building society lending was also exceptionally strong. As Table 6.1 shows, the expansion of the building societies' business has been more than that of the banks' since the Thatcher Government came to power. In real terms building societies' net mortgage advances were not just greater in 1985 and 1986 than in 1972 and 1973, but virtually twice as high.

These figures are both an eloquent tribute to the Thatcher Government's determination to promote home-ownership and a disturbing commentary on the consequent problems of financial management. It was almost as if, once Treasury ministers had liberalized the market in mortgage finance and so enabled more people to buy a house, they felt obliged to make people happy with their investment. Since the start of the credit boom in mid-1985 the national rate of house price increase has gone up from under 10 per cent a

Table 6.1   The growth of credit over the last 20 years

	Bank lending in sterling to UK private sector (£million, current prices)	Net mortgage advances by building societies (£million, current prices)	GDP deflator (factor cost, expenditure data) 1980 = 100	Bank lending in sterling to UK private sector (£million, 1986 prices)	Net mortgage advances by building societies (£million, 1986 prices)
1967	511	823	22.9	3182	5125
1968	538	860	23.7	3237	5175
1969	429	782	24.5	2497	4552
1970	678	1088	26.4	3662	5877
1971	1776	1576	29.3	8644	7670
1972	5511	2215	32.3	24330	9779
1973	5671	1999	34.8	23238	8191
1974	3734	1490	40.7	13083	5220
1975	−367	2768	51.8	−1010	7620
1976	3081	3618	59.3	7409	8700
1977	3492	4100	66.6	7477	8779
1978	4710	5115	74.7	8991	9764
1979	8573	5271	84.2	14519	9078
1980	9622	5722	100.0	13721	8160
1981	8633	6207	110.3	11161	8025
1982	13055	8147	118.0	15777	9845
1983	13628	10928	124.6	15597	12507
1984	13479	14572	130.4	14740	15935
1985	19839	14711	138.5	20426	15146
1986	30005	19072	142.6	30005	19072

Source: Financial Statistics, Economic Trends

year to almost 15 per cent, while in some parts of London property prices have doubled. It is not coincidence that those areas of the country with the highest proportion of owner-occupied housing were the same areas which saw a swing towards the Conservatives in the election.

As in the Heath/Barber boom of the early 1970s, the explosion in credit has led to accelerated growth of broad money. For some time now the money supply has been expanding at an annual rate of about 20 per cent. There may be some doubts about the precise nature of the link between broad money and money national income, but that does not mean there is no link at all. It is almost incredible that the Mr Lawson who now as Chancellor of the Exchequer is so insouciant about the fastest monetary growth for 15 years is the same Mr Lawson who as Financial Secretary to the Treasury in June 1980 declared that 'in order to reduce the inflation rate on anything more than an ephemeral basis it is necessary to reduce the rate of monetary growth'. As Professor Charles Goodhart has remarked in the latest *Gerrard & National Economic Viewpoint*:

> The capacity of the present Conservative Government, and of the Treasury, to move from the (invalid) viewpoint that the growth of broad money is an exact determinant of the growth of nominal incomes to the (invalid) viewpoint that the growth of broad money has no relationship at all with the growth of nominal incomes is staggering with respect both to its speed and to the comprehensive nature of the intellectual somersault involved.

Those who are perplexed by broad money might like to reflect on the more accessible idea that house prices and the general price level tend to move together over periods of several years. (As with the money/incomes relationship, there are many short-term disturbances to the long-term link.) It follows that, if the present disparity between the behaviour of house prices and prices in the shops is to end, either the rate of house price inflation has to be reduced to 5 per cent or the rate of retail price inflation has to move up.

What is to be done now? How can an authentic anti-inflation policy be restored? There is not much to be expected from the Opposition parties. Since their leaders have variously derided monetary control as mumbo-jumbo, punk economics, a 'fashion' and the like, and since they have shown in their election manifestoes that they would be happy to trade more inflation for less unemployment, they are unlikely to become credible guardians of sound money. The Government bamboozled them into thinking that it was rigidly anti-inflationary, when in fact it was manipulating the financial environment for its own electoral benefit. But they have only themselves to blame for their inability to criticize the Government. Having said that irresponsible monetary policies do not matter, they of course have no right to challenge the Government for the irresponsibility of its monetary policies.

The best hope in the short run is that the Thatcher Government, which had such an excellent record on inflation in its first term, restores the system of monetary control which was working well in 1983 and 1984. That means bringing back broad money targets and demonstrating a preparedness to deter private sector credit by an appropriately high level of interest rates. In the long run, however, the answer is to give the Bank of England greater independence from government. In a well-ordered country, decisions on monetary policy should not be subject to the vagaries of the electoral cycle, and fluctuations in credit growth should not reflect politically-motivated calculations about house price increases and the voting propensities of home-owners. The Bank of England should be privatized, its autonomy from government should be protected by statute, and both the tactics and strategy of monetary policy should be determined by the Governor of the Bank of England in consultation with its Court of Directors. The Chancellor of the

Exchequer would be left with the humdrum but necessary task of keeping the Government's finances in good shape.

The most widely canvassed alternative to domestic monetary control on traditional lines is that Britain become a full member of the European Monetary System. Has none of its many advocates noticed that the pivotal institution of the EMS is the Bundesbank, the only truly independent central bank in the EEC? Has none of them wondered why the Bundesbank, so unlike its counterpart in Britain in the last two months, was able to ignore the course of the West German election during December and January? And has none of them realized that the superiority of West Germany's inflation record is not due to some innate national characteristic, but to a constitutional arrangement which Britain could readily imitate? Indeed, has none of them remembered that before 1946 Britain had its own independent central bank, that Britain's currency – not Germany's – was the hub of a major international trading area, and that Britain's inflation record had long been better than that of any other European nation?

Stop-Go Returns

From an article 'The return of stop-go?' in The Times *of 20 October 1987.*

This article said that the boom of late 1987 resembled the 'go' phases of previous stop-go cycles. The likely antidote was a sharp rise in interest rates after 'shock trade figures' in accordance with 'the classic pattern'. (This did indeed happen in late 1988.) Some people have tried to excuse Lawson for his misjudgements in this period by saying that he believed, genuinely, that Britain's underlying rate of output growth had increased to 4 or 5 per cent a year. But similar illusions had been held by other unsuccessful Conservative Chancellors at the same stage of their booms.

It is becoming increasingly clear, as they recede into the past, that the five years from mid-1981 to mid-1986 were a golden age of macroeconomic management. National output grew steadily at a sustainable rate of about $2^3/4$ per cent a year, while inflation was moderate and declining gradually, and the balance of payments usually in small surplus. Few periods in our history have been characterized by greater economic stability. It is also becoming increasingly clear, as the months go by, that the stability of the 1981–86 period has been ruptured. The growth of national output in 1987 is projected at an above-trend and unsustainable 4 per cent, while manufacturing production is increasing even faster. There is a general mood of excitement.

Unemployment is going down, profits are going up and property speculators are making lots of money.

Why is the economy booming more vigorously now than at any time since the early 1970s? It cannot be because the UK is reflecting international trends, since the world economy has made indifferent progress in the last couple of years. Nor can it be due to fiscal reflation, as public expenditure has been kept under such a tight rein that there is a chance of a budget surplus in both 1987/88 and 1988/89. The answer is instead to be sought in the behaviour of credit and money.

In the golden period of economic stability in the early 1980s the Treasury and the Bank of England watched trends in bank lending with great care, mainly because each new bank loan creates a new bank deposit and so adds to the money supply. It is true that both bank lending and the money supply increased faster than originally expected, and that monetary control often gave the appearance of incoherence and muddle. But it is also true that the growth rate of the money supply (on its broad M3 definition) was kept down to a level consistent with a stable economy and moderate inflation. The system of monetary control operating in the early 1980s, widely labelled 'monetarist', was a success in its own terms. Despite much pragmatic compromising and frequent technical embarrassments, it was the key to the Government's principal economic achievement, the reduction in inflation to under 5 per cent. But – for reasons that are not altogether clear – the system was abandoned about two years ago.

Since then Britain has had the strongest surge in private sector credit in its history and the annual rate of money supply growth has increased from about 12 per cent to over 20 per cent. Today sees the publication of the September money supply figures. Analysts are expecting another massive lending total of about £3 billion and money supply growth in the month of about $1^1/2$ per cent. It is interesting and legitimate to make comparisons with the Heath–Barber boom of the early 1970s, when the growth rate of the money supply peaked at over 25 per cent. Without doubt, it is the flood of credit and money into the economy which explains the current boom in output. This boom has an all too obvious resemblance to the 'go' phases of the many previous stop–go cycles in the post-war period. Like its predecessors in 1955, 1959, 1964 and 1973, it will eventually have to be restrained.

It is not going too far to describe the Government's performance – in this central area of economic policy – as bewildering to the point of perversity. In 1979 and 1980 it instituted rules of economic management that were intended to combat inflation and eliminate the stop–go cycle. These rules achieved most of what the Government asked of them. In 1984 and early 1985 Nigel Lawson could claim, without being frivolous, that the cycle had been relegated to the history books. Moreover, in business circles there was a general expectation that the next few years would be as stable as the previous three. But then, just at the moment of apparent triumph, the Government scrapped its own rules. Instead of adhering to the broad money targets that had existed for almost a decade, it embarked on a credit binge certain to lead to unsustainably rapid economic growth. Whether by accident, design or mere inadvertence, it had restored the stop–go cycle.

At this stage of the earlier cycles there have always been a few economists prepared to advocate permanent boom and there have sometimes been Chancellors of the Exchequer foolish enough to believe them, at any rate for a few months. But, sooner or later, common sense has prevailed. The classic pattern is that shock trade figures and/or a car strike initiate a sterling crisis and oblige the government to slow the economy, with an interest rate hike the most familiar weapon.

The sudden collapse in share prices yesterday suggests that investors are beginning to fear deflationary measures of the traditional kind. As the stock market normally anticipates developments in the economy, the largest-ever one-day fall in share prices is worrying. Comparisons with 1974 – when share prices dropped by 60 per cent – are unjustified, since the economic and political background is much more favourable than it was then. But a milder 15 to 25 per cent downward adjustment to share prices would be similar to that seen in the concluding stages of most post-war stop–go cycles.

Lawson has recently shown disturbing signs of believing, if not in permanent boom, that nothing much is wrong. In particular, he has implied that growth will moderate to a lower and more sustainable pace in 1988, without corrective action by the Government and without any inflationary repercussions from the 1987 boom. In the Autumn Statement early next month he is expected to be more complacent than ever, with several newspapers suggesting that he will promise more tax cuts in the 1988 Budget.

In fact, no part of the economy (except, ominously, exports) is weakening and several pointers to faster growth have emerged. In particular, it should be noted that a number of large construction projects (the Channel Tunnel, Canary Wharf, the Stansted Airport expansion) will add $1/2$ to $3/4$ per cent to gross domestic product next year. The question is not *if* the boom will have to be checked by the Government, but *when*.

On Friday the September trade figures will be announced, while the car strike at Vauxhall may be joined in the next few weeks by one at Ford. If these events are followed by a sterling crisis, they would fit an old and familiar pattern; and, if sterling depreciation and excessive pay awards in the car industry lead to higher inflation, the recent mistakes in monetary policy would meet with the usual retribution. Lawson, who has had more than his fair share of good fortune in his years as Chancellor, will be lucky if his boom does not end in the same manner as Butler's in 1956, Heathcoat-Amory's in 1960, Maudling's in 1964 and Barber's in 1974.

The Lawson Boom in the Light of the Crash

From an article of the same name in Economic Affairs, *February/March 1988.*

This piece was critical of the easing of monetary policy which followed the stock market crash of October 1987. As I pointed out, most indicators of domestic demand were rising strongly at the beginning of 1988. The post-Crash loosening of monetary policy would therefore aggravate the rise in inflation that was already inevitable. The inflation forecast in this article, 'that inflation will increase significantly, but should not move above the 8 to 10 per cent area', was largely correct. Nevertheless, the peak in headline retail inflation in late 1990 was over 10 per cent because of higher oil prices and the effect of increased interest rates on mortgage costs. (Incredible though it may seem now, most of the so-called 'leading forecasting bodies' expected in early 1988 that inflation would fall in 1989 and 1990!)

In its section on the UK, the Group of Seven (G7) statement of 23 December 1987 remarks that 'The Government, in the context of the British economy's vigorous growth of output and domestic demand, coupled with sound public finances, will continue to strive to reduce inflation by pursuing a prudent monetary policy.' The bland and colourless phrasing, presumably the work of senior Treasury officials, may seem appropriate coming from an august international gathering. In fact, it is a tribute to its authors' sense of humour. The remarks on vigorous output growth and sound public finances are fair enough, but the reference to 'prudent' monetary policy must have been written with mandarin tongues firmly in embarrassed official cheeks. The truth is that monetary growth in the UK is grossly excessive, that excessive monetary growth is fuelling an unsustainable boom in the economy and that the boom will be followed by a significant increase in inflation. There are ample grounds for calling the current period of economic excitement the 'Lawson boom', just as its forerunners in 1964 and 1973 are associated with the names of Maudling and Barber.

However, the G7 verdict on the UK is not altogether facetious. There was a period, in the very recent past, when it was legitimate to talk of the prudence of British monetary policy. In early 1985 the Government could fairly claim to have reduced the rate of inflation by the determined and consistent pursuit of a responsible monetary policy. At that time, as for nearly all of the previous decade, the centrepiece of monetary policy was a target for the growth of broad money which was intended to constrain, in a rough-and-ready way, the rate of increase in nominal gross domestic product. With the underlying growth rate of output set by the economy's supply-side characteristics, the limit on nominal GDP secured control over inflation. It was essential to the whole approach that the budget deficit, as measured by the public sector borrowing requirement, was not used to manage the amount of demand in the economy, but was restricted to a level compatible with the monetary targets. But in mid-1985 broad money targets, and most of the so-called 'monetarist' framework of financial control, were abandoned.

At the end of 1984 broad money was under reasonably good control, with sterling M3 showing an annual growth rate of about 10 per cent. The figure of 10 per cent was at the top end of the official target range of 6 to 10 per cent, but was broadly comparable to a figure of 11 per cent recorded at the end of 1983 and 9 per cent at the end of 1982. As high real interest rates and certain institutional changes in the banking system were tending to increase the economy's propensity to hold money, money supply growth of about or slightly above 10 per cent was consistent with inflation of 5 per cent and real growth of 3 per cent. Indeed, the economic stability of these years was an impressive endorsement of the monetarist system of financial control which by then seemed well established.

Despite the sound financial environment, officials in Whitehall and the Bank of England became dissatisfied with monetary policy. Exactly why they became dissatisfied is far from obvious, but Mr Lawson, as Chancellor of the Exchequer, was readily persuaded that change of some kind was needed. In May 1985 he gave a foretaste of what was to come by stating that the significance of sterling M3 had 'somewhat diminished'. Shortly afterwards the authorities decided to end a method of determining official gilt sales, known as 'overfunding', which had been essential to monetary control over the previous four years. The demise of overfunding – which was confirmed in the September 1985 *Bank of England Quarterly Bulletin* – was made to appear purely technical in import and not given much attention in the financial press. But it had a crucial consequence. The Government could no longer adjust gilt sales flexibly to meet broad money targets. In the Mansion House speech on 17 October Mr Lawson announced that the sterling M3 target for 1985/86 had been suspended.

The scrapping of the monetarist policy framework was soon followed by an acceleration in broad money growth. In the six months to January 1986 sterling M3 grew at an annualized rate of 15 per cent. This was followed by 18 per cent in the year to January 1987 and over 20 per cent in the year to November 1987. By the beginning of 1988 the economy had had two-and-a-half years of broad monetary growth in the region of 15 to 20 per cent. The contrast with the preceding four years of 10 to 12 per cent growth is clear and definite. Moreover, this contrast is not an accident, but the logical result of a deliberate shift in Government policy. Mr Lawson was very articulate in his justification of this policy shift when it was made.

No one – and certainly none of the small and dwindling band of 'monetarist' commentators in the City – expected the acceleration in monetary growth to be followed in short order by an exactly commensurate acceleration in inflation. On the contrary, past experience suggested that the initial impact of excess monetary growth would be felt on asset prices (houses, commercial property and shares) and on economic activity. The usual pattern was that output growth picked up nine to 18 months after the increase in monetary growth, while inflation responded after a long lag of three or more years.

The behaviour of the economy in 1986 and 1987 fitted in neatly with the standard monetarist timetable. Output started to move ahead strongly about three quarters after the acceleration in monetary growth. Gross domestic product (as measured by the output estimate) increased by 1.3 per cent in the second quarter of 1986, by 1.2 per cent in the third quarter and 1.0 per cent in the fourth, implying an annualized rate of advance in every quarter of over 4 per cent. The most buoyant component of expenditure was consumption, which soared by 6 per cent in the year. The consumption boom was widely attributed to the ready availability of personal loans and was associated in the public mind with the proliferation of credit cards. While these were notable aspects of the consumer scene, they were completely overshadowed in scale by an upturn in mortgage lending. Net mortgage advances totalled £19.1 billion in 1985 and £25.8 billion in 1986, a multiple of borrowing on credit cards which was under £1 billion in both years. Through a process known as 'equity withdrawal' a high proportion of mortgage finance escaped from the housing market and was used to finance increased purchases of consumer durables. In this way the high level of mortgage lending was a major reason for an extraordinary leap of 17 per cent in sales of consumer durables between the second quarter of 1985 and the third quarter of 1986. Nevertheless, there was still enough money remaining in the housing market to initiate a surge of house price increases. According to the Building Societies' Association index, house prices were 13.9 per cent higher in December 1986 than a year earlier.

Houses were not the only assets to increase sharply in price. As rapid monetary growth meant that people had a far higher level of bank deposits than they needed to carry out their usual transactions, they were keen to transfer the excess deposits into more attractive investments. Inflows into unit trusts soared, while insurance companies found it easy to sell policies and put on record amounts of new business. Because of all this extra money, the long-term savings institutions (insurance companies, pension funds, unit trusts) had £24 billion to invest in 1986, significantly higher than the £20.9 billion in 1985. Here was the financial raw material to support a substantial rise in share prices. The stock market advanced particularly briskly in the months leading up to March 1986, when the *Financial Times* industrial ordinary index stood almost 50 per cent higher than nine months earlier.

Faster output growth in 1986 cannot be attributed to an easing of fiscal policy, since public sector borrowing was kept under tight control, or to more buoyant international economic conditions, since the growth of the world economy was roughly the same in 1986 as in 1985. Instead the upturn in Britain bore the strong imprint, in both its timing and character, of the increase in broad money growth. There were obvious parallels with the Barber boom of the early 1970s, which saw a jump in sales of consumer durables of 28 per cent in the year to the second quarter of 1972, a rise of almost 40 per cent in house prices in the year to December 1972, and a spectacular bull market in equities with the *Financial Times* industrial ordinary index up by 65 per cent between March 1971 and May 1972.

In 1987 the expansion broadened and gathered pace. Investment overtook consumption as the most dynamic category of demand, with construction activity showing particular vigour. The buoyancy of sales and orders came as a surprise to most businessmen, who initially met higher demand partly by running down their stocks. By the end of the second quarter the stock/output ratio to manufacturing was at its lowest level in the post-war period. It was necessary and inevitable that companies rebuild their stocks. The process began in the third quarter and caused output growth to move into a yet higher gear. The average measure of GDP went up by 2.2 per cent, implying an annualized growth rate of 9 per cent.

As the economy gathered momentum, the private sector's demand for bank credit strengthened and the pace of monetary growth increased. In these circumstances institutional cash again grew very rapidly, propelling a further surge in share prices. In July the *Financial Times* industrial ordinary index was 45 per cent higher than at the end of 1986 and almost double its level of two years earlier. House price inflation also accelerated, suggesting a generalized condition of 'too much money chasing too few assets'. The speed of economic growth in the third quarter was not known in full until the release of the relevant GDP data in December. But there were many symptoms of excessive demand. Fears about future inflationary trouble gained new cogency when information became available about a £4.5 billion leap in bank lending in July. At the behest of the Bank of England, clearing bank base rates were raised from 9 to 10 per cent on 9 August, with domestic monetary conditions cited as the principal justification. Bad August trade figures, released in September, were another warning that the boom was running out of control. Despite these jolts to confidence share prices remained at such high levels that companies felt they had to raise money by rights issues. At the same time the Government was eager to press ahead with its privatization programme. In the three months from August to October about £7 billion was taken out of institutional cash holdings by rights issues, new privatizations, calls on old privatizations, offers for sale and other kinds of corporate money-raising. By mid-October, for the first time in several years, the institutions were short of cash. The scale of the cash drain left the stock market vulnerable to disappointments. On 19 October – ahead of a week which included potentially troublesome statistics on the money supply, bank lending and the trade balance – share prices collapsed. Although foreign stock markets also fell heavily, worries about domestic inflationary trends within the UK were undoubtedly a bearish influence on London equity prices.

But Mr Lawson and his advisers did not see it that way. In their view the economy was growing at about the right rate and the prospect, even before the Crash, was for a slowdown in 1988. Their new anxiety was that the drop in share prices would seriously undermine economic activity, turning the slowdown into a recession. Instead of interpreting the Crash as a warning about excessive growth, they saw it as liable to precipitate unnecessary contraction. They reacted by reducing interest rates. Base rates were lowered to $9^1/_2$ per cent on 23 October and to $8^1/_2$ per cent in two further falls in the next few weeks.

It soon became obvious that these interest rate cuts were inappropriate. At the time of writing (early January 1988) there are few indications of weakening demand and many signs that demand is growing faster than ever. Retail sales and car registrations in November showed increases from October and very large increases compared to a year earlier; the trade figures for November were disturbingly bad, with a current account deficit of almost £600 million in the month and of £1,800 million (the equivalent of 1 per cent of gross domestic product) in the most recent four months; labour shortages are being widely reported, with concern over a shortage of nursing staff being given considerable media coverage; and retail spending over Christmas and at New Year sales appears to have been unusually buoyant. Moreover, the portents are for an intensification of excess demand pressures in the early months of 1988. The December CBI survey had the highest proportion of companies reporting above-normal order books since the mid-1970s; the rise in mortgage credit, arguably the financial dynamo behind the Lawson boom, is due to gain momentum in the next few months because of promises to lend already made by building societies and banks. Manpower, the staff consultancy, has said that more companies plan to recruit people in early 1988 than at any time in 1987, while the number of vacancies notified to

Jobcentres is rising every month, and is now higher than for most of the late 1960s.

At this point in a standard UK stop–go business cycle the pound usually suffers a speculative attack on the foreign exchanges. A sterling crisis is the financial markets' characteristic reaction to loose monetary policy and the Government responds by raising interest rates. Higher interest rates then serve the dual function of bolstering the international value of the pound and moderating the growth of domestic credit. However, at present the pound is very firm on the foreign exchanges, largely as a by-product of dollar weakness. The dollar's problems are therefore disguising the irresponsibility of UK policy and allowing the Government to postpone the necessary restrictive action.

A strong pound contains the domestic price level because it reinforces foreign competition. For the time being the excessive growth of credit and money will tend to damage the balance of payments rather than inflation. But the foreign exchanges will not forever remain indifferent to the UK's worsening payments position. As long as the growth of the money supply continues to be three or four times faster in the UK than in West Germany and the USA, and the trend in the balance of payments is remorselessly into more substantial deficit, a sterling crisis is inevitable. After sterling has fallen in value, inflation will increase. Precise medium-term inflation forecasts are difficult to make because the price level is subject to random influences such as world commodity prices and Government policy towards public sector pricing. All one can say on past form is that an acceleration in monetary growth normally hits the inflation rate about three years after it began. A reasonable expectation is that sterling will weaken in early 1988, perhaps in conjunction with falling oil prices, and that the inflation rate will rise for much of late 1988 and 1989. Alternatively, the weakness in sterling may be combined with a transitory phase of renewed confidence in the dollar.

Since monetary growth has been 5 to 10 per cent more than in the stable period before the middle of 1985, it would be logical to envisage the rate of increase in nominal GDP also rising 5 to 10 per cent above the 8 per cent figure associated with that period. But this may overstate the inflationary threat. The last three years may have seen a continuing and more pronounced increase in the economy's propensity to hold money, because of institutional changes. Moreover, because unemployment was so high before the Lawson monetary stimulus, much of its impact will be felt in higher output rather than a rise in the price level. A cautious view is that inflation will increase significantly but should not move above the 8 to 10 per cent area. Although that would be modest by the standards of the last 15 years, it would be regarded as a major setback for the Government. In particular, it would cast doubt on the wisdom of the strategic decision to abandon broad money targets in mid-1985 and on the tactical decision to cut interest rates in October and November 1987.

The Government made two mistakes after the Crash. The first was to underestimate the vitality of the pre-Crash economy. This is clear enough, both from the pattern of events and from official statements. The Chancellor and his colleagues failed to recognize that – in the absence of the Crash – the economy would have had considerable forward impetus. Growth, even though it might have moderated to less than the startling 9 per cent annualized rate seen in the third quarter, would still have remained much above the trend rate of about 3 per cent. The second mistake was to overestimate the effects of the Crash. A fall in share prices does – by itself – tend to slow the economy down, but its impact is marginal. As direct personal sector holdings of shares are less than a tenth of total personal wealth, it is implausible to expect changes in their value to have a particularly powerful effect on consumer attitudes or behaviour. Indirect holdings (through insurance companies, pension funds and other institutional intermediaries) are more significant, but one of the purposes of investment in these channels is to muffle the impact of market volatility on the individual saver. (Most unit trusts carry a specific 'health warning' that share prices can go up as well as down, and that investment should be regarded as long term in nature; pension funds typically determine their solvency position not by looking at the market value of their equity holdings, but by applying a discount rate to expected dividend receipts.)

In any case, direct and indirect share holdings combined are overshadowed in terms of value by the housing stock and other kinds of property (agricultural land, buildings and plant owned by unincorporated businesses, commercial buildings). In the year to October 1987 house prices, as measured by the Building Societies' Association average house price series, rose by 18.3 per cent, indicating a massively positive 'wealth effect' on consumption. Two further points should be emphasized: first, despite the October Crash, share prices were higher in November 1987 than in November 1986; and, second, since the gilt market rallied on the news of the equity slump, higher gilt prices partly outweighed the effect of lower equity prices on personal wealth.

The Crash is an important incident in the Lawson boom. But it is no more than an incident. If the 30 per cent fall in share prices had been spread over six months instead of compressed into two days, it is unlikely that economists would have made much fuss. (Most of the major macroeconomic models do not have share prices as an independent variable in their consumption or investment equations, or, indeed, anywhere else.) The key problem for the British economy today is to rein in the excessive growth of credit and so curb the rapid monetary growth which lies behind an unsustainably rapid increase in demand and output. It would be a tragedy if the Lawson boom of 1986–88 follows largely the same course as the Barber boom of 1971–73. But, in the words of the American philosopher George Santayana, 'those who cannot learn from history are condemned to repeat it.'

Even the Housing Boom can Turn to Bust

Reprinted from an article of the same name in The Spectator *of 14 May 1988.*

Perhaps this article says nothing more than 'what goes up must come down'. But it needed to be said. Four years after the article was written the residential housing market in most of England (particularly Conservative-voting England, i.e., London, the South-East, the South-West and East Anglia) was in a more traumatized state than at any time in the post-war period.

The success of market-based, free-enterprise economies depends on people with long memories and a deeply ingrained financial scepticism. If the majority of investors are instead always carried away by the enthusiasms of the moment, the economy is liable to suffer from wasteful excesses of over- or under-investment.

These remarks may seem trite. But it is remarkable how often they are forgotten. The most vivid, and the most socially costly, illustrations come from industries requiring large and bulky investments with long lead times. Property development brings out the general idea very clearly. The risk of a large error in calculating demand is compensated by the possibility of vast speculative gains for entrepreneurs who judge correctly. Over the last 20 years enormous personal fortunes (Donald Trump, the Reichmann brothers, Godfrey Bradman) have been made in real estate by borrowing to purchase cyclically unpopular and under-valued assets. The scale of these fortunes and the apparent ease of their acquisition have encouraged many imitators. Nowhere has this been more true than in North America, with the late 1970s and the early 1980s the peak period of excitement.

Office buildings received particularly favourable tax treatment in the early years of the Reagan presidency, partly as a by-product of the supply-siders' tax cuts, and were the focus of considerable tax-assisted speculation. By the second quarter of 1985 new office building in the USA was virtually three times higher than five years earlier. More space was coming on to the market than ever before. Unfortunately, the demand for new space did not stay in line. An office vacancy index compiled by Coldwell Banker, a Chicago-based real estate service, rose from 5 per cent in early 1982 to 11.7 per cent in 1983, 13.9 per cent in 1984 and 16.1 per cent in 1985. Not surprisingly, rental growth stopped.

The price of office buildings, which had been rising (apart from minor regional variations and very temporary interruptions) for over 40 years, began to fall. Even worse, in 1986 Congress, dismayed by the grotesque waste evident in so many empty buildings, passed a tax reform package which ended the indulgent fiscal treatment enjoyed by the real estate industry. Since then, financial strains in cities with particularly high office-vacancy levels, notably such former models of Sun Belt prosperity as Houston and Dallas, have intensified. Today virtually the entire Texan banking industry is crippled by bad real estate loans. Whereas in the 1960s and 1970s many Texan families grew rich by the far from arduous practice of watching their office blocks increase in value by 20 per cent a year, they are now helpless as interest mounts remorselessly on old debts. The moral of the Texan real estate misfortunes is that no asset price can forever rise faster than interest rates. The success of the astute (or lucky) few who borrow to buy at the bottom cannot be repeated by the mediocre (or unlucky) many. When the mediocre many do try to join in, they may further inflate a speculative bubble, but the bubble still has to burst sooner or later.

Empty office space in Texas may seem remote from the problems of the British economy today. But there is mounting evidence that a speculative boom is also under way in this country. It is not as wild or as extreme as the mania for Houston office blocks in the late 1970s. Nor will it be followed by such a precipitous slump in the value of the assets which are the object of the speculative excitement. But it is driven by a similarly unsustainable pattern of expectations. Moreover, whereas credit-based purchases of Houston office buildings involved only the rich (or the once rich), the boom in the UK affects – at least indirectly – millions of people. The boom is in credit to purchase houses and other forms of property, particularly in the southern half of England. The existence of this credit boom, and of the related surge in property values, has been recognized by the media for some time. But they do not yet seem to have noticed that the boom, far from fading away, is set to gather extra momentum in the next few months.

In Greater London the price of residential property rose on average by 17.3 per cent a year between 1982 and 1987. Over the same period the cost of borrowing to buy a house – as measured by the mortgage rate adjusted for tax relief – averaged a little less than 8.5 per cent. In other words, someone who took out a 100 per cent mortgage in 1982 typically received, in each of the next five years, an increment in wealth equivalent to almost 10 per cent of the value of the property. If the mortgage was originally set at two-and-a-half times income (as would be common), this increment in wealth amounted each year to about a quarter of income. This bonus was achieved without effort and was free of tax.

The potential for capital gains on residential property in London is a matter of common observation. It is a constant topic of conversation at dinner parties and business lunches, and is encouraged by glossy controlled-circulation property magazines and estate agents' sales material. Outside London the enthusiasm for property is also intense, if a little less frenzied. In the South-East house prices rose by 14.8 per cent a year between 1982 and 1987, in East Anglia by 13.4 per cent, in the South-West by 12.3 per cent and in the East Midlands by 10.3 per cent. The numbers are lower than in London, but they are still above the post-tax mortgage rate.

Because of this background the middle class in the south of England takes it for granted that the rate of appreciation on their houses will always exceed the rate of interest. In other words, here is another example of a widespread expectation, indeed almost an assumption of thought, that a major asset will continue to rise in price at a faster rate than the cost of borrowing to purchase it. This set of beliefs has permeated so widely and become so firmly entrenched that mortgage credit has risen in every year since 1974. In 1987 net mortgage advances were five times higher than in 1979.

It might have been reasonable to expect that, in the first year of its third term, the Thatcher Government would want a cooling-off period in the housing market. However, because of the Chancellor's anxiety about the dangers of a strong pound for British industry, interest rates have been cut to the lowest level since 1978. In response, mortgage credit is growing more rapidly than ever before. In February the building societies promised an astonishing 74.9 per cent more in new mortgage commitments than a year earlier. This seemed a bit freakish, but in March the figure approached 85 per cent. When account is taken of the role of the banks and specialist mortgage intermediaries, net mortgage advances in 1988 are likely to be £40 billion – £10 billion more than in 1987 and nearly seven times higher than in 1979.

Of course, it would be far-fetched to claim that house prices in southern England could behave in as erratic a fashion as the price of Texan office buildings. House prices have never fallen by much in the UK and their rate of change is sedate compared with most commodity or financial markets. It should be noted, nevertheless, that the bouyancy of the London property market has recently attracted an adventurous form of speculation, the property futures market. The standard operation is to put up the deposit (of, say, 10 per cent) on a flat or house still in the course of construction and then to sell it some months later when prices are higher. (If prices have risen 10 per cent, the profit is 100 per cent.) There is some similarity to highly geared trading in American real estate, particularly if the 'purchasers' of the properties are financing the deposits with borrowed money.

It is inescapable, almost as a matter of logic, that the mortgage credit boom of 1987 and 1988 will have to be followed by a few years in which house prices rise by less than the post-tax mortgage rate. Unless house price increases fall behind the cost of borrowing, the temptation to borrow more will overwhelm the Government's attempts to moderate credit demand and destroy its anti-inflationary monetary policies. The unfortunate truth is that the English middle class looks on continually rising house prices with considerable affection. It does not want to understand that rising house prices are an aspect of more general inflation. Nor will it like to be told – either by Mr Lawson's successor (whoever that may be) or by a Prime Minister who has extolled the virtues of home ownership – that a serious attempt to restore price stability must mean a few years with a less overheated housing market. But Conservative Cabinet ministers with long memories and a deeply in-grained political scepticism ought to have realized months ago (and perhaps even before June 1987) that the sequel to the current housing boom was bound to be electorally inconvenient. They must be hoping that the belt of affluence now covering most of southern England does not end up in a financial mess similar to that in such former bywords of economic dynamism as Houston and Dallas.

7.   I told you so

Anyone who says 'I told you so' too often is liable to make himself unpopular. But, as the Lawson boom disintegrated in 1988 and 1989, my forecasts of rising inflation were vindicated. I felt justified in pointing out that I had warned the Government, well in advance of the event, that its economic policies would end badly.

In 1988 and 1989 the 'leading forecasting groups' (i.e., the London Business School and the National Institute of Economic Research), the Treasury and Government ministers had forgotten about monetarism, broad money targets and the like. Instead they had reverted to their practices in the early and mid-1970s, using forecasts from a large-scale macroeconomic model as the basis for short-term decisions about interest rates, tax changes and budgetary policy. They seem to have forgotten the catastrophe suffered by macroeconomic forecasting during and after the Barber boom, when all the models utterly failed to foresee either the severity of the fall in output in late 1974 and early 1975, or the scale of the concurrent increase in inflation. The late 1980s were a very similar period. Once again the mainstream economic forecasts were hopelessly wrong and policy decisions based upon them were often inappropriate.

Two of the four pieces in this section refer to macroeconomic forecasting. The first, 'Quick, quick, slow, stop–go', from *The Times* of 25 July 1988, was probably my sharpest attack on Lawson personally. He ought to have known, from many years of experience as a financial journalist and politician, that Treasury forecasts were not to be taken too literally. But he was clearly duped by the inept and totally wrong forecast produced by his Treasury officials before the 1988 Budget. The forecast was that the economy would slow down to a moderate rate of growth, with no significant rise in inflation and no large change in interest rates. Lawson, still relying on his Treasury forecasters, continued to promise this so-called 'soft landing' until his resignation in 1989.

The second article, 'Scribblers in the stocks', from *The Times* of 27 September 1988, turned its attention to the large number of 'publicity-seeking "teenage scribblers"' who began to jeer at Lawson and the Treasury's forecasting record in late 1988. My point was that virtually all of them had produced the same forecast as the Treasury in late 1987 and early 1988!

Sadly, these economists had a 'propensity, when asked about the future, to transform themselves into computerized sheep'.

Quick, Quick, Slow, Stop–Go

Reprinted from the an article of the same name in The Times *of 25 July 1988.*

Note the reference to the change in monetary policy in mid-1985, followed by 'a clear change in the behaviour of all the relevant variables – bank lending, mortgage credit, M3, M4 and M5 – by early 1986', as the start of Lawson's troubles. By late 1988 most politically-aware economists realized that Lawson had mishandled the economy, but many attributed higher inflation to the 1988 Budget. In my view, the causes of rising inflation had to be sought much earlier.

At long last the Government has accepted what most economic scribblers, from the teenage to the geriatric, have known for many months. The British economy has enjoyed a full-scale boom since mid-1986, with domestic demand rising more strongly than at any time since the Heath–Barber 'dash for growth' of the early 1970s. The Treasury has spent most of the last two years wrongly forecasting an imminent and spontaneous slowdown in economic activity. By endorsing the Bank of England's recent moves to raise clearing bank base rates by 3 per cent in a mere six weeks, it has finally approved action which makes a slowdown conceivable.

But there is still a debate about how smoothly the economy will return to a moderate pace of expansion. Mr Lawson, and presumably most of his Cabinet colleagues and Treasury advisers, believe there will be a gentle touchdown to the sustainable medium-term growth rate of about $2\frac{1}{2}$ to 3 per cent. In their view, this touchdown can be achieved without an intervening recession or even a short period of beneath-trend growth, while the inflation rate will remain at about 5 per cent and the balance of payments, although in deficit, will not be a problem.

The alternative view is that the economy will suffer a hard landing. In this argument, the pressure of excess demand is bound to cause persisting balance-of-payments weakness and a sharp rise in inflation. Once the severity of the inflation difficulties is recognized, the Government will be obliged to engineer a further deceleration in the speed of economic expansion. A year or two of slow growth, involving some rise in unemployment, will be needed to eliminate the labour and capacity shortages which are the immediate causes of more inflation. It will seem retrospectively that the Lawson boom, like its many predecessors in the post-war period, was part of just another stop–go cycle.

The strategic disagreement between the optimists and pessimists will not be settled conclusively until the end of 1989, if not later. But the optimists at the Treasury have already suffered heavy tactical defeats from the economic data of the last few months. The official Budget-time forecasts of a £4 billion current account deficit and year-end 4 per cent inflation have already had to be revised upwards. The Treasury has rather shamefacedly declined to give a precise figure for its new payments forecast, but a £10 billion deficit is quite possible. (More will be known with the publication of the June trade figures on Wednesday.) Meanwhile several private forecasters envisage a $5^1/2$ to 6 per cent increase in retail prices this year.

Indeed, the scale of the mistake with the payments forecast has been such as to raise doubts about the basis for the Chancellor's continuing complacency. It needs to be emphasized that this is not the first time in recent years that the official forecast has gone astray. At Budget time last year the Treasury expected gross domestic product to rise by 3 per cent in 1987. In fact growth was about $4^1/2$ per cent.

The forecasting errors made in the Budgets of both 1987 and 1988 point to two conclusions. The Treasury completely failed to appreciate the vigour of the upturn in economic activity which began in mid-1986; and most members of the Government, including the Prime Minister, had no advance warning that there was going to be a boom on the scale actually experienced. In the circumstances it is not surprising that Mrs Thatcher is more worried about overheating and inflation than her Chancellor, or that she is seeking new sources of advice.

Why have Lawson and the Treasury been so badly wrong? By far the most convincing general explanation is that the Chancellor stopped paying much attention to credit and broad money about three years ago and attached no importance to the accelerating growth of both which began in late 1985. This acceleration was foreshadowed in both the 1985 Budget and the Mansion House speech of October 1985, and can reasonably be described as the inevitable consequence of the change in policy approach. There was a clear change in the behaviour of all the relevant variables – bank lending, mortgage credit, M3, M4 and M5 – by early 1986.

It is not possible in a short article to review all the evidence. Instead we will focus on just one statistic, the increase in M3 adjusted for inflation, which may be called the 'real money supply'. It is perhaps the best indicator of the influence being exerted on economic activity by changes in personal and corporate liquidity. In periods of monetary relaxation it measures the stimulatory push coming from excess money growth. In the five years to the beginning of 1986 the real money supply increased on average by 5 per cent a year, with only small annual variations. This growth rate was associated with impressive economic stability and was only slightly higher than the $2^1/2$ to 3 per cent growth of output. The whole period was the heyday, indeed almost the golden age, of the Medium-Term Financial Strategy, with ministers, from Mrs Thatcher downwards, trumpeting the success of their anti-inflationary policies.

By contrast, since the beginning of 1986 the real money supply has increased by an average annual rate of 17 per cent. This upturn was particularly marked in early 1986, mainly because the oil price fall led to an exceptional fall in inflation, but it has continued until the present. The economy has been asked to absorb an injection of liquidity out of all proportion to the sustainable rise in output. This total change in the monetary environment is the main cause – indeed, practically the only cause – of the Lawson boom. It is by far the most important reason that house prices are rising by more than 20 per cent a year; that fewer companies consider themselves to have excess capacity than at any time in the last 30 years; that pay settlements are edging up after the largest two-year fall in unemployment in our history; and that of the balance-of-payments current account has worsened by the equivalent of more than $^1/2$ per cent of GDP in each of the last six quarters.

If the essentials of this argument are accepted, a precondition for a return to sustainable $2^1/2$ to 3 per cent growth is that monetary expansion falls back to the rate seen in the five years to 1986. That rate is at most about 5 per cent a year in inflation-adjusted terms and about 10 to 12 per cent a year in terms of actual numbers. The latest monthly figures are disturbing since they suggest that this goal is remote. Bank lending in June was at an all-time record of £6.1 billion, the boom in mortgage credit continues and M3 growth over the last year is still at 20 per cent. Since there is some short-term inertia in credit trends, it will take several months and a few additional interest rate rises before the pace of economic expansion does moderate significantly. The Government will be lucky if, after virtually three years of monetary excess, the inflation rate can be easily held near to the 5 per cent figure. A hard landing, with an awkward phase of economic adjustment, coming at an inconvenient stage in the electoral cycle, is more probable than a smooth touchdown.

Lawson's personal attitude towards the events of the last three years is a puzzle. In the early 1980s he was the most vocal 'monetarist' in the Government; in the mid-1980s he was its most deliberate pragmatist; but in a speech earlier this month he is said to have reiterated, apparently with a straight face, that 'inflation is pre-eminently a monetary phenomenon'.

It has been an extraordinary performance. A few months ago the right image for the Chancellor's intellectual evolution would have been a somersault, as he turned on its head the official orthodoxy of the Government's early years. But, if the latest shift in his statements is to be taken at face value, this would be greatly to underestimate his gymnastic abilities. A more appropriate image now is the pirouette, as he swirls round trying to find a credible theoretical justification for the latest twist in the erratic course of macroeconomic policy. In the last three years he has effectively destroyed all that he stood for, in terms of the structure of policy, in the previous five. It is an impressive tribute to his skills of presentation that he is still regarded by the media, and the majority of Conservative MPs, as the most successful Chancellor since the war and, by the Prime Minister, as 'quite brilliant' in his recent conduct of policy.

On Teenage Scribblers and Computerized Sheep

From an article 'Scribblers in the stocks' in The Times *of 27 September 1988.*

This article was another polemic, but I think it made some useful points. In particular, it asked why so many economists could be wrong so often in more or less the same way. The answer was, at least in part, that 'the computerized sheep' shared the same 'framework of thought and the model which incorporates it'. The argument is developed below on pp. 191–4 in an article on 'The importance of money in macroeconomic forecasting – part 2', based on an article in The Spectator *of 11 March 1989, and it harks back to the article 'A lesson from the Treasury on how to be precisely wrong' in* The Times *of 28 August 1975.*

It has become fashionable to sneer at Mr Lawson and the Treasury. Why, it is asked, did the Government fail to anticipate the excessive domestic demand and a widening payments deficit? Lawson, who was even more self-confident than usual about the economy earlier this year, has been censured for pushing his luck too far by cutting taxes in the middle of a consumer boom. Meanwhile the Treasury, whose Budget-time expectation of a slowdown in the economy was largely responsible for the Chancellor's complacency, has been criticized for bad forecasting.

Some of the most articulate critics have been City economists whose attacks have been given a sharper edge by Lawson's description of them two months ago as publicity-seeking 'teenage scribblers'. As the Government's own economic forecast for 1988 has proved increasingly inaccurate, the City scribblers have hit back by condemning official policy as irresponsible. The press has portrayed the argument between Lawson and the analysts as a high-grade Punch and Judy show: the analysts bash him with the July trade figures and the August money supply numbers. In reply, Lawson biffs the analysts, apparently on the grounds that they have not grown up.

The histrionics are great fun, but the press reporting is misleading in its assumption that the Chancellor has been wrong and the City scribblers right. The truth is that the City has been slightly more wrong than the Treasury in its appraisal of the economy this year. Although Lawson has every reason to be embarrassed about the forecasts he made in the Budget, the scribblers, instead of mocking the official errors, ought to be apologizing for theirs.

The facts are easy to check. In addition to preparing its own forecasts, the Treasury compiles a survey of independent forecasts, of which nine come from the City. An average of these nine can be regarded as the 'City consensus'. The forecast given by this consensus in March can readily be compared with the Treasury's own much derided figures. The Treasury view was that 1988 would see 3 per cent growth in gross domestic product, a 4 per cent rise in the retail price index in the year to the fourth quarter, and a current account deficit of £4 billion. In less than three months it had become clear that this forecast was grossly wrong. A more plausible assessment now is that growth will be 4 to $4^1/2$ per cent, while inflation will reach 6 to $6^1/2$ per cent and the current account deficit may exceed £12 billion.

The analysts could justifiably jeer if their forecasts for these three key variables had been higher. In fact, the City consensus in March was that growth would be 2.7 per cent, inflation 3.8 per cent and the current account deficit £4.1 billion. So, on growth and inflation, the City was lower (and therefore more wrong) than the Treasury, while on the balance of payments the City and the Treasury were practically identical. The City scribblers may not be able to resist the temptation to trade insults with a Chancellor who has made a fool of himself, but they have no right to ridicule the Treasury's forecasting ability.

Of course, this indictment of the City's forecasting record would be less compelling if there had been a wide dispersion of views in the nine forecasts collected by the Treasury. At least one or two brave souls might then have come close to forecasting, in broad terms, what was going to happen to the economy. Sadly all the nine forecasts were closely bunched together and were therefore equally inaccurate. (This is not to say that all City forecasts were unsatisfactory. There may have been others, not included in the nine, which were reasonably correct.)

Indeed, the gap between the City consensus and the likely out-turn is far greater than the gap between the nine separate forecasts. A cynic new to the forecasting game, unaware of the great skill and care with which City analysts carry out their work, their undoubted intellectual courage and the enormous salaries which reward their efforts, might conclude that they are much better at copying each other than at predicting the future course of the economy.

These remarks may seem snide and unnecessary. But there is an important point at issue.

The so-called 'debate' between Mr Lawson and his City critics hides the failure of virtually the entire British economics profession to foresee, at a sufficiently early stage, how strong the 1988 boom would be. Since policy is driven by forecasts, this failure is largely responsible for the difficult problems of financial adjustment Britain now faces. The tendency of forecasters to imitate one another, rather than to say what they really think, can be blamed for a current account payments deficit exceeding 3 per cent of GDP and a worrying rise in inflation.

Of course, there are more charitable explanations for the lack of differentiation between forecasts than economists' propensity, when asked about the future, to transform themselves into computerized sheep. It may be that the Treasury and the various City firms share the same underlying framework of thought so fully that, by genuinely independent processes of reasoning, they arrive at broadly identical and equally wrong forecasts. It may be, in other words, that the problem does not arise because the modellers are copy-cats, but because they have the same inadequate model.

If so, the important task now is to find out what is wrong with the existing shared framework of thought and with the model which incorporates it, and then to propose a superior method of analysing the economy. Silly name-calling, from either the Chancellor or his critics, is not the way forward.

The Lawson Boom: Not Quite as Bad as the Barber Boom

From an article 'Will the Lawson boom cause as much inflation as the Barber boom?' in Economic Affairs, *April/May 1989.*

The figures for broad money growth were remarkably similar in the Barber and Lawson booms. However, the Lawson boom caused much less inflation. There were a number of reasons for the contrast, which I discussed in this article. The conclusion of the article, that 13 per cent base rates 'will cause a recession if they continue for very long', was – I now think – not quite right. In fact, base rates had to reach 15 per cent before the economy's slowdown became incontrovertible.

Over the last three years monetary growth has been extremely fast. The rapid expansion of the money supply reflects a deliberate decision in mid-1985 by the Chancellor of the Exchequer, Mr Lawson, to downgrade broad money in economic policy decisions. The result has been a vigorous and well-defined boom in economic activity, which has obvious parallels with a previous boom in the early 1970s when Mr (now Lord) Barber was Chancellor. Will the Lawson boom be followed by an upturn in inflation similar to that after the Barber boom? Is the monetary overhang today as dangerous as it was in the mid-1970s?

Table 7.1   A comparison of monetary growth in the Barber and Lawson booms

Ratio of broad money to gross domestic product		
Broad money on M3 definition (£b[1])	GDP, on expenditure basis, at current market prices (£b[2])	Ratio of broad money to GDP
The Barber boom		
1970 4th qt. 18.2	54.1	0.336
1973 4th qt. 33.6	76.2	0.441
The Lawson boom		
1985 2nd qt. 118.0	351.3	0.336
1988 2nd qt. 201.2	448.2	0.449

Growth rates of broad money and money GDP	
Average annual increase in broad money, on M3 definition (%)	Average annual increase in money GDP, expenditure basis (%)
Three years to 4th qt. 1973 22.6	12.1
Three years to 2nd qt. 1988 19.5	8.5

Notes
[1] The figures in 1970 and 1973 have been adjusted upwards by a factor of 1.0976 to make them comparable with those in 1985 and 1988. The upward adjustment reflects a reclassification in the fourth quarter of 1981. Other reclassifications have been ignored.
[2] At an annualized rate.

Source: Economic Trends, various issues

Some key facts are set out in Table 7.1. There are uncanny resemblances between the two periods. The rise in the ratio of broad money, on the M3 definition, to gross domestic product was almost the same in the three years to end-1973 as it was in the three years to mid-1988, while the ratio of broad money to GDP was only a touch higher in mid-1988 than at end-1973. The annual growth rates of both broad money and money GDP were rather lower, by about 3 per cent and $3^1/_2$ per cent, respectively, in the second episode than in the first, but the difference in growth rates was small compared to their absolute level. In fact, the impression conveyed by Table 7.1 is that the monetary indiscretions of the Lawson boom have been remarkably similar to those of the Barber boom.

If the two booms really are similar, there is a frightening message for future inflation rates. It is clear in retrospect that at the end of 1973 the economy had grossly excessive liquidity and that this excess liquidity could be eliminated only by a large increase in the price level. In the three years to end-1976 the price level rose by 70 per cent, which – in conjunction with a sharp deceleration in monetary growth – brought the ratio of broad money to GDP down to 0.321. This was roughly the same as it had been six years earlier before the Barber boom began. If an analogous sequence of events were now to unfold, inflation rates of almost 20 per cent would be needed in 1989, 1990 and 1991 to absorb the surplus liquidity in the economy. Is that possible? Could the situation really be as bad as that?

Inspection of monetary data is very important. It is a truism that the behaviour of all economic agents, including individuals, companies and the long-term savings institutions, is profoundly influenced by their financial circumstances. In this context the state of anyone's bank balance is obviously crucial. But the link between money and other economic variables is not mechanical. The monetary acceleration since mid-1985 has already caused an increase in inflation, and it will remain a source of inflationary pressure for several years to come. But judgement and analysis are needed to temper inflation forecasts based on crude extrapolations of recent M3 figures.

There are three uncontroversial points which suggest that recent M3 growth rates will not be as inflationary in the next three years as the M3 growth rates of the Barber boom were in the mid-1970s. The first is that the underlying growth rate of the economy is somewhat more now than it was then. Although a precise estimate is difficult, it seems plausible that the trend growth in productive potential is now about 3 per cent to $3^1/_2$ per cent a year, whereas in the mid-1970s it was about 1 per cent a year. Monetary growth can therefore be 2 per cent to $2^1/_2$ per cent a year higher without inflationary consequences.

Secondly, deregulation and innovation in the financial system has made it more attractive to hold money assets. For example, as lending restrictions have been removed, competition between banks has intensified and a larger number of banks pay interest on a wider range of deposits. The impact of financial innovation in raising the demand to hold money is difficult to assess exactly, but a reasonable 'guesstimate' is that in the early 1980s it had the effect of raising the desired ratio of money to GDP by about 3 per cent or 4 per cent a year. In the mid-1980s an even higher figure may be sensible, because of a special development in the building society movement. As the supply of short-dated government securities diminished, the building societies switched their liquidity from gilts to bank deposits. In mid-1985 the building societies held £3,507 million deposits with the monetary sector and £991 million certificates of deposit (CDs); in mid-1988 their deposits with the monetary sector were £9,914 million and their CDs £7,582 million. This change in the societies' portfolio preferences has no obvious implications for spending behaviour, but it has accounted for over 15 per cent of the increase in M3 in the three-year period. When allowance is made for it, the desired ratio of money to GDP may have been rising by about 6 per cent a year during the Lawson boom. Of course, financial innovation was also at work in the Barber boom and the mid-1970s, but it does not seem to have been so powerful.

Finally, people and companies are more willing to hold their wealth in monetary form because of a more favourable macroeconomic environment than ten or 15 years ago. Not only does a higher proportion of bank deposits pay interest, but also real interest rates are higher and inflation expectations lower. However, the importance of this influence depends very much on the level of interest rates prevailing at the time. It is not obvious that there has been any significant structural change here compared with mid-1985. If clearing bank base rates were less than the 13 per cent figure now prevailing, economic agents' preparedness to hold bank deposits would be reduced.

In summary, underlying output growth and financial innovation might in recent years have permitted 9 per cent or 10 per cent a year growth in broad money without inflationary consequences. Broad money growth of 13 per cent or 14 per cent would therefore have been consistent with the actual inflation rate of 4 per cent or 5 per cent. Since the growth rate of broad money was in fact 19^1/$_2$ per cent, excess money was being injected into the economy at a rate of about 5 per cent a year. This boost to liquidity, and the consequent extremely healthy condition of personal and corporate balance sheets, was one of the driving forces – indeed, arguably the key driving force – behind the Lawson boom.

The monetary impulse to higher spending was most potent in the first half of 1988, because the cut in interest rates encouraged people to move out of interest-bearing financial assets (such as bank deposits) into real assets (such as houses and consumer durables). It was logical that the Lawson boom should reach its crescendo at about the same time and that the balance of payments should, in the standard cyclical manner, plunge heavily into deficit shortly afterwards. In mid-1988 the ratio of broad money to GDP was probably about 15 per cent to 20 per cent higher than sustainable in the long run. Since then a very large increase in interest rates has neutralized, at least temporarily, the inflationary threat posed by the excess liquidity.

But the situation is precarious. One of the reasons that the Lawson boom has not led to more inflation is that domestic demand has been diverted overseas by a high exchange rate. The balance of payments, rather than the inflation rate, has acted as the main shock absorber for excess expenditure. Heavy capital inflows, particularly through the banking system, are financing a current account deficit of more than 3 per cent of GDP. These inflows, like the willingness of money-holders to keep surplus balances idle, rely on the extremely high level of interest rates now in force.

But clearing bank base rates of 13 per cent will cause a recession if they continue for very long. A safe conclusion is that 10 per cent inflation, which would be a fitting retribution for the monetary excesses of the Lawson boom, can be avoided only by two to three years of beneath-trend output growth. The monetary legacy of the Lawson boom is less traumatic than that of the Barber boom. But who would have thought three years ago, when the present Conservative Government was so proud of its financial record, that it would so soon face problems of cyclical adjustment similar in character to those of the mid-1970s?

On Property Speculation and Business Entrepreneurship

From an article 'Boxed in by the boom' in The Times *of 25 October 1988.*

This article is also self-explanatory, but it was undoubtedly influenced by my involvement as an outside investor in a small business being started up by some friends. The success of the business depended less on their basic competence than on their ability to time correctly decisions to borrow and buy property. This was the microeconomic result of Mr Lawson's macroeconomic mismanagement.

Most British companies nowadays are involved in two distinct activities. The first is creating a product or service and selling it to their customers. The second is amateur property speculation.

This may seem a startling remark, but a little reflection shows how important property is to corporate success in modern Britain. A lively market in commercial and industrial property gives all companies the option to own their premises instead of renting, while a highly competitive banking system enables them to finance property acquisition by borrowing rather than from the owners' equity. Land and buildings are often worth much more than stock, machinery and goodwill. Decisions about property and its financing can therefore have a greater influence on profitability than decisions about technology and marketing. Managements with a naive focus on their own business can be bamboozled by managements with a greater awareness of property opportunities. A recent illustration is British Aerospace's coup in obtaining large chunks of under-valued land with its purchases of Royal Ordnance and the Rover Group. But there are countless earlier examples. In the 1960s and early 1970s the City pages were full of stories about easy fortunes made from asset-stripping.

Property matters less to big business than to small, new businesses. Typically, a small company starts up with a loan from a local bank manager secured against either the premises or the businessman's own house. The interest on the loan is usually a high proportion of costs and may sometimes be the largest single expense. In extreme but not uncommon cases the viability of the business depends only marginally on the ability to make and sell something. Far more crucial is the relationship between interest rates and the rate of increase in property prices, including house price inflation.

The argument should not be pressed too far. It is not valid at all times and in all places. If Britain had been better governed over the last 40 years it would not be of much relevance here. The pivotal role of property management in contemporary business success is not inevitable, but the result of inflation, volatile interest rates and erratic financial policies. Inflation is a nuisance because it is accompanied by high nominal interest rates, needed to compensate savers for the fall in the value of money. High interest rates bite into cash flow and can cripple new businesses, which nearly always have an initial period of liquidity strain.

True enough, the interest charges are offset by the increase in the value of any land and buildings which the business owns. Perhaps, in an ideal world, it ought not to be necessary to pay interest in full. Since both the nominal interest rate and the appreciation of property values reflect general inflation, the inflation component in both cancel out and can be ignored. But in the rough and tumble of everyday business life, banks are not so understanding. They still adhere to the primitive belief that customers ought to repay loans, including accumulated interest. Their difficulty, and also the borrowers', is to know how to assess the true cost of a loan. Is it best measured by the excess of interest rates over the increase in the retail price index, or over the increase in property prices generally, or over the increase in the value of the specific loan and buildings which represent collateral? Everyone agrees that inflation reduces the real burden of any given level of nominal interest rates. But how much?

These uncertainties help to explain why interest rate volatility is such a curse. Over the last 11 years clearing bank base rates have varied between 5 per cent and 17 per cent. No one knows with any confidence, whether interest rates 12 months from now will be 3 per cent more or less than they are today. Since the rate of property price appreciation is high when interest rates are low, and vice versa, it is critical to the small businessman when he establishes his company. An investor in, say, a restaurant or hotel at a favourable point in the property cycle (for example, 1970 or 1981), is far more likely to make money than someone who instead chose an unlucky moment (1973 or 1979).

Management skill benefits society. If industry makes more high-quality products and markets them successfully, national output increases. By contrast, astuteness in predicting interest rates adds little or nothing to economic welfare. It is, in economists' jargon, a zero-sum game. It may yield positive returns to certain individuals (those who invested in 1970 or 1981), but these must be offset by negative returns to others (those who invested in 1973 or 1979). Because of macroeconomic turbulence, a fixation with the property market and interest rate gyrations has become part of the British way of life. A return to price stability and an associated move in interest rates to lower and more settled levels are needed if genuine entrepreneurship is to replace small-time property speculation.

It is here that we see the connection between three well-known Thatcherite themes: the case for a sound currency, the virtues of effort and thrift, and the enthusiasm for small business. It is here also that we see just how damaging that Lawson boom has been to the Conservatives' long-term economic programme. The wild increase in London office prices in 1986 and 1987, the 40 per cent surge in house prices nationally over the last 18 months and the recent $4^1/2$ per cent jump in interest rates will all reinforce the widely-held belief that correct timing in the property market is essential to business success. The eradication of the boom–bust mentality was central to the present Government's original agenda. But the excesses of the last three years have obliged businessmen once again to worry more about the stop–go cycle and less about the really important tasks of managing, producing and selling.

8. Some initial theorizing

In 1989 I wrote a pamphlet, entitled *Monetarism Lost*, for the Centre for Policy Studies. It gave a narrative account of how and why the monetarist approach to economic management had been dropped in 1985, and attributed the subsequent boom to excessive monetary growth. It was very thin on theory. In his review of the pamphlet in the *Financial Times* (on 6 June 1989) Mr Samuel Brittan nevertheless remarked: 'Tim Congdon deserves credit for spotting the present UK inflationary boom long before most others, at least partly for the right reasons. The difficulty of presenting him with his Oscar is that he insists on using the award ceremony to promulgate his general system, which is more dubious.' I assume Mr Brittan's reference to a 'general system' may have been prompted by some of my other writings, although I am not sure which ones. In this chapter I give an attempt to set out, in loosely theoretical terms, how I think the economy works. The main paper is based on a lecture on 'Money' I gave in 1988 at the invitation of the Economic Research Council, and published in 1990 in a book, *Reflections on Money*, edited by Professor David Llewellyn.

It is indeed possible – as Mr Brittan implies – that I was right about the Lawson boom because of a fluke. However, I would like to think that my accurate prognosis reflected a good analytical understanding of how the economy works. If it were impossible to identify in general terms what had gone wrong with official policy in these years, there would be little hope of avoiding similar mistakes in the future. There should be some mileage in trying to extract wider lessons from recent experience. I believe that my approach to analysing the British economy in the 1970s and 1980s, with its strong emphasis on credit and broad money, was better than the alternatives.

The focus of recent debates has been the importance of monetary policy for the economy's behaviour. There are two main schools of thought, although each has several variants. According to the first ('monetarist'), the level of spending in the economy is determined mainly by monetary variables and, usually, by a particular monetary aggregate. I tend to be categorized as a 'monetarist' in public debate and have been unable to avoid this practice in previous chapters. But, in fact, this label is misleading and a nuisance. I would like the sort of monetarist who thinks that money GDP is determined by M0 (or M3 or M4) to be called a 'naive monetarist' and his sort of analysis 'naive monetarism'. According to the second school of thought ('Keynesian'), the level of spending is determined by a number of variables (such as tax rates, world trade and interest rates), whose relative importance is best assessed by carrying out statistical tests on past data. (In Britain this 'Keynesianism' has become so diluted from the original Keynes that it might as well be called 'pragmatic' or 'pragmatic Keynesian'.)

The naive monetarist approach is very simple in structure. It is judged – from econometric estimation – that one monetary aggregate (M0, M1, non-interest-bearing M1 or whatever) has a particularly reliable link with expenditure and incomes. So, if economists track this aggregate, they should have a good idea of what is happening to the economy now, and what will happen in the future. The approach includes among its supporters Professor Patrick Minford of Liverpool University (who is keen on M0), Sir Alan Walters (who is also keen on M0, but admires M1 as well) and Professor Gordon Pepper (who sometimes prefers narrow money to broad money). Typically, monetarist economists of this kind do not feel obliged to produce forecasts of the various components of demand, such as consumption and investment, because they are doubtful that enough is understood to make sensible statements about the detailed national income arithmetic.

By contrast, Keynesian/pragmatic analysis can become quite complicated. Spending is split into various categories, such as consumption, investment, stockbuilding, exports and imports, and government spending. The key is to identify the major influences on these various categories of expenditure. These influences are called 'exogenous variables' and can be quite various. Once econometric tests have established which exogenous variables have been most important in the past, their role is incorporated into a set of equations (known as 'expenditure equations'). Usually econometric work is unable to identify a strong link between any monetary aggregate and any category of spending. The role of money in the economy comes to be regarded as incidental and is sometimes dismissed as of no importance. The National Institute of Economic and Social Research exemplifies this point of view most completely, although there are traces of it in a number of City analysts, including, for instance, Mr Gavyn Davies of Goldman Sachs, who often pours scorn on the Ms.

My approach is different from that of both naive monetarism and pragmatic Keynesianism. The starting-point of my analysis is that money is of great importance to the economy, which sets me apart from the Keynesians. But unlike the naive monetarists I try to explain how the quantity of money is determined, and I agree with the Keynesians about the need to have expenditure equations determining consumption, investment and so on. Moreover, I am not happy to use a monetary aggregate because it has had a good relationship with national income in the past. The trouble here is that the monetary aggregate may be determined by money national income, rather than national income by the monetary aggregate. For me it is essential also to look at the balance sheets of particular agents in the economy – that is, individuals, companies, financial institutions and so on. Sharp changes in monetary growth and asset prices can disturb balance sheets, and provoke major changes in behaviour. In this context the only relevant definition of money is a broad measure, which includes all deposits. I therefore pay great attention to the growth of credit, because it is this which determines the growth of broad money. The structure of my approach to macroeconomic analysis is contrasted to that of the naive monetarists and pragmatic Keynesians in Figs 8.1–8.3.

My approach is certainly not 'monetarist' in the strict Chicago sense of the term. It does not see the quantity of money as being determined by some multiple of the banks' cash reserves and it identifies monetary disequilibrium as a key motive force behind macroeconomic fluctuations. It might be better seen as harking back to the trade cycle literature before the development of Keynesian macroeconomics in the 1950s and 1960s, even perhaps to the Banking School of the early 19th century. (There was a debate between the Banking and Currency Schools about how best to conduct monetary policy.)

Figure 8.1   Structure of naive monetarist model

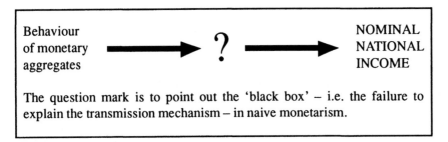

Figure 8.2   Structure of standard Keynesian/pragmatic model

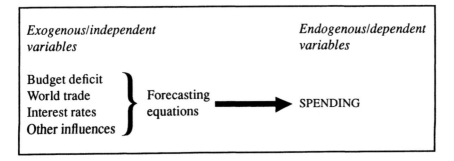

Figure 8.3   An alternative approach: how credit, money and balance sheets affect economic activity

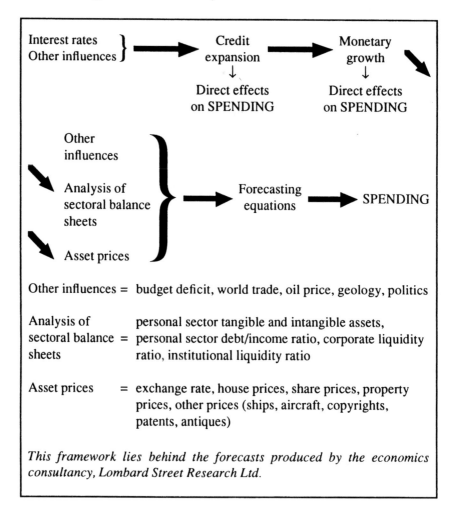

Other influences = budget deficit, world trade, oil price, geology, politics

Analysis of
sectoral balance = personal sector tangible and intangible assets, personal sector debt/income ratio, corporate liquidity
sheets   ratio, institutional liquidity ratio

Asset prices   = exchange rate, house prices, share prices, property prices, other prices (ships, aircraft, copyrights, patents, antiques)

This framework lies behind the forecasts produced by the economics consultancy, Lombard Street Research Ltd.

Further, an argument could be made that my line of thought is closer to Keynes than Keynes is to the so-called 'Keynesians' today.

Although I am sceptical about large-scale econometric models, I decided in 1986 that I would have to develop one. Participants in the public debate are hallucinated by their computer power, econometric jargon and apparent precision into believing that forecasts from such models have a stronger claim to be taken seriously than other kinds of statement about the economy. For my so-called 'monetarist' warnings to be given any credence, I felt that I also had to produce a large-scale macroeconomic forecast. I was very fortunate that Dr Peter Warburton (now Chief Economist at Robert Fleming) joined my economics team at L. Messel & Co. and later Shearson Lehman. (L. Messel & Co. was taken over by Shearson and lost its identity in 1987.)

Dr Warburton had considerable econometric experience in building the London Business School model in the late 1970s and early 1980s. With his help, I prepared macroeconomic forecasts from October 1986 to June 1988. I am glad to say that we produced the most accurate forecasts of the British economy for both 1987 and 1988. After leaving Shearson Lehman, I established in 1989 a small economic forecasting consultancy, Lombard Street Research Ltd, with help from Gerrard & National. Its forecast of the British economy for 1990 was also excellent and came close to being the most accurate available.

The other piece reprinted here, 'The importance of money in macroeconomic forecasting – part 2', explains – in a journalistic way – why the Treasury misled Mr. Lawson with its economic forecasts in the late 1980s, just as it had misled Mr. Barber in the early 1970s.

Credit, Broad Money and Economic Activity

Reprinted from a paper, 'Credit, broad money and the economy', published in D. Llewellyn (ed.) Reflections on Money *(London: Macmillan), 1990, with minor amendments.*

The key point of this paper is that macroeconomic analysis cannot proceed sensibly without a discussion of monetary equilibrium. (I would guess that 90 per cent of practising British macroeconomists hardly ever think about 'monetary equilibrium'. Many of them would not even know what is meant by the phrase.) Moreover, the attainment of monetary equilibrium is only interesting if the monetary concept under consideration is broad money. In a modern economy the growth of broad money is determined by the growth of bank credit.

British macroeconomics is in a mess. There is much confusion about how demand, output and inflation are determined, with economists constantly squabbling among themselves about the relative importance of different influences. The disputes are not of merely academic and theoretical interest. The lack of a consensus about 'how the economy really works' was largely responsible for the failure of both official and private forecasters to see that the financial excesses of 1987 and 1988 would lead to the inflation and balance-of-payments problems of 1989 and 1990. This failure also had vital implications for financial markets. The credit and monetary excesses had to be countered by an increase in interest rates in late 1988 which was a shock in its scale and timing, and interest rates have subsequently had to stay higher for longer than anyone expected. The focus of these debates has been the importance of monetary policy for the economy's behaviour. One source of disagreement has been the lack of clarity about the precise meaning of credit and money, and about their implications for the economy.

The objective of the present paper is to clarify and resolve some of the key issues. It has two main themes. The first is that, in modern circumstances, the growth of money is driven by the growth of credit. Money and credit are nevertheless distinct and separate categories, and should not be confused. The second is that, in any economy, the amount of money has a strong and definite link with the amount of spending. As a result, when the amount of money changes sharply, there are profound short-run effects on the way people and companies behave, and so on the level of economic activity. In the long run, however, money cannot alter the economy's ability to produce real output, and changes in the quantity of money mainly affect the price level.

Professor Goodhart has noted that historically money has taken a great variety of exotic forms, including such objects as red feathers and cowrie shells.[1] The evolution of money is a fascinating and important subject, and one of its main lessons needs to be strongly emphasized. This is that in the past societies have used such a diverse range of things as 'money' that grand generalizations in monetary economics should be treated with suspicion. The discussion here will be confined to the circumstances of a modern economy with banks and a central bank. The aim will be to provide an account (a 'special theory') of credit and money that is valid in contemporary market-based industrial economies. The same story could not be told in a pre-modern economy without banks or central banks; nor would it be alto-gether convincing today in a poor developing country or in a command economy like the former Soviet Union's; and it might be totally misleading as a description of the operation of high-tech economies in the future.

Money is a liability of the financial system

The first point to highlight in a definition of money is that money has to be recognized as such by large numbers of people. Esoteric objects such as Chinese porcelain vases or Byzantine icons may be 'worth a lot of money', but they are not money as such. They could not be used to buy groceries from a corner shop or timber from a builders' merchant. Instead money comprises a fairly limited range of assets which can be used to pay for goods and services everywhere within a particular monetary area.

There is another key dimension to the definition of money. Goodhart has argued that money consists of 'those assets that represent a means of payment'.[2] The remark might seem straightforward enough, but he added a subtle and vital amplification. This was to say that one characteristic of such assets was that their transfer 'completes a transaction'. By so doing, Professor Goodhart excluded credit facilities, which allow a transaction to take place but still leave a debt to be settled.

It is obvious that notes and coin are money under this definition. If payments are made with notes and coin, purchases are completed when they are handed over to the vendor. The purchaser has the goods, the vendor has the money and nothing remains to be done. Again, if payments are made by cheque against bank deposits, the purchaser has the goods, the vendor has the cheque, the purchaser's bank deposit is debited by a particular amount, the vendor is credited by the same amount, and nothing remains to be done. But, if payments are made by cheque against a loan facility, the purchaser has the goods, the vendor has the cheque, the purchaser's loan account is debited by a particular amount, the vendor is credited by the same amount *and the purchaser has to repay the bank at some future date*. In this final example, the transaction is not completed even when the cheque has been cleared. It follows that notes, coin and bank deposits are money, but loan facilities are not. Similarly, proofs of creditworthiness (such as credit cards) may greatly reduce the inconvenience of buying and selling, but they are not money. We have here a very sharp distinction between credit facilities and money assets. There is no need for confusion.

Indeed, it is sufficient for most purposes to think of money as constituted by notes, coin and deposits. The issue can be complicated by devising different definitions of money, each of which includes a specific range of monetary assets. Thus, we can think of an aggregate which consists of only notes and coin, and call it M0. Or we can think of another which includes notes, coin and deposits (so-called 'sight deposits') which can be spent without giving advance notice to a bank, and call it M1. In fact, in the UK today there are six Ms, ranging from M0 to M5. The higher is the number attached to an M, the greater is the range of money assets included and the larger is the money supply concept under consideration. M0 and M1 are commonly called the 'narrow' definitions; M2 is an intermediate measure, usually described as consisting of transactions balances; and M3, M4 and M5 are measures of 'broad money'. But the basic idea – that money consists of notes, coin and deposits, and the money supply may be defined as some mix of these ingredients – is straightforward.

It is clear that notes, coin and deposits share the characteristic that they can be used to pay for goods, services and assets. But, in a modern economy, they also have something else in common. This is that they are liabilities of financial institutions, particularly the banks. Thus, notes are issued by, and are a liability of, the Bank of England. Similarly, if money is held in a bank deposit, the bank owes money to the depositor and must follow instructions with regard to payments. The bank deposits are evidently the banks' liabilities. Finally, since it is increasingly possible nowadays to write cheques against building society deposits, they are beginning to resemble bank deposits and can properly be regarded as money. But they also are liabilities, this time of the building societies.

It may seem unnecessary to labour the point that nowadays all forms of money are liabilities of financial organizations. But there is an important reason for emphasizing it. By so doing, we are alerted to the uniqueness of the monetary system in a modern economy. In earlier times (such as the eras of red feathers and cowrie shells), money was not a liability of financial systems, but a commodity. In other words, money had value not because a particular bank recognized an obligation to its depositors or holders of its notes, but because the commodity had intrinsic worth. The realization that money could perform its functions without being a specific commodity was one of the key institutional innovations which made possible the emergence of advanced industrial economies.

Despite the benefits of modern monetary arrangements, nostalgia for commodity money is widespread and deeply rooted. It takes two particularly notable forms. First, sceptics of governments' ability to manage 'paper money' yearn for the financial stability commonly, although perhaps mistakenly, attributed to the gold standard. Secondly, some economists (including such well-known monetarists as Milton Friedman and Karl Brunner) continue to theorize about economies with commodity money, apparently unaware that this approach is not fully applicable to economies with paper money. There is not enough space here to explain the difficulties to which this confusion gives rise. It is sufficient to say that many of the most heated debates in monetary economics stem from a lack of clarity about whether propositions relate to commodity-money or paper-money economies.[3] The discussion in the rest of this chapter relates to a modern economy in which money is explicitly a liability of financial institutions.

A key distinction

Before we discuss the creation of money, one more idea needs to be developed. Although notes, coin and bank deposits are all money, a sharp distinction should be drawn between two forms that they take. Certain kinds of money are legal tender and must be accepted in law as a means of payment. In the UK today, these are represented by coins (a liability of the Royal Mint) and notes (a liability of the Bank of England). But there are other kinds of money which are not legal tender, and it is not an offence to refuse payment in them.

Thus, I am fully within my rights to turn down someone's cheque. The writer of the cheque has no legal redress against me or against his bank. In effect, when I refuse a cheque I am indicating two things. First, I am not convinced that the writer of the cheque has enough legal tender in his bank account to honour the cheque and, secondly, if he does not in fact have enough legal tender, I am not prepared to hold a claim on the bank concerned. In some circumstances – for example, when a cheque is drawn on a bogus bank without capital or assets – I would be a fool to accept a cheque instead of legal tender. In the UK today we can, for virtually all practical purposes, regard notes and coin as legal tender, while other forms of money (bank deposits, building society deposits) are not.[4]

The last two paragraphs have a critical implication for the behaviour of interest rates. When I write a cheque, I am giving someone a mere scrap of paper. Why does this piece of paper have any value? The answer is that it is an instruction to my bank to pay the person or company named a sum in legal tender. An obvious corollary is that the bank could not conduct its business unless it held legal tender among its assets. It is true that nowadays the practice of modern banking is so sophisticated that most cheques are cleared by the cancellation of debits and credits between the banks themselves. Banks do not need to make large and cumbersome payments in notes and coin either to each other or to their customers. Nevertheless, they must have the ultimate ability to make payments in legal tender.

The imperative need for banks to meet demands on them in notes and coin is the origin of the Bank of England's power to determine interest rates. The Bank is the monopoly issuer of legal tender notes. It can therefore fix the interest rate at which these notes are borrowed and lent.[5] Since bank deposits are expressed in terms of legal tender and should be fully substitutable with them, the Bank of England's interest rate (variously described as 'Bank rate', 'Minimum Lending Rate', 'seven-day dealing rate' and so on over the years) is the key interest rate in the monetary system. Since there is no other issuer of legal tender, there is no other institution which can dispute the Bank's sway over interest rates.

This conclusion is of great significance. The operation of monetary policy has been a constant topic of debate in the UK in recent years, with uncertainty about how interest rates are set being a leading source of contention. There is no need for this uncertainty. Although there are a number of details to fill in, the essential message of our argument is plain and should be uncontroversial. In a modern economy interest rates are decided by the central bank. The power to determine interest rates is derived from the central bank's position as the monopoly supplier of legal tender. Its influence over interest rates is not based on convention and it does not survive because of the commercial banks' inertia.[6] Moreover, in principle, the central bank does not have to pay the slightest attention to 'market views'. It is true that, in the real world, central bankers are not known for intellectual iconoclasm and therefore try to respect the market consensus about where interest rates should be. But it is also true that there is nothing logically inevitable about this interplay of ideas between the markets and the authorities.[7]

Money is created by credit

The nature of money in a modern economy – that it is a liability of financial organizations – has an important consequence. The liability side of any balance sheet can expand only if the assets side also expands. Banks and building societies increase their assets by making loans to their customers. It follows that money is created as a result of this extension of credit, while the rate of monetary growth is governed by the rate of credit expansion. In a pre-modern economy more money could come into being only if more of the monetary commodity was actually produced. Credit expansion, on the other hand, requires merely the simultaneous registration of debts (i.e. deposit liabilities) and assets (i.e. bank loans, mostly). The ability to create money by a stroke of a pen is strikingly efficient in cutting down on the quantity of resources needed to operate a system of payments. It constitutes a major advance in a society's productivity.

Unhappily, the negligible cost of producing money in a modern economy has the drawback that the issuers of money may be tempted to create an excessive amount. The result may be an inflationary process, with money losing value relative to other things and a consequent loss of confidence in the currency. This risk exists with privately owned banks, but it is subject to a tight constraint. Because their deposit liabilities are not legal tender, they must not allow their deposits to increase too much in relation to their holdings of legal tender. The quantity of bank deposits therefore cannot expand without limit if the quantity of legal tender is fixed or rising only gently over time. In fact, the historical record shows that bank deposits tend to be a fairly stable multiple of the amount of legal tender money over a period of five or ten years, although in the very long run institutional change can alter the relationship radically.

However, central banks are not subject to the same discipline as privately-owned banks. If they (or their political masters) decide to issue legal tender money in reckless and inflationary profusion, they are not breaking the law and neither do they (or their political masters) have to worry about going out of business. The dangers of an inflationary overissue of credit-based money have to be balanced against the benefits to society from the trifling cost of creating it. This dilemma, which is at the heart of the controversies over monetary policy in a modern economy, is neatly captured in the title of a pamphlet, *Proposals for an Economical and Secure Currency*, written by the famous British economist, David Ricardo, in 1816. Credit-based money is economical in terms of the resources required to make it. But it is potentially insecure in value if too much of it is made. The responsibility for prudent monetary management ultimately falls on the central bank, since – as we have seen – the quantity of bank deposits cannot run out of control if the quantity of legal tender is limited.

The key points of the discussion so far may now be summarized. In a modern economy money is a liability of the financial system, particularly of the banks. Because of this property the growth of money is governed by – indeed, for many practical purposes, can be equated with – the growth of bank credit. The central bank, notably the Bank of England in the UK, can try to control the quantity of money by varying the rate of interest. It has the power to determine interest rates because it is the monopoly supplier of legal tender. Privately-owned commercial banks, whose deposits are not legal tender, must kowtow to the Bank of England's interest rate decisions as they dare not risk being unable to convert their liabilities into legal tender.

We must emphasize, before we proceed to consider the impact of money on economic activity, that there is no muddle about the relationship between credit and money in our theory. To say that 'money is created by credit' is not equivalent to saying that 'money is credit'.

Money and monetary equilibrium

Once money has been brought into being by credit expansion, what is the relationship between money and economic activity? Before answering this question, it is best to digress briefly to consider the relationship between any set of objects in the economy. For example, the economy produces each year a certain number of apples and pears. Market forces – the laws of supply and demand – establish a price ratio between the two fruits which keeps their producers profitable and their consumers happy. We can call this ratio, which satisfies buyers and sellers so fully that they have no wish to change the situation, an equilibrium ratio.

If the quantity of apples rises or falls dramatically (because of the discovery of a new seed, a crop disease or whatever), but the quantity of pears stays the same, we would expect the relative price of apples and pears to change sharply. There will be another equilibrium price associated with the new supply conditions. But the passage from one equilibrium price to another may involve disturbance and uncertainty, and we would not expect the new equilibrium to be attained instantaneously.

We could tell the same story about the relative price of bricks and mortar, or coal and electricity, or any other combination of goods and services we care to think of. Associated with each equilibrium price are also particular quantities of each good. If the quantities change, it is likely that the relative price must also change. The essential point is that there is an equilibrium relationship, in terms of both price and quantity, between any good and all other goods. When this equilibrium holds, there is no tendency for people or companies to try to upset it. The same set of prices and quantities continues from one period to another. The economy is at rest. Only if there is an unexpected change (in demand or supply conditions) is the equilibrium broken.

It does not take much imagination to think of money as just another 'good'. Indeed, it is particularly easy to think of it in this way since the prices of all goods are expressed in terms of money. If market forces establish the relative price of apples and pears (i.e. the number of apples required to buy one pear, say, $1^1/_2$), they also establish the relative price of apples and money (say, 6p) and the relative price of pears and money (4p). The idea can be extended and generalized. If there is an equilibrium relationship between money and any particular good, there must also be an equilibrium relationship between money and national output as a whole. When this equilibrium holds, there is a particular level of national output (expressed in terms of £ billion, to put the idea in a UK context) and a particular amount of money (also in £ billion). Associated with the equilibrium is a price level of all goods and services taken together. In monetary equilibrium the demand for money (i.e. the quantity of notes, coin and bank deposits people want to hold) is equal to the money supply (i.e. the quantity of notes, coin and bank deposits actually in existence).

The concept of monetary equilibrium is not universally respected in the economics profession. Some of its critics think that it leads on too readily to the ambitious – and politically controversial – claim that the money supply and money national income tend to move together over time. In fact, any careful statement of the meaning of monetary equilibrium recognizes that there are many influences other than income on the amount of money people want to hold.

Three such influences deserve to be separately identified. The first comes under the general heading of 'payments technology'. The more efficiently payments can be completed, the less money is needed in relation to income. For example, a society in which credit cards are widely used is unlikely to need as much ready cash (in proportion to national income) as one where they are unknown. Also important in this context are such institutional characteristics of the economy as the frequency with which people receive wages and salaries, and the preparedness of companies to defer payments to each other (e.g. by extending trade credit).

Secondly, the rate of interest people and companies receive on money affects how much of it they wish to hold. Interest is not paid at all on notes and coin, and there are still some bank accounts (e.g. the traditional current account) which do not pay interest. But nowadays the majority of bank deposits and practically all building society deposits, pay interest. When we are considering people's desire to hold money relative to other assets, the key consideration is the rate of interest received on money *relative to the rate of return on these other assets*. When the general level of interest rates rises, people will want to cut down on their holdings of notes and coin because the relative attractiveness of these non-interest-bearing assets has declined. *But it is possible, indeed quite likely, that the return on interest-bearing bank deposits will have improved relative to the return on other assets, and that people will want to hold a higher ratio of interest-bearing money to income.* (We will return later to this point, which has an important bearing on the interest rate sensitivity of the economy.)

Thirdly, it is clear that the expected rate of inflation affects attitudes towards holding money, since every increase in the price level reduces the real value of money balances. A high rate of expected inflation makes it worthwhile to keep wealth in the form of goods and tangible assets rather than money.

In fact, there are so many potential influences that we cannot hope to be comprehensive in a short discussion. But we can give an adequate summary by saying that the desired ratio of money holdings to national income depends on three main considerations: transactions technology, the rate of interest (or, better, the interest rate differential between money and non-money assets) and inflation expectations. *If these influences are stable, it is reasonable to expect the desired ratio of money to income to be constant.* This is not a particularly bold or ideological statement. It is plain common sense to say that the number of apples people wish to consume depends on how tasty they are, how expensive they are compared to pears and oranges, and how quickly they rot if they are not stored properly. Our remarks on money run on very similar lines. We can analyse the demand for money in much the same way as we analyse the demand for other things.

Some implications of monetary equilibrium

Once we accept that, with certain conditions satisfied, the desired ratio of money to income is constant, some vital consequences follow. The most important is that an increase of x per cent in the money supply must be followed by an increase of x per cent in money incomes, and so in the nominal value of expenditure and output, if people are again to be happy with their money holdings. If national income does not rise by x per cent immediately, monetary equilibrium has been violated and people will change their behaviour until national income does rise by x per cent. We can think of an increase in national income as having two parts, an increase in output and an increase in the price level. If output is fixed, it is only the price level that can respond to the monetary injection. Indeed, monetary equilibrium requires that the x per cent increase in the money supply must be matched by an x per cent increase in the price level.

This does sound like a bold and ideological statement. It is undoubtedly very 'monetarist' in flavour. But our argument does not imply that, in any examination of actual data over a period of years, there will be a precise link between the money supply on the one hand and national income and the price level on the other. First, it has been emphasized that a precise link would be found *only if influences such as transactions technology, the rate of interest and inflation expectations were stable.* In practice, the character and strength of these influences are always changing, and their changes greatly complicate the relationship between money and prices. Secondly, the statement about money and prices is valid *only if monetary equilibrium has been established.* We have explained that people are always trying to move towards equilibrium. But in the real world the economy may not be in equilibrium. Just as it takes a period of microeconomic disturbance before the relative price of apples and pears adjusts to the discovery of a new seed or a crop disease, so there may be a period of macroeconomic disturbance before national income and the price level adjust to an increase in the money supply. During this interval of monetary disequilibrium, the connection between money and prices may be difficult to identify.

We will discuss monetary disequilibrium in the next section. But before doing so, some consequences of the argument in the last paragraph need to be emphasized. It is possible both to believe that inflation is always and everywhere essentially 'a monetary phenomenon' (in Friedman's words) and to expect to observe, in the real world, considerable fluctuations in the ratio of money to national income. In policy debates the behaviour of the ratio of money to national income – and of its inverse, the velocity of circulation of money – attracts considerable attention. Many critics of a monetary approach to inflation claim that changes in velocity demonstrate the irrelevance of the money supply. But we can see that these claims are exaggerated and misleading. Indeed, the relevance of the money supply stems, at root, from a belief that the demand for money – like the demand for fruit, building materials or energy – can be analysed with the standard tools of microeconomic theory. All the interesting conclusions about money and prices are derived from the concept of monetary equilibrium. To deny the validity of this concept is also to deny the premise of rationality which is basic to all economic analysis.

The concept of monetary disequilibrium
The notion of monetary disequilibrium is best understood in relation to that of monetary equilibrium. We have said that when an economy is in equilib-

rium all prices and quantities set in one period are repeated in the following and subsequent periods. In monetary equilibrium, the demand for money is equal to the money supply and the ratio between money and income is stable over time.

Monetary disequilibrium arises when the demand for money is not equal to the money supply and people are changing their behaviour in order to restore equilibrium. In more familiar language, the amount of money people are willing to hold differs from the amount of money actually in the economy. If people have excess money balances they will seek to reduce them by, for instance, buying goods and services or financial and real assets. Decisions about spending and saving are adjusted until a more settled position, with desired money holdings equal to actual money holdings, is restored.

This may sound strange and, indeed, some economists have questioned the legitimacy of the idea of 'monetary disequilibrium'. In all economies at all times there is a particular quantity of notes, coin and bank deposits in existence, and this quantity is held by people, companies and financial institutions. Surely, the sceptics might say, if the money is held at all, it is held willingly. There cannot be a mismatch between the demand for money and the money supply. In this view, the notion of 'monetary disequilibrium' is incoherent and an intellectual cul-de-sac.

But to dismiss monetary disequilibrium so abruptly is superficial. A modern economy is extremely complex, with millions of prices being fixed every day only to be changed tomorrow, the day after tomorrow and so on into the indefinite future. At any given moment, the price level – and many other characteristics of the economy (including, perhaps, transactions technology, the interest rate and the inflation rate) – may differ from the expectations prevailing when people last took action to adjust their money holdings. Moreover, very few economic agents know precisely how large their money holdings are at every instant in time. It is clear that actual money holdings can differ from the desired level. Monetary disequilibrium is a viable concept.[8]

With this idea accepted as part of our analytical tool-kit, we are almost ready to shift the discussion away from the abstract plane to a practical, real-world level. But there is one further argument to develop. Our interest is in how decisions motivated by the behaviour of credit and money impact on output, employment and prices. We are not particularly interested in the behaviour of credit and money for its own sake. A transfer of money from one bank account to another, or from notes to bank deposits, is tangential to our main concern, since these transactions are purely monetary and do not affect the 'real economy'. It follows that we need to identify and monitor a measure of the money supply which can make people reconsider their patterns of expenditure and saving. There is no point tracking a measure of money which is irrelevant to expenditure decisions. Which measure of money is relevant?

Narrow money vs broad money

The notion of monetary disequilibrium gives us the clue to making the right selection. In equilibrium the demand for money is equal to the money supply, monetary variables are neutral in their impact on the economy, and it does not make much difference which particular monetary variable (notes, coin or deposits; M0, M1, M3 or whatever) is the focus of attention. It is only in disequilibrium that money can disturb behaviour. Our question therefore becomes: 'For what measure (or measures) of money is there a possibility that the holdings people want to have differ significantly from the holdings that they actually do have?' This question could be rephrased more briefly as: 'What measures of money can behave in ways which surprise people and make them re-assess their decisions to consume and invest?'.

Notes and coin are the small change of the economy. If people find that their holdings of notes and coin are too small for their requirements (to buy goods and services, mostly), they go to their banks and convert part of their deposits into notes and coin. (If, on the other hand, notes and coin are too large, they leave them on deposit with their banks.) The adjustment occurs through purely monetary transactions, which we have already said are incidental to our main concerns. It is also obvious that no person or business organization allows holdings of notes and coin to affect any major decision about the purchase or sale of large assets (shares, factories, buildings). In an advanced industrial economy, with its massive accumulation of capital assets, these decisions about asset disposition are critical to the economy's behaviour.

We have said enough to reject notes and coin (M0) from consideration. M0 cannot surprise people and make them review their decisions to consume and invest. This narrow aggregate has one further characteristic which needs to be emphasized. We have said that when individuals find that their holdings of notes and coin are out of line with their requirements, they restore equilibrium by transfers into and out of bank deposits. That could leave the banks with too much or too little cash, which creates another problem of adjustment. The banks respond by approaching the Bank of England in order to persuade it either to absorb the excess cash or to eliminate the deficiency. The Bank, which of course issued the notes in the first place, accommodates the banks' requirements as a matter of routine. *A large number of individual decisions to increase (reduce) holdings of notes and coin do lead to an increase (reduction) in the aggregate amount of notes and coin in the whole economy. M0 adjusts to events in the economy; events in the economy do not adjust to M0.*

Nowadays, the contacts between the banking system and the Bank of England are so harmonious, and the Bank's operations are so finely tuned, that the amount of M0 in the economy rarely differs from the amount people want to hold. M0 is virtually always in or near to equilibrium. One consequence is that econometric work typically identifies a good, close-fitting statistical relationship between M0 and money national income.[9] *But this does not mean that M0 has a strong influence on decisions to spend or on the level of money national income. The direction of causation is rather from money national income to M0.*

Similar remarks apply to other measures of narrow money. M1 is larger than M0 because it includes bank accounts which can be spent without giving notice (sight deposits). But, again, if such bank accounts are too large or small, the natural response is to shift a sum of money to or from accounts which require notice (term deposits). An example is when an individual transfers funds from a current account at a clearing bank to a deposit account. This is clearly a financial transaction without implications for the real economy. Moreover, a host of such individual transfers will change the aggregate amount of M1. If M1 is too high or too low in relation to money national income, it is M1 which adjusts, not money national income.

We can summarize the last three paragraphs by saying that the various measures of narrow money are rarely in major disequilibrium, and even when they are, people and companies bring them back into equilibrium by purely monetary transactions. The narrow money aggregates – such as M0 and M1 – are therefore not the money supply concepts that we are seeking. Instead we need to look at broad money, notably M3 and M4.

Broad money and expenditure decisions
We have seen that when people and companies have too much or too little narrow money, a more appropriate holding is restored – at the level of the whole economy – by switching between different categories of deposit or between deposits and notes or coin. The position is quite different with broad money. Broad money (on the M3 definition) includes all bank deposits in the economy. If the nominal quantity of such bank deposits is fixed by a separate and independent influence (such as the level of bank credit), a host of individual decisions to switch to and fro between different agents' bank deposits or between one type of bank deposit and another cannot change that nominal quantity. It follows that if the nominal quantity of broad money is too high or too low in relation to income, interest rates or other macro-economic variables, equilibrium can be re-established only by changes in these variables. This property explains why we must concentrate on broad money, not narrow money, if we wish to understand the link between money and economy activity.

The point may need a little elaboration. Suppose I discover, when I check my bank statement, that my holding of bank deposits is higher than I expected and require. Then I will attempt to shift the excess holding somewhere else. It will not solve the problem to transfer money from a deposit account to a current account (or vice versa) since that would leave the total of my deposits unaffected. The only way I can eliminate my excess money is to spend it on goods and services, or acquire an asset. Both these transactions will add to someone else's deposit, but they will not reduce the aggregate amount of bank deposits in the economy. Moreover, although I may eliminate my own excess money holding, the sudden addition of money to someone else's deposit may result in his having excess money holdings. Any one person may think that he can control the amount in his bank account, but:

> For all individuals combined, the appearance that they can control their money balances is an optical illusion. One individual can reduce or increase his money balance only because another or several others are induced to increase or reduce theirs; that is, they do the opposite of what he does. If individuals as a whole were to try to reduce the number of dollars [or pounds] they held, they could not all do so, they would simply be playing a game of musical chairs.[10]

This game of musical chairs is the economy's attempt to move from monetary disequilibrium to equilibrium. It is not futile. If everyone considers their broad money holdings excessive, they will all, more or less simultaneously, try to disembarrass themselves of the excess by increasing their spending on goods and services, or by purchasing more assets. These efforts will lead to higher aggregate expenditure and, in due course, probably raise the price level. At the new, higher price level, it may well be that the nominal quantity of bank deposits is again appropriate. Indeed, expenditure decisions will keep on being revised until the right balance between money and incomes is restored. While individuals may be

> frustrated in their attempt to reduce the number of dollars [or pounds] they hold, they succeed in achieving an equivalent change in their position, for the rise in money income and in prices reduces the ratio of these balances to their income and also the real value of these balances. The process will continue until this ratio and this real value are in accord with their desires.[11]

We may summarize the message of this section. *A large number of individual decisions to increase (reduce) nominal holdings of broad money does not lead to an increase (reduction) in the nominal aggregate amount of broad money, but instead causes changes in expenditure on both current and capital items. The behaviour of the economy therefore adjusts to broad money, rather than broad money to the behaviour of the economy.*

Interest rates and prices

There has now been enough analytical preparation for a rough and ready account of how interest rates, credit and money affect economic activity and the price level. It can be related, if rather casually, to the position of the UK economy over the last 20 or 30 years. Let us suppose that the economy is in approximate monetary equilibrium. Interest rates are set at a level where both the growth of credit and the associated growth rate of broad money are such as to keep output expanding at about its trend rate (say, 3 per cent a year) and inflation is at its average value in recent years (say, 5 per cent). Let us also suppose that – perhaps under political pressure to promote faster growth – the Bank of England cuts interest rates substantially. How would we expect the economy to respond?

First, the growth of credit is stimulated. The explanation is simply that with lower interest rates the attractions of borrowing are increased. If interest rates are cut, there will be a wider range of assets where the return exceeds interest costs and there will also be higher borrowing. Experience in the UK suggests that two kinds of credit – mortgage borrowing for residential property and borrowing by property companies to invest in offices and other kinds of commercial property – are particularly susceptible to interest rate changes. Increased expenditure on these assets often represents the economy's earliest 'real' response to lower interest rates.

Secondly, the faster growth of credit leads to faster growth of broad money. If broad money growth was previously appropriate to maintain a steady rate of increase in money national income of about 8 per cent a year (i.e. 3 per cent increase in output, 5 per cent increase in prices), it must now be too high. Economic agents discover – because of the quicker increase in the nominal amount of bank deposits – that their money holdings are excessive. For this reason they must think about how their money holdings can be brought into a better relation to their expenditure and income.

But there is yet another reason for adjusting behaviour. As mentioned earlier, in the UK today most deposits are interest-bearing. When interest rates are cut, the desired ratio of interest-bearing deposits to income is lowered. This effect would stimulate expenditure even if the nominal amount of broad money were constant. Since there is actually more rapid growth of nominal money due to the extra buoyancy of bank credit, the urge to move out of money assets into either current expenditure or non-money assets is doubly strong.

We have explained – in the last section – why the excess holdings of broad money cannot be eliminated except by changes in incomes, interest rates or other macroeconomic variables. In practice, the economy's efforts to restore monetary equilibrium are very complicated and work initially via asset markets (the stock market, the property market) rather than goods markets (i.e. through immediate changes in consumption and investment). For example, when they have 'too much' money in the bank, private individuals switch much of the excess balances to building societies (where they finance the purchase of houses), to financial institutions such as unit trusts and insurance companies (where they become available to buy shares and government bonds) and to companies. Companies can then use the money either to finance stockbuilding and investment, or to purchase more assets (the shares of other companies, or commercial and industrial property such as offices, warehouses and factories). Typically, in the early stages of an upturn, when there is only nascent optimism about future output growth, companies are more eager to buy existing assets than commit themselves to increased expenditure on new capital equipment and buildings.

In other words, a cut in interest rates is often followed in the first instance more by a surge in asset values than by an upturn in output growth. But just as there is an equilibrium relationship between money and national income, so there are an assortment of equilibrium relationships between the market values of capital assets and their replacement values. If the market value of capital assets is driven far in excess of replacement value by a boom in credit and money, more new investment becomes worthwhile. To talk in terms of 'market value' and 'replacement value' may sound technical, but the underlying economic logic is obvious. After all, if house prices soar above the cost of building new ones, it is only common sense that there should be a surge in housebuilding. In due course, the jump in asset values stimulates higher investment.

The length of the lag between the interest rate cut and the revival in most forms of capital expenditure may confuse economists into thinking that investment – and therefore the economy as a whole – is not sensitive to interest rate changes. Indeed, it needs to be recognized that a standard feature in the early stages of a boom is that only one kind of investment, in private residential houses, is notably strong. Consumers' expenditure, which is often regarded by economists as little affected by interest rates, may show a more definite response than investment. Closer examination is nevertheless likely to demonstrate that the increase in consumption is concentrated in long-lived items like cars and durables (e.g. furniture, carpets, washing machines). These items are effectively investment by the personal sector and the increased demand for them may be motivated, in large part, by the cut in interest rates.

Once the boom has started it becomes difficult to stop. Indeed, the rise in asset values which reflects attempts to redispose wealth holdings more effectively may give further impetus to credit demand. Some businessmen may be tempted to project a rate of asset price appreciation persistently above the rate of interest, and they borrow even more heavily to capture the expected capital gains. Unless interest rates are raised, speculative excitement becomes self-feeding. Credit growth – and therefore the growth of broad money – accelerates further.

Eventually the economy reaches a condition of boom. The rate of real demand growth may be between 5 and 7 per cent a year, far in excess of the 3 per cent trend growth rate. Output may grow at an above-trend rate of 5 or even 6 per cent for a time, but in due course signs of strain emerge. In the UK, which has a medium-sized economy highly exposed to international influences, a classic symptom of excess demand is balance-of-payments deterioration. But other indicators, such as a sharp fall in unemployment and a rise in the proportion of companies reporting capacity shortages, usually tell the same story. The lack of spare capacity in factories now leads to the rapid growth in manufacturing investment which was missing at an earlier stage in the cycle.

Companies and individuals are, throughout the upswing and the boom, attempting to bring their money holdings into line with their incomes. But with credit growth strengthening because of the emergence of speculative activities in the property and other asset markets, they may find that every time they adjust their behaviour, a new and unexpected addition to their bank deposits throws them out of equilibrium again. The ratio of broad money to their incomes may rise to levels far above the long-run figure they regard as sensible. To put the same point in more technical terms, the velocity of circulation of M3 and M4 may fall substantially beneath its equilibrium value. Strangely, a repetitive pattern in UK cycles at this stage – indeed, virtually a recurrent cyclical phenomenon in its own right – is that economic commentators point to the drop in velocity as evidence of the poor relationship between the money supply and economic activity.

Sooner or later inflation spreads from asset markets to the prices of goods leaving factories and appearing in the shops. The excess demand for all types of products causes shortages which can only be eased by price increases; the decline in unemployment leads to tightness in the labour market, which provokes higher wage increases and aggravates the spiral in industrial costs; and the worsening external payments position undermines the pound on the foreign exchanges, which increases the price of imported goods, including the costs of many of the raw materials and inputs used in UK factories. At this point the growth rates of M0 and M1 – which were probably unaffected by the asset price surges in the early stages of the boom, but are highly responsive to the higher money value of transactions consequent on rising inflation – may accelerate markedly.

Now, with inflation as well as real output growth moving above its previous trend figure, the Government becomes alarmed. It mandates the Bank of England to raise interest rates to restrain the pace of expansion. The higher level of interest rates causes falls in asset prices and deters the more speculative forms of credit. But broad money growth remains high for several quarters, as companies complete the expansion programmes initiated during the boom and take up banking facilities already arranged. Beneath-trend output growth of under 3 per cent is needed for a time to compensate for the excesses of the boom. If the Government is lucky, credit expansion, money growth and inflation return – without too much fuss or delay – to the values associated with the previous condition of approximate monetary equilibrium. However, the price level is x per cent higher than it would have been if interest rates had not been cut in the first place. The value of x is likely to be very close to the excess of broad money growth over the figure that would have occurred if interest rates had been kept constant throughout. The episode of excessive credit and monetary expansion has achieved nothing positive in real terms. But it has imposed on society, even if only temporarily, all the awkwardness and inconvenience of coping with higher inflation.

Conclusion: money does matter

The sequence of events described in the last section may sound familiar. It is, in the form of a simplified idealization, the story of the UK economy between mid-1986 and mid-1988. The early 1980s had been a rather tranquil period for the UK economy, as output grew at about the trend rate of $2^3/_4$ per cent a year and inflation was steady at about 5 per cent. But a marked upturn in demand and output growth in the second half of 1986 followed a reduction in interest rates from the rather high levels of 1985 (when clearing banks' base rates averaged $12^1/_4$ per cent). It gathered dangerous momentum in early 1988 after base rates had dropped to $8^1/_2$ per cent and below. Share prices soared in the initial phase of above-trend output growth, while property values rose sharply throughout the boom. Serious financial problems eventually emerged, with inflation on the rise and the current account of the balance of payments lurching heavily into deficit. Between June and August 1988 base rates were raised eight times from $7^1/_2$ per cent to 12 per cent, as the Bank of England tried to compensate for previous monetary looseness.

The behaviour of both real and financial variables during this period is inexplicable except in terms of interest rates, credit and broad money. Some economists have suggested other causes for the rapid expansion of demand and output, but these are all implausible. The world economy was not notably vigorous over these years and, in any case, such strength as it had cannot account for the UK growing faster than the rest of the industrial world. Fiscal policy was somewhat contractionary in effect, even when adjustment is made for the impact of cyclically strong tax revenues in forging a large budget surplus. The claim that the oil price fall of 1986 caused a significant sterling depreciation, which then stimulated exports, is valid up to a point.[12] But over the two years to mid-1988 imports rose much faster than exports and the change in the balance of payments actually withdrew demand from the economy. The non-monetary explanations of the 1986–8 boom (which may be fairly called the 'Lawson boom' after the Chancellor of the Excheq-uer who presided over it) are random and miscellaneous; the monetary explanation – which focuses on official interest rate decisions, the upturn in credit expansion in late 1985 and 1986, and the subsequent acceleration in broad money growth – fits the essential facts.

Indeed, the Lawson boom has several incontestable similarities to the Barber boom of 1971–3 and what might be termed the 'Healey boomlet' of 1977–9. At some point in all three of these episodes, base rates dipped beneath 8 per cent and gave a clear stimulus to credit and monetary expansion. Apart from these instances, base rates were never at 8 per cent or less in the 17 years from 1971. The year 1971 is an important landmark since it saw the abolition of artificial restrictions on bank balance sheet growth. When the low level of interest rates had been established, share and property prices rose quickly, demand and output moved forward at above-normal rates, and financial difficulties developed. Interest rates then had to be raised to cool the economy down.

If the general outline of our analysis is accepted, it is evident that the Bank of England has enormous power over the economy. Interest rates are under its absolute control, while interest rate changes cause fluctuations in the growth of credit and broad money, and these in turn cause fluctuations in the growth of demand and output. The Bank of England may abuse its power, perhaps under pressure from over-optimistic Chancellors of the Ex-chequer. But there should be no doubt about the extent of its ability to determine macroeconomic outcomes. It would be of great benefit to society if the Bank of England's power were exercised more responsibly in future than it has been in recent years.

Notes

1. Strictly, changes in the quantity of money are matched by changes in output and the price level. The effect on prices dominates only in an inflationary economy, where the rate of increase in prices is two, three or more times the rate of increase in output. See pp. 116–20 of Sir Alan Walters's *Britain's Economic Renaissance* (Oxford: Oxford University Press, 1986) for an example of the claim that money and credit are frequently confused.
2. 'Central bank' is a generic term for the bankers' bank. Nowadays it is invariably banker to the Government and its note liabilities are legal tender. But there is nothing pre-ordained about these arrangements which, have evolved over centuries. See Tim Congdon, 'Is the provision of a sound currency a necessary function of the state?', pp. 2–21 in *National Westminster Bank Quarterly Review* (August 1981), for an outline of the his-torical development of the existing system.
3. Monetarist economists are known for emphasizing that control of the money supply is necessary and sufficient for the control of inflation. Associated with this essentially technical proposition are a number of political beliefs, including a particularly hostile attitude towards state intervention in the economy.
   The author registered his own protest against the failure to differentiate between commodity and paper-money economies in his 'Has Friedman got it wrong?', pp. 117–

25 in *The Banker* (July 1983). The same theme appears in Kaldor's 1980 evidence to the House of Commons Treasury and Civil Service Committee, reprinted in N. Kaldor, *The Scourge of Monetarism* (Oxford: Oxford University Press, 1986).

4.   There is a trivial exception. The Scottish banks issue notes which, although they are perfectly acceptable for most payments throughout the UK, are not legal tender.

5.   In practice, the Bank of England expresses its wishes on interest rates more by setting the price at which it buys and sells seven-day bills (seven-day dealing rate) than by announcing the rate of interest at which it will lend money. The detailed institutional arrangements for money market operations are extremely complicated, but it would not change the basic argument if they were described here. The two key articles are: 'The management of money day by day', in *Bank of England Quarterly Bulletin* (March 1963) and 'The role of the Bank of England in the money market', in *Bank of England Quarterly Bulletin* (March 1982). They are reprinted in the Bank of England's *The Development and Operation of Monetary Policy* (Oxford: Oxford University Press, 1984).

6.   This statement is intended as a direct contradiction of the general argument in Chapters 3 and 4 of J. C. R. Dow and I. D. Saville, *A Critique of Monetary Policy* (Oxford: Oxford University Press, 1988), and of the particular statement on p. 61 that 'bank base rates are determined by conventions that are largely historically determined, and thus subject to considerable inertia'.

7.   The view that short-term interest rates are strongly influenced by market sentiment, and are not therefore under full Bank of England control, has been argued by Professors David Llewellyn and Brian Tew in 'The Sterling Money Market and the Determination of Interest Rates', in *National Westminster Bank Quarterly Review* (May 1988).

8.   The idea of disequilibrium money is associated in the UK at present particularly with Professor Charles Goodhart of the London School of Economics and Professor David Laidler of the University of Western Ontario. See, for example, Chapter 10 of C. A. E. Goodhart, *Monetary Theory and Practice* (London: Macmillan, 1984). But it can be traced back a long way. Arguably, it is implicit in the distinction between long-run and short-run monetary equilibria in D. Patinkin, *Money, Interest and Prices*, 2nd edn (New York: Harper & Row, 1965), particularly on pp. 50–9, and perhaps can be found in Keynes (notably, according to Richard Coghlan, in two articles Keynes wrote in 1937). (See R. T. Coghlan, *Money, Credit and the Economy* (London: Allen & Unwin 1978, p. 27).

9.   See, as regards M0, R. B. Johnston, *The Demand for Non-Interest-Bearing Money in the UK* (London: Government Economic Service Working Paper, No. 66, H.M. Treasury, 1984) and, for M1, R. T. Coghlan, 'A transactions demand for money', *Bank of England Quarterly Bulletin* (March 1978).

10.   See M. Friedman, 'Statement on monetary theory and policy' given in Congressional hearings in 1959, reprinted on pp. 136–45 of R.J. Ball and Peter Doyle (eds), *Inflation* (Harmondsworth: Penguin Books, 1969). The quotation is from p. 141.

11.   Again, the quotation is from p. 141 of Friedman, 'Statement on monetary theory and policy'.

12.   As argued by Mr Philip Stephens, the Economics Correspondent of the *Financial Times*, in an article in the *Financial Times* of 6 August 1988.

The Importance of Money in Macroeconomic Forecasting – Part 2

*From an article 'A new and compleat economic model for the Chancellor'
from* The Spectator *of 11 March 1989.*

*This article was a sequel ('part 2)' to that on the Treasury's forecasting
failures in the early 1970s, published in* The Times *of 28 August 1975. (See
pp. 30–35.)*

As the annual pre-Budget guessing game becomes more technical by the day,
it needs to be remembered that the 1988 Budget was a disaster for the clever
civil servants who advise the Chancellor. The economic forecast published by
the Treasury with the Budget last year was so wrong as to make a mockery of
the considerable effort, in terms of professional time, bureaucratic manpower
and computer gadgetry, which went into producing it. Indeed, the mistakes
were so large as to cast doubt on the legitimacy of the whole exercise.

The official view was that there would be a significant slowdown in
output growth from $4^{1}/_{2}$ per cent in 1987 to 3 per cent in 1988, with only a
mild deterioration in the balance of payments from a current account deficit
of £2.5 billion in 1987 to £4 billion in 1988. In the event, national output
again grew by about $4^{1}/_{2}$ per cent and the balance of payments lurched into
massive deficit, with the current account deficit reaching £14 billion. The net
effect of these errors is that the Treasury underestimated the growth of
domestic demand by almost 5 per cent of national output. A mistake on this
scale – equivalent to more than one year's normal growth – can be fairly
described as gross professional incompetence. Parallels in other walks of life
would be a civil engineering contractor building one more storey on an
office building than in the architect's plans, or a doctor telling a patient that
he has mild angina just before he suffers a massive heart attack.

The blunders were not just in predicting demand, output and the balance
of payments. The forecasts of financial variables were also completely adrift.
Whereas the official Budget-time view was that 1988 would see stable
inflation and little change in interest rates, the increase in the retail price
index went up from 4 per cent at the end of 1987 to $6^{1}/_{2}$ per cent at the end of
1988, and clearing bank base rates soared from $8^{1}/_{2}$ per cent in March to 13
per cent in November. If one believes with Mr Lawson that high interest
rates are a cure-all for excess demand, the incompetence of the Treasury's
forecast is re-emphasized. The move to higher base rates ought to have
caused the growth in demand to be smaller than expected, but it turned out to
be more.

The Treasury was embarrassed by last year's events, but private sector
economists ought to be even more apologetic. For 1988 was a catastrophe

not just for the Government's advisers in Whitehall, but for British macroeconomics. At the beginning of the year the average of City forecasts was that growth would be a little beneath 3 per cent and inflation lower than 4 per cent. Although the City 'scribblers' have been derisive about Mr Lawson, their view was for less even growth and less inflation than the Treasury's estimates; they were actually more inaccurate than the Chancellor. According to Mr Christopher Smallwood writing in *The Sunday Times*, 'For economic forecasters 1988 will go down as the *annus horrendus*. It was the year they all got it wrong. And not just a little bit wrong, but spectacularly wrong.'

But this is an exaggeration. They did not all get it wrong. There was an exception. In late 1986 my economics team at the stockbrokers, L. Messel & Co. prepared a forecast which argued that, without big changes in Government policy, the next two years would see a boom in output followed by an intensification of inflationary pressures. The forecast was not perfect, and indeed it could not have been, since there is always much that is uncertain about government policy, the world economy, the oil market and the like. But it did capture the main features of the economy in 1987 and 1988.

The forecast was updated quarterly, to reflect new data and policy developments. (It also appeared under a different name, as L. Messel & Co. was integrated into the American securities house, Shearson Lehman Hutton. The detailed statistical work was done by Dr Peter Warburton, who has since moved to Robert Fleming Securities.) In February 1988 we envisaged $3\frac{1}{2}$ to 4 per cent growth in output, retail price inflation of $6\frac{1}{2}$ per cent, short-term interest rates by the end of the year of 12 per cent, and a large current account deficit of £6 billion. These numbers were not 100 per cent exact, but they proved to be broadly right. In particular, we made the key strategic judgement that the pace of spending growth would accelerate unless interest rates were raised substantially. This point was essential in understanding what was to happen in the rest of the year.

The important issue here is: why were our forecasts right (more or less) and the mass of other forecasters so badly wrong? If it were simply a matter of good guesswork and better luck, there would not be much more to say. If the forecasting game were largely random, every participant would have a brief moment of glory like this. But there is another possibility – that our model for forecasting the economy was different from and superior to that used by other economists. If so, the approach we adopted should in future be able to provide, on a fairly systematic basis, better insights into how the economy works.

In fact, our approach was quite different, and we were very self-conscious about it. In a standard model, output is determined by total spending in the economy and total spending is seen as the sum of various components of demand, such as consumption, investment and exports. Equations are used to calculate the most likely values of these components, on the assumption that underlying behaviour will be the same in future as in the past. It is a characteristic of the standard models that financial variables such as money supply growth are seen as being determined by, rather than determining, spending, while interest rates have only weak effects on the demand components. As a result, the standard models regard interest rates, credit growth and the money supply as trivial and subordinate. The prices of such assets as houses, shares and industrial and commercial property are also largely ignored. (One mainstream forecaster told me about 18 months ago, just as the house price boom was gathering dangerous momentum, that house prices were 'a fifth wheel' in any forecasting exercise.)

By contrast, our model started with interest rates, which were taken as being determined by the Bank of England. The level of interest rates was judged to be a powerful influence on credit to the private sector, particularly mortgage credit. Since every new bank loan creates a new bank deposit, credit growth determined the growth of the money supply. (The money supply, on its broad definition, is dominated by bank deposits.) Unexpected changes in the money supply then made people and companies alter their spending patterns, with strong effects on both asset prices and the demand components which comprise total spending. In two respects, therefore, our model diverged radically from that used by other forecasters. First, the financial variables drove the real variables forward, rather than the other way round. Secondly, changes in broad money were central to the economy's behaviour.

All these technicalities may sound complicated and tedious, and of only marginal relevance to the political debate. In fact, they are crucial to understanding the future of both economic policy and the politicians who shape it. The skirmish between our forecast and the standard forecast over the last two years has been another episode in the protracted intellectual battle fought between Keynesians and monetarists since the early 1970s. The standard forecast was derived from a model in which money does not really matter, whereas our forecast was based on a model in which money mattered vitally. The breakdown of the conventional models and the success of our alternative approach suggest that the money supply (on the much despised broad definitions, M3 and M4) remains as important now as it was when the monetarists first presented their case.

This is not the first humiliation suffered by the standard models. In 1974 and 1975 they completely failed to recognize the scale of the inflationary threat implicit in the monetary growth of the Heath–Barber boom and to appreciate just how bad a recession would be needed to bring inflation down again. Interestingly, a small group of monetarists at Manchester University, under the leadership of Professors David Laidler and Michael Parkin, were the only economists who predicted both the rise in inflation to over 20 per cent and a sharp fall in output.

The Heath–Barber boom was a watershed in Britain's post-war political economy. It was as a reaction to the wild monetary adventurism of 1972 and 1973 that Sir Keith Joseph gave his Preston speech of September 1974 which insisted that, 'our inflation has been the result of the creation of new money...out of proportion to the additional goods and services available. When the money supply grows too quickly, inflation results. This has been known for centuries.' The Preston speech was effectively the beginning of Thatcherism as a political movement. By 1979 it had become a cliché that monetary control was integral to contemporary Conservativism.

This intellectual environment gave Nigel Lawson, with his unusually extensive knowledge of the economy, based on many years as a financial journalist, the opportunity to cultivate a reputation as an expert on monetary questions. He became Thatcherism's financial technician. As Financial Secretary to the Treasury in the early years of the Thatcher Government, he championed strict control of broad money as the key to inflation control. But, as Chancellor in the mid-1980s, he appeared to renounce what he had once stood for. He scrapped broad money targets and engineered the greatest surge in private sector credit this country has ever seen. The boom made him popular for a time. But the inevitable sequel of rising inflation and balance-of-payments deterioration has now tarnished his reputation, probably for good.

There is a growing enigma about Mr Lawson's performance and motives. It would be easy to attribute the somersault in his policies to an excess of political cynicism, a lack of economic understanding or simple folly. But there may be a more straightforward and charitable explanation. This is to see the Chancellor as someone highly susceptible to the latest advice from the clever Treasury civil servants who prepare the official economic forecasts. If so, there is an obvious need for British macroeconomists to change the way they analyse the economy and to incorporate monetary variables more fully into their models. Unless this is done, the next Chancellor – who will have a weaker grasp of technicalities than Mr Lawson – may be misled even more badly by his advisers.

PART THREE

Keynes and British Monetarism

9. Keynes and British monetarism

These three papers, which are the most 'academic' in this volume, largely speak for themselves. Their main point, as explained in the Introduction, is to demonstrate that Keynes, unlike the so-called 'Keynesians' in the Treasury, British universities and elsewhere, was very concerned about how interest rates, credit growth and the money supply affected economic activity, employment and inflation.

Are We Really All Keynesians Now?

From an article of the same name in the April 1975 issue of Encounter.

In the mid-1970s, when Britain's inflation ran at an annual rate of over 15 per cent for extended periods of time, a particularly common position in the public debate was that inflation should be reduced by an incomes policy. The phrase 'incomes policy' meant that controls should be imposed by the Government over particular wages, dividends and prices, in order to restrict the overall rate of inflation. Economists urging this policy usually called themselves 'Keynesian'. They were distinguished from the 'monetarists' who thought that excess demand was responsible for rising prices and that slower monetary growth was the right answer to inflation.

Having been an avid reader of Keynes as a student, I was puzzled that the advocates of an incomes policy should adopt the 'Keynesian' label, because I could not recall Keynes recommending an incomes policy during peacetime at any stage in his career. I therefore wrote the following article for Encounter. *It argued that the 'Keynesians' had no textual basis in Keynes's opus for their policy prescriptions, and that his own views on inflation control were conventional, with a strong emphasis on the value of monetary policy.*

Tribal warfare is not the most attractive feature of contemporary economics, but it is much the most exciting. A BBC2 'Controversy' programme on inflation in September last year had much to recommend it as a sporting occasion. But the vigour of debate occasionally makes it less careful and

precise; distinguished economists become misled by their own slogans and
tend to assert glibly what they know should be argued cautiously. One
particular vice is the habit of attaching a brand-name to a school of thought,
not with the intention of designating a common theme, but with that of
heightening rhetorical impact. It is right to be suspicious of this tendency
because it conveys a possibly spurious impression of unanimity, of a confederation of intellects, which can persuade non-participants in the debate by
sheer force of numbers. But there can be a still more serious reason for
distrust. When the confederation becomes known by a special name there is
a danger that the name can give a distorted idea of the quality of its intellectual weaponry. The danger is greatest when the name used is that of a much
revered warrior, now dead, who achieved a number of famous victories in
his lifetime.

In economics, the revered warrior in all confrontations is still John Maynard
Keynes. A quote from Keynes, no matter how slight and trivial, appears to
silence opposition. It has the same force as an appendix of mathematical
reasoning or a half-dozen learned articles. It can be a powerful blow in
debate and, indeed, it can sometimes serve as a substitute for thought. It is
important, therefore, to examine carefully the credentials of any group which
calls itself 'Keynesian'. At present the Keynesian label has been attached to
a body of economists in England, principally from Cambridge University,
who have certain special views on the problem of inflation control. In choosing
this label they have – or believe they have – a great advantage. It is a
commonplace that Keynes was worried above all by the depression of the
1930s and the attendant unemployment, and that his work on inflation was
insubstantial and can be neglected. The Keynesians therefore have freedom
to propound their own views as those of Keynes. This freedom amounts to a
licence to counterfeit his intellectual coinage.[1]

In fact, it is not true that Keynes was uninterested in inflation. He lived
through the most rapid inflation of the 20th century: that between 1914 and
1920, which ravaged the British financial system and devastated the currencies of most European countries. His writings on inflation are extensive. The
consistency of modern Keynesian views on inflation with Keynes's own
position can be checked. It emerges that several leading strands in Keynesian
thought cannot be said to have their origins in Keynes's work. The claim that
there is a close correspondence between the two is based on a myth – a myth
which has been carefully nurtured by a number of English economists who
collaborated with Keynes in the 1930s, but who have outlived him and
propagated an influential, but spurious, oral tradition. Tribes, even tribes of
economists, need myths. They are a form of emotional nourishment, a sort of
spiritual subsistence level. It is important that this particular myth be exploded.

It may help the argument along if a summary of the Keynesian position is provided. I hope that this summary does justice to Keynesian thought, despite the obvious and unavoidable danger that, by highlighting its central elements, its variety and subtlety will not be sufficiently acknowledged.

The inflationary process is seen as basically a question of 'cost–push'. There are a number of forces which are said to raise costs of production throughout the economy. Prices are then raised in response to preserve profit mark-ups. This cost–push process has to be contrasted with 'excess demand' explanations of inflation, in which the causes are said to be too much demand for labour (which, then, raises wages and costs) and goods (which enables firms to raise prices without fearing loss of business).

The initial impulse behind the cost–push process comes from the trade unions. The Keynesians are somewhat ambivalent in their attitude to the union movement, because it is regarded as both the cause of a self-defeating jostling between different groups for a higher share of the national cake (which they deplore) and the agent of income redistribution in favour of the lower classes (which they applaud). An insistence on the villainy of the trade unions is, however, common to all the Keynesians in some form or other. At one extreme there is Lord Balogh who is outspoken and unhesitating in his condemnation. Others are more reserved. Dr Roger Opie, in his contribution to a new book on *Keynes: Aspects of the Man and his Work* (based on the first Keynes seminar held at the University of Kent in 1972), attributes their behaviour to the economic context in which they operate. It is, he says, the experience of past high employment which has given unions the taste of power; and the combination of organized labour and oligopolized industry which has given them the opportunity to exercise it without limit.[2] Professor Joan Robinson recognizes the conflict between the public aims of the labour movement as a whole and the private, self-interested objectives of the individual union. Although the vicious inflationary spiral caused by wage-bargaining 'does no good to the workers', nevertheless 'it remains the duty of each trade union individually to look after the interests of its own members individually'.[3]

Accompanying this hostility, open or disguised, to the trade unions, is a set of beliefs about the operation of the labour market. Wages are set, not by demand and supply, but by bargaining. Workers do not move from industry to industry and from firm to firm in response to the incentives of better pay and prospects. The labour market is characterized by rigidities and imperfections, and wage-determination takes place in an environment of 'countervailing power', without respect for fairness or for social justice. ('Countervailing power' is a phrase invented by the American Keynesian, Professor Kenneth Galbraith.) The imperfections in the labour market are matched by imperfections in the production and supply of goods. Opie's reference to 'oligopolized industry' is typical. Occasionally even the retailers have to take their share of the blame. As Sir Roy Harrod puts it, the distributors are 'sometimes up to a little mischief'.

In short, 'the core' of cost–push inflation is the conflict between 'managers, trade unionists, and the non-unionized' as they 'all struggle endlessly to increase, or at least preserve, their share of the national product'. The timing and size of the demands placed on the economy do not have a primarily economic explanation. The principal influences are, instead, social and psychological; and they operate continuously. The outcome of the distributional struggle is not determined by productivity, but by power. The crucial determinant is the strike threat.

What, then, is the answer to cost–push inflation? It is direct intervention by the Government in the form of prices and incomes policies. The Keynesians are united in this, and they would appear to have convinced a majority of the academic economics profession. There are few clearer statements of support than that from Sir Roy Harrod in *Keynes: Aspects of the Man and his Work*, where he writes, 'I am myself a definite advocate of what we call an "incomes policy". I believe there must be direct interference'. A prices and incomes policy serves many functions. It is, first and foremost, a weapon to fight inflation. But it is more than that. By enabling a central authority to monitor price movements, it supersedes – or, at least, overrides – the monopoly bargaining power of large firms and the trade unions. It can thereby contribute to attempts to distribute economic rewards more fairly. It is a means of attaining social justice.[4]

What of the uses of monetary correctives? These are scorned. To quote Harrod again:

> I do not think it is any good saying that banks can stop inflation – saying, let them reduce the money supply. How can the poor banks reduce the money supply? What actually happens is that wage-earners get a demand granted which must raise costs.[5]

If monetary methods were adopted they would cause unemployment, and this is thought to be unacceptable. It would be the negation of Keynesianism if unemployment were the best method of fighting rising prices.

There is no doubt that the Keynesian position is internally consistent. If one believes that 'greed' and 'envy' are the causes of inflation, one is likely to be sceptical of the use of such indirect methods of control as changes in taxation and interest rates. It is much easier to legislate against greed and envy directly, by laying down statutory limitations on their effects. It is also consistent with a particular perception of reality. If monopoly power is pervasive, if markets are stunted by imperfections and rigidities, it is futile to apply those remedies which work on the assumption that the economic world is competitive and responsive to supply-and-demand pressures. But the Keynesian position is not, as we shall see, consistent with that of Keynes. It has no foundation in his written work and is not, indeed, compatible with fundamental aspects of his economic philosophy.

But surely, it might be said, the Keynesians must be basing their case on some element of Keynes's thinking. Is there any kinship between their arguments and his?

In fact, there is an assumption common to their way of thinking and the most important part of Keynes's work. It is a technical assumption, slipped into the interstices of the theoretical structure; and, for that reason, one whose significance is easily overlooked. It is the assumption throughout *The General Theory of Employment, Interest and Money* (1936) that the analysis can be conducted in terms of 'wage-units'.

Keynes was not concerned in his investigation of unemployment with the relationship between capital inputs and output. The vital relationships were those between employment, output and demand. The function of the wage-unit assumption was that it enabled his analysis to focus on these relationships 'provided we assume that a given volume of effective demand has a particular distribution of this demand between different products uniquely associated with it'. The wage-unit was defined as the sum of money paid to each 'labour-unit' or, in effect, each worker.[6] This was a very useful assumption. Keynes could proceed to the determination of output and employment without needing a prior theory of the determination of the money wage and without troubling himself too much over microeconomic details. It might seem to follow that Keynes considered money wages to be given exogenously, perhaps as a result of bargaining.

The subtle effect of the wage-unit assumption on later thinking is exposed in an important new book on *The Crisis in Keynesian Economics* by Sir John Hicks. The validity of analysis conducted in wage-units turns on what Sir John calls 'the wage theorem', that 'when there is a general (proportional) rise in money wages, the normal effect is that all prices rise in the same proportion'.[7] Given the wage theorem it is immaterial what the particular money wage is. The relationships between liquidity preference, the investment function, and the rest, which are the hub of Keynes's economics, are unaffected. Consequently, it is a convenient and innocuous simplification to assume a fixed money wage. Consequently, the relationship between aggregate demand and the money wage can be neglected.

This chain of thought – or, rather, this compound of faulty thought-habits and pseudo-empirical hunches – is the source of all the trouble. Keynes made the wage-unit assumption because it facilitated his theoretical task. He could grapple more quickly with the issues of demand and employment, once the awkward (but, to him, supererogatory) problem of money wage determination was put to one side. But this does not mean that he thought money wages were determined exogenously in the real world. Unfortunately, the Keynesians have come to think just that. It is almost comical to picture Sir Roy Harrod indulging in an elaborate exegetical hunt to find some justification for his conjecture:

> I have searched through his writings very carefully, not long ago –for the purpose of discovering anything he had to say about what we call 'cost–push inflation'. I could find only one short passage in Keynes, just a couple of sentences, where he said, 'Of course the wage-earners might demand more than corresponding to their rise in productivity, might demand more and get more.' You can find those words if you search; I ought to give you chapter and verse, but I have not put down the page reference; they are there all right.[8]

The fact is that Keynes wrote almost nothing about 'what we call "cost–push inflation"'. The 'one short passage' may or may not be a figment of Sir Roy's imagination. The many thousands of words written by Keynes on inflation as an excess demand phenomenon are palpable and, to anyone who 'searches through his writings very carefully', rather obtrusive.

There is, however, a certain agreement between the Keynesians' and Keynes's views on social fairness. His writings at times resemble a roll-call of the class structure of a late industrial society, with references to profiteers, rentiers and unions scattered throughout the pages. The passages on income distribution in *How to Pay for the War* describe the upward swirl of the wage–price spiral particularly well. Here, indeed, it might be said, is the endless social struggle for a higher proportion of the national income.[9] But it is difficult to infer Keynes's attitude to the labour movement from his writings. He was certainly alerted to its potential impact on the organization of the markets in factor services. In one of his public speeches he described trade unionists as, 'once the oppressed, now the tyrants, whose selfish and sectional pretensions need to be bravely opposed'.[10] But the harshness of the observation is unusual. It may be an isolated piece of bravura intended more for public relations purposes than as an expression in inner conviction. In *The General Theory* (and elsewhere) the unions are a fact of life; they are not the subject of a favourable or adverse judgement.

But, if there are some reasons for attributing Keynesian views to Keynes's intellectual legacy, there are many more reasons for denying a strong connection between the two.

Before moving on to an examination of Keynes's theory of inflation, it is essential to challenge a widespread misapprehension: that Keynes knew nothing about, and was uninterested in, the price mechanism or, more generally, in what we would now call microeconomics. This is simply untrue.[11] His awareness of the virtues (within limits) of the price mechanism saved him from the common assumption among the Keynesians that official interference to restrain rises in the absolute price level – or, more explicitly, prices and incomes policies – has no damaging repercussions on the configuration of relative prices. Equally, he was sceptical of the effectiveness of price controls, a scepticism formed by knowledge of conditions in the inflation-ridden European economies of the early 1920s. In *The Economic Consequences of the Peace* (1919), he wrote:

> The preservation of a spurious value of the currency, by the force of law expressed in the regulation of prices, contains in itself, however, the seeds of final economic decay, and soon dries up the sources of ultimate supply.

A page later he added, 'The effect on foreign trade of price-regulation and profiteer-hunting as cures for inflation is even worse'.[12] An even more contemporary ring attaches to his derision of the 'bread subsidies' which were common at the time.

Similarly, he did not consider wage control to be feasible. There are recurrent passages in Keynes – particularly when Britain returned to the gold standard (in 1925) – where the need to bring down the level of wages is stressed (if the exchange rate had to be unnecessarily raised). But it was precisely the impracticality of efforts to depress the general wage level which was the problem (and, therefore, made adjustments of the exchange rate expedient). In 1931, just before Britain left the gold standard, he wrote that the reduction of all money wages in the economy

> if it were to be adequate would involve so drastic a reduction of wages and such appallingly difficult, probably insoluble, problems, both of social justice and practical method, that it would be crazy not to try [the alternative of import restrictions].[13]

Of course, the Keynesians could argue that today the community has become habituated to directives from the centre. The improvement in communications has made it that much easier to administer and to police a prices and incomes policy. It might be contended that in these altered circumstances Keynes would revise his views, acknowledging some merits in legally-imposed limitations on wage and price rises.

It is impossible to argue with this. It might well be true. But surely no one can give a definitive answer one way or the other. What is clear is that there is nothing in Keynes's writings which explicitly envisages and endorses a prices and incomes policy, and there is much in their mood and tenor which is contemptuous of its makeshift predecessors in the 1920s.

What, then, of Keynes's views of the inflationary process?

The first point is that Keynes regarded inflation as an excess demand phenomenon. There is very little, if anything, in his writings to suggest that he regarded it as something else. Perhaps the most lucid and consecutive discussion to be found in his work is in Chapter 21 of *The General Theory* on 'The theory of prices' (and, more especially, between pages 295 and 303). Paradoxically, however, it is rather hard to use this section for our purposes. The difficulty is that Keynes thought the proposition that inflation was due to excess demand so self-evident that he did not bother to argue it. The discussion consists of permutations of assumptions, all of which derive from a theoretical position of extreme orthodoxy. No alternative to excess-demand inflation is contemplated, let alone explored.

The form of the discussion is to put forward, as a pivot for further argument, the principle that:

> So long as there is unemployment, employment will change in the same proportion as the quantity of money; and when there is full employment, prices will change in the same proportion as the quantity of money.[14]

The validity of this principle is shown to depend on five assumptions. Only one of the five assumptions is concerned with the institutional context of wage-bargaining. It is the tendency for the wage-unit – or, in effect, money wages – to rise before full employment has been reached. Let me quote the relevant passage in full:

> In actual experience the wage-unit does not change continuously in terms of money in response to every small change in effective demand; but discontinuously. These points of discontinuity are determined by the psychology of the workers and by the policies of employers and trade unions.[15]

In other words, the significance of the union movement is recognized. But the exercise of bargaining power depends on prior changes in 'effective demand'.

This was plainly thought to be the normal run of events. These 'discontinuities' represented 'semi-inflations' which 'have, moreover, a good deal of historical importance'. It is not surprising that Keynes saw unions as susceptible to the same economic pressures as firms or individuals. In his lifetime, the membership of the union movement was substantially reduced on two distinct occasions – between 1921 and 1924, and between 1929 and 1932. In both instances the cause was the downturn in demand. To summarize, Keynes believed there to be an interplay between institutions and economic forces; but he did not believe, as do the Keynesians, that institutions dictate to or overwhelm these forces.[16]

Whereas Keynes hardly ever attributed trade unions a causal role in inflation, there are an abundance of passages in which inflation is 'a monetary phenomenon'. (The claim that inflation is 'a monetary phenomenon' is associated with the famous American economist, Professor Milton Friedman.) Indeed, on one occasion Keynes gave a definition of inflation which was stated in terms of the money supply. He did not dither between two competing modern definitions – of 'rising prices' and 'aggregate demand in excess of aggregate supply'. Instead:

> From 1914 to 1920 all countries experienced an expansion in the supply of money relative to the supply of things to purchase, that is to say Inflation.

Moreover, the emphasis on money in the inflations of the First World War is consonant with the dominant themes of Keynes's depression economics. In the more simplistic explanations of Keynes's theory there is often undue concentration on the need for public works to raise spending. But this neglects the cause of inadequate private investment, which was too much liquidity preference or, roughly speaking, the behaviour of the demand for money.[17] When savings take the form of liquid holdings (such as bank deposits) rather than illiquid holdings (like plant and machinery), the demand for goods declines and there is unemployment. The traditional answer was to lower the rate of return on liquid holdings, until savers shifted back into illiquid. But Keynes saw that, in certain extreme circumstances, there might be psychological and institutional barriers to a sufficient downward reduction in the rate of interest. It followed from this that monetary policy, intended to engineer changes in interest rates, could not by itself cause a recovery of demand. Hence, there was a need, in his words, for 'a somewhat comprehensive socialization of investment'. If investment were in state hands, it could be undertaken with larger ambitions than mere profit-maximization. In particular, it could be stepped up in order to promote higher employment.

However, if the impotence of monetary policy in a depression is one of the principal conclusions of Keynes's economics, there is no foundation for the widespread Keynesian attitude that 'money does not matter'. Keynes's writings are replete with references to the banking system and financial assets. It would be remarkable if he thought them irrelevant to problems of economic policy in normal circumstances. (The 1930s, of course, were not normal circumstances. But it should be remembered that three out of the eight historical illustrations in Chapter 30 of *A Treatise on Money* were analyses of inflations. Keynes did think about the longer time span.[18])

In Keynes, the monetary variable under discussion was usually the rate of interest (the price of money) rather than the money supply (its quantity). This has subsequently been a fertile and persistent source of disagreement between the Keynesians and others. The Keynesians say that no support is to be found in *The General Theory* or elsewhere for the mechanistic rules advocated by, for example, Milton Friedman of the Chicago school, in which the monetary variable emphasized is the quantity of money. It is true that nowhere in Keynes is there a forthright recommendation for stable growth of a monetary aggregate. But there are sections of *A Tract on Monetary Reform* which come remarkably close to this standard monetarist position.[19]

Of course, Keynes was in no position to talk with confidence about fluctuations in money supply growth, because he lived in an age before full statistics were available. The rate of interest, on the other hand, was something known and observable. There are some intriguing passages in *A Treatise on Money* (1930) where Keynes plainly was searching for a measure of the money supply and trying to identify a relationship with nominal national income. The two most interesting cases were in Britain in the decade after the First World War and in the USA between 1925 and 1930.[20] There were mismatches between changes in the money supply and nominal national income changes, which, interestingly, he attributed to 'lags' between 'profit' and 'income inflations'. The discussion in these pages is a fascinating attempt to understand the transmission mechanism of monetary policy.

Keynes's tendency to focus on the price of money, rather than its quantity, may also have reflected his involvement in insurance and fund management. He was active in City finance and speculation throughout the 1920s and 1930s, and looked at monetary policy as City men do. Bankers, who have to arrange loans from day to day, think of the demand for credit as fickle and volatile, while economists, who look at broad monetary aggregates and long-run time series, regard it as continuous and stable. Bankers see interest rates, which give signals of credit availability, as the determining variable, while economists tend to regard the money supply as all-important and are inclined to downplay the significance of transient price incentives. Keynes mostly thought in interest rate terms. But this does not mean that, in the general run of events, he distrusted the effectiveness of monetary policy as a method of changing demand, output and employment. A clear statement of his position is again to be found in *A Treatise on Money*. The authorities have, he said, no control over individual prices (like those of cars or meat) in the economic system. Nor do they have *direct* control over the money supply because the central bank must act as lender of last resort. But they do determine one price, 'the rate of discount', or the rate of interest; and it is this which gives them leverage on the system as a whole.[21]

One final point, which is perhaps decisive in refuting the Keynesians, needs to be made: it is that when Britain was confronted with nasty outbreaks of inflation during his lifetime, Keynes supported policies of a traditional, demand-restrictive nature. It has been too readily assumed that the years from 1914 to 1945 were of prolonged and unremitting depression, characterized by falling or stable prices, and that Keynes was therefore never called upon to offer advice on the control of inflation. This is quite wrong. In early 1920, Britain was in the midst of an inflationary boom of proportions which have never been paralleled before or since. (Conditions in 1973 and 1974 were, in some respects, rather similar.) In both 1918 and 1919 money wages soared by nearly 30 per cent a year, and even by February 1920 there seemed no sign of an early release from the grip of the price explosion which had inevitably followed.

The Chancellor of the Exchequer, Austen Chamberlain, asked for an interview with Keynes to obtain his opinion on the right course of action. Chamberlain later summarized his impression of the interview as:

> K. would go for a financial crisis (doesn't believe it would lead to unemployment). Would go to whatever rate is necessary – perhaps 10 per cent – and would keep it at that for three years.[22]

Shortly afterwards Keynes prepared a 15-point memorandum in which he amplified his advice. Perhaps its most startling feature is the similarity between the economic issues of early 1920 and those of late 1974, and only a little less startling is Keynes's set of recommendations to deal with the problems. He wanted stiff and harsh deflation.

Is this document an aberration? Would Keynes have retracted it with the benefit of hindsight and of the breakthroughs in economic thought he pioneered in the 1930s? In 1942 he was shown his 1920 memorandum. He was not in the least repentant. Far from thinking his position too iconoclastic, he acknowledged that other economists at the time had thought exactly the same and that they had been equally right. To quote:

> As usual the economists were found to be unanimous and the common charge to the contrary without foundation! I feel myself that I should give today exactly the same advice that I gave then, namely a swift and sharp dose of dear money, sufficient to break the market, and quick enough to prevent at least some of the disastrous consequences that would then ensue. In fact, the remedies of the economists were taken, but too timidly.[23]

There is no need to go any further. The argument could be reinforced by an analysis of Keynes's views of war finance, but there is already enough evidence to validate the main contentions of this article.

There is nothing in Keynes's writings, philosophy, or work which coincides with the present-day Keynesians' viewpoints on inflation policy. They favour direct government interference to keep prices down. Keynes scorned price regulation as ineffective and harmful. They consider inflation to be a cost–push phenomenon. He never envisaged it as anything but a phenomenon of excess demand. They dismiss monetary policy. He thought the one sure answer to inflationary excesses was 'a swift and severe dose of dear money'.

Are we really all 'Keynesians' now?

Notes

1. The best-known Keynesians in this country are Sir Roy Harrod, Lord Kahn and Joan Robinson. Lord Kahn and Mrs Robinson have stayed at Cambridge, but Sir Roy Harrod has taught at Oxford for most of his academic career. Although Cambridge is the centre of Keynesianism, many economists in universities throughout England would profess themselves as Keynesians; and it is, perhaps, slightly misleading to locate it too precisely in geographical terms.

   Throughout the article, Keynesianism will mean the body of beliefs of this group of economists, and Keynesians will be these economists. A distinction will, therefore, be drawn between Keynesian economics and Keynes's economics. A similar distinction is to be found in A. Leijonhufvud's, *On Keynesian Economics and the Economics of Keynes* (1968), although Leijonhufvud is concerned with the whole body of Keynes's economics whereas I am only interested in his work on inflation.

2. Roger Opie, 'The political consequences of Lord Keynes', in D. E. Moggridge (ed.), *Keynes: Aspects of the Man and his Work* (Macmillan Press, 1974), p. 87.

3. Joan Robinson, *Economic Philosophy* (1962), p. 131.

4. Sir Roy Harrod, 'Keynes's Theory and its applications', in D. E. Moggridge (ed.), Keynes, pp. 9–10; and Opie, p. 86. There have been suggestions that there is such a thing as a 'just price' and that 'social considerations' should enter into price determination. See A. Jones, *The New Inflation* (1973), particularly Chapters 5 and 6.

5. Sir Roy Harrod in D. E. Moggridge (ed.), *Keynes*, p. 9.

6. J. M. Keynes, *The General Theory of Employment, Interest and Money* (1936), pp. 41–43. See, particularly, the footnote on pp. 42–43.

7. Sir John Hicks, *The Crisis in Keynesian Economics* (Blackwell, 1974), pp. 59–60.

8. Sir Roy Harrod in Moggridge (ed.), *Keynes*, p. 9. Other examples: 'It would be most inappropriate for me to stand up here and tell you what Keynes would have thought. Goodness knows he would have thought of something much cleverer than I can think of' (pp. 8–9); and: 'I do not think we can tackle it without direct interference. They do seem to be doing this rather more effectively in America now than here having tribunals, boards, call them what you will, responsible for fixing maximum price increases. I am sure we have got to come to that, and, as our Chairman very kindly hinted, I had a letter in *The Times* on this very subject yesterday.'

9. J. M. Keynes, *How to Pay for the War* (1940), of which pp. 61–70 are reprinted in R. J. Ball and Peter Doyle, *Inflation* (1969), pp. 21–27.

10. J. M. Keynes, 'Liberalism and Labour' (1926), reprinted in *Essays in Persuasion* (1931), p. 341.

11. There is an extremely tart and amusing footnote on pp. 70–71 of D. E. Moggridge (ed.), *Keynes: Aspects of the Man and his Work* on this theme, which I strongly recommend to the connoisseur. It is at Joan Robinson's expense. She had supported the notion that 'Maynard had never spent the 20 minutes necessary to understand the theory of value', sublimely unaware that as a matter of fact (as is clear from one of the notes to her publisher) he had acted as referee to her very book on the subject.

12. E. Johnson and D. E. Moggridge (eds), *The Collected Writings of John Maynard Keynes: Vol. 2, The Economic Consequences of the Peace* (London, 1971), pp. 151–2.

13. J. M. Keynes, *Essays in Persuasion* (1931), p. 284. The alternative of import restrictions is the one preferred in the context of the passage quoted, but Keynes was, of course, in favour of a devaluation if it was politically possible.

14. Keynes, *The General Theory of Employment, Interest and Money* (1936), p. 296.
15. Keynes, *The General Theory*, pp. 301–302.
16. The frailty of institutions in the face of economic imperatives is one of the themes of an interesting new book: G. A. Dorfman, *Wage Politics in Britain*, Charles Knight (1974). See, particularly, Chapter 2 on the inter-War period.
17. Keynes, *Essays in Persuasion* (1931), p. 81. There is a fascinating discussion of the notion of liquidity preference, and its connection with investment flexibility, in the second part of Sir John Hicks, *The Crisis in Keynesian Economics*.
18. E. Johnson and D. E. Moggridge (eds), *The Collected Writings of John Maynard Keynes: Vol. 6, A Treatise on Money: The Applied Theory of Money* (1971), pp. 132–186.
19. See below pp. 240–42.
20. *Treatise*, pp.155–61 and pp.170–75.
21. Keynes himself put 'direct' in italics (p. 189) of the *Treatise*, presumably because he thought that a rise in the price of money would cause people to economize on its use and, therefore, the authorities could indirectly control the money supply. The belief that a central bank should not hold down the money supply directly, because it has the lender-of-last resort function, is a very typical banker's attitude. Incidentally, it is one reason why Friedmanite economists and central bankers often do not see eye to eye.
22. Susan Howson, '"A dear money man"?: Keynes on monetary policy, 1920', in *The Economic Journal* (June 1973), p. 458.
23. Susan Howson, *The Economic Journal*, p. 461.

Keynes, British Monetarism and American Monetarism

From a paper 'British and American monetarism compared' in R. Hill (ed.)
Keynes, Money and Monetarism *(1989) London and Basingstoke: Macmillan.*

This paper has several echoes to other pieces in the book, particularly in its discussion of the tension between external and domestic objectives in monetary policy. This tension was one of the most important and consistent themes in Keynes's writings, and it is easy to show that Keynes wanted British monetary policy to be based on domestic considerations, not external. This paper, which was given at a one-day conference on Keynes at the University of Kent in 1987, argues that Keynes's recommendation of 'a managed currency' in his 1923 A Tract on Monetary Reform *is similar to the targeted money growth which was the centrepiece of the Thatcher Government's Medium-Term Financial Strategy. (The argument is also made, in a somewhat different context, in the following paper based on my Cardiff inaugural lecture in November 1989.) The Kent paper also discusses Keynes's remarks, at various points in his work, on the mechanics of monetary control, a subject which caused antagonism between British and American monetarists in the early 1980s.*

The spread of monetarism in the 1970s did not occur by a simple process of intellectual conquest. In most countries monetarist ideas could not be incorporated in policy formation until they had adapted to local economic conditions and recognized existing traditions of monetary management. Although the framework of financial control assumed some monetarist characteristics in virtually all the industrial nations, each nation still retained distinctive institutional arrangements and policy approaches. The UK posed a particular problem. With its long history of monetary debate and practice, and with its unusually well-established institutional structures, it did not readily assimilate Chicago School doctrines. Nevertheless, in the late 1970s and early 1980s the media, leading politicians and the public at large believed that British macroeconomic policy was becoming progressively more monetarist. Perhaps the apex of monetarist influence on policy came in the Budget of 1980 with the announcement of the Medium-Term Financial Strategy, in which targets for both monetary growth and the budget deficit were stated for four years into the future. In a statement to regional city editors on 9 June 1980, Nigel Lawson, Financial Secretary to the Treasury (later to be Chancellor of the Exchequer), said that the 'Medium-Term Financial Strategy is essentially a monetary – or, if you like, monetarist – strategy'.[1]

The purpose of this paper is to compare the 'monetarism' referred to by Nigel Lawson with the 'monetarism' which is conventionally associated with the Chicago School. The monetarism which once dominated policy formation in the UK is called British monetarism, and the monetarism of the Chicago School, American monetarism. Of course, these simple labels are to a degree misleading. So many ideas have been in play, and they have undergone such constant evolution, that there is an inevitable arbitrariness in talking of this monetarism, that monetarism or the other monetarism. Despite the difficulties, a short description of British monetarism is ventured in the next section. No precise definition is given of American monetarism, but Friedman's work and Mayer's book on the structure of monetarism are taken as broadly representative.[2] In the following four sections contrasts are drawn between British monetarism and American monetarism. The tensions between them were reflected in a number of perplexities which are critical to understanding the decline and fall of monetarism in UK policy formation in the mid-1980s. The final section therefore discusses, among other things, the corrosive impact of certain distinctively Chicagoan beliefs on the staying-power of British monetarism in the policy debate.

It would be wrong to give the impression that there has been a bitter transatlantic intellectual duel. The recent divergence between British and American monetarism certainly has not reflected a controversy as intense or long-standing as that between monetarism and Keynesianism. However, there are points of contact between the two debates. Perhaps it is not surprising, in view of the range of his work, that Keynes himself touched on several of the topics which have subsequently been disputed between American and British monetarists. As we shall see, the relationship between his views and recent Anglo-American monetary disagreements turn out to be complex and ambivalent.

The opening months of 1980, coinciding with the introduction of the Medium-Term Financial Strategy, have already been mentioned as a period of particular confidence in the virtues of monetary policy. Two official documents prepared at the time may be regarded as defining statements of British monetarism. The first is the March 1980 Green Paper on *Monetary Control*, which was the joint work of the Treasury and the Bank of England; the second is the *Memorandum on Monetary Policy* prepared by the Treasury for the Treasury and Civil Service Committee in June 1980.[3]

The focus of both documents was a target for the growth of broad money, measured by sterling M3. Sterling M3 consisted of notes and coin and nearly all deposit liabilities of the banking system. (Certificates of deposit were included, but both deposits and CDs with an original term to maturity of over two years were excluded. Sterling M3 was renamed M3 in May 1987.) Sterling M3 was not monitored for its own sake, but as an intermediate target thought to have a definite – if rather elusive – relationship with the ultimate target of inflation. The Government's faith in this relationship was expressed strongly in the Treasury's *Memorandum on Monetary Policy*. While conceding that the mechanisms linking money and prices change over time and space, the *Memorandum* insisted that 'the proposition that prices must ultimately respond to monetary control holds whatever the adjustment process in the shorter term may be'.[4] An accompanying note on 'The stability of the income velocity of circulation of money supply' stated that, although velocity had fluctuated in the previous 17 years, 'at times quite sharply', there appeared to be 'a clear tendency for the series to return to the underlying trend'.[5]

If the monetary targets were to be achieved, it was essential to understand what caused monetary expansion. The favoured account of the money supply process gave pride of place to bank credit. With the deposit liabilities of the banking system representing the greater part of broad money, it was logical to attempt to limit the growth of bank assets. Since the growth of bank assets depended on the extension of new credit to the public, private and overseas sectors, monetary control was guided by an analysis of the so-called 'credit counterparts'. More specifically, the authorities used a credit counterparts identity which set out the relationship between, on the one hand, the public sector borrowing requirement, sales of public sector debt to non-banks, bank lending to the private sector and a variety of external and other influences; and, on the other hand, the growth of broad money.[6]

The chosen approach to managing monetary growth was therefore to operate on the credit counterparts. Bank credit to the public sector could be influenced by varying the PSBR and the amount of public debt sold to non-banks; bank credit to the private sector was thought to be responsive to changes in interest rates; and bank credit to the overseas sector was related to intervention tactics on the foreign exchanges.[7] In this spirit, the Green Paper on *Monetary Control* began with the observation that: 'There are a number of policy instruments available to the authorities in influencing monetary conditions. Of these the main ones are fiscal policy, debt management, administered changes in short-term interest rates, direct controls on the financial system and operations in the foreign exchange markets'.[8]

Officials at the Treasury and the Bank of England had few illusions about the precision of monetary management by these means. Indeed, there is an uneasy slide from the use of the ambitious words 'control' in the title of the Green Paper to the more modest notion of 'influence' in the key opening paragraph. Nevertheless, the authorities were confident that, with their 'basic weapons', they could 'achieve the first requisite of control of the money supply – control, say, over a year or more'.[9]

Restraint over the budget deficit was seen as integral to monetary control over such annual periods. At Budget time a careful assessment was made of the consistency of the PSBR estimate with the broad money target, and the tendency of policy was to subordinate fiscal decision to the monetary targets. The humbling of fiscal policy was regarded as almost revolutionary, since it appeared to end the Keynesian demand-management role traditionally assigned to the Government in post-war British political economy. The intention was not to vary the PSBR to counter cyclical ups and downs in the economy, but to ensure – in the words of the Treasury *Memorandum* – that 'the trend path' of the PSBR be 'downwards'.[10]

If the authorities were sceptical about their ability to target broad money over short-run periods of a few months, the Government was reluctant to make exact predictions about how long it would take for inflation to respond to monetary restraint. The emphasis was very much on the medium-term nature of the commitment to monetary targets. It was readily conceded that a check to broad money this year would be followed by slower inflation not in the immediate future, but in two, three or perhaps even four years' time. This was, of course, consistent with the belief that the relationship between broad money and inflation was medium-term in character.

One consideration thought particularly likely to confuse the money/inflation link in the UK was the influence of a powerful trade union movement on wages and prices. This influence was sometimes regarded as having autonomy from strictly economic variables, such as the state of demand and the level of unemployment. The size of the public sector, and its insensitivity to monetary conditions, was a special problem.[11]

To ask what Keynes would have thought about British monetarism, in its 1980 version, may seem an ahistorical impertinence. However, it is not far-fetched to see similarities between the system of monetary management envisaged by the Thatcher Government in its early years and the idea of a managed currency advocated by Keynes throughout his life. Indeed, in one particularly interesting respect they coincided. The proposal for a managed currency was first made in *A Tract on Monetary Reform* (published in 1923), which was intended as a reasoned polemic against the gold standard. It contrasted the gold standard ('a barbarous relic') focusing on the stability of foreign exchange, and a managed currency ('a more scientific standard') with its goal of 'stability in an index number of prices'.[12] A preference for domestic price stability over a fixed exchange rate was also embodied in the Medium Term Financial Strategy, as originally formulated. In the 1981 Mais lecture Sir Geoffrey Howe, the Chancellor of the Exchequer, remarked that, if monetary targets had been adopted, 'you cannot have it both ways and also hold the exchange rate at a particular level. If any inconsistency emerges, the monetary targets have to come first'.[13] In accordance with this prescription exchange intervention was minimal for several years in the early 1980s.

In summary, British monetarism could be said to have four distinctive features: (1) the selection of broad money as the appropriate intermediate target, and a consequent emphasis on the control of bank credit as the central task of monetary management; (2) as part of the overall control of credit, a belief that fiscal policy should be made consistent with monetary policy and lose the demand-management functions attributed to it in the 1960s and early 1970s; (3) an admission that the link between money and inflation was medium-term in nature and difficult to predict, partly because of the strength of British trade unionism; and (4) the avoidance of any specific exchange rate objective, for reasons which Keynes would probably have understood and approved.

The first area of disagreement between British and American monetarism lies in the emphasis placed on broad and narrow money, and in related questions about the implementation of monetary control. As we have explained, in Britain in the early 1980s broad money was the focus of policy-makers' attention. Although Friedman himself is agnostic about the issue and believes that all measures of money convey a valuable message, there is no doubt that the majority of American monetarists favour the monetary base or a narrow money aggregate as the best policy indicator. According to Mayer, the monetary base is chosen for two reasons. One is that the American monetarist's 'analysis of the money supply process tells him that this is the variable which best reflects monetary policy actions'; the other is that 'he believes the monetary base to be the best indicator of future changes in the money stock'.[14] Both aspects of Mayer's statement are important and need to be discussed, but to understand them a sketch of the American monetarists' view of the money supply process is required.

American monetarists, like their British counterparts, normally include bank deposits in their definition of the money supply.[15] Since banks have to be able to repay deposits with cash, they are obliged to hold a fraction of their assets in the form of cash or balances with the central bank. Empirical investigation is said to demonstrate that the ratio between cash and deposits is reasonably stable over the long run, while the quantity of cash is a liability of the central bank and fully under the monetary authorities' control. It follows that changes in the quantity of cash, reflecting central bank operations, determine the level of bank deposits and, hence, of the money supply. Cash (that is, notes, coin and balances with the central bank) is also known as 'high-powered money', the 'monetary base' or the 'reserve base'. Economists who believe in this account of the money supply process tend also to favour deliberate variations in the quantity of cash as the main instrument of monetary policy. This system, known as monetary base control, has been widely advocated by American monetarists.

The first part of Mayer's statement is therefore readily explained. Changes in the monetary base are taken, by American monetarists, as the clearest guide to what the central bank has been doing, and so to the intended thrust of monetary policy. It is quite clear – from the previous section – that the approach of British monetarists is quite different. With bank deposits viewed as the counterpart to bank credit, British monetarists concentrate their attention on variables believed to be relevant to the behaviour of bank credit. By far the most important of these is the short-term rate of interest, set by Bank of England operations in the money market. The contrast with the American monetarist position, with its concern over the quantity of reserves rather than the price at which they are made available to the banking system, is virtually total. Moreover, whereas in British monetarism the level of bank lending to the private sector is seen as critical to the monetary outlook, American monetarists are largely indifferent to it.

Some doctrinal purists might protest at this stage that a preference for the interest rate over the monetary base cannot plausibly be attributed to monetarists of any kind, not even to 'British monetarists'. They might say that, if that is the implication of our definition of British monetarism, the definition is too idiosyncratic and peculiar to be taken seriously. The answer to this objection is to recall the pattern of public debate in the early 1980s. The official policy framework prevailing at that time, and the attitudes informing it, were labelled as 'monetarist' in the media, in Parliament and in many other contexts. Furthermore, its emphasis on broad money and the credit counterparts arithmetic did logically entail that close attention be paid to interest rates. Of course, to say that interest rates mattered was not to make them a target of policy. On the contrary, the intention was that interest rates (the instrument) were to be varied to influence credit and money (the intermediate targets) in order to exert leverage over the inflation rate (the ultimate target).

American reaction to monetary control procedures in Britain has varied from technical puzzlement to frank outrage. A consequence of the British arrangements was that official sales of gilt-edged securities to non-banks often had to be stepped up in order to reduce the excessive quantity of deposits created by bank credit. In other words, long-term funding was a basic instrument of monetary policy. An official at the Federal Reserve Bank of New York remarked at a conference in May 1982 that this 'emphasis on selling intermediate and long-term securities to mop up money balances always sounds a bit strange to us'.[16] Friedman's comments to the Treasury and Civil Service Committee in 1980 were much sharper. He expressed incredulity at the opening paragraph of the Green paper on Monetary Control. In his view: 'Only a Rip Van Winkle, who had not read any of the flood of literature during the past decade and more on the money supply process, could possibly have written' the key sentence with its list of instruments for influencing monetary conditions. He judged that: 'This remarkable sentence reflects the myopia engendered by long-established practices, the difficulty we all have of adjusting our outlook to changed circumstances.' He declared strong support for direct control of the monetary base instead of the British system.[17]

The dismay that many American monetarists felt – and still do feel – about the Bank of England's monetary control procedures did not go unnoticed in the UK. Several economists advocated that Britain adopt some form of monetary base control. The most notable were Professor Brian Griffiths of the City University (later to be head of the Prime Minister's Policy Unit at 10 Downing Street), Professor Patrick Minford of Liverpool University and Professor (later Sir) Alan Walters who was appointed the Prime Minister's Economic Adviser in 1981. As all three are British and have been called monetarists, it may seem odd that in this paper 'British monetarism' is associated with broad money, credit control and funding. It perhaps needs to be repeated that British monetarism is defined here as the system of macroeconomic management established in the late 1970s and early 1980s, not a set of beliefs held by self-professed monetarist economists. In fact, as we shall see, the views of Minford and Walters became important as much because they challenged the existing policy framework as because they supported it.

What about the second part of Mayer's statement, that American monetarists follow the monetary base because it is 'the best indicator of future changes in the money stock'? It may or may not be true that the monetary base has this property in the USA; much depends on whose econometrics one chooses to trust. But it is certainly not true in the UK, where the institutional apparatus is such that the monetary base is not a reliable guide to future changes in the money stock, on any definition. Under the British arrangements the Bank of England supplies cash in the required amounts to keep banks' balances at the daily clearing just adequate for them to fulfil their obligations.[18] In consequence, the quantity of cash held by the banks adjusts to the size of their balance sheets rather than the other way round. The monetary base is determined by what is happening in the economy today; it does not determine what banks, the money stock or the economy will do in future.[19] Indeed, one of the remarkable features of the British system is that – because of the flexibility of official money market operations – the banks can keep very low ratios of cash reserves to deposit liabilities. Since cash does not pay interest, this feature is attractive to profit-seeking overseas bankers, and is one reason for the intensity of foreign competition in the British financial system.

American economists do not appear fully to understand either the method of operation or the purpose of the British practices. The same Federal Reserve official who was puzzled by the significance of funding in the UK was also 'struck by the minimal role that reserve requirements play in the monetary control process'. He wondered whether 'the amount of leverage available' was 'sufficiently large for the central bank to pursue monetary and other policy targets effectively in all seasons'.[20] But the point of the British system is that – in contrast to the situation in the USA – the quantity of cash reserves is not supposed to exert any leverage on the monetary targets.

Friedman, in his evidence to the Treasury and Civil Service Committee, proposed some reforms which he thought would tighten the link between the base and the money supply. He noted that, in 1981, banks could hold a variety of assets to meet reserve requirements in the UK and suggested that:

> It would be highly desirable to replace this multiple reserve system by one in which only a single asset – liabilities of the Bank of England in the form of notes and coin (that is, base money) – satisfies reserve requirements. This is probably the most important single change in current institutional arrangements that is required to permit more effective control of the money supply.[21]

The problem here was that Friedman had become confused between a $12\frac{1}{2}$ per cent reserve asset ratio which served an essentially prudential function and a $1\frac{1}{2}$ per cent cash ratio which was the operational fulcrum of monetary policy. Since the confusion has been shared to some degree by British economists and officials, it was perhaps excusable. But Friedman's imperceptiveness on the question reflected a wide gap between American and

British approaches to monetary management and undoubtedly symptomized a certain amount of mutual incomprehension.

The differences between central bank techniques in the UK and USA are not new, but can be dated back to the early years of the Federal Reserve system. Unlike some recent participants in the debate, Keynes was well aware of their nature and origins, and devoted many pages of his *Treatise on Money* (published in 1930) to their analysis. He drew a contrast between 'the bank-rate policy' applied in Britain and the 'open-market policy' adopted in the USA. Essentially, the bank-rate policy involved a varying bank rate in order to control 'the aggregate of the central bank's assets', whereas open-market operations of the American kind produced 'a direct effect on the reserves of the member banks, and hence on the volume of deposits and of credit generally'.[22] Although Keynes saw some merits in a bank-rate policy, it is quite clear that he preferred an open-market policy. He expressed great admiration for Governor Strong of the Federal Reserve, whom he regarded as the pioneer of scientific open-market operations, remarking that:

> open-market operations can be so handled as to be quite extraordinarily effective in managing the currency. The successful management of the dollar by the Federal Reserve i.e. from 1923 to 1928 was a triumph – for the view that currency management is feasible, in conditions which are virtually independent of the movements of gold.[23]

The sympathy here for the American approach connects with some of his later themes, since he also considered that, 'whilst the bank rate may be the most suitable weapon for use when the object of the central bank is to preserve international equilibrium, open-market sales and purchases of securities may be more effective when the object is to influence the rate of investment'.[24] This fits in neatly with Keynes's emphasis in *The General Theory* on the need to influence investment in order to mitigate fluctuations in output and employment.

However, it should be noted that in *The General Theory* Keynes says rather little about central bank techniques and almost nothing about the Federal Reserve. There is a short comment, in the 'Notes on the trade cycle' in Chapter 22, about how 'the most enlightened monetary control might find itself in difficulties, faced with a boom of the 1929 type in America, and armed with no other weapons than those possessed at the time by the Federal Reserve System'.[25] But that is all. The implication seems to be that the severity of the American slump in the early 1930s, particularly by comparison with the mildness of the contemporaneous downturn in Britain, undermined the prestige of the Federal Reserve's procedures. Nevertheless, it is reasonable to conclude that – in this area of the technicalities of monetary control – Keynes inclined more towards American monetarism than British.

In qualification, it also needs to be said that throughout this work Keynes refers repeatedly, and with evident belief in its importance, to 'credit', while in virtually all his discussions about monetary practice he is concerned about the behaviour of bank deposits and so of broad money. The focus on broad money is particularly obvious in his distinctions between income, business and savings deposits, and between industrial and financial 'circulations', in the first volume of the *Treatise on Money*.[26]

Basic to the Medium-Term Financial Strategy, and indeed to the monetarist enterprise in Britain more generally, was control over the fiscal position. Recognition of the importance of restricting public sector borrowing can be dated back to the mid-1970s, when extremely large budget deficits were accompanied by difficulties in controlling the money supply and by fears that the substantial demands made by the public sector on the savings pool were crowding out private sector investment. Targets for the PSBR were included in the International Monetary Fund's Letter of Intent in December 1976, which set out conditions for its loan to the UK. In his speech to the Lord Mayor's dinner on 19 October 1978, Denis Healey – as Chancellor of the Exchequer in the then Labour Government – said that the Government was 'determined to control the growth of public expenditure so that its fiscal policy is consistent with its monetary stance'.[27] The stipulation of precise numbers for the PSBR in the Medium-Term Financial Strategy from 1980 onwards should not be seen as a surprise innovation, but as the logical culmination to events over several years.

The thinking behind this approach was implicit in the credit counterparts arithmetic. If bank lending to the private sector, external influences on money growth and public sector debt sales to non-banks were all given, there was – and, of course, still is – a direct accounting link between the PSBR and the growth of the money supply. For every £100 million of extra PSBR there was an extra £100 million of M3. If an excessive PSBR threatened the monetary target, high interest rates would be needed to discourage lending to the private sector or encourage more buying of public sector debt. According to Peter Middleton (later to become Sir Peter and also Permanent Secretary to the Treasury), in a seminar paper given in the 1977/78 academic year, 'as a general proposition, a big fiscal deficit will tend to lead to a rapid growth of money supply and/or to higher interest rates... It follows that it is essential to examine fiscal and monetary policy simultaneously and co-ordinate them as far as practicable.'[28]

This relationship between flows of public sector borrowing and the growth of the money supply can be easily reformulated in terms of the stocks of public sector debt, bank lending to the private sector and money.[29] The main conclusion is that, if the ratios of public debt and bank lending to gross domestic product are constant, a higher ratio of the PSBR to GDP is associated with a higher growth rate of broad money and so with more inflation. In practice, ratios of public sector debt and bank lending to GDP fluctuate substantially over time. But it is plausible that a government committed to extensive privatization of productive assets would favour, over the medium term, a rising ratio of private sector bank borrowing to GDP, rather than a high ratio of public debt to GDP. In the early 1980s, that implied a need for the PSBR/GDP ratio to be maintained at a low level for several years.

What about the American monetarists' attitude towards fiscal policy? In the late 1960s there was a fierce debate in the USA – known as the 'Battle of the Radio Stations' after the initials of the main researchers involved (AM, FM, for Ando–Modigliani, Friedman–Meiselman) – about the relative effectiveness of fiscal and monetary policy.[30] Arguably, it was the starting-point of monetarism. Not only did it prompt Professor Karl Brunner to coin the term 'monetarist', but also it revolved around the idea – later to become a commonplace in the British policy debate – that discretionary changes in fiscal policy were misguided as a means of influencing the economy.

In view of this background, American monetarists might reasonably have been expected to welcome the demotion of fiscal policy in the Medium-Term Financial Strategy. Curiously, that has not been the reaction. Friedman, in his evidence to the Treasury and Civil Service Committee, said that the attention paid to the PSBR targets was 'unwise', partly 'because there is no necessary relation between the size of the PSBR and monetary growth'.[31] Friedman's remarks were picked up by British critics of monetarism, notably by the Oxford economist, Christopher Allsopp, who was emboldened to claim that: 'The standard monetarist line is that it is only the money supply that matters for inflation control, and that fiscal policy has little direct effect on the economy, or on the ease or difficulty of controlling money.'[32] Although Friedman may be extreme in denigrating the place of PSBR control in British monetarism, there is no doubt that most American monetarists do not integrate fiscal policy into their thinking and policy advice. Thus a prescription for fiscal policy does not figure in Mayer's list of key monetarist propositions. The explanation is perhaps to be sought in the separation of powers between the Federal Reserve (responsible for monetary policy) and the Treasury (which, along with other agencies, controls the Budget) in the American system. For these institutional reasons it makes less sense to attempt to co-ordinate fiscal and monetary policy in the American macro-economic context than in the British.

There was never any pretence in British monetarism that *x* per cent growth of broad money over the next year would be followed by an exactly predictable *y* per cent growth of money GDP at an exactly known date in the future.

It was readily admitted that the link between money and inflation was imprecise, while there were no illusions that the impact of monetary restraint on inflation would assert itself – or even be identifiable – over periods of time as short as three to six months. Instead, the connection between broad money and the price level was regarded as rather difficult to forecast and essentially medium-term in nature. When British monetarism was at its most influential, policy-makers probably thought in terms of an x per cent rate of broad money growth leading to an inflation rate of x plus or minus 2 or 3 per cent at some date two to four years away. That may sound too flimsy as a basis for decision-taking; but it is vital to remember the context in which British monetarism first made headway in the public debate. In the mid-1970s, when the inflation rate was frequently at about 20 per cent or more, politicians were less fussy about a 2 or 3 per cent error in forecasting it than they are now. Moreover, there was little respect for computer-based macroeconomic forecasting methods which promised great exactitude. Such methods had totally failed to predict the scale of the inflationary retribution for the monetary policy mistakes of the Heath–Barber period.

American monetarists also refuse to make bold claims about the precision of monetary impacts on the economy. Friedman coined an often-repeated phrase when he said that the relationship between money and inflation was marked by 'long and variable lags'. In his evidence to the Treasury and Civil Service Committee, he cautions that 'failure to allow for lags in reaction is a major source of misunderstanding'. After suggesting that 'for the US, the UK and Japan, the lag between a change in monetary growth and output is roughly six to nine months, between the change in monetary growth and inflation, roughly two years', he immediately inserted the qualification that, 'of course, the effects are spread out, not concentrated at the indicated point of time'.[33] Arguably, this reluctance to be specific reflects an aspect of monetarism highlighted by Mayer, a preference for small reduced-form models over large-scale structural models of the economy. According to Mayer, monetarists believe that the money supply affects the economy in so many ways that 'even a large structural model is not likely to pick them all up'.[34]

The differences between American and British monetarists in this area may not, therefore, seem to be all that wide. Keynes also recognized, although with reservations, the medium- and long-term validity of the money/inflation link. In Chapter 21 of *The General Theory*, he said that the question of the relationship between money and prices outside the short period is 'for historical generalizations rather than for pure theory'. He continued by observing that, if liquidity preference (that is, the demand for money) tends to be uniform over the long run, 'there may well be some sort of rough relationship between the national income and the quantity of money required to satisfy liquidity preference, taken as a mean over periods of pessimism and optimism together'.[35] This is an interesting quotation because it shows that Keynes never dismissed the relevance of money to the long-run behaviour of prices, not even after the refinement of his theoretical ideas on the short-run determination of output in *The General Theory*. However, the section which contains the quotation also makes several references to wages and productivity as fundamental influences on prices. Keynes may have been reluctant to give a wholehearted endorsement to either a monetary or a wage-bargaining theory of the price level. Perhaps he thought that both had something to say.

Keynes's equivocation on the subject may have reflected the central position of the trade unions in British society. A strong and influential trade union movement has continued for most of the 50 or so years since the publication of *The General Theory* and obliged economists in the UK to pay trade unionism more attention than their counterparts in the USA. Not surprisingly, therefore, greater anxiety in the UK about the trade unions' impact on the labour market and the economy has differentiated American and British monetarism, although the differences are more matters of emphasis than of substance.

British monetarists are more prone to claim that trade unions, by disrupting the setting of market-clearing wages, aggravate the problem of unemployment. This argument is integrated into a specifically monetarist framework by saying that trade union activity increases the natural rate of unemployment. The point is that, in a situation such as the UK's where there have traditionally been strong political pressures to reduce unemployment below the natural rate, inflation expectations have been contaminated by occasional phases of excess demand. As long periods of unemployment above the natural rate have then been needed to remove the inflationary virus, and as these have always involved restrictive and unpopular monetary policies, trade union activism has indirectly stigmatized the deliberate use of monetary policy. British monetarists therefore accord trade unions a more prominent and active role in the inflationary process than American monetarists.[36]

Friedman's position on the trade unions is that they can alter relative wages (that is, the ratio between union and non-union wages), but they cannot influence the absolute level of wages (that is, union and non-union wages combined) which is determined by, among other things, the money supply. Moreover, a given amount of trade union power cannot explain continuing inflation. When asked at an Institute of Economic Affairs lecture in 1974 whether trade unions could increase the natural rate of unemployment, Friedman acknowledged that this was 'a very difficult question to answer', but reiterated that 'what produced...inflation is not trade unions, nor monopolistic employers, but what happens to the quantity of money'.[37]

The problem posed by trade unionism for British monetarism has been exacerbated by the dominance of trade unionism in the public sector. While there are reasonably obvious transmission mechanisms between monetary policy and private sector inflation, it is far from evident how monetary policy affects the public sector. Wages and prices in government and nationalized industries are typically set by administrative fiat and are remote from market forces. One exercise on the demand for money in the UK recognized this by regressing the money supply on private sector GDP, not GDP as a whole.[38] It would not occur to American monetarists – with the USA's small government sector and weaker trade unions – to be so fastidious.

The British economy also differs from the American in being smaller and more susceptible to international influences. Since this difference has made British monetarists more concerned about external pressures on domestic monetary policy than their American counterparts, it has stimulated a lively debate about the appropriateness of alternative exchange rate regimes. This debate has continued over many decades, with Keynes's argument for a managed currency in *A Tract on Monetary Reform* being one of the most seminal contributions. Indeed, it could be claimed that when Sir Geoffrey Howe expressed such a decided preference for monetary targets over a fixed exchange rate in 1981 he was echoing a famous passage in the *Tract* where Keynes set up an opposition between stability of prices and stability of exchange. In his words, 'If the external price level is unstable, we cannot keep both our own price level and our exchanges stable. And we are compelled to choose'.[39]

In the mid-1970s, however, Mr Healey failed to choose one or the other. Some interest rate changes were motivated by external factors, some by domestic considerations and some by both. The result was rather unhappy not just intellectually, but also practically, with 1976 seeing the most prolonged and embarrassing sterling crisis in the post-war period. The monetarist commitment to floating exchange rates in the early 1980s can be interpreted largely as a reaction to the muddles of the first three years of Mr Healey's Chancellorship. But a number of key theoretical inputs also moulded the climate of opinion and need to be mentioned. They can be dated back to the late 1960s, when leading economic journalists – egged on by Professor Harry Johnson of the University of Chicago and the London School of Economics – thought that the abandonment of a fixed exchange rate would remove an artificial barrier to British economic growth. More immediately relevant in the late 1970s was work done by Laidler and Parkin at the Manchester Inflation Workshop.[40]

An episode in late 1977 is basic to understanding the fervour of the monetarist support for a floating exchange rate in 1980 and 1981. After the excessive depreciation of 1976 the pound revived in 1977, and for much of the year its rise was restrained by heavy foreign exchange intervention. This intervention had the effect of boosting the money supply, which in consequence grew much faster than envisaged by the official target. (The target was for an increase of 9 to 13 per cent in sterling M3 in the 1977/78 financial year. The actual result was an increase of 15.1 per cent.) Monetarist economists argued that the high monetary growth jeopardized the financial progress achieved under the International Monetary Fund programmes and, after the usual lag, would be punished by higher inflation; more conventional economists at the Treasury and elsewhere thought that a 'low' exchange rate was needed for reasons of export competitiveness. The debate was conducted at several levels and is reported to have been particularly intense within the official machine.

When the Government stopped intervening and allowed the pound to float upwards in October 1977, the monetarists seemed to have won. But their victory was not final. Although they were vindicated by a sharp upturn in inflation in late 1979 and early 1980 (after a fairly standard Friedmanite two-year lag), there were constant complaints that the Government's permissive attitude towards the exchange rate allowed undue exchange rate appreciation. Among the most active participants to the 1977 debate were economists at the London Business School. On the whole they favoured adhering to the money supply targets and allowing the exchange rate to float. A particularly notable contribution was made by Terence (later Sir Terence) Burns, who was to become the Government's Chief Economic Adviser in 1979.[41]

The views of British monetarists in the late 1970s and early 1980s were not radically different from those of their American counterparts. Perhaps the most classic statement of the merits of floating was given by Friedman in his 1950 paper on 'The case for flexible exchange rates'.[42] This paper was perfunctory in its treatment of the impact of foreign exchange intervention on money growth, which was basic to the UK debate in the late 1970s. But its mood, with its aspersions on the forecasting ability of central bank officials and its praise for market forces, was close to that of the Thatcher Government in its early years. In his evidence to the Treasury and Civil Service Committee in 1980, Friedman said that 'of course' an attempt to manipulate the exchange rate would limit the authorities' ability to control the money supply. He also criticized the Government's announced policy of preventing excessive fluctuations in the exchange rate. In his opinion, 'this exception is a mistake; better to leave the market entirely free ... certainly for such a broad and efficient market as exists in British sterling'.[43]

As it happened, the Government in 1980 and early 1981 did not make an exception, even for a patently excessive fluctuation in the exchange rate. The pound became seriously over-valued, reaching $2.42 in October 1980 compared to $1.63 in October 1976, and in February 1981 almost 5 to the

Deutschmark compared with 4 one year earlier. These exchange rate antics have subsequently been singled out as the principal policy disappointment of the monetarist experiment. Inevitably, there has been much soul-searching about the suitability of monetary targets in a small economy subject to all the volatilities of contemporary international finance. It is interesting that Keynes, when describing the alternatives of price stability and exchange stability in the *Tract*, conceded that the right choice must 'partly depend on the relative importance of foreign trade in the economic life of the country'.[44] Indeed, the book's final paragraph suggested that 'there are probably no countries, other than Great Britain and the United States, which would be justified in attempting to set up an independent standard'. Other countries could decide to peg their currencies to either sterling or the dollar until, 'with the progress of knowledge and understanding, so perfect a harmony had been established between the two that the choice was a matter of indifference'.[45]

The period of strong monetarist influence over policy-making was short-lived, although its precise length is a matter for discussion and depends on whose version of events one selects. At one extreme it has been argued that broad money targets were discredited in July 1980 when the abolition of the 'corset' was followed by a jump of over 5 per cent in sterling M3 in only one month. (The corset was an artificial device for restricting credit, which imposed penalties on banks when their balance sheets increased faster than given percentage figures.) Officials quickly realized that the original sterling M3 target for the year to March 1981, which was for growth of between 7 and 11 per cent, was unattainable. They therefore sought forms of words to explain away – and, as far as possible, divert attention from – a serious monetary overshoot. In the end sterling M3 rose by 19.4 per cent in the 1980/81 target period. This wide divergence from target, combined with the apparent failure of high interest rates to bring M3 back under control, is said by some authors to have caused monetarism to be abandoned only a few months after it had been publicly proclaimed as official dogma.[46]

However, a more plausible account would treat the erosion of the system set up in early 1980 as a gradual process. There are various possibilities, but mid-1985 is probably best regarded as the terminal phase. It was then that broad money targets, and hence the defining features of British monetarism, were scrapped. Just as monetarism did not gain ground by a simple process of intellectual conquest, so it did not retreat through a straightforward failure to meet key practical tests. Instead there were a number of distinct and intermittent challenges to monetarist arrangements. Although none of them individually might have been decisive, their cumulative impact was difficult to resist.

The first major problem was the pound's clear overvaluation in late 1980 and early 1981. The reasons for sterling's appreciation have been much debated, but one thesis – that above-target broad money growth obliged the Government to maintain high interest rates, and high interest rates drove up the sterling exchange rate – had obvious cogency and relevance. As we have seen, both Sir Geoffrey Howe and Keynes had argued, in their different ways, that 'you cannot have it both ways', and simultaneously control the domestic price level and the exchange rate. But the experience of 1980 and 1981 suggested that Britain should try to have it both ways. It was better to have an intellectually muddled monetary policy than a politically unacceptable industrial recession. In 1982 and 1983 official thinking was that the exchange rate should have some role in assessing monetary conditions, while the monetary targets should be retained. After severe exchange rate overvaluation had caused a drastic fall in industrial production between mid-1980 and mid-1981, the Government was less concerned about the logical niceties of the matter than about avoiding further damage to the manufacturing base.

The second difficulty was that sterling M3 proved awkward to manage. The 1980 Green Paper on *Monetary Control* may not have been particularly optimistic about month-by-month control, but at least it thought that sterling M3 could be brought within target 'over a year or more'. The large overshoot in 1980/81 undermined the credibility of even that rather unambitious statement. When there was another overshoot in the 1981/82 financial year, with sterling M3 up by 13 per cent compared to a target range of 6 to 10 per cent, many economists agreed with the then chief Opposition spokesman on Treasury and economic affairs, Peter Shore, that sterling M3 had become 'a wayward mistress'. There was a widely-held view that sterling M3 was no longer a reliable intermediate target and that policy should be stated more flexibly. For those who still favoured monetary targets in some form, the disappointments with M3 targeting implied that monetary base control deserved more sympathetic consideration. The disillusionment with broad money was accompanied by increased interest in narrow money, either in the monetary base itself (also known as 'M0') or in M1 (cash in circulation with the public, plus sight deposits).

These changes in official allegiances and informed opinion, away from money targets to the exchange rate and from broad money to narrow money, were largely determined by the pattern of events. But intellectual rationalization was not far behind. A key figure in the dethronement of sterling M3 was Sir Alan Walters. Although his credentials when appointed as the Prime Minister's Economic Adviser in 1981 were avowedly 'monetarist', his monetarism was very different in character from the 'British monetarism' described here. He had been much influenced by the American enthusiasm for monetary base control and was doubtful about the merits of operating on the credit counterparts to achieve broad money targets. His preference was for a measure of money used in transactions, which he thought was best approximated in the UK's case by M1. Despite problems because of institutional change, he believed that, 'It is money in this transactions sense that plays the central role in the theoretical structure and the propositions of monetarism.' He judged that credit had 'but a minor role' and was correspondingly sceptical about 'such credit magnitudes as M3'.[47]

A consequence of the demotion of broad money was that less concern was felt about the rapid growth of credit in the private sector. Indeed, there was a school of thought – best represented by the Liverpool Research Group under Professor Patrick Minford – that bank lending to the private sector was always good for the economy, since it made possible more private sector spending and investment. High levels of lending were therefore welcomed, irrespective of the monetary repercussions. In some of its publications this group also suggested that large increases in broad money contained no inflationary threat. According to one issue of its *Quarterly Economic Bulletin*, credit – even credit in the form of bank lending – cannot be inflationary. Its argument was that, since borrowing by some individuals must be accompanied by lending by others, there is no net addition to or subtraction from wealth, and there should be no effect on behaviour. Thus, when both sides of a balance sheet increase: 'This is a straightforward portfolio adjustment and is not inflationary'.[48] Professor Minford, like Sir Alan Walters, had been much influenced by the American literature. As a reflection of this background, he regarded narrow money (particularly M0) as the most trustworthy money supply indicator and favoured monetary base control.

By 1983 and 1984 the views of Walters and Minford had been important in undermining the original monetarist arrangements. These arrangements suffered most from policy surprises and disappointments, and from criticisms from non-monetarist or frankly anti-monetarist economists. But the willingness of two economists carrying the 'monetarist' label to denigrate certain aspects of the existing policy framework reinforced the suspicion and distrust with which British monetarism had always been viewed by the press, Whitehall and the majority of academic economists. Since Walters and Minford had undoubtedly been keen students of monetarist thought coming from the other side of the Atlantic, their susceptibility to its teachings meant that American monetrarism contributed – if somewhat indirectly – to the decline of British monetarism.[49]

In another respect, however, Walters and Minford were loyal to the policy structure envisaged in 1980 and 1981. Although Walters promoted a 1981 report by Jurg Niehans which identified sterling's sharp appreciation as a symptom of monetary tightness, he was adamantly opposed to attempts to manage the exchange rate by foreign exchange intervention. He wanted policy to be geared towards domestic monetary objectives and not towards the preservation of a fixed exchange rate or a target exchange-rate band. Indeed, he thought that these conditions still 'broadly' applied to the UK in 1985 when he wrote, in *Britain's Economic Renaissance*, that: 'The authorities announce that the level of short-term interest rates will depend primarily on the assessment of the movement in the monetary aggregates. The exchange rate is to be the object of benign neglect.'[50] Minford was equally hostile to systematic foreign-exchange intervention. In a paper first presented in 1980, he took it for granted that an 'independent monetary policy is possible' and noted that this 'presupposition is only valid under floating exchange rates'.[51]

Unlike the tendency to play down the significance of credit and broad money, the increasing official preoccupation with the exchange rate in the early and mid-1980s therefore cannot be ascribed to pressure from Walters and Minford, or to the influence of American monetarist ideas. In the end it was the completeness of the shift in official priorities from domestic monetary control to exchange rate stability which was primarily responsible for monetarism's downfall. Although several official statements had already hinted at the precedence of exchange rate stability as a policy goal, the Plaza Accord of September 1985 may have been the key turning-point. At the Plaza meeting the finance ministers of the five leading industrial nations decided that in future they should co-operate more actively to achieve an appropriate pattern of exchange rates. Thereafter the Chancellor of the Exchequer, Nigel Lawson, was constantly mindful of this international responsibility and gave less attention to domestic monetary issues.

Other considerations, more local and humdrum, pointed policy in the same direction. The standard British practice of long-term funding, which had so bewildered Federal Reserve officials in 1982, was beginning to cause technical problems in the UK's short-term money markets by mid-1985. The authorities decided that they could no longer 'overfund' the PSBR in order to keep broad money on target. Without this technique, which had proved immensely useful as a means of curbing the growth of the monetary aggregates, there were likely to be great difficulties meeting broad money targets.[52] In addition to all the other supposed weaknesses of broad money, sterling M3 was now condemned for complicating the management of the money markets. In his Mansion House speech on 17 October 1985 Nigel Lawson suspended the broad money target for the 1985/86 financial year.

This was effectively the end of British monetarism. Although ostensibly only 'suspended', broad money targets had in fact been abandoned. A broad money target was announced in the 1986 Budget, but the envisaged growth rate was so high that it was not a worthwhile constraint on inflation. Despite that, the target was soon exceeded and Mr Lawson suspended it again. By late 1986 the UK was in the early stages of a vigorous boom driven by extraordinarily rapid growth in bank lending and broad money. Although the Government refrained from fiscal reflation, the credit and money excesses of 1987 and early 1988 were curiously similar to those seen in the Barber boom of the early 1970s. This was richly ironic, since the inflation which followed the Barber boom had been largely responsible for policy-makers' initial receptiveness to American monetarist ideas in the late 1970s.

The Government did announce and observe narrow money targets, expressed in terms of M0, throughout 1986 and 1987. But, as its champions ought to have known, M0 tracks recent movements in money transactions and does not influence the future behaviour of the economy. The behaviour of narrow money completely failed to warn the Government about the widening payments gap and rising inflation trend which emerged in late 1988. If Nigel Lawson had a meaningful anti-inflation policy in these years, the key instrument was the exchange rate for the pound and the central idea was that exchange rate stability would ensure rough equivalence between inflation in the UK and other industrial countries. As the dollar was falling heavily from early 1985 because of the USA's enormous trade and current account deficits, it seemed sensible to watch the pound/Deutschmark exchange rate more closely than the pound/dollar rate or, indeed, the effective exchange rate against a weighted basket of other major currencies. Throughout 1987 sterling was held fairly stable in a band of 2.85 to 3 Deutschmark.

This shadowing of the Deutschmark meant that the UK was virtually a participant in the exchange rate mechanism of the European Monetary System. Nigel Lawson had opted for an external financial discipline in preference to the domestic focus associated with money supply targets. Since this was obviously a major change in strategy from the early years of the Thatcher Government, an active public debate developed about the advantages and disadvantages of full EMS membership. Most academic economists approved of Lawson's new approach and thought it a welcome change from the doctrinaire monetarism he had espoused as Financial Secretary to the Treasury in 1980. But old-style monetarists (as they now were being called) were mostly hostile to EMS membership, while Walters and Minford were particularly outspoken in their attacks on it. In *Britain's Economic Renaissance*, Walters described the EMS as 'rather messy' and remarked that the periodic exchange rate realignments, far from being determined in an economically rational way, were 'grand political events which present many opportunities for horse-trading, threats, counter threats, bluff, etc.'.[53] In his view, it would be best if the UK had nothing to do with it. In adopting this position, Walters was following the mainstream monetarist tradition, in favour of freely floating exchange rates, associated with Friedman and Johnson.

After Walters had persuaded the Prime Minister, Margaret Thatcher, that the EMS was a bad idea, she was increasingly worried about how Lawson was organizing monetary policy. Although at the time of writing (September 1988), the precise terms of their discussions are largely a matter of conjecture, it is clear that their private disagreements became steadily more acrimonious and eventually could not be hidden from the press or their Cabinet colleagues. On 7 March 1988 Margaret Thatcher indicated to the Bank of England her wish that foreign exchange intervention be more limited in scale. The pound soon appreciated sharply against the Deutschmark. However, this did not foreshadow a return to money supply targets. In the Budget on 15 March Nigel Lawson did not reinstate a broad money target and even narrow money received a sharp snub. The M0 target was rendered ineffective, if only temporarily, by the admission, in the Treasury's *Financial Statement and Budget Report*, that no specific action would be taken to correct an overshoot which was expected to emerge early in the coming financial year.

By mid-1988 economic policy was in a fairly standard British muddle. The coherence and relative simplicity of the 1980-style monetarist framework had been replaced by a confusion and complexity highly reminiscent of the Healey Chancellorship in the mid-1970s. Government policy involved 'looking at everything' (the exchange rate, bank lending, house prices and the trade figures) and decisions were often the result of a lucky dip between options suggested by events in the financial markets. The UK had dropped broad money targets of a kind favoured by British monetarists; it had not adopted monetary base control as recommended by American monetarists; it had had an unsatisfactory experience with narrow money targets supported by American-influenced monetarists such as Walters and Minford; and it had equivocated before rejecting, at least provisionally, full membership of the EMS.

The many fluctuations in policy fashion in the 1980s should not be allowed to disguise a number of successes which were clearly attributable to the original monetarist programme. Most obviously, the inflation rate was reduced from an average of almost 15 per cent in the late 1970s to about 5 per cent in the five years from 1982. In view of the substantial monetary overshoots in 1980/81 and 1981/82, this achievement may have seemed more due to serendipity than scientific management. But in all of the next three financial years the broad money target was met, and in early 1985 the annual growth of sterling M3 was down to under 10 per cent. Meanwhile the Government broadly adhered to the fiscal side of the Medium-Term Financial Strategy.

The result was that in the years of moderate growth from 1982 to 1986 the ratio of public sector debt to national output was falling, while in the Lawson boom of 1987 and 1988 tax revenues were so buoyant that the Government actually ran a large budget surplus. The UK was therefore saved from the worries about long-run fiscal solvency which troubled some other European nations.[54] The soundness of the UK's public finances was also, of course, in sharp contrast to the USA's problems with budget deficits throughout the 1980s. With the benefit of hindsight, fiscal issues seem to have been handled more prudently by British monetarists than their American counterparts.[55]

Indeed, there is something of a puzzle about the Government's – or, at any rate, Nigel Lawson's – decision in 1985 to scrap the monetarist machinery with which it (and he) had been so closely associated five years earlier. As we have seen, there were many pressures tending to undermine the monetarist approach throughout the early 1980s, but one central point could not be overlooked. Monetarism had accomplished most of the original objectives held by its supporters as set out in the key policy documents of 1979 and 1980. Why, then, had the monetarist approach to macroeconomic policy disintegrated so quickly?

Perhaps the main solvents were the hostility of the traditional policy-making establishment, particularly academic economists in the universities, and the incomprehension of many influential commentators in the media. The aversion of the policy-making establishment may have had political roots. It is a safe sociological generalization that the majority of university teachers in Britain do not like Mrs Thatcher and do not vote Conservative. They are more sympathetic to socialism or the mixed economy than to competitive capitalism. It would be consistent if they disliked monetarism as much for the free-market evangelism of its high priests as for its technical content. Also important in explaining their attitudes is that British economists had become habituated to basing macroeconomic policy on external criteria, notably the exchange rate, instead of analysing domestic monetary conditions. Officials at the Bank of England, which for most of its history had been charged with keeping the pound stable in value against gold or the dollar, undoubtedly found it more natural to adjust interest rates in response to exchange rate movements than to deviations of the money supply from its target level.

In this context the debates between British and American monetarists were important. In the circumstances of the early 1980s, when monetarism was very much on trial, the new system needed to be defended with simple and convincing arguments by a cohesive group of advocates. Instead the arguments were typically of extreme complexity, while often they were more heated between rival members of the monetarist camp than between monetarists and non-monetarists. The differences betwen the British and American methods provided material and personnel for these disputes, and therefore weakened the monetarist position in public debate. Samuel Brittan of the *Financial Times*, the UK's most influential economic commentator, referred dismissively on several occasions to 'monetarist mumbo-jumbo', well aware that most of his readers were bored by technicalities. To him, and to many other people, membership of the EMS – with its uncomplicated exchange rate disciple – had great appeal.

There is a paradox here. Many critics of monetarism assumed the label of 'Keynesian' and clearly believed that their views were in a direct line of descent from Keynes himself. But, as we have seen, this is questionable. One consistent theme throughout Keynes's career was that monetary policy should be directed to the attainment of domestic policy objectives (price stability and full employment), not to fixing the international value of the pound (either in terms of gold or another currency). In 1923 he mentioned in *A Tract on Monetary Reform*, with evident approval and sympathy, 'the pioneer of price stability as against exchange stability, Irving Fisher'.[56] (It is intriguing that Irving Fisher is usually seen as an intellectual ancestor of Milton Friedman. It is certain that he wanted monetary policy geared to domestic economic goals, not to a numerically arbitrary exchange rate. Indeed, this is the central policy implication of his idea of a managed currency.)

After the abandonment of monetarism in the mid-1980s, there is little prospect that the UK will ever adopt Keynes's managed currency or anything resembling it. When he wrote the *Tract* in 1923, Britain had extensive commercial influence throughout the world. Its size relative to other countries justified it 'in attempting to set up an independent standard' as a complement to the dollar area. By contrast, in the late 1980s the UK is in a transitional and historically ambiguous position. It is no longer large enough to dominate a supra-national currency area, but it is not so small that membership of a European currency arrangement is self-evidently optimal. This dilemma, posed by the decline in British economic and financial power in the 65 years since the publication of the *Tract*, is basic to understanding policy-makers' resistance to a managed currency over the whole period. Perhaps the detailed blueprint for a managed currency would still have been unattractive if it had come not in the form of monetarism, but in a less ideologically unpalatable and far-reaching package. The trouble was that the Treasury and the Bank of England, knowing that the UK was in long-term financial retreat, lacked the self-confidence to make a managed currency work. American monetarists, coming from a large, self-contained economy, could more confidently recommend an ambitious and independent style of monetary policy than their British equivalents. It may always have been rather naive to expect that ideas nurtured in the University of Chicago could be easily transplanted to Whitehall and Threadneedle Street.

Notes

1. H.M. Treasury press release, 9 June 1980. Statement by Nigel Lawson, MP, Financial Secretary to the Treasury during his meeting with regional city editors.
2. T. Mayer, *The Structure of Monetarism* (New York and London: Norton, 1978). See, particularly, p. 2 for a list of 12 characteristic monetarist propositions.
3. *Monetary Control*, Cmnd 7858 (London: H.M.S.O., 1980), and Memorandum of H.M. Treasury, pp. 86–95, in Vol. II, *Minutes of Evidence of Third Report from the House of Commons Treasury and Civil Service Committee*, Session 1980–1 (London: H.M.S.O., 1981).
4. Ibid., p. 90.
5. Note by H.M. Treasury on 'The stability of the income velocity of circulation of money supply', pp. 126–7, in *Third Report from the Treasury and Civil Service Committee*, Session 1980–1.
6. For an example of the approach see the chapter on 'Bank lending and monetary control' in C. A. E. Goodhart, *Monetary Theory and Practice* (London, Macmillan: 1984), pp. 122–45.
7. It should be added that interest rate changes act not only on bank lending, but also on the ability of the authorities to sell gilt-edged securities as part of the funding programme.
8. *Monetary Control*, p. 1.
9. *Monetary Control*, p. 2.
10. Memorandum by H.M. Treasury, p. 89.
11. See, for example, J. Burton, 'Trade unions' role in the British disease: "An interest in inflation"', pp. 99–111, in A. Seldon (ed.), *Is Monetarism Enough?* (London: Institute of Economic Affairs, 1980), particularly pp. 105–6; and T. G. Congdon, 'Why has monetarism failed so far?', in *The Banker* (April 1982), pp. 43–9. The subject is also discussed in T. G. Congdon, *Monetarism: An Essay in Definition* (London: Centre for Policy Studies, 1978), particularly pp. 53–6.
12. J. M. Keynes, *A Tract on Monetary Reform* (1923), reprinted in *The Collected Writings of John Maynard Keynes* Vol. IV, ed. D. Moggridge and E. Johnson (London: Macmillan for the Royal Economic Society, 1971), pp. 126, 132 and 138.
13. H.M. Treasury press release, 12 May 1981. The Mais Lecture given by Sir Geoffrey Howe, QC, MP, Chancellor of the Exchequer, at the City University, p. 11.
14. Mayer, *Monetarism*, p. 27.
15. Few economists would regard the monetary base by itself as constituting a measure of the money supply. The Treasury is therefore rather iconoclastic in its attitute toward M0, which has been regarded as the full-scale aggregate since 1983.
16. The quotation comes from p. 71 of P. Meek, 'Comment on papers presented by Messrs. Forece and Coleby', in P. Meek (ed.), *Central Bank Views on Monetary Targeting* (New York: Federal Reserve Bank of New York, 1983), pp. 70–1.
17. The quotations are from p. 57 of M. Friedman, 'Response to questionnaire on monetary policy', in House of Commons Treasury and Civil Service Committee (Session 1979–80) *Memoranda on Monetary Policy* (London: H.M.S.O., 1980), pp. 55–62.
18. The arrangements are described in 'The role of the Bank of England in the money market', in *The Development and Operation of Monetary Policy 1960–83* (Oxford University Press for the Bank of England, 1984), pp. 156–64.
19. Econometric work may identify a contemporaneous link between the monetary base and one or other measure of the money supply, but that does not mean that the base 'explains' money rather than the other way round. If one wanted to predict the growth of M3 over the next six to 12 months, the level of monetary base today would not be much help, but forecasts of bank lending and the PSBR would be.
20. Meek, 'Comment', p. 70.
21. Friedman, 'Response', p. 58.

22. J. M. Keynes, *A Treatise on Money: 2. The Applied Theory of Money* (1930) reprinted in *Collected Writings*, Vol. VI (1971), pp. 224 and 225.
23. Ibid., p. 231.
24. Ibid., p. 225.
25. J. M. Keynes, *The General Theory of Employment, Interest and Money* (1936), reprinted in *Collected Writings*, Vol. III (1973), p. 327.
26. Keynes, *Treatise 2*, in *Collected Writings*, Vol. V (1971), pp. 30–2 and pp. 217–30. These distinctions anticipate the more celebrated analysis of the motives for holding money in *The General Theory*.
27. H.M. Treasury press release, 19 October 1978. Speech by Rt Hon. Denis Healey, MP, Chancellor of the Exchequer, to the Lord Mayor's dinner.
28. The quotation is from p. 97 of P. E. Middleton, 'The relationship between fiscal and monetary policy', in M. J. Artis and M. H. Miller (eds), *Essays in Fiscal and Monetary Policy* (Oxford University Press, 1981), pp. 95–116.
29. See pp. 21–3 of T. G. Congdon, 'The analytical foundations of the Medium-Term Financial Strategy', in M. Keen (ed.), *The Economy and the 1984 Budget* (Oxford: Basil Blackwell for the Institute of Fiscal Studies, 1984), pp. 17–29.
30. Mentioned on p. 5 of J. L. Jordan, 'The Anderson Jordan approach after nearly 20 years', in *Federal Reserve Bank of St Louis Review* (October 1986), pp. 5–8.
31. Friedman, 'Response', p. 56.
32. The quotation is from p. 2 of C. J. Allsop, 'The assessment: monetary and fiscal policy in the 1980s', in *Oxford Review of Economic Policy*, 1, 1 (Spring 1985), pp. 1–19.
33. Friedman, 'Response', p. 59.
34. Mayer, *Monetarism*, pp. 24–5.
35. Keynes, *General Theory*, p. 306.
36. Thus, for example, Laidler's awareness of trade union power may have been one reason for his advocacy of a 'gradualist' approach to the elimination of inflation. See D. Laidler on the case for gradualism, in Laidler, *Monetarist Perspectives* (Oxford: Philip Allan, 1982), Ch. 5, pp. 176–7.
37. M. Friedman, *Unemployment verus Inflation?* (London: Institute of Economic Affairs, 1975), pp. 30–5. The quotations are from pp. 32 and 33.
38. A. Budd, S. Holly, A. Longbottom and D. Smith, 'Does monetarism fit the UK facts?' in B. Griffiths and G. E. Wood (eds), *Monetarism in the United Kingdom* (London: Macmillan, 1984), pp. 75–119.
39. Keynes, *Tract*, p. 126.
40. See, for example, M. Parkin and G. Zis (eds), *Inflation in Open Economies* (Manchester University Press and University of Toronto Press, 1976).
41. See R. J. Ball and T. Burns, 'Long-run portfolio equilibrium and balance-of-payments adjustment in econometric models', in J. Sawyer (ed.), *Modelling the International Transmission Mechanism* (Amsterdam: North-Holland, 1979) for an example of his writings at that time.
42. Reprinted in M. Friedman, *Essays in Positive Economics* (University of Chicago Press, 1953).
43. Friedman, 'Response', p. 53.
44. Keynes, *Tract*, p. 126.
45. Ibid., pp. 159–60.
46. G. Maynard, *The Economy under Mrs Thatcher* (Oxford: Basil Blackwell, 1988), p. 100.
47. A. Walters, *Britain's Economic Renaissance* (New York and Oxford: Oxford University Press, 1986), pp. 117 and 121. The description of M3 as a 'credit aggregate' is surprising. M3 consists of notes, coin and bank deposits. To say that its growth is driven by bank credit is *not* to say that bank deposits are the same thing as bank loans. (They evidently are not.) In any case, the growth of M1 – or, indeed, even of M0 – is also driven by credit. T. G. Congdon, 'Credit, broad money and the economy', in D. Llewellyn (ed.), *Money* (London: Macmillan, for the Economic Research Council), forthcoming [at the time of writing, September 1987, and reprinted here on pp. 171–90].

48. Liverpool Research Group in Macroeconomics *Quarterly Economic Bulletin* (October 1987), p. 13. If this proposition were true, it would have drastic implications for economic theory and policy. But it overlooks the banks' liquidity-transformation role. Since cheques can be written against bank deposits and there is no loss of cheque-writing ability because of the existence of bank loans, the simultaneous expansion of deposits and loans increases the economy's liquidity and can change behaviour.

49. More direct damage to British monetarism came in other ways; for example, *The Observer* – which, under the lead of its Economics Editor, William Keegan, was strongly anti-monetarist – reprinted Friedman's 1980 evidence to the Treasury and Civil Service Committee. It correctly judged that this evidence would weaken the credibility of official policy.

50. Walters, *Renaissance*, p. 135.

51. P. Minford, 'The exchange rate and monetary policy', pp. 120–42, in W. A. Eltis and P. J. N. Sinclair (eds) *The Money Supply and the Exchange Rate* (Oxford: Clarendon Press, 1981). The quotation is from p. 121.

52. Again, see the chapter on bank lending and monetary control in Goodhart, *Monetary Theory*. On p. 126 Goodhart noted that 'official reactions in the gilts market to developments in the monetary aggregates ... have been relatively successful in offsetting unforeseen variations' in bank lending and other influences on broad money growth.

53. Walters, *Renaissance*, pp. 128 and 131.

54. These worries, which were particularly serious in Italy, Ireland and Belgium, are discussed in Chapters 1–3 of T. G. Congdon, *The Debt Threat* (Oxford: Basil Blackwell, 1988).

55. Perhaps it should not come as a surprise, after his remarks to the Treasury and Civil Service Committee in 1980, that Friedman should claim in a letter to *The Wall Street Journal* on 4 September 1984 that he did not regard the USA's budget deficit as a major issue or a cause for concern.

56. Keynes, *Tract*, p. 147.

The Exchange Rate in British Monetary Policy – or Where British Economics Went Wrong

From an inaugural lecture at Cardiff Business School in November 1990.

My 1975 article in Encounter *protested against the inaccuracy of labelling advocates of incomes policy as 'Keynesian'. An even stranger practice in the nomenclature of British economics is that many 'Keynesians' have been happy, even keen, to base interest rates on the exchange rate. (The latest illustration of this tendency is that the great majority of British economists have supported full participation in the European exchange rate mechanism.) In fact, as both this paper and the 1987 paper at the University of Kent show, Keynes was consistently opposed to subordinating British monetary policy to the exchange rate.*

Indeed, many British economists seem unwilling to appraise monetary policy in terms of its domestic consequences. They think of monetary policy solely as a means of influencing the exchange rate. The interesting question is, then, why they think about monetary policy in such a narrowly confined way. In my lecture I suggested that the answer be sought in the history of monetary policy in Britain.

One of the most-quoted remarks in economics comes in the final chapter of Keynes's *General Theory of Employment, Interest and Money*, where he says:

> the ideas of economists, both when they are right and when they are wrong, are more powerful than is commonly understood. Indeed the world is ruled by little else. Practical men, who believe themselves to be quite exempt from any intellectual influences, are usually the slaves of some defunct economist. Madmen in authority, who hear voices in the air, are distilling their frenzy from some academic scribbler of a few years back.[1]

Keynes believed that his book would be a particularly powerful 'intellectual influence' on such 'practical men'. He hoped that, by adopting his recommendations of increased state ownership and the counter-cyclical variation of public investment, the Government would in future be able to prevent large swings in unemployment. He wanted to make the trade cycle obsolete.

For about 25 years after the Second World War British economists thought that Keynes's ambition had been largely fulfilled. Of course, there were fluctuations in economic activity in the 1950s and 1960s. But these fluctuations, known as 'stop–go cycles', were mild by comparison with those in the inter-war period or the 19th century. Although unemployment varied in the course of the stop–go cycle, it never – even at the most immobile point of the 'stop' – amounted to more than a fraction of what it had been in the 1930s. This achievement, the so-called 'Keynesian Revolution', was taken to be the triumph of modern economic theory over a number of ancient financial prejudices, notably the doctrine that the Government should balance its budget. In the late 1960s no British economist expected the next 25 years to see large cyclical fluctuations in economic activity. The trade cycle may not yet have been obsolete, but it was thought to have depreciated to the point of insignificance.

Unhappily, these expectations were to prove wrong. The next 25 years were to see three major cyclical episodes. The first was the Barber boom of 1972 and 1973, followed by the severe downturn of 1974 and 1975; the second, from early 1978 to mid-1979, could be called the Healey boomlet, and gave way to the recession of 1980 and early 1981; and the third was the Lawson boom of mid-1986 to mid-1988, which preceded the current recession. These episodes were not as extreme as the slump of the early 1930s, but they were comparable – in the amplitude of the fluctuations and other characteristics – to the trade cycles of the 19th century. They were certainly more noticeable than the stop–go cycles of the immediate post-war decades. The questions arise, 'why have these large cyclical fluctuations come back?', 'what mistakes have governments been making?' and 'have their mistakes been tactical and accidental in nature, or the result of a strategic misunderstanding of how the economy works?'. More pointedly, why did the madmen in authority behave as they did? And to which defunct economists were they listening?

In attempting to answer these questions the approach in this lecture will be largely historical. As we shall see, the reference to 'defunct economists' will not be purely rhetorical. The aim will be to consider why British economists, and hence the British Government, have been so unprepared for the problems of the last 25 years. The underlying assumption is that events cannot be understood without an explanation – or at least an interpretation – of why people thought in the way they did. The lecture will therefore be mostly an exercise in the history of ideas, particularly ideas about macroeconomic policy.

The notion of 'macroeconomic policy' is very modern. In the 18th century no one believed that the Government had either the ability or the responsibility to manage the economy. Cyclical fluctuations in economic activity were sometimes pronounced, but these were regarded as Acts of God like the weather or earthquakes. In particular, theorizing about the role of money in the trade cycle was rudimentary. In previous centuries the money stock had consisted entirely of metals, particularly gold and silver, and the quantity of money had therefore been determined by the past production of gold and silver mines. There had been little scope to substitute paper for these metals, because of the lack of trust in paper alternatives. However, as the 18th century wore on, Britain's political stability and the development of a satisfactory legal framework encouraged people to carry out an increasing proportion of their transactions in bank notes and bills of exchange. These paper instruments – whose validity depended on credit – came increasingly to perform the monetary functions of the precious metals.

But the growth of paper credit carried a risk. This risk was that the individuals and organizations that issued these paper alternatives to the precious metals might not be able to redeem them at their face value. A goldsmith banker might issue a note recognizing an obligation to repay the bearer on demand a particular weight of gold or silver, and the note might circulate widely and with perfect creditworthiness for many months. But, if one of its holders presented it to the goldsmith banker and he was unable – for any reason – to pay over the stated quantity of precious metal, his entire note issue would fall into disrepute and this part of the money stock would be removed from circulation. Sudden collapses in the creditworthiness of paper lay behind some of the most severe cyclical fluctuations of the 18th century, even though precious metals continued to be the most important monetary asset. London bankers tried to anticipate the dangers by opening accounts and establishing a good relationship with the Bank of England, on the understanding that the Bank would act as a source of precious metals in an emergency. Country bankers in turn opened accounts and established good relationships with the London bankers.

The Parliamentary response to these developments was twofold. First, restrictions were placed on the ability of private banks to issue notes, although these restrictions were surprisingly late in coming and were more a feature of the 19th than the 18th century. Secondly, the Bank of England – which was seen as the core institution from an early stage – was required in successive Bank Charter Acts to redeem its liabilities at a fixed price in terms of the precious metals. The price of gold was fixed at £3. 17s. 10^{1}/2d. an ounce by Sir Isaac Newton in 1717, while the first denominationalized notes were printed in 1725.[2] In other words, the Bank of England was mandated to protect a fixed exchange rate between its paper liabilities and the precious metals. After the Napoleonic Wars Parliament deprived silver of much of its former monetary role and established gold monometallism as the basis of Britain's money in 1821. Thereafter the essential features of Britain's monetary arrangements, and indeed the defining characteristics of the classical gold standard in this country, were the fixed gold price of £3. 17s. 10^{1}/2d. an ounce and the ready convertibility of notes into gold and vice versa.

The logic of this system is easy to analyse and defend. Let us take it for granted that the public at large wants a money which is fairly reliable in terms of its ability to purchase non-monetary things. Precious metals have the key merit as a monetary asset that, because they are highly durable, their quantity is fairly stable from one year to the next. As long as mining technology changes only slowly and there are no new discoveries, this year's production of new gold is likely to be only a small fraction of the existing stock of the metal. In such circumstances the price of commodities in general should be roughly stable in terms of gold.

From this point of view, the introduction of paper alternatives to be precious metals is potentially a dangerous nuisance, because it could undermine the rigidity of the metallic money stock which explains its anti-inflationary virtue. So the right public-policy response is to insist that paper be convertible into gold at a fixed price. If the fixed exchange rate between paper and gold is maintained, and the value of gold remains reasonably stable in terms of commodities, then the value of paper should also remain reasonably stable in terms of commodities. The rationale for the gold standard in the 19th century was therefore very straightforward. With paper anchored to gold at a fixed exchange rate the growth of paper money could not have systematic inflationary consequences. Of course, this is also the essence of the more recent argument for fixed exchange rate arrangements with reputedly strong currencies, such as the dollar in the Bretton Woods era or the Deutschmark in the European Monetary System.

The gold standard was a success. Although the economy was subject to occasional cyclical disturbances and the price level varied both within these cycles and over longer periods, 19th-century Britain was a model of financial stability. Such was the admiration for Britain's achievement that by the 1880s most other major industrial countries had also adopted gold as the basis for their monetary systems, creating the international gold standard of the late 19th century. The 'rules of the game' were well known. The central bank of every participating country had to preserve the convertibility of its note liabilities into gold at the agreed fixed exchange rate. The paper/gold exchange rate within each country implied certain exchange rates between the paper currencies of the participant countries. If an exchange rate came under pressure, the consequent external drain on the central bank's gold reserve had to be countered by raising interest rates. On the other hand, when a central bank's gold reserve was ample, it could cut interest rates. In the case of the Bank of England, its interest rate decisions were determined fairly mechanically by watching the Proportion between its gold holdings and its deposit liabilities.[3] By the late 19th century its gold holdings varied mainly because of international pressures, rather than domestic changes in financial confidence. The practice of relating interest rate decisions to external developments became deeply entrenched.

But another and quite different approach to monetary policy would have been possible, and had indeed been intimated by some economists many years before. It would have relied on two revolutionary ideas which emerged in the debates on British financial policy during the Napoleonic Wars, debates which in their complexity and sophistication can fairly be described as the matrix of modern monetary theory. The urgency of those controversies arose because, under the strains of war, the Bank of England had been forced to suspend the convertibility of its notes into gold in 1797. There was widespread public concern that the value of the notes, which continued to circulate as currency, would decline steadily. The vital question was how to stabilize the real value of the notes in the absence of the fixed paper/gold anchor.

The first of the two revolutionary ideas was that of the 'general price level'. Nowadays the concepts of an overall price level, of a price index which quantifies it and of an inflation rate measured by changes in the index are so commonplace that we rarely stop to think about them. That was not so in the 1790s. People were aware of the need to have a reliable monetary unit and standard of value, but they were not sure how best to formalize this need in precise numerical terms. Thus, when David Ricardo wrote about the depreciation of the currency in a famous pamphlet of 1810 he gave it the title, *The High Price of Bullion, a Proof of the Depreciation of Bank Notes*. He thought of currency depreciation in terms of the price of gold, not in terms of a general price level. However, there had already been innovators who had seen the potential for applying index numbers to the problem. According to Schumpeter, 'A great step toward full realization of the importance of the method was made in 1798, when Sir George Shuckburgh Evelyn presented a paper to the Royal Society in which, with apologies for treating a subject so much below the dignity of that august body, he used an index number – of a primitive kind no doubt – for measuring the "depreciation of money".'[4] The approach became progressively more refined in the course of the 19th century and in 1922 the American economist, Irving Fisher, published a monumental work on *The Making of Index Numbers*. One of the motives of this work and, indeed, one of Fisher's strongest professional interests – was to define a price index whose stability would be the prime objective of monetary policy.

The second revolutionary idea, and perhaps an even more fundamental one, was to recognize that the nature of the inflationary process was radically changed by the introduction of paper money. With the functions of money increasingly being performed by paper instruments, the quantity of such instruments could affect the prices of goods and services. The link between the quantity of gold and its price had been the central interest of earlier monetary commentators. But, as more notes and bills of exchange entered the circulation, economists began to think of a connection between the quantity of all forms of money, both gold and paper, and the price level. The starting-point for their analyses was the crude but serviceable principle that the greater the quantity of paper credit, the higher the price level. By extension, the higher the rate of increase in paper credit, the faster the rate of inflation.

The seminal work on these ideas was *An Inquiry into the Nature and Effects of the Paper Credit of Great Britain* by Henry Thornton, published in 1802. The timing of this great book, five years after the Bank of England's suspension of gold convertibility, was not an accident. Thornton was convinced that the widespread acceptability of paper in payments was an advantage to a country and, in particular, that it helped Britain to face wartime pressures on its economy. 'Paper credit has...been highly important to us. Our former familiarity with it prepared us for the more extended use of it. And our experience of its power of supplying the want of gold in times of difficulty and peril, is a circumstance which...may justly add to the future confidence of the nation.'[5] Nevertheless, Thornton was aware of the dangers inherent in a system of paper credit. He emphasized that an excessive issue of bank notes would lead to rises in the price level, while warning, on the other hand, that sharp contractions of the note issue could cause downturns in economic activity. His advice to the Bank of England was therefore to 'limit the amount of paper issued, and to resort for this purpose, whenever the temptation to borrow is strong, to some effectual principle of restriction; in no case, however, materially to diminish the sum in circulation, but to let it vibrate only within certain limits' and 'to afford a slow and cautious extension of it, as the general trade of the kingdom enlarges itself'.[6]

Here is the kernel of a new approach, the beginnings of the idea of 'monetary policy' or even 'macroeconomic policy'. The guideline for monetary management is no longer stated in terms of a gold price or an exchange rate between paper and a metal. Instead the central bank is understood to have fairly deliberate goals, to stabilize the price level and, as far as possible, to avoid large fluctuations in economic activity. Moreover, it is to achieve these goals by trying to control 'the sum in circulation' or, as we would now say, by regulating the money supply. This way of conducting monetary policy – where the quantity of paper money is the target of central bank action – is clearly quite different from the earlier approach, with its focus on a particular gold price or exchange rate.[7]

Thornton's hint of a new style of monetary regulation was not taken up in his lifetime. On the contrary, the gold standard became established, gained increasing credibility and flourished until the First World War. But after 1918 another phase of intense monetary controversy began. The problem – just as it had been after the Napoleonic Wars – was whether Britain should restore the gold standard at the pre-war parity.

The majority of bankers, politicians and so-called 'practical men' associated the gold standard with the stability and prosperity of the Victorian period. Perhaps without thinking very hard about the issues, they wanted to return to the gold standard. This point of view was expressed officially in the Reports of the Cunliffe Committee, in 1918 and 1919, which said that restoration should occur as soon as possible. However, a small group of economists were sceptical, believing that the success of the gold standard in the 19th century had been largely a fluke and preferring a more deliberate and (as they described it) scientific approach to monetary policy. Their inspiration was the great tradition of *ad hoc* and more or less amateur theorizing on the trade cycle in the 19th century, which had begun with Thornton and was developed in later decades by such authors as Tooke, Overstone, John Stuart Mill, Alfred Marshall, Bagehot and Hartley Withers. The key idea was that fluctuations in demand, output and the price level were driven by changes in business confidence and variations in credit growth.

The foremost sceptic was John Maynard Keynes. In his *Tract on Monetary Reform*, published in 1923, he scorned the gold standard as a 'barbarous relic', pointing out the risk that gold could be kept in line with output only through chance discoveries of the metal. In any case, since Britain held only a small part of the world's gold stock, a return to the pre-war standard would leave it vulnerable to changes in other countries' demand for gold. There was no alternative to managing the currency:

> If providence watched over gold, or if Nature had provided us with a stable standard ready-made, I would not, in an attempt after some slight improvement, hand over the management to the possible weakness or ignorance of boards and governments. But this is not the situation. We have no ready-made standard. Experience has shown that in emergencies ministers of finance cannot be strapped down. And – most important of all – in the modern world of paper currency and bank credit there is no escape from a 'managed' currency, whether we wish it or not; convertibility into gold will not alter the fact that the value of gold itself depends on the policy of the central banks.[8]

The answer, then, was not to go back to a fixed gold price, but to have a 'managed currency'. But how, in more specific terms, should a managed currency work? What objectives should policy-makers have and how should these objectives be achieved?

Keynes was clear about what he wanted. He was against not only the gold standard, but also a fixed exchange rate between the pound and the dollar, since this would leave Britain too much at the mercy of the American Federal Reserve. Although he recognized that 'an internal standard, so regulated as to maintain stability in an index number of prices, is a difficult scientific innovation never yet put into practice', that was nevertheless the ideal he favoured: 'I regard the stability of prices, credit and employment as of paramount importance.'[9] He referred with enthusiasm to Irving Fisher, as the pioneer of price stability as against exchange stability.

The *Tract* also devoted much space to the principles and practice of monetary management. In Keynes's view, 'The internal price level is mainly determined by the amount of credit created by the banks, chiefly the Big Five' and 'The amount of credit...is in its turn roughly measured by the volume of the banks' deposits'.[10] There is a certain lack of clarity in these remarks, since it is not obvious whether it is the assets or liabilities side of banks' balance sheets that Keynes wanted to emphasize. But, if we agree that new lending creates deposits, this would be no great problem.

The discussion of the mechanics of monetary control was also rather confusing. Keynes seemed to oscillate between two views, one that the size of banks' balance sheets is a multiple of their cash reserves, which can be determined by open-market operations, and another that 'adequate control' over an important part of banks' assets (i.e., their advances and bills) 'can be obtained by varying the price charged, that is to say the bank rate'.[11]

But the technical complications should not be allowed to hide the essence of the 'managed currency' as Keynes envisaged it. The ultimate target should be the stability of the domestic price level, not the gold price or the exchange rate; and that target should be attained by managing the growth rate of banks' balance sheets, through interest rate variations if appropriate. It would be a matter of comparative indifference in practical terms whether the inter-mediate target here were taken as bank credit, bank deposits or a broad measure of the money supply, although the relevant pages in the *Tract* are a little muddled and ambiguous on the subject. It might also not add much to say that Keynes's managed currency had a certain amount in common with latter-day 'monetarism', since that begs the question of how monetarism should be defined.[12] But there cannot be much doubt that Keynes disliked having a fixed exchange rate as a policy target and paid close attention to credit and monetary variables when assessing economic prospects. That, on a careful reading of the texts, should be uncontroversial.

At first Keynes's proposals for a managed currency got nowhere. Britain returned to the gold standard in 1925, with unhappy consequences for eco-nomic activity and employment, just as Keynes had expected. But after the departure from the gold standard in 1931, and the subsequent disintegration of international monetary order, Britain willy-nilly had the managed currency that Keynes advocated. Domestic objectives, not the gold price or the ex-change rate, dominated policy-making in the 1930s. Keynes never changed his mind on the relative priority of external and internal objectives. In a speech on the proposed International Monetary Fund in the House of Lords in May 1943, he said:

> We are determined that, in future, the external value of sterling shall conform to its internal value, as set by our own domestic policies, and not the other way round. Secondly, we intend to keep control of our domestic rate of interest. Thirdly, whilst we intend to prevent inflation at home, we will not accept deflation at the dictates of influences from outside. In other words, we abjure the instruments of bank rate and credit contraction operating through an increase in unemployment as a means of forcing our domestic economy into line with external factors. I hope your Lordships will trust me not to have turned my back on all I have fought for. To establish these three principles which I have just stated has been my main task for the last 20 years.[13]

It would be natural to assume that the post-war 'Keynesian Revolution' would reflect the implementation of a macroeconomic policy directed to domestic priorities. That, indeed, is how some of the hagiographers have seen it. They have claimed that official policy in the first 25 years after 1945 was dominated by the aim of maintaining the domestic goal of full employ-ment. Since a closer approximation to full employment was achieved in these years than before or since, that may seem a reasonable assertion. However, monetary policy was certainly not organized in the way that Keynes had recommended in the *Tract on Monetary Reform* or in his 1943 speech to the House of Lords.

On the contrary, the lodestar for interest rate decisions was the pound's exchange rate against the dollar. For almost 20 years, from 1949 to 1967, the pound was constrained by the Bretton Woods regime of fixed exchange rates and kept close to its central parity of $2.80. It was true that sterling's explicit link with gold had been broken. But the pound was tied to the dollar and the dollar was fixed to gold at the official price of $35 an ounce. Britain may no longer have been on the gold standard, but sterling maintained a constant, if indirect and perhaps rather clandestine, relationship to gold for many years after Keynes's death. As we shall see, the final break came only in the early 1970s.

In these years of fixed exchange rates, academic and official interest in monetary policy dwindled steadily. Indeed, it could be argued that Keynes's *General Theory* was both the climax and the terminus of the 19th-century tradition of trade cycle theorizing, in which credit and money had been so important. Afterwards British economists downplayed the significance of credit and money in macroeconomic fluctuations and inflation. There were at least three reasons for the new neglect of monetary analysis.

The first was that Keynes himself had been moving in this direction late in his career. At the time of the *Tract* he believed, with few qualifications, in the ability of interest rate changes to manage the currency and so to achieve desired macroeconomic outcomes. But in the 1930s very low interest rates were unable to prevent the persistence of high unemployment. One task of *The General Theory* was therefore to identify those circumstances in which low interest rates would be ineffective in stimulating investment and encouraging employment. He suggested that there could be a situation, a so-called 'liquidity trap', where people were so shell-shocked by the deflationary environment around them that they could not be induced to move out of cash into other assets. The deflation could not be countered by central bank action to cut interest rates. Keynes went on to advocate that the Government take direct responsibility for investment in order to offset the possible impotence of interest rates. In his words, 'it seems unlikely that the influence of banking policy on the rate of interest will be sufficient by itself to determine an optimum rate of investment. I conceive, therefore, that a somewhat comprehensive socialization of investment will prove the only means of securing an approximation to full employment.'[14]

This argument – linking the alleged ineffectiveness of monetary policy to wholesale nationalization – was one of the most influential and important in Britain's post-war political economy. In the 1950s and 1960s it gave economists a rationale both for a modishly left-wing sympathy towards state ownership, and for suppressing the teaching of monetary economics. It is far from clear that this is altogether what Keynes wanted. As the *Tract* made clear, a managed currency would have required a strong and detailed understanding of monetary institutions. Even *The General Theory* says far more about interest rates and monetary policy than it does about nationalization. But that Keynes contributed to the diminishing of monetary economics, even of his own great work in the area, cannot be denied.

The second reason for the growing indifference towards monetary policy was that for almost 20 years, from 1932 to 1951, interest rates were virtually constant. Bank rate was held at 2 per cent throughout the period, apart from a brief (and insignificant) interruption at the beginning of the Second World War. Since hardly any interest rate changes occurred, there seemed little practical benefit in analysing the results of such changes. As interest rates had clearly not been much of an influence on business conditions for such a long period, economists thought they could ignore the possibility that interest rates might become important in the future. Even in the 1950s and 1960s interest rate variations were small for most of the time. In British universities theorizing about interest rates – and so about monetary policy in the large – became moribund.

Thirdly, during the War, and for many years afterwards, the British economy was subject to a wide variety of administrative controls of one sort or another. Rationing, conscription and the requisitioning of resources for the armed forces had a clear military function and could not be accepted for long in peacetime. But other restrictions – such as exchange controls, tight planning controls on building materials, controls on new issues and so on – survived long after the War had ended. Governments thought that the economy could be run better by relaxing or tightening these controls than by relaxing or tightening monetary policy. Their ideal was not Keynes's 'managed currency', which would have been fully compatible with market capitalism, but a semi-socialist mixed economy with extensive economic planning. In the late 1940s and 1950s the majority of British economists undoubtedly welcomed the retention of controls and a commitment to planning.

If this seems a strong statement, it needs to be emphasized that 1963 saw the publication of an official document on *Conditions for Faster Growth*, which enjoined a more active government role in industry, with the full blessing of the then Conservative Government. In 1964 the Department of Economic Affairs, with even more interventionist objectives, was established by the newly-elected Labour Government of Mr Harold Wilson. Mr Wilson had previously been an economics don at Oxford University and his Government introduced large numbers of academic economists into Whitehall. It is a fair comment that none of these economists was much bothered by monetary policy, but all of them were fascinated – in one way or another – by the potential of 'economic planning'. One kind of control was particularly important in the monetary field; direct quantitative restrictions on bank lending. With credit kept under control by such means, the role of interest rates in macroeconomic policy was rarely discussed.

By the late 1960s hardly any British economist thought that interest rates could or should be varied to influence domestic economic variables. The immensely influential National Institute of Economic and Social Research never mentioned the money supply, on any of its definitions, in its *Reviews*. It only occasionally referred to credit variables and even then the focus was on hire purchase rather than mortgage lending. Whole volumes were written on macroeconomic policy with hardly any comment on money. For example, in a book on *The Labour Government's Economic Record: 1964–70*, edited by Wilfred Beckerman and published in 1972, there was only one index reference to 'the money supply', whereas there were 17 to the National Economic Development Council, 21 to the National Board for Prices and Incomes, and no less than 41 to the National Plan and 'Planning'.[15] In the early 1970s the Cambridge Economic Policy Group was established with the support of such well-known figures as Lord Kaldor and Professor Robert Neild. The much-publicized recommendations in its *Economic Policy Reviews* almost never contained remarks on monetary policy, unless they were dismissive. According to one article in its March 1977 issue, 'In our view there is no justification at all for incorporating a target for domestic credit expansion in official economic policy'.[16]

An extraordinary somersault had been accomplished. Whereas in 1923 the managed currency favoured by Keynes had seen the restraint over credit growth as central to monetary regulation, in the 1970s Cambridge economists and, indeed, most economists in British universities saw no merit in targets for credit and monetary growth. Many of them saw no point in analysing credit or monetary trends at all. Inflation was better understood, in their view, by watching the behaviour of wages and the exchange rate. The irony was heightened by the readiness of staff at the National Institute and the Department of Applied Economics to adopt the label of 'Keynesian'. These economists did not seem to appreciate that their ways of thinking were a betrayal of Keynes's own ideas. Instead their loyalty was to second-rate textbooks which regurgitated, for decades after they had lost any practical relevance, the dangers of the liquidity trap and interest-inelastic investment.

The questions arise, 'how then was the Keynesian Revolution accomplished?' and 'what were the techniques of economic policy which gave the British economy its stability in the first 25 years after the War?'. If Keynes's managed currency was forgotten by most British economists, who or what should be awarded the medals for the relative financial tranquillity of the immediate post-war decades? It is here that we come to a yet greater paradox. There can be hardly any doubt that the key economic constraint on British governments in those years was the avoidance of sterling devaluation. Whenever policy-makers embarked on unduly stimulatory policies, the pound would come under downward pressure on the foreign exchanges and the resulting 'sterling crisis' would oblige the Government to think again. It was the succession of sterling crises, and the need to check them by credit restrictions and/or higher interest rates, which kept inflation under control.

Since the pound/dollar rate was the lynchpin of the system, American monetary policy determined British monetary policy. Fortunately, American monetary policy in the first 25 years after the War was a model of anti-inflationary prudence and counter-cyclical stability. The outcome was that 'the instruments of bank rate and credit contraction', dictated from outside Britain, not only forced the domestic economy into line with external factors, but also delivered the full employment, low inflation and cyclical moderation of the post-war period. The exchange rate played a benign role in British macroeconomic management. Keynes's suspicion of international financial influences on monetary policy-making proved misplaced.

Before we discuss what happened after the pound/dollar link was broken, there is another irony to be mentioned. American monetary policy in the first two decades after the Second World War was unquestionably a success compared with other periods, both before and after. But why? Many of the good decisions can be attributed, of course, to the professionalism of the staff of the Federal Reserve System and the budgetary restraint of Presidents Truman and Eisenhower. But there was another factor at work. One of the reasons for the Federal Reserve's tightening of monetary policy in the late 1950s was to protect the dollar on the foreign exchanges and, in particular, to preserve the $35-an-ounce gold price. Gold was still the bedrock of the Bretton Woods system.

Does it follow from this argument that the Keynesian Revolution was not the result of the discretionary demand management and fiscal fine-tuning so much praised in the textbooks? Can the happy stability of the 1950s and 1960s instead be seen to rest on two fixed exchange rates, the $2.80 rate between the pound and the dollar, and the $35-an-ounce official price of gold? Was the prosperity of that period due not to the final abandonment of the 'barbarous relic', but rather to the world's last inarticulate clinging to a gold anchor?

The two exchange rates were scrapped in the early 1970s. In August 1971 the American government suspended the dollar's convertibility into gold, because of the rapid decline in its gold reserve, while in June 1972 the pound left the embryonic European 'currency snake', after belonging for less than two months. Sterling's exit from the snake was to inaugurate a period of deliberate floating. We have already seen that one of the key preconditions for wise domestic monetary management – namely, a deep and extensive understanding of monetary economics among professional economists – no longer existed in Britain. Very few academic economists were interested in the pre-Keynesian tradition of trade cycle analysis, the acknowledged classics of monetary theory or contemporary monetary institutions. As a result there was no longer any heavy-weight intellectual obstacle to rapid domestic credit and monetary expansion. The external barrier to inflationary policies, which had been imposed by a fixed exchange rate for over 20 years, was now also removed.

The scene had been set for the Barber boom of the early 1970s. There is little point in describing that boom in detail once more. Suffice it to say that credit and monetary growth were extraordinarily fast by any previous standards. But the overwhelming majority of British economists were not worried by the potential inflationary repercussions and celebrated the very rapid output growth from mid-1972 to mid-1973. (The level of GDP, at factor cost, expenditure-based, was 8.6 per cent higher in real terms in the middle two quarters of 1973 than in the middle two quarters of 1972. Domestic demand grew even faster.) On 7 May 1973 Mr Peter Jay, the Economics Editor of *The Times*, wrote an isolated article entitled 'The boom that must go bust'. *The National Institute Economic Review* judged in the same month that, 'there is no reason why the present boom should either bust or have to be busted'. The *Review* was undoubtedly representative of professional economic opinion.

Later it became uncontroversial that something had gone horribly wrong. The current account deficit on the balance of payments was a post-war record in 1974 and in early 1975 the inflation rate hit 25 per cent. In 1976 Mr Healey, the Chancellor of the Exchequer, introduced money supply targets in order to establish a monetary framework for reducing inflation. These targets opened up the possibility that interest rate changes might be determined by the behaviour of monetary growth rather than by the exchange rate. The targets were expressed in terms of broad money, which is dominated by bank deposits. Broad money targets were to survive for almost a decade, until they were abandoned in late 1985. Although the need for some kind of money target, or a so-called 'nominal framework', was widely accepted, it would be wrong to think that academic economists were much involved in its introduction. On the contrary, the case for money targets was urged most vigorously in the financial press, particularly in *The Times*.[17]

The heyday of broad money targets was in early 1980, only a few months after the Thatcher Government had come to power. At about the same time as the announcement of the Medium-Term Financial Strategy in the Budget of that year, the Government published a Green Paper on *Monetary Control*. It set out the rationale and the method of operation of broad money targets. In its words, 'The Government's policy is...to sustain downward pressure on prices by a progressive reduction of the rate of growth of the money supply over a period of years'. (This statement clearly implied that monetary growth caused inflation.) The reduction in monetary growth was to be accomplished partly by curbing public sector borrowing from the banks (which depended on the total amount of public sector borrowing minus sales of public sector debt to non-banks) and partly by discouraging bank lending to the private sector. Although sceptical that the private sector's demand for bank finance was responsive to interest rates in the short run, the Green Paper's aversion to quantitative credit restrictions left interest rates as the only instrument available to regulate credit expansion. It followed that interest rates were to be raised if monetary growth was ahead of target, but lowered if it was behind target.

In effect, the Green Paper on *Monetary Control* set out an approach to monetary policy which – in its emphasis on the credit counterparts to deposit growth and its focus on domestic rather than external objectives – had clear similarities to Keynes's scheme for a 'managed currency' in the *Tract on Monetary Reform*. Moreover, in a number of speeches Sir Geoffrey Howe, the then Chancellor of the Exchequer, argued that the exchange rate had to be allowed to float if the Government was to have the freedom over interest rates required to achieve its money supply targets. Interest rates were to be governed by domestic criteria, with a view to attaining price stability, rather than by the exchange rate.

The question of what happened to broad money targets, and the system of financial control associated with them, is not much debated now. There is hardly time here to provide a detailed history of British economic policy in the early 1980s.[18] However, certain salient points are essential to the argument of this lecture. In late 1980 monetary growth ran far ahead of target, obliging the Government to keep interest rates high despite a deepening industrial recession. The exchange rate rose to remarkable levels and by early 1981 was clearly over-valued. Most economists, appalled by this turn of events, urged the Government to ease the deflationary pressures. They wanted it to pay more attention on the exchange rate and less (or none at all) to domestic monetary trends.

But in the Budget of March 1981 the Government raised taxes in order to keep public sector borrowing within the targets stated in the Medium-Term Financial Strategy. Two professors of economics at Cambridge – Frank Hahn and Robert Neild – organized a letter to *The Times* from 364 economists at British universities, which claimed that the Government's policies 'will deepen the depression, erode the industrial base of the economy and threaten its social and political stability'. They also warned that, without any change in policy, the economy would never recover. In their view, a permanent slump was in prospect. The letter from the 364 was the most emphatic possible denunciation of the attempt to manage the economy by reducing and stabilizing the rate of growth of the money stock.

The 364 economists were wrong. The British economy began to recover only a few months after it had been written. But to assume therefore that the letter had no influence would be a very serious mistake. It accurately reflected the overwhelming consensus of British academic opinion. Whenever officials from the Treasury or the Bank of England took part in academic conferences, both in these years and later, they were subjected to a barrage of scorn for obeying their political masters and implementing money supply targets. The constant sniping undoubtedly took its toll. Perhaps even more important, there was only limited academic interest in the technical operation of the system of monetary management actually at work in the early 1980s. An enormous literature developed on the merits of an alternative system of monetary base control, but this was not strictly relevant to the day-to-day problems facing the Treasury and the Bank of England. For example, whereas City newsletters and circulars discussed the problem of 'overfunding' in some detail in 1984 and 1985, it received hardly any comment in academic journals. The reason was straightforward. There were very few university economists who respected what the Government was trying to do, namely, to combat inflation by reducing the rate of broad money growth.

So when broad money targets were scrapped in late 1985 there was general relief in university economics departments that, at long last, the Government had returned to sanity. 'Sanity' was to be understood, in their view, as the former style of macroeconomic management with interest rate changes determined largely by the pound's fortunes on the foreign exchanges. The Government nevertheless retained monetary targets, at least in form. Few people outside the Treasury took these targets, which came to be expressed in terms of narrow money rather than broad money, all that seriously. City commentators noted that the quantity of notes and coin, which is the main constituent of the officially-favoured narrow money measure, M0, is determined by the current economic situation, rather than being a determinant of the future behaviour of demand and output. It followed from this that narrow money could not have any causal role in the inflationary process.

Keynes had, in fact, made precisely the same point in the *Tract* over 60 years earlier. He remarked that, in the circumstances of the early 1920s, 'Cash, in the form of bank and currency notes, is supplied *ad libitum*, i.e. in such quantities as are called for by the amount of credit created and the internal price level established'. It followed that:

...the tendency of today – rightly I think – is to watch and control the creation of credit and to let the creation of currency follow suit, rather than, as formerly, to watch and control the creation of currency and to let the creation of credit follow suit.[19]

Keynes's preference for watching credit rather than currency was a by-product of his aversion to gold. Under the Bank Charter Act of 1844 the Bank of England had been required to restrict the fiduciary note issue (i.e., that part of the note issue not backed by gold holdings in its Issue Department) and gold had remained, in principle, the ultimate regulator of the quantity of notes. But Keynes wanted 'the volume of paper money' (i.e., notes) to be 'consequential...on the state of trade and employment, bank rate policy and Treasury bill policy', so that the 'governors of the system would be bank rate and Treasury bill policy'. He therefore made 'the proposal – which may seem, but should not be, shocking – of separating entirely the gold reserve from the note issue'. If this were done, monetary policy would be free to serve the Government's proper objectives, which in his view were, of course, the 'stability of trade, prices and employment'.[20]

As Keynes would have expected, the Treasury's preoccupation with M0 since the mid-1980s has turned out to be unfortunate. Because it is an indicator rather than a cause of inflation, it has failed abjectly to give advance warning of future inflationary trouble. The role of two self-styled 'monetarist' advisers to the Government, Sir Alan Walters and Professor Patrick Minford, in this failure needs to be mentioned. In the early 1980s they were both critical of the importance attached to credit and broad money, and advocated that narrow money be given a more prominent role. Conservative politicians did not trust the great mass of left-leaning British academic economists, but they did consult the ideologically sound Walters and Minford. The advice of these two economists was therefore instrumental in undermining the frame-work of monetary management which was in existence *before* Mrs Thatcher and her Treasury ministers started listening to them.

In his book *Britain's Economic Renaissance* Sir Alan Walters observed that it is money in the 'transactions sense that plays the central role in the theoretical structure and the proposition of monetarism'. He gives paying a bus fare as an example of the kind of transaction he has in mind, and distinguishes this sharply from 'credit'. (To quote, 'You pay your bus fare with money; you do not offer the fare collector a promissory note.'[21]) But, whatever the role of money in this 'transactions sense' in either Walters's or the British Government's understanding of monetary economics during the 1980s, it had actually been superseded several decades earlier by the leaders of economic thought.

The whole point of Keynes's critique of classical monetary theory was that it overlooked the position of money in a portfolio of assets. If the demand to hold money rose for reasons of increased liquidity preference, the demand to buy goods and services would fall. In Keynes's extreme case of the liquidity trap, the ability of money's non-transactions role to expand indefinitely could become the jinx of the capitalist system. Hicks also saw the need to locate money in a framework of portfolio choice, proposing that the principle of marginal maximization should be borrowed from microeconomics.[22] Friedman's attempt to restate the quantity theory related the demand for money to wealth, as well as income and other variables.[23] Walters's neglect of these basic ideas, and their many implications, is further testimony to British economists' lack of insight into the role of credit and money in macroeconomic fluctuations.

Walters and Minford undoubtedly agreed with the majority of Keynesian economists in British universities that Nigel Lawson, as Chancellor of the Exchequer, was correct to abandon broad money targets in late 1985. They were part of the extensive coalition of academic economists which regarded the monitoring of trends in credit and broad money as unnecessary. In retrospect, it may surprise laymen that this coalition was largely silent about the practical outcome of the currency management of the decade from 1976 to 1985.

In 1976 Britain had one of the highest inflation rates in the industrial world, a universally despised currency, a budget deficit of almost 10 per cent of gross domestic product and an associated long-term problem of fiscal unsustainability. Moreover, after the most violent cyclical upheaval of the post-war period, there was pervasive private sector distrust of the Government's ability to deliver stable, non-inflationary growth. By contrast, in 1985 British inflation had been reduced to a trend rate of about 5 per cent, sterling was one of the most respected currencies in international finance, public debt was falling as a share of GDP and the economy had enjoyed four years of steady growth more or less in line with its trend rate of $2^1/_2$ per cent a year. Whatever the academic economics profession thought about the matter, there can surely be little question that the decade of broad money targets had gone far to solving Britain's macroeconomic problems. If Keynes had still been alive, he would surely have been pleased to see the idea of a 'managed currency' so amply vindicated.

The sequence of events after the scrapping of broad money targets in 1985 had clear similarities to that after the abandonment of a fixed exchange rate in 1971 and 1972, except that the boom evolved somewhat more slowly. The focus of monetary policy again became the exchange rate. In late 1985 and early 1986, with the dollar falling rapidly on the foreign exchanges, the exchange rate did not signal a need for higher interest rates. The pound itself fell heavily in late 1986, particularly against the Deutschmark, but this was interpreted as the result of lower oil prices.

From March 1987 to March 1988 sterling was deliberately kept in a band of 2.95 to 3 against the Deutschmark. However, with German interest rates so much beneath those in Britain, this external factor argued for an easing, rather than a tightening, of domestic monetary policy. In effect, from late 1985 to early 1988 there was no meaningful external constraint on domestic monetary policy. The external environment was as permissive to monetary expansion as that which had prevailed after the ending of the dollar's convertibility into gold in August 1971.

Interest rates fell, credit growth accelerated and the growth rate of broad money – no longer dampened by overfunding – also increased. By late 1986 the economy was undoubtedly growing at an above-trend rate. By mid-1987 it was in a full-scale boom. The mood of businessmen, particularly get-rich-quick property speculators, was an almost exact replica of that in the Barber boom 15 years earlier. Indeed, the bank lending and broad money numbers themselves were remarkably similar. But did British economists, of either the Keynesian or narrow money schools, object? Did they warn that the boom would inevitably end in a worse payments deficit, a rising inflation rate and a need for a sharp cyclical downturn to offset the excesses of the boom? Sadly, it is hardly necessary to answer these questions. As is well known, the overwhelming majority of them – in the universities, the official policy-making machine and the City – raised no objections and issued no warnings. On the contrary, the consensus macroeconomic forecast in 1986, 1987 and early 1988 was that the economy was about to slow down to a trend rate of output growth without any rise in interest rates. All of the so-called leading forecasting bodies – the London Business School, the National Institute, the Treasury and their many imitators – believed that the inflation rate in the late 1980s would be similar to, or lower than, that in mid-1980s.[24]

Without an appropriately valued fixed exchange rate to guide interest rate decisions, academic economists were very casual about the medium-term implications of grossly unsustainable domestic monetary trends. The indifference of academic opinion gave economic advisers in the civil service and the Bank of England a pretext for not alerting their political masters to the foolishness of policy.[25] The Lawson boom of the late 1980s – like the Barber boom of the early 1970s – was the result of British economists' lack of recognition of how credit and money affect demand, output, employment and inflation. It was due, above all, to a great vacuum in intellectual understanding. The Lawson boom has been followed, like the Barber boom, by a sharp rise in inflation and a recession. It has wrecked the greatest asset the

Thatcher Government had in the general elections of 1983 and 1987, a high reputation for managerial competence in running the economy and controlling inflation. These consequences can be fairly described as the revenge of the 364.

The argument of this lecture is that there is no excuse for the vacuum in intellectual understanding. Keynes set out over 60 years ago in his *Tract on Monetary Reform* how a system of monetary policy focused on domestic objectives should work. The key intermediate indicators in the *Tract* were the growth rates of credit and bank deposits (or, as we would now say, broad money), just as they were in the original Medium-Term Financial Strategy declared in 1980. Keynes's agenda in the *Tract* should be seen as the logical culmination of many decades of analysis and theorizing about the trade cycle. This tradition of British monetary economics began with Thornton and Ricardo, and proceeded through (among others) John Stuart Mill, Bagehot and Alfred Marshall, to Keynes's contemporaries, Dennis Robertson and Ralph Hawtrey. But it withered and died in the 1940s and 1950s. It suffered, most of all, from the deliberate and ideologically-motivated neglect of an economics profession far more interested in planning how a semi-socialist economy might work in the future than in understanding how a free-market economy had operated in the past.

Perhaps this lecture has been too nostalgic and backward-looking. Perhaps it should have been less about 'what might have been' and more about 'what we have to do now'. The mainstream academic economist would probably reply that its central argument has been made redundant by British entry into the exchange rate mechanism of the European Monetary System. Surely, he would claim, from here on we can rely on the German efficiency in monetary management to remedy British inefficiency in inflation control. That may or may not be right as a statement about the real world. But what a strange conclusion to the debate! Having finally unshackled themselves from gold in the early 1970s and made a complete hash of domestic monetary management in the subsequent 20 years, the British economics establishment now warms to the embrace of the Deutsche Bundesbank.[26]

It should be easier now to identify the 'defunct economists' who have made the internal value of the pound conform to its external value, lost us control of our interest rates, and made us subject to inflation and deflation dictated from outside. The indictment relates not to one or two hare-brained theorists with a Rasputin-like influence over certain 'madmen in authority', but to an entire profession, the profession of academic economists in this country. We have to ask them, with the British Government actively contemplating proposals which would mean the end of the pound sterling as an independent currency, 'was this how the "Keynesian Revolution" was supposed to end?'.

Notes

1. D. Moggridge and E. Johnson (eds), *The Collected Writings of John Maynard Keynes*, Vol. VII: *The General Theory of Employment, Interest and Money* (London: Macmillan, 1964, originally published 1936), p. 383.
2. V. H. Hewitt and J. M. Keyworth, *As Good as Gold: 300 Years of British Bank Note Design* (London: British Museum Publications in association with the Bank of England, 1987), p. 27.
3. C. A. E. Goodhart, *The Business of Banking, 1891–1914* (London: Weidenfeld and Nicolson, 1972), pp. 195–208.
4. J. A. Schumpeter, *History of Economic Analysis* (London: George Allen & Unwin, 1954), p. 526.
5. H. Thornton, *An Enquiry into the Nature and Effects of the Paper Credit of Great Britain* (Fairfield: August M. Kelly, 1978, reprint of version edited by F. A. v. Hayek and published by George Allen & Unwin in 1939; originally published 1802), p. 276.
6. Thornton, *Paper Credit*, p. 259.
7. I am not suggesting that Thornton was opposed to the gold standard. In fact, his 1811 contributions to two House of Commons debates show that he was strongly in favour of it. See *Paper Credit*, p. 346. I am claiming only that his writings hinted at the possibility of a different approach.
8. D. Moggridge and E. Johnson (eds), *The Collected Writings of John Maynard Keynes:* Vol. IV, *A Tract on Monetary Reform* (London and Basingstoke: Macmillan, 1971, originally published 1923), p. 136.
9. Moggridge and Johnson (eds), *Keynes: Tract*, pp. 126–7 and p. 140.
10. Moggridge and Johnson (eds), *Keynes: Tract*, pp. 141–2.
11. Moggridge and Johnson (eds), *Keynes: Tract*, pp. 142–5.
12. I discussed some of the definitional problems in my contribution 'British and American monetarism compared', pp. 38–72, in R. Hill (ed.), *Keynes, Money and Monetarism* (London and Basingstoke: Macmillan, 1989). (This paper is reprinted in this volume as 'Keynes, British monetarism and American monetarism', on pp. 209–34.)
13. Lord Kahn, *On Re-reading Keynes* (London: Oxford University Press for the British Academy, 1975), pp. 22–3.
14. Moggridge and Johnson (eds), *Keynes: General Theory*, p. 378.
15. W. Beckerman (ed.), The *Labour Government's Economic Record: 1964–70* (London: Duckworth, 1972), pp. 340–41.
16. F. Cripps and M. Fetherston, 'The role of monetary policy in economic management' in *Economic Policy Review*, March 1977 (Cambridge: University of Cambridge, Department of Applied Economics), p. 54.
17. T. Congdon, *Monetarism: an Essay in Definition* (London: Centre for Policy Studies, 1978), pp. 11–13.
18. See my pamphlet, *Monetarism Lost* (London: Centre for Policy Studies, 1989), for a description of the evolution of monetary policy in the 1980s.
19. Moggridge and Johnson (eds), *Keynes: Tract*, pp. 145–6.
20. Moggridge and Johnson (eds), *Keynes: Tract*, pp. 153–4.
21. A. Walters, Britain's *Economic Renaissance* (New York: Oxford University Press, 1986), pp. 116–7.
22. This is a reference to Sir John Hicks's famous paper on 'A suggestion for simplifying the theory of money', written before Keynes's *General Theory.*
23. Milton Friedman's 'The quantity theory of money: a restatement', a paper originally published in 1956, said that 'the demand for money is a special topic in the theory of capital'. It was the theoretical launching-pad of the so-called 'monetarist counter-revolution'.
24. Professor Patrick Minford of Liverpool University argued late into the boom that slow growth of M0 presaged an early return to 3 per cent inflation. This was not the first time that Minford had been disastrously wrong by using M0 for forecasting purposes. He warned in late 1985 that, because of slow M0 growth, 'we now have the tightest

monetary policy we have ever had' and maintained that 'a stalling in the growth rate, unless immediate action is taken to reduce interest rates, is now increasingly likely'. See p. 45 of J. Bruce-Gardyne and others, *Whither Monetarism?* (London: Centre for Policy Studies, 1985). These remarks were made on the eve of the strongest boom for 15 years.

25. According to one former civil servant, even Mr Denis Healey – who had been responsible for introducing broad money targets – did not really believe in them. 'To ascribe paternity for the MTFS to Denis Healey seems to me to be going too far. He was described at the time as an unbelieving monetarist, meaning that he adopted monetary targets only with a view to inspiring confidence in the financial world, which did believe in them.' L. Pliatzky, *The Treasury under Mrs Thatcher* (Oxford: Basil Blackwell, 1989), p. 122.

26. In any case, other European countries do not suffer the illusion that full membership of the EMS specifies a complete anti-inflationary policy. They also follow domestic financial targets stated in terms of credit and/or broad money. In their regard for narrow money, it is British economic policy-makers and their advisers who have become idiosyncratic.

PART FOUR

Two Period Pieces

10. Two period pieces

As mentioned in the Introduction, these two final pieces do not fit neatly into the previous sections of the book. Although they were prompted by contemporary developments, they cannot be easily related to specific events. Since both have been widely referred to by other economists, it seemed appropriate to include them in this volume.

The first of these pieces was published in the *Lloyds Bank Review* of October 1982 as 'A new approach to the balance of payments' and is republished here under the more challenging title 'The intelligent radical's approach to the balance of payments'. Its key message is very simple and may be quickly summarized, as follows:

> Where payments imbalances between countries reflect the free decisions of private sector agents, such imbalances cannot be a policy problem for governments. There is no such thing as a balance-of-payments problem between consenting adults. Payments deficits may nevertheless be a genuine policy problem when they are due to excessive budget deficits. The implication in that case is that policies specifically aimed at the payments deficit as such (like tariffs and quotas) are wrong-headed. The only cause of an external payments problem is mistaken fiscal policy and the only remedy for it is to adjust fiscal policy.

That may sound straightforward, but it has drastic consequences for a substantial body of economic theory and policy-making. In particular, it implies that the balance-of-payments problems suffered by Britain for much of the post-war period were due to over-expansionary fiscal policy alone. Since the Keynesian establishment in Britain has traditionally seen active fiscal policy as the correct way to maintain high employment, this approach to balance-of-payments analysis is most unsettling for them. Sir James Meade, one of the most distinguished of the British Keynesians, responded very critically to the ideas and wrote in protest to *Lloyds Bank Review*. A lively debate with an exchange of letters followed in the April 1983 issue.

Paradoxically, the new 'radical liberal' approach to the balance of payments proved to be very convenient to policy-makers during the Lawson boom. The excess demand generated by rapid monetary expansion was partly responsible for a sharp deterioration in the balance of payments in 1987 and 1988, but the fiscal position became extremely strong. In fact, a large budget surplus was recorded in 1988 and 1989. Mr Lawson was therefore able to use the new approach to the balance of payments to give legitimacy to the large current account deficit. After Sir Terence Burns, the Government's Chief Economic Adviser, had articulated it as a justification for Britain's external deficit at the 1988 meeting of the International Monetary Fund and World Bank in Berlin, Mr Brittan of the *Financial Times* called the ideas 'the Burns doctrine' or 'the Lawson/Burns doctrine'. (In fact, the new approach was first suggested in some lectures given by Professor Max Corden at Chicago in 1976. But Corden's remarks were quite brief, and I believe that my 1982 article was the first extended treatment.)

The second period piece is a reprint of a paper I wrote jointly with my former colleague, Mr Paul Turnbull, at L. Messel & Co., again in 1982. One puzzle at that time was that rapid growth of mortgage credit was not leading to a sharp rise in house prices. Mr Turnbull had done some work on mortgage lending while working at the Building Societies' Association in the 1970s, and had seen a similar pattern during previous episodes of buoyant mortgage lending. Meanwhile the clearing banks were lobbying the Government to remove informal restrictions on their mortgage lending. As part of this campaign Mr David Lomax of National Westminster Bank wrote an article in the February 1982 issue of the *National Westminster Bank Quarterly Review* which gave a very lucid description of how funds circulate in the housing market, including the statement, 'apart from mortgage lending used for new construction, for transactions costs, and for buying houses from the public sector, every penny of net additional credit for house purchase is taken out in equity from the housing market'. The idea of 'equity withdrawal' was born.

The paper I wrote with Mr Turnbull took the analysis further in three ways. It used the actual phrase 'equity withdrawal', I believe for the first time; it quantified the relative sizes of net mortgage credit and equity withdrawal; and it showed that there was nothing sinister about the phenomenon. On the face of it, the main conclusion was shocking, that – even when the mortgage market was subject to severe restrictions of various sorts in the late 1970s – equity withdrawal exceeded investment in the housing stock. So more than half of net mortgage credit, highly tax-privileged because it was supposed to promote home ownership, was, in fact, not staying in the housing market at all. But we demonstrated through some familiar real-world transactions sequences, such as those following the death or retirement of homeowners, that equity would inevitably be withdrawn in the process of buying and selling houses. 'People quitting the housing market rightly regard the equity in their homes as their own property. They are entitled to do with it whatever they wish. It would be wholly wrong for the monetary authorities to impede them.'

The ideas in the paper were quickly taken up by the Bank of England, in its August 1982 *Quarterly Review,* without (I am afraid to say) any acknowledgement, and became staples in the academic analysis of savings and consumption in the rest of the 1980s. Sadly, however, the warning against single-digit interest rates in the final paragraph of the paper was not heeded by Mr Lawson in 1987 and 1988, with very harmful effects on the housing market and the economy. To quote the final paragraph: 'Credit is pouring into residential property at present [i.e., 1982]. The associated rapid growth of bank and building society deposits is threatening the Government's [broad money] targets. If interest rates come down quickly to 10 per cent or less, we can be confident that those targets would be unattainable and that an unsustainably vigorous upturn in housing market activity would develop.'

It seems a safe assumption that his advisers never brought the passage to Mr Lawson's attention. We have to ask him, as he prepares his memoirs, 'what advice were you receiving when you cut interest rates to under 8 per cent during the strongest credit explosion for 15 years?'. We might also ask, 'to which academic advisers were you listening most attentively and why?'. Did those advisers believe, in all seriousness, that annual monetary growth of 20 per cent would not have disastrous results both for the economy and the Thatcher Government?

The Intelligent Radical's Approach to the Balance of Payments

Reprinted from an article 'A new approach to the balance of payments' in the October 1982 issue of Lloyds Bank Review.

The balance of payments remains in the forefront of policy-makers' attention in many countries, particularly in the Third World. Discussion has been given new urgency by the prospect of default by sovereign borrowers, unable to repay substantial bank debts incurred in the 1960s and 1970s. As these practical problems have been subjected to considerable theoretical analysis, it may seem surprising that there is anything novel to say. However, the argument of this article is that valuable insights can be gained by a new method of formulating the balance of payments. The critical point of departure from previous work is to divide the economy into the public and private sectors, and to assess their contribution to a nation's overall balance of payments separately. By suggesting that a deficit incurred by the private sector results from freely-taken decisions by individuals and is not a problem for policy-makers, the spotlight is turned onto the deficit incurred by the public sector. A government's payments difficulties are interrelated with fiscal and debt management problems. Indeed, we shall claim that the central misunderstanding of traditional theories has been to regard the balance-of-payments problem as distinct from the problems of the budget deficit and government debt sales. The provocative conclusion reached here is that these supposedly independent problems are, in fact, one and the same.

This has drastic implications. The most important is that restrictions on international trade and financial flows are of little value in curing payments imbalance. They help only insofar as they improve tax revenues or increase domestic acquisition of public sector debt or, in other words, only because they affect fiscal and monetary variables. It would be more honest, and also less prone to cause distortions, to operate on these variables directly. There is an obvious message for the many Third World nations which, in response to balance-of-payments weakness, are now busy erecting tariff and non-tariff barriers to trade. But the point is equally relevant for advanced industrial countries. In Britain, the Cambridge Economic Policy Group has warned that the balance of payments is damned beyond redemption by adverse long-term import trends, and that the only reliable method of countering these trends is import control. Although its prognosis has not so far proved correct, the Group's work has attracted much comment and seems to have encouraged the Labour Party to favour import restrictions. The ideas developed in this article suggest that, on the contrary, import restrictions would be almost useless as an antidote to international payments imbalance.

To help organize the argument we start with the familiar flow-of-funds identity. It states that the foreign sector's financial position is the counterpart to that of the public and private sectors combined:

Overseas sector's net acquisition of financial assets (NAFA) = public sector's NAFA + private sector's NAFA

When the overseas sector's net acquisition of financial assets is positive, a country is running a current account deficit. The conventional view is that a 'problem' exists if the deficit is unsustainably large and must be corrected by policy action. We may break down the total current account deficit into two parts:

Current account deficit = public sector deficit + private sector deficit

This is not strictly accurate because the public or private sector might have a positive net acquisition of financial assets outweighed by a negative NAFA by the other, but it simplifies the discussion to assume that both sectors contribute – at least, in an arithmetical sense – to the current account deficit. Let us suppose initially that the current account deficit is attributable to the private sector. The private sector is running into debt with the rest of the world.

Why does this matter? Within an economy it is an everyday event for companies and individuals to borrow from one another. They do so with advantage because they have different time preferences, different production opportunities or different cash flow patterns. Equally, it is possible for the set of private companies and individuals which comprise one economy to incur debt to the set of private companies and individuals which comprise another economy. Although every agent is acting independently, in the aggregate the private sector agents in one country have a current account deficit. Since the numerous borrowing decisions responsible for the deficit are taken freely, it is unclear why the government should be concerned or why policy needs to be amended. Perhaps, as Corden has remarked, 'One should...just assume for the purposes of discussing balance-of-payments issues that the private sector knows what it is doing, and what is good for it, as far as its spending and savings decisions are concerned.'[1]

The objection might be raised that private sector agents may not be properly informed about the eventual results of particular financial transactions across frontiers. But the domestic and foreign agents concerned have to make their own judgement about the creditworthiness of the debt incurred. The task of ensuring that it can be serviced and repaid falls on them, not the government.

In the past, many countries have registered persistent private sector current account deficits with no detriment to their economies. The characteristic explanation is that they have been able to cover the deficits by capital inflows, normally attracted by a better rate of return than in the source country. The consequent higher level of capital accumulation has accelerated the growth of output, including exports, and enabled the debts to be repaid without difficulty. A classic illustration is provided by the USA in the 19th century. In the decade to 1878 its trade deficit averaged 0.8 per cent of net national product and the current account deficit, boosted by interest and dividend payments to foreign investors, was even larger. But in the early 20th century it began to earn substantial trade surpluses and became a capital exporter.[2]

Another possibility is that the domestic private sector may experience a temporary dip in income due, for example, to an adverse terms-of-trade shift. If consumption is related to 'permanent income', private individuals may wish to borrow from abroad in the expectation of better times ahead. If their expectations prove correct, and no one should be able to make forecasts better than themselves, they will be able to repay when the improvement materializes. ('Permanent income' is a concept advanced by Friedman in his 1957 study on *A Theory of the Consumption Function*. It abstracts from 'accidental' or 'chance' influences on income.)

But some economists might protest that these arguments are based on too sharp a differentiation between public and private sector decision-taking. What happens if a private sector current account deficit emerges because companies and individuals misinterpret macroeconomic signals given by unsound official policy? When these signals are shown to have been wrong and the private sector cannot repay, should not the blame be placed on the government? And does not this carry the implication that policy-makers should be worried about a private sector current account deficit and take remedial measures if they think it excessive?

These questions raise some potentially awkward issues. The most troublesome example is where a central bank keeps interest rates 'too low', promoting heavy borrowing by the private sector and hence leading to a current account deficit. But it is necessary to remember that, unless they are prevented by official restrictions, private sector agents have discretion about the currency in which debts are denominated. Suppose that interest rates in, say, Brazil are 'too low', that bank credit, and so the money supply, is expanding quickly, and that the cruzeiro is under pressure. The probability of depreciation is known to private agents at home and abroad. Foreign lenders and Brazilian borrowers can intermediate in cruzeiros or, if they wish, in dollars or another recognized convertible currency. The foreigners – aware that depreciation of claims expressed in cruzeiro terms is likely – will take this into account when drawing up debt contracts. If they have little trust in the Brazilian bank because it is setting 'too low' interest rates, Brazilian individuals will be unable to borrow in cruzeiros from foreigners. It is a mistake to imagine that central banks can saddle residents of their country with huge foreign debts by tampering with interest rates in home currency terms. Of course, if Brazilians borrow in dollars they will have to pay a more appropriate interest rate and any exchange rate loss due to cruzeiro depreciation.[3]

The plain fact is that risk attaches – and, in a market economy, is understood to attach – to every credit transaction between private agents. Part of this risk stems from the difficulty of forecasting macroeconomic trends. This element in risk is found in borrowing and lending between residents of the same country. The main new dimension in borrowing and lending between residents of different countries is exchange rate variation. But, just as a central bank is not responsible for compensating agents in its own country when they have been upset by an unexpected interest rate change, so it should not be responsible for compensating agents at home or abroad because of an unexpected exchange rate change. The Federal Reserve need be no more involved if a company in Brazil defaults on a dollar loan than if a company in Massachusetts does so. By extension, why should a current account deficit between the private sectors of the USA and Brazil be of any

more interest to it than a current account deficit between the private individuals of Massachusetts and California?

It is quite possible that, after international financial flows, private sector
agents in both debtor and creditor countries find they have made mistakes.
But, when one party to a credit transaction undertaken between nationals of
one country defaults, there is no presumption that the government will
automatically help the other party. It is therefore unclear why the government of one country should intervene if its citizens fail to honour their
foreign debts. Apart from providing law courts to arbitrate on disputes, the
state has no particular duty or obligation. To put the argument at its most
polemical, there is no such thing as a balance-of-payments 'problem' between
consenting adults.

The matter is quite different when we consider a current account deficit
attributable to the government's behaviour. The deficit can be covered either
by drawing down foreign currency reserves or by increasing external indebtedness. Reserve depletion is a finite process and must, at some stage, be
reversed. There must also be some upper limit to the external indebtedness a
government can tolerate, although the scope for debate about what that limit
may be is considerable. Since both reserve depletion and foreign borrowing
cannot continue for ever, a public sector current account deficit poses a
genuine problem for policy-makers. They must sooner or later take action to
solve it. But what action is needed?

The answer is contained by the identity:

Public sector current account deficit = Public sector financial deficit −
sales of public sector debt to the domestic private sector (including
money creation)

This makes the obvious statement that the public sector's contribution to a
current account deficit is equal to the total increase in its financial liabilities
minus that part of the total increase taken up by domestic savings. It is also
clear that the external deficit can be reduced in two ways − by reducing the
public sector financial deficit (which, from now on, we shall call 'the budget
deficit' for brevity) or by increasing domestic sales of public sector debt.
Any policy measure which does not affect the budget deficit or the domestic
demands for government debt is futile as a response to balance-of-payments
difficulties; any measure which does affect these two variables also changes
the public sector's current account deficit. As we have already argued that
the private sector's current account is not a relevant concern for policy-
makers, it follows that the solution to payments imbalance is to be sought

only in fiscal or debt management policy. This is a strong assertion. If it is accepted, much previous analysis of the balance of payments is superseded.

There is no doubt that economists have not in the past seen balance-of-payments problems exclusively in fiscal terms. In the next two sections we shall, therefore, consider the characteristic symptoms of payments imbalance in two recent periods, the fixed exchange rate regime before 1971 and the floating exchange rate regime subsequently, and relate these symptoms to fiscal and debt management policies.

In the Bretton Woods system of fixed exchange rates one key pressure-gauge for assessing balance-of-payments difficulties was the movement in foreign currency reserves. Central banks were expected to sell foreign currency and buy their own if the exchange rate was in trouble. By using their ammunition of accumulated dollars they could fight back against speculative attacks on their currency; if the ammunition was exhausted they had to admit defeat and accept the ultimate disgrace of devaluation. According to Johnson, writing during the period, the balance-of-payments concept relevant to 'policy properly defined and to the corresponding instruments of macroeconomic policy is the net inflow or outflow of international reserves'.[4] The theme can be dated back to his celebrated 1958 paper, 'Towards a general theory of the balance of payments', in which he stated that the 'balance of payments relevant to economic analysis' was the difference between residents' receipts from and payments to foreigners, with a deficit being 'financed by sales of domestic currency by residents or foreigners to the exchange authority in exchange for foreign currency'.[5] Johnson clearly assumed the presence of an exchange authority, in the form of a central bank, acting as the principal intermediary between the citizens of one country and those of another. The pivotal role of such an authority was emphasized by the 'official settlements' definition of the balance of payments, which for several years in the late 1960s and early 1970s was deemed the best indicator of the need for policy adjustment. It corresponded roughly to the change in reserves, although it also included items which would alter the monetary authorities' international creditor/debtor position without affecting the reserves.

The need was to derive a theory which accounted for changes in the reserves. The monetary approach to the balance of payments was developed, notably by Johnson, in response to this need. It explained how the official settlements balance of payments was determined by the difference between the increase in the demand for money and domestic credit expansion. As such, it was 'a monetary phenomenon, representing a disequilibrium in the demand for money'. Johnson made strong claims for the monetary approach – for example, that it debunked much Keynesian analysis which had paid excessive attention to aggregate expenditure decisions as an influence on international payments.

But our formulation contains an alternative explanation of the official settlements balance. We make the assumption that the central bank has only two assets – claims on the domestic government and foreign currency reserves. In the 1950s and 1960s this would have been a realistic assumption in the overwhelming majority of countries. We also assume that the central bank is reluctant to expand its liabilities because additions to high-powered money may become the raw material for excessive growth of bank credit. In this case, if the government fails to borrow from the domestic private sector to cover its budget deficit, it must appeal to the central bank. The central bank can meet the demand only by selling foreign exchange – and any sales represent a deficit on official settlements. We seem to have turned Johnson's argument on its head. Far from being a monetary phenomenon, the official settlements balance of payments can be interpreted in fiscal terms. The solution to unfavourable official settlements is to be sought in reductions in the budget deficit or more aggressive attempts to sell government debt to domestic entities other than the central bank.

In fact, our conceptual somersault is only apparent. It is largely a semantic artefact and should not be taken too seriously. The budget deficit itself constitutes part of domestic credit expansion and may therefore be regarded as a monetary variable, while the demand for public sector debt is susceptible to monetary policy shifts, particularly changes in interest rates. There is no abrupt cleavage between monetary and fiscal instruments.

However, by stating the problem in fiscal terms some fresh insights have been generated. We have identified the government as the most likely culprit for an unsustainable imbalance on official settlements. The sequence of sterling crises in Britain illustrates the point clearly. Following recommendations from its Keynesian advisers, the government from time to time embarked on fiscal reflation which involved a deliberate increase in the budget deficit. After a relatively short period, often no more than a year or 18 months, there was a run on the reserves. The official reply was typically a 'package' of public expenditure cuts, taxation increases and higher interest rates. The balance of payments then convalesced and the reserve position improved. A rise in unemployment followed, prompting another bout of fiscal reflation, another sterling crisis and another 'package'. In Brittan's words, 'Chancellors behaved like simple Pavlovian dogs responding to two main stimuli: one was "a run on the reserves" and the other was "500 000 unemployed" – a figure which was later increased to above 600 000.'[6] The stop–go cycle may be interpreted as reflecting the incompatibility of increased budget deficits with the maintenance of a fixed exchange rate against the dollar. This incompatibility was signalled by a fall in reserves.

The Bretton Woods regime of fixed exchange rates was effectively termi-
nated by the USA's decision to suspend the convertibility of the dollar into
gold in August 1971. Since then the major currencies have for most of the
time been floating against each other. This has changed the form of the
typical balance-of-payments crisis. In the 1950s and 1960s, when the reserves were both the first and last line of defence, a run on the reserves
necessitated early action on the budget deficit or interest rates. Today the
option of devaluation is also available. The environment for deficit countries
has become more permissive in another respect. Large international capital
markets with the capacity to lend to governments for balance-of-payments
financing have developed, with OPEC members being an important source
of funds after the oil price rise of 1973/4. Instead of having to appeal to the
International Monetary Fund, which imposed conditions to ensure a return
to payments balance within a set timetable, deficit countries have been able
to borrow from private commercial banks. As long as the banks have been
persuaded that their loans will be repaid eventually, they have not been as
rigorous as the IMF in expecting responsible macroeconomic policies.

The two new choices – devaluation and borrowing – have changed governments' perceptions about how they should meet payments difficulties.
Particularly in the Third World, but also among many industrial countries,
attitudes have become more lax. Budget deficits represent a much higher
proportion of national income in nearly all countries. Are the frequency of
devaluation and the scale of borrowing for balance-of-payments purposes
related to these large budget deficits and, if so, in what ways?

We stated earlier that the public sector current account deficit was equal to
the budget deficit minus domestic debt sales. At first sight, devaluation is
not much help in curing the deficit because it has no obvious repercussions
on either the budgetary position or debt sales. However, this is too superficial a view. There are indirect relationships, working through the balance
sheets of the central bank and the domestic commercial banks, between
devaluation and a government's ability to finance its deficit internally.

Devaluation is usually followed by a rise in the price level. The higher
price level is accompanied by an increased demand for both the monetary
base and money (i.e. an increased willingness to hold the liabilities of the
central bank and the commercial banks). As a result the banking system can
expand its assets without disturbing monetary equilibrium. The central bank,
as banker to the government, is always under an obligation to take on more
public sector debt. In an economy free from official regulations, the commercial banks might refuse to lend to government if they thought the loans
would be unprofitable. But in most Third World countries the banks are
either nationalized or subject to some degree of official arm-twisting. They
have to accept new public sector debt in their balance sheets.

In other words, devaluation enables a government to increase its domestic debt sales. The high price level associated with it causes the private sector to wish to hold more notes and coin, and more bank deposits. By holding more monetary assets economic agents are – through a circuitous route – purchasing more government debt. Notes and coin are claims on the central bank, but the central bank matches them by claims on government; and deposits are liabilities of banks, but banks match them by investing in government paper.

Indeed, it is an open question whether devaluation should be regarded as a method of promoting domestic debt sales or as a way of levying the inflation tax. An econometric analysis of Italy's exchange rate movements in the 1970s concluded that: 'The monetary financing of over one-third of the government's deficit effectively implied that...nine-tenths of the increase in the total monetary base was accounted for by the Treasury, causing an expansion in high-powered money well in excess of that which would have been consistent with a reasonable stability in the value of the lira.' Its author judged that 'the sharp increase in the monetary base plus inflation meant that the public paid a growing part of taxes in the form of the inflation tax on money balances. Indeed, according to some rough estimates I have made in the three years 1972–75, the yield from this tax turned out to be almost equal to that from income tax.'[7]

But Italy is only a mild example of the problems which can arise. In many Third World countries, particularly in Latin America, devaluation is almost synonymous with inflation. Consequently, it may seem preferable for a government with a large budget deficit to borrow abroad. No hard and fast criteria for deciding whether a government's external debt is excessive have been agreed. Clearly, one requirement for the sustainability of a foreign borrowing programme is that the citizens are willing to pay sufficient taxes to cover interest charges and maturing capital payments. But the question of the government's ability to repay principal is more awkward and problematic. There is no obvious rule which says whether a particular ratio of public sector foreign debt to taxable capacity (usually proxied by national income) is too high. Sovereign risk is a very controversial subject among bankers. In principle, a government could be running a continuous current account deficit as long as the resulting growth of its foreign debt and servicing costs is no faster than the growth of its national income. The situation becomes unsustainable only when this condition is violated. In that case the government must sooner or later take measures to reduce its foreign borrowing. If no measures are taken, the government will finally be unable to pay interest and will have to seek rescheduling of its debt.

Balance-of-payments crises since 1971 have, therefore, been rather different dramas from those in the 1950s and 1960s. Whereas the main actors in the play used to be the government and the IMF, and the most absorbing item of stage scenery a change in the reserves, today international bankers have been added to the cast, and devaluation and debt service ratios to the props. But the responsibility for balance-of-payment problems still rests with governments and their budget deficits.

Direct restrictions imposed for balance-of-payments reasons are of two main kinds – import controls and exchange controls. Are either of any value in solving a public sector current account deficit?

Import controls on private sector transactions are by themselves of little use. A public sector current account deficit is equal to the difference between two numbers – the public sector financial deficit and sales of public sector debt to the domestic private sector. Import controls can reduce it only insofar as they affect these variables. Tariffs yield revenue to the government and therefore lower the budget deficit. But otherwise there are no obvious linkages at work.[8] Some favourite Third World responses to payments imbalance, such as quotas or placing luxuries on a list of prohibited imports, are futile, as public sector finances are unaffected. Aside from the boost to revenue from tariffs, import controls are pointless as an instrument for reducing the public sector's current account deficit. Nothing more needs to be said.

Exchange controls are more interesting. The most characteristic exchange control is a requirement that the private citizens of a country keep no foreign exchange in their own names and transfer any holdings to the central bank in return for domestic currency. Two observations may be made here.

First, exchange control may be viewed as serving the same function as devaluation. It increases the private sector's demand for government debt. When private sector agents are legally obliged to surrender foreign exchange to the central bank, they receive central bank liabilities in return (i.e. high-powered money in the form of notes or balances at the central bank). More frankly, they are forced to invest in the central bank. The central bank, as banker to the government, in turn invests in public sector debt. The private sector has indirectly financed the public sector deficit and may, to that extent, have reduced the public current account imbalance. However, this arrangement, which in any case is rather distasteful since it rests on compulsion, is unstable. If the private sector's holdings of high-powered money are above desired levels because of exchange controls, it attempts to reduce them. It can do so most obviously by using the excess high-powered money as the base for inflationary credit expansion. The monetary authorities may hinder this by introducing credit restrictions on private banks. This reaction is extremely common and helps to explain why so many central banks throughout the world are to be seen enforcing exchange controls and administrative credit restrictions simultaneously. The panoply of controls may be interpreted as the result of competition between the government and the private sector for foreign exchange and, at a deeper level, for resources of any kind.

Secondly, exchange control resembles inflation in that it is a form of taxation. Without exchange control, private sector agents would not convert their foreign currency into domestic. It follows that, after compulsory conversion, there is excess supply of the domestic currency, and its market-clearing price (in terms of foreign currency) is beneath the official price. The difference between the market-clearing and official exchange rates is an incentive for the creation of black markets. It is also a measure of the government's exchange control tax. As an instrument of taxation, exchange control enables governments to finance their foreign purchases at a lower price in domestic currency terms than would otherwise be the case. In this sense, it reduces the public sector financial deficit. The success of exchange control as a tax is, however, hazardous to estimate in advance, since the government cannot know what proportion of the private sector's foreign exchange may seep out through the black market. The existence of black markets is another symptom of competition between the government and the private sector for resources; it is the result of government failure to pay for its expenditure by more visible and honest forms of taxation.

We have to concede that exchange controls, if they are effective, may cut the public sector's current account deficit. But they do so through means – taxation and increasing domestic demand for public sector debt – which have always been available to governments in more transparent forms. Exchange controls have no merits compared to the conventional techniques, and they suffer from several obvious disadvantages. Not least among these disadvantages is the contempt for government aroused by the arbitrary character of the exchange control tax.

In summary, the messages of the new approach to the balance of payments are that only foreign debts incurred by the public sector constitute a balance-of-payments problem, and that the only solution is the pursuit of more appropriate fiscal and debt management policies. A further implication is that a country whose government has adopted responsible budgetary policies cannot have external payments difficulties. The new approach provides reinforcement for the 'old-time religion' of sound finance and balanced budgets.

But the contrast between the white of private sector deficits and the black of public sector deficits should not be exaggerated. There are grey areas. Two deserve particular mention, as they are of some topical interest. The first is where public sector agencies borrow abroad to finance capital projects. If these are expected to generate a rate of return above the cost of funds, no extra burden is imposed on the taxpayer and no strong case for differentiating this form of public foreign borrowing from private can be argued.

The second arises when heavy overseas borrowing is conducted by private banks, which on-lend to companies and individuals. This should be distinguished from credit flowing directly from foreign entities to the domestic private sector because bank deposits are in most countries guaranteed by the central bank, which is a public sector body. If the companies and individuals who ultimately receive the funds are unable to repay the banks, the central bank has to interfere to protect depositors' interests. Central bank interference is necessarily a matter of public policy. This unintentional involvement of government in private sector financial transactions has occurred in some Latin American countries. A notable example is Chile which, in 1980 and 1981, simultaneously had a budget surplus and a big current account deficit stemming from heavy private sector borrowing abroad. In 1982, many of the private sector loans went wrong and central bank refinancing of the bad debts contributed to a sizeable budget deficit. Despite cautious fiscal policies, excessive borrowing by the private sector eventually undermined the country's credit rating.

These two special cases are only minor qualifications to the central theme. They in no sense invalidate the emphasis on fiscal policy as the key to the balance-of-payments 'problem'. Indeed, if bankers want to avoid some of the sovereign debt difficulties they are now facing, they should in future focus on fiscal variables to assess a government's ability to repay. The abundance of a country's natural resources is of limited value unless they can be translated into tax revenue. Assertions such as 'Mexico has oil' and 'Argentina's agricultural potential is so great its finances can always be turned round' have been heard to justify the large loans extended to these two nations over the last decade. But Mexico's oil and Argentina's agricultural potential are not by themselves any help to foreign bankers holding claims on their governments. Bankers need dollars, not oil or beef. The only way, apart from borrowing, that the Mexican or Argentine governments can obtain dollars is by purchasing them with local currency; and the only way, apart from printing, that these governments can acquire surplus local currency is by having an excess of tax receipts over expenditure. If there is no prospect of a Third World government reorganizing its public sector finances after a foreign borrowing programme, it is unwise for banks to participate in that programme while it is under way.

Although reschedulings of Third World debt are the most topical application of the new approach to the balance of payments, it is also relevant to recent policy debates in the developed countries. It shows, for example, that the Cambridge Economic Policy Group's advocacy of import controls as an answer to future payments imbalance in Britain is misguided and unsound.

There is a balance-of-payments problem only if the government has a financial deficit which it cannot cover by domestic debt sales. Paradoxically, a reliable method of creating such a problem would be fiscal reflation of the kind proposed in the 'alternative economic strategy' and supported by the Cambridge Economic Policy Group. A further irony might be mentioned. There is a resemblance between our approach to the balance of payments and the New Cambridge School theory of the mid-1970s. The gravamen of this theory, also developed by the Cambridge Economic Policy Group, was that the government's budget deficit – and only the government's budget deficit – was responsible for payments imbalance. Cambridge economists seem not to have recognized that this conclusion is inconsistent with their subsequent enthusiasm for import controls. Tariffs on finished manufactures would mitigate the problem to the extent that they boosted tax revenue, but otherwise they would be quite pointless.

If the British Government wants to avoid external constraints on economic policy, it should ensure that budgetary policy remains responsible. As long as the public sector borrowing requirement is a low and declining proportion of national income, Britain will not suffer from a balance-of-payments problem.

Notes

1. W. M. Corden, *Inflation, Exchange Rates and the World Economy*, Oxford 1977, p. 45. The aim of the present article can be regarded as giving Corden's insight further elaboration.
2. G. E. Wood and D. R. Mudd, 'The recent US trade deficit' *Federal Reserve Bank of St Louis Review*, April 1978, p. 3.
3. I have clarified my thinking on this point after correspondence with Professor W. M. Corden. There is a special difficulty if the central bank, a public sector entity, is borrowing abroad at high interest rates and then extending cheap credit to the domestic private sector.
4. See H. G. Johnson, 'The monetary theory of balance-of-payments policies', pp. 262–84, in J. A. Frenkel and H. G. Johnson (eds), *The Monetary Approach to the Balance of Payments*, London 1976. The quotation is from p. 262.
5. H. G. Johnson, 'Towards a general theory of the balance of payments', pp. 153–68, in *International Trade and Economic Growth* (London: Allen & Unwin 1958), reprinted on pp. 237–55 of R. N. Cooper (ed), *International Finance* (Harmondsworth: Penguin 1969). The quotations are from p. 239 of Cooper's collection.
6. S. Brittan, *Steering the Economy* (Harmondsworth: Penguin 1971). The quotation is from p. 455.
7. R. Masera, 'The interaction between money, the exchange rate and prices: the Italian experience in the 1970s', pp. 233–47, in A. S. Courakis (ed.), *Inflation, Depression and Economic Policy in the West*, London 1981. The quotations are from p. 244.
8. In countries where collection costs of domestic taxes are high, 'tariffs and export taxes may form part of a first-best tax package'. (W. M. Corden, *Trade Policy and Economic Welfare*, Oxford 1974, p. 66.) In fact, there are many developing countries where tariffs are introduced or raised explicitly for revenue-raising rather than protectionist purposes.

Introducing the Concept of 'Equity Withdrawal'

From a paper of 4 June 1982 'The coming boom in housing credit' from the stockbroking firm, L. Messel & Co., written by Tim Congdon and Paul Turnbull.

Several signs of a very large increase in finance for house purchase have appeared recently. The building societies promised a record £1,491 million to mortgage applicants in March and £1,416 million in April. (The previous high was £1,210 million in March 1981.) Meanwhile the April London clearing banks' statement referred to 'a further sharp rise in house mortgage finance'. Mortgage lending by banks and building societies combined is likely to be about 40 per cent higher in the second quarter of 1982 than a year earlier, and roughly double that in the second quarter of 1980.

The boom in housing credit has created problems of both analysis and policy. The analytical problem is to reconcile the volume of funds now pouring into the housing market with the relative stability of house prices. It seems that a significant, and perhaps rising, proportion of loans designated for 'house purchase' are actually being used for other purposes. We will argue strongly that there is nothing sinister in this and it would be quite wrong for the Bank of England to stop it. The policy problem is that there are domestic constraints on further large interest rate reductions. Of course, if the economy can recover with the base rates of 12 per cent or 13 per cent which currently prevail, that is not by itself a cause for anxiety. But investors' hopes of short-term interest rates of 10 per cent or less in 1982 will be disappointed. Before we draw our conclusions for interest rates we need to identify the influences on the boom in housing credit and see how they are likely to unfold in coming quarters.

The main cause of the housing credit boom is the liberalization of the financial system. In 1981 the banks, already freed from 'corset' restrictions, were allowed to ignore the qualitative guidelines on personal sector lending originally imposed by the Bank of England in December 1973. (No formal announcement of the change was made.) They sought new business in the home mortgage market, putting the building societies under severe competitive pressure. The societies have retaliated by actively marketing their mortgage facilities.

Recent developments are in sharp contrast to the post-war norm. In the 1960s and 1970s there was a continuous excess demand for housing finance. The most well-known symptom was the mortgage queue, taken for granted as natural and inevitable by all home-buyers. The explanation for excess demand was that building societies and banks were unable to lend as much as they wished because of a variety of official restrictions. The societies, which are mutual associations and do not maximize profits anyway, could lend all the deposits they received. But for most of the 1970s the Government wanted to prevent a house price explosion similar to that in 1971–73. Restrictions on mortgage advances, laid down by a government-backed body called the Joint Advisory Committee, were in operation on several occasions. The societies, with the scope of their activities necessarily limited in this way, discriminated in favour of small and first-time borrowers. For example, they charged a differential (i.e., higher) rate for mortgages above a certain size.

The position of the banks was even more straightforward. In December 1973, following the notorious excesses of the Barber boom, the Bank of England issued a notice which said that, 'Banks and finance houses are asked to reinforce strongly their restraints on lending to persons generally, to property companies and for purely financial transactions.' This was taken to indicate that home mortgage lending was 'low priority' and would be disapproved by the Bank of England. The banks therefore undertook virtually none in the 1970s, except on behalf of their own staff.

The relaxation of regulations in 1981 changed the situation radically. The banks entered the mortgage market in a big way – and, for reasons which remain unexplained, the Bank of England did nothing to stop them. In the quarter to November 1980 they lent £124 million for house purchase; in the quarter to November 1981 they lent £920 million. By the end of the year the building societies were in the unusual position of not being able to lend out all the money they had available. Several of them responded by ending the differential rate structures so that they could compete more effectively at the top end of the market. There was also a weakening of the cartel arrangements on deposit inflows. In theory, the share rate (i.e. for deposits withdrawable on demand) is agreed by the Building Societies' Association and applies to all societies. But, in practice, societies have in recent years offered different rates to savers on term shares. Not only has new competition between banks and building societies emerged, but also competition between the societies themselves has developed in an unexpected way.

The result of the liberalization moves is that excess demand for housing finance is now being eliminated. Anyone who wants to buy a residential property can find the funds – if he is prepared to pay the price. The volume of money entering the housing market has therefore risen massively. This is an undoubted improvement in the structure of the financial system. An efficient financial system allocates funds (and, implicitly, real resources) by price; it does not ration them by queues. The latest changes should be seen as a further extension of the Competition and Credit Control reforms which began in 1971 and have done so much to strengthen competition between financial intermediaries.

Largely because of the liberalization of housing credit the total amount of house purchase advances by all institutions was nearly 30 per cent higher in 1981 than in 1980. The quarterly pattern of the increase is shown in Table 10.1. But there seems to have been remarkably little effect on the housing market. Indeed, the Building Societies' Association index of all house prices was 4.4 per cent lower in January 1982 than a year earlier. How can the surge of new credit and the static property market be reconciled?

Table 10.1   The quarterly pattern of borrowing for house purchase in 1981

		Borrowing (in £million) for house purchase from					% rise on year earlier
		Building societies	Banks	Local authorities	Others	Total	
1980	4th qtr	1 708	130	71	229	2 138	+28.6
1981	1st	1 561	210	11	201	1 983	+23.7
	2nd	1 808	390	25	207	2 430	+41.9
	3rd	1 560	730	65	208	2 563	+32.9
	4th	1 270	870	149	153	2 442	+14.2

Source: Financial Statistics, April 1982

The key to the reconciliation must be that much of the money was destined for purposes other than house purchase. A very clear statement of how funds circulate in the housing market was given by David Lomax in an article in the February 1982 *National Westminster Bank Quarterly Review:*

> The essential point is that apart from mortgage lending used for new construction (new houses or extensions), for transactions costs, and for buying houses from the public sector (council house sales), every penny of net additional credit for house purchase is taken out in equity from the housing market. This is an arithmetic identity, stemming from the fact that if one is trading a given stock of assets among the population, then by definition if somebody increases his or her net debt to buy into the existing stock, somebody else must be taking that amount out of the system. One does not know at which point in the chain the equity is taken out of the housing market, but the amount taken out must be equal to the total net additional credit, subject to the adjustments mentioned above.

Table 10.2 The destination of mortgage funds

	Total net mortgage advances	Advances on new houses	Advances to buy council houses	Increase in mortgage debt on existing homes ((1) minus (2) and (3))	Mortgage lending for home improvement	Equity withdrawal ((4) minus (5))	Equity withdrawal as proportion of net mortgage advances
	(1)	(2)	(3)	(4)	(5)	(6)	(7)
1975	3.7	1.3	0.1	2.3	0.3	2.0	54%
1976	3.9	1.2	0.1	2.6	0.4	2.2	56%
1977	4.4	1.3	0.1	3.0	0.4	2.6	59%
1978	5.5	1.6	0.2	3.7	0.5	3.2	58%
1979	6.6	1.9	0.3	4.4	0.6	3.8	58%
1980	7.4	1.8	0.5	5.1	0.8	4.3	58%
1981	9.4	2.2	0.7	6.5	0.9	5.6	60%

All figures in £ billion.

Notes
(1) Figures are provided by the Building Societies' Association showing a breakdown of building society lending between new and existing properties. The amounts in col. (2) assume that the lending division between new and existing properties is the same for all institutions as for building societies.
(2) Figures are not available showing the amount of mortgage lending used to purchase council houses. Our estimates are based on Department of the Environment data for the number of council house sales. For example, in 1980, there were 80,000 sales. Assuming an average mortgage of £6,000 we obtain the £500 million figure shown.
(3) Data for the value of home improvement loans are not available. Our figures are necessarily rough estimates. Nevertheless, the primary purposes of our 'destination of mortgage funds analysis' is to illustrate that a substantial part of mortgage lending becomes available to finance consumption. In this respect, the split between cols (5) and (6) is unimportant since spending on home improvement is classified as part of consumer expenditure.

Source: Financial Statistics, April 1982 and L. Messel & Co. estimates

The items in the 'arithmetic identity' mentioned by Lomax can be estimated and some conjectures made about the size of equity withdrawn from the housing market. The estimates are presented in Table 10.2.

As can be seen, equity withdrawn has in recent years continuously been more than half of net mortgage advances. In other words, most of the mortgage credit extended by building societies and banks does not increase the housing stock owned by persons – even though the funds are categorized as being for 'house purchase'. Moreover, a big rise in net mortgage advances may not be translated into higher house prices if there is a change in the level of equity withdrawn. In 1981 the proportion of equity withdrawn to net advances seems to have increased, although not very dramatically. This, combined with the absorption of significant funds by council house purchases, prevented the quite strong growth in mortgage lending having much impact on house prices. (The method of calculating the split between increase in equity and equity withdrawn is explained in the notes to Table 10.2.)

It may seem odd that so much mortgage money does not end up – or, at least, does not appear to end up – in residential property. How is this at first sight very curious phenomenon to be explained? What are the main forms of equity withdrawal? Four should be mentioned:

1. Departures from the owner-occupied market.
2. Trading down.
3. Sales of formerly rented houses by private landlords.
4. Equity release in house transfer.

Each may be analysed in more detail.

Departures from the owner-occupied market   These arise most commonly on the death of an owner-occupier when the sales proceeds are distributed to next of kin and other beneficiaries in the will. The money received by the legatees may be spent on consumption or invested in other assets rather than retained in the housing market.

Trading down   There are two principal examples here. First, on retirement or in old age households often move into smaller and less expensive properties. Secondly, in mid-career many individuals may unfortunately suffer a major deterioration in their economic prospects because of redundancy, bankruptcy and so on. Again they are obliged to live in more modest accommodation.

Sales of formerly rented houses by private landlords   These have proceeded steadily over the years, with occasional encouragement (such as the 1974

Rent Act) from legislation against the private landlord. The remaining stock of privately rented accommodation is now down to almost 12 per cent of all households.

Equity release in house transfer   The mechanics of equity-releasing transactions are quite straightforward. Suppose someone has owned a property for five years which he bought for £10,000 with a mortgage of £8,000. The house is now worth £20,000 and the mortgage has been reduced to £7,000 by repayments. He receives a promotion and is able to buy another house worth £30,000 with a mortgage of £24,000. Although he has moved into a larger property, he has withdrawn equity because the increase in borrowing exceeds the increase in the value of his home. The opportunity is created because borrowing can be swapped for equity. The equity released becomes available for consumption or investment in other assets. It should be emphasized that building societies have traditionally hindered equity-releasing transactions by existing borrowers because it reduced the amounts they could lend to first-time buyers.

Why should any of these four types of equity withdrawal have been greater in 1981 than in previous years? Both departures from the owner-occupied market and sales of rented accommodation should be stable from year to year, the first being determined by demographic trends and the second by institutional factors. The scope for variation in equity withdrawal arises in trading down and equity release in house transfer. There is, in fact, likely to have been a substantial increase in both categories in 1981. Because of the recession, which involved a very high level of redundancies and early retirements, trading down must have been more frequent than ever before. Equity release in house transfer may also have been on a much increased scale. In the much more competitive environment in housing finance last year, the building societies were probably less concerned about having enough money for first-time buyers and less fussy about whom they lent to. The banks also may have taken a relaxed attitude about the ultimate destination of their loans.

The potential for equity release in house transfer depends on the gap between mortgage debt and the current market value of residential property. After the two house price booms of 1971–73 and 1978–79 this gap is now very large. Some relevant figures are given in Table 10.3. The personal sector's net equity in the housing stock amounted to nearly £250 billion at the end of 1980. In principle, the whole of it is available for consumption or reallocation into different assets. In practice, of course, if everyone tried to sell their houses and there was not simultaneously a flood of credit to enable them to buy others, house prices would collapse. However, there is obvious

Table 10.3   The value of the personal sector's equity in the housing stock

	Holdings (in £million) at 31st December					
	1975	1976	1977	1978	1979	1980
Value of dwellings	137 525	152 960	167 794	218 352	270 949	300 707
Liabilities incurred in house purchase						
to building societies	18 882	22 500	26 600	31 712	36 981	42 696
to banks	1 310	1 390	1 510	1 780	2 370	2 860
to insurance companies	1 520	1 563	1 577	1 623	1 847	2 107
to public sector	3 254	3 381	3 403	3 377	3 744	4 446
to TSBs	—	—	10	15	22	115
Total liabilities for house purchase	24 966	28 834	33 100	38 507	44 964	52 224
Equity in housing stock (i.e. value of dwellings minus liabilities incurred)	112 559	124 126	134 694	179 845	225 985	248 483
Personal disposable income	78 448	89 276	103 176	121 808	150 676	168 560
Ratio of equity in housing stock to personal disposable income	1.43	1.39	1.31	1.48	1.50	1.47

Source: Financial Statistics, February 1982

scope for the personal sector in certain years to borrow more than the increase in its housing investment, while retaining massive net equity. Indeed, residential property represents ideal security for consumer credit from banks, finance houses and retailers. Loans granted for 'house purchase' and then used for another end are indistinguishable, in economic terms, from loans for consumer credit made against the security of residential property.

There is no doubt that in 1981 the banks were allowed much more freedom to make consumption loans to individuals than they had been in the past. The absence of a formal relaxation of the official qualitative guidelines imposed in December 1973 does not invalidate the point. It is therefore more than a little curious that on 20 January 1982 the Bank of England issued a statement that it was 'concerned to ensure that lending on mortgage for house purchase should in fact be applied to the purchase or improvement of residential property and not to the realization of capital profits on their houses by the borrowers'. Ordinary consumer loans, which the Bank certainly now permits, are almost identical in their effects to equity release in house transfer, about which it has expressed its disapproval. We shall say more on this subject in a later section.

In summary, there is no puzzle about a 30 per cent jump in housing credit coexisting in 1981 with little change in house prices. Our estimate in Table 10.2 is that because of more trading down and equity release on house transfer a smaller proportion of net mortgage advances ended up in the housing market than in 1980. With money being absorbed to buy council houses and to eliminate part of the unsold stock of new private sector houses, little movement occurred in house prices despite much increased flows through the main house mortgage institutions. The housing market has not defied the laws of supply and demand.

But what will happen in 1982? The indications are that in the second quarter net mortgage advances by all institutions might amount to £3.45 billion. Over the year as a whole a figure of £13 billion is quite feasible. Interesting comparisons can be made with previous experience.

In the 1971–73 boom equity withdrawal was an unusually high proportion of funds entering the housing market. Between 1970 and 1972 net mortgage advances by building societies more than doubled from £1,088 million to £2,215 million, while the amount channelled towards purchasing new dwellings went up less than 70 per cent from £510 million to £862 million. The discrepancy implies that much of the leap in building society lending found its way into consumption or other investment. If our estimates are correct, the rise in net mortgage advances between 1981 and 1982 will be less than in the early 1970s, but still spectacular. We would therefore expect equity withdrawal again to absorb an increasing proportion of mortgage funds. As a working hypothesis, we suggest 62 per cent, compared with 60 per cent in 1981. Another outlet is mortgage money to buy council houses. Sales of council houses are running at a higher level than the Government or the local authorities expected. Newspaper reports suggest that the total may reach 160,000 in 1982, compared with 104,000 in 1981. Assuming the average mortgage is about £6,000, we obtain an estimate of nearly £1 billion for advances to buy council houses in 1982. Some mortgage lending is for home improvement and, in effect, adds to equity in the property market. As no precise statistics from the Building Societies' Association are available of its scale, the figures in Table 10.2 are our own estimates. A sharp rise seems likely in 1982 because both building societies and banks are marketing facilities for this fringe form of finance quite hard. We suggest £1.1 billion in 1982 compared to £0.9 billion in 1981.

We are now in a position to prepare an estimate for mortgage funds to be directed towards the acquisition of new houses in 1982. The calculation is given below:

		£bn
	Total net mortgage advances in 1982	13.0
less	62% of total to finance equity withdrawal	−8.0
	(Increase in housing market equity	5.0)
less	Purchases of council houses	−1.0
less	Mortgage lending for home improvement	−1.1
	Mortgage funds to purchase new houses	£2.9 billion

The £2.9 billion 1982 total is a striking improvement on the £2.2 billion figure in 1981. Of course, it is not the same as all personal sector investment in dwellings because most homebuyers also put in part of their own savings. In 1980, for example, the average mortgage advance on new properties by building societies was £14,696, compared to an average new house price of £26,131. Typically, therefore, mortgage funds to purchase new houses are equivalent to between 55 and 60% of private sector investment in dwellings.

Table 10.4   Private sector investment in dwellings: the record in recent years and a projection for 1982

	Advances on new houses (£billion, current prices)	Proportion of advances to total investment (%)	Private sector investment in dwellings (£billion, current prices)
1975	1.3	59	2.2
1976	1.2	50	2.4
1977	1.3	52	2.5
1978	1.6	50	3.2
1979	1.9	58	3.3
1980	1.8	51	3.5
1981 first 3 qts	1.7	68	2.5
1981 estimate	2.2	60	3.7
1982 projection	2.9	60	4.8

Source: L. Messel & Co. estimates and *Monthly Digest of Statistics*

Using this ratio, we give in Table 10.4 an estimate of private housebuilding investment in 1982 and compare it to recent years. There is a big jump – from £3.7 billion to £4.8 billion, equivalent to almost 30 per cent – between 1981 and 1982. As substantial spare capacity persists in the construction industry and no serious land shortages are to be found, this increase will feed through mainly into housing starts rather than house prices. The evidence available so far in 1982 supports this interpretation. In the first quarter the number of private sector housing starts was 38,700 (seasonally adjusted), compared to an average of 29,100 per quarter in 1981. House prices have edged up, but not significantly. According to Building Societies' Association statistics, the average price of a new house was 2.9% higher in March 1982 than in December 1981. Since then there may have been some further movement. The *Financial Times* (25 May) reported the most recent quarterly survey of the Royal Institution of Chartered Surveyors (RICS), many of whose members are estate agents. The RICS was said to be looking for a change in market sentiment. According to Mr John Thomas, RICS spokesman on the housing market, the figures for April and May 'will probably illustrate that the harassed sellers of 1981 are gradually being replaced by those eager to buy while prices are still reasonably competitive'. An increase in house prices of between 5 per cent and 10 per cent between the end of 1981 and the end of 1982 seems the most likely outcome.

The projections made here rest on many assumptions, all of which can be questioned. Perhaps the most important is that we are not expecting any major change in interest rates from their present levels. A drop in base rates to 12 per cent seems likely in the next few weeks, but interest rate declines thereafter would undermine even further the Government's chances of staying within its sterling M3 and PSL2 targets. But what would happen if the Government placed more emphasis on the recovery and allowed interest rates to drop to, say, 10 per cent at some stage in the third quarter?

Before the liberalization of the housing market it was easy to work out the relationship between interest rates and net mortgage advances. The building society share rate lagged other interest rates and the changed differential between it and these other rates affected the volume of inflows into the societies. All the money taken by the societies could be lent. Today circumstances are different because banks are in the market, and they can expand their loans and deposits by a stroke of the pen. The key question has become 'how responsive is the demand for bank mortgage finance to interest rates?'. Obviously, we cannot tell because our experience of a free housing finance market is so limited.

But we can make some rough estimates. Before liberalization, a 1 per cent change in the differential between building society share rate and the banks' deposit rate would induce new inflows of about £75 million a month. A cut in rates would mean, however, that less interest was paid by existing mortgage borrowers – leaving about £50 million a month extra available for mortgages. The underlying demand for finance is bigger than that which passed through building societies. We would suggest that a 1 per cent drop in interest rates adds £70 million to £80 million a month to the demand for mortgage finance, equivalent to £850 million to £950 million at an annual rate.

If interest rates fell to 10 per cent in the third quarter and stayed there, we would have about £1³/₄ billion extra finance compared to our base estimate. In the year from mid-1982 to mid-1983, this would suggest net mortgage advances of about £15¹/₄ billion. On plausible assumptions about equity withdrawal similar to those above, finance available for buying new houses would amount to £3.5 billion, significantly more than the £2.9 billion projected for calendar 1982.

In January the Bank of England admonished the banks that mortgage lending should be for the purchase or improvement of residential property – and for no other purpose. Moreover, such lending should not allow 'the realization of capital profits on their houses by the borrowers'.

Our analysis shows that this warning is misconceived. For many years more than half of mortgage lending by the building societies has not actually been for 'the purchase or improvement of residential property'. The proportion of net mortgage advances used for equity withdrawal was consistently between 55 per cent and 60 per cent during the 1970s. Banks' entry into the housing market may have been followed by a small increase in the proportion in 1981, but the change was very marginal. The siphoning-off of mortgage funds into consumption or other investment was not caused by anything sinister or imprudent. It was the consequence of building society managers doing their job in the normal way. There are entrants and quits in the housing market, just as there are entrants and quits in the labour market. People quitting the housing market rightly regard the equity in their homes as their own property. They are entitled to do with it whatever they wish. It would be wholly wrong for the monetary authorities to impede them. For example, an elderly couple nearing retirement may decide to sell their home, which they own outright, for £50,000 and use the proceeds to generate income to supplement their pension. The purchase may be granted a 90 per cent mortgage by a bank. The personal sector's equity in the house has been cut from £50,000 to £5,000. But who could object to this sequence of transactions? Everyone concerned – the elderly couple, the homebuyer and the bank – is happy with its results. Why stop it?

Some Bank of England officials might say that they have no objection to individuals taking out equity when they are trading down, as they clearly are in the elderly couple case. There is misbehaviour, so they might claim, only when equity is released by trading up, where borrowing increases by more than the change in the value of one's home. But it would be very difficult in practice to differentiate between equity release due to trading down and trading up. For example, a young married couple may have two homes – a small flat in London and a cottage in the country. They decide to have children and move into one large house. Is this trading up or trading down? Or consider the case of an entrepreneur who wants to take money out of his home and put it into a new company. He sells his house and buys business premises, with some rooms for accommodation, for a higher sum. Again, is this trading up or trading down? Even if it were possible to distinguish clearly between the two kinds of equity release, the notion of Bank of England officials checking individual mortgage loans by banks and building societies is mind-boggling.

There is, in any case, the wider and more fundamental question of why it matters that mortgage loans enable people to consume more. The idea that consumption is by itself improper and harmful has been heard over the ages from a variety of cranks, but so far no central bank has provided a persuasive theoretical rationale. The Bank of England – or, at least, some of its officials – seems not to like consumption, particularly when financed by bank loans. We have not been told why. In fact, personal sector bank borrowing was extremely helpful last year in sustaining consumption while real incomes were under pressure. Without it the recession would have been far worse and prospects for an economic upturn more remote than they currently are.

Of course, there is nothing particularly wicked about loans for consumption or particularly virtuous about loans for investment. The personal sector is in no sense less worthy – or a less fitting destination for credit – than the corporate sector. This was tacitly recognized last year when all restraints on conventional bank loans to persons for consumption were removed. Whatever the formal position, the December 1973 guidelines are defunct. Bank managers often require that equity in a house be collateral for consumption loans. As explained earlier, such loans are economically indistinguishable from using mortgage funds to take out equity from a home and spending the proceeds. Why is the Bank of England permissive towards one type of loan and disapproving towards the other? Its attitude seems muddled and illogical.

Perhaps the most disquieting aspect of the Bank of England's warning is its indifference to the principles of private property and personal freedom. As David Lomax remarked in his *National Westminster Bank Quarterly Review article*: 'A person's equity in a house is his or her own property, and provided the financial transaction is within the law there is no reason at all why he or she should not make use of his or her own equity. If the lending behaviour of certain institutions were clearly irresponsible and/or illegal, then appropriate regulatory or legal action should be taken against them. But that is a different matter from using extremely fragmented and hearsay evidence to build up a climate of criticism of lending institutions where there is no evidence at all from the economy itself, or from the movement of house prices, that any financial or economic disequilibrium is being generated.'

The liberalization of housing finance in 1981 was a welcome and logical continuation of the Competition and Credit Control reforms first introduced in September 1971. It will be followed by a minor boom in housing credit, with net mortgage advances likely to total £13 billion in 1982 compared with £9.4 billion in 1981. The new funds will help stimulate private housebuilding and also, through the subsequent increased withdrawal of equity from the housing market, promote consumption. In the present depressed economic environment, both developments are fortunate. They should certainly not be deterred by artificial official restrictions, such as those hinted at in the Bank of England's warning to the banks in January this year. Equity withdrawal from housing has accounted for 55 per cent to 60 per cent of net mortgage advances over many years. It has permitted those quitting the housing market to consume or redispose of their wealth, a very normal and healthy characteristic of a free-market economy with extensive private ownership of property. Recent changes are certainly not a radical new departure. There does seem to have been some rise in the rate of equity withdrawal in 1982, probably because of trading down connected with the recession. It helps to explain the apparent anomaly of a sizeable rise in mortgage finance having little effect on house prices; it should certainly not be a cause of Government anxiety or official complaint.

The other message which emerges from our analysis is that the economy is very sensitive to interest rate changes. The linkages between interest rates, mortgage credit flows and private sector housebuilding are strong and identifiable. But much more can be said. Because interest rate reductions encourage credit flows through banks and building societies, they are often accompanied by an acceleration of house price inflation. This tends to be followed by a rise in the proportion of mortgage funds which home-owners use to withdraw equity. There is a consequent fall in the savings ratio and boost to consumption. Unfortunately, statistical evidence on the responsiveness of consumption to interest rate changes is weak, perhaps a reflection of the long period when the financial system was highly regulated and interest rates were not fully operative as allocative signals.

If the economy does react powerfully to changes in the cost of money, there must be constraints on large interest rate reductions in the rest of 1982. Credit is pouring into residential property at present. The associated rapid growth of bank and building society deposits is threatening the Government's sterling M3 and PSL2 targets. If interest rates come down quickly to 10 per cent or less, we can be confident that those targets would be unattainable and that an unsustainably vigorous upturn in housing market activity would develop.

Index